A·N·N·U·A·L E·D·I·T·I·O·N·S

Western Civilization Volume I

13th Edition

The Earliest Civilizations Through the Reformation

EDITOR

Robert L. Lembright

James Madison University

Robert L. Lembright teaches World Civilization, Ancient Near East, Byzantine, Islamic, and Greek/Roman history at James Madison University. He received his B.A. from Miami University and his M.A. and Ph.D from The Ohio State University. Dr. Lembright has been a participant in many National Endowment for the Humanities Summer Seminars and Institutes on Egyptology, the Ancient Near East, Byzantine History, and the Ottoman Empire. He has written several articles in the four editions of *The Global Experience*, as well as articles in the *James Madison Journal* and *Western Views of China and the Far East*. His research has concentrated on the French Renaissance of the sixteenth century, and he has published reports in the *Bulletins et memoires, Societé archaeologique et historique de la Charente*. In addition, Dr. Lembright has written many book reviews on the ancient world and Byzantine and Islamic history for *History: Reviews of New Books*.

McGraw-Hill/Dushkin

2460 Kerper Blvd., Dubuque, Iowa 52001

Visit us on the Internet
http://www.dushkin.com

Credits

1. **The Earliest Civilizations**
   Unit photo—© Getty Images/PhotoLink/R. Strange
2. **Greece and Rome: The Classical Tradition**
   Unit photo—© PhotoDisc, Inc
3. **The Judeo-Christian Heritage**
   Unit photo—National Gallery of Art, Washington, DC
4. **Muslims and Byzantines**
   Unit photo—Aramco photo
5. **The Medieval Period**
   Unit photo—© Getty Images/Life File/Andrew Ward
6. **Renaissance and Reformation**
   Unit photo—Library of Congress photo

Copyright

Cataloging in Publication Data
Main entry under title: Annual Editions: Western Civilization, Vol. I: The Earliest Civilizations Through the Reformation. 13/E.
   1. Civilization—Periodicals. 2. World history—Periodicals. I. Lembright, Robert L. *comp.* II. Title: Western Civilization Vol. I.
ISBN 0–07–296879–6   901.9'05   82–645823   ISSN 0735-0392

Thirteenth Edition

Cover image © Andrew Ward/Life File/Getty Images

Printed in the United States of America   1234567890QPDQPD987654   Printed on Recycled Paper

Editors/Advisory Board

Members of the Advisory Board are instrumental in the final selection of articles for each edition of ANNUAL EDITIONS. Their review of articles for content, level, currentness, and appropriateness provides critical direction to the editor and staff. We think that you will find their careful consideration well reflected in this volume.

To the Reader

In publishing ANNUAL EDITIONS we recognize the enormous role played by the magazines, newspapers, and journals of the public press in providing current, first-rate educational information in a broad spectrum of interest areas. Many of these articles are appropriate for students, researchers, and professionals seeking accurate, current material to help bridge the gap between principles and theories and the real world. These articles, however, become more useful for study when those of lasting value are carefully collected, organized, indexed, and reproduced in a low-cost format, which provides easy and permanent access when the material is needed. That is the role played by ANNUAL EDITIONS.

What does it mean to say that we are attempting to study the history of Western civilizations?

A traditional course in Western civilization was often a chronological survey in the development of European institutions and ideas, with a slight reference to the Near East and the Americas and other places where Westernization has occurred. Typically it began with the Greeks, then the Romans, and on to the medieval period, and finally to the modern era, depicting the distinctive characteristics of each stage, as well as each period's relation to the preceding and succeeding events. Of course, in a survey so broad, from Adam to the atomic age in two semesters, a certain superficiality was inevitable. Main characters and events galloped by; often there was little opportunity to absorb and digest complex ideas that have shaped Western culture.

It is tempting to excuse these shortcomings as unavoidable. However, to present a course in Western civilization which leaves students with only a scrambled series of events, names, dates, and places, is to miss a great opportunity. For the promise of such a broad course of study is that it enables students to explore great turning points or shifts in the development of Western culture. Close analysis of these moments enables students to understand the dynamics of continuity and change over time. At best, the course can give a coherent view of the Western tradition and its interplay with non-Western cultures. It can offer opportunities for students to compare various historical forms of authority, religion, and economic organization, to assess the great struggles over the meaning of truth and reality that have sometimes divided Western culture, and even to reflect on the price of progress.

Yet, to focus exclusively on Western civilization can lead us to ignore non-Western peoples and cultures or else to perceive them in ways that some label as "Eurocentric." But contemporary courses in Western history are rarely, if ever, mere exercises in European tribalism. Indeed, they offer an opportunity to subject the Western tradition to critical scrutiny, to asses its accomplishments and its shortfalls. Few of us who teach these courses would argue that Western history is the only history which contemporary students should know. Yet it should be an essential part of what they learn, for it is impossible to understand the modern world without some specific knowledge in the basic tenets of the Western tradition.

When students learn the distinctive traits of the West, they can develop a sense of the dynamism of history. They can begin to understand how ideas relate to social structures and social forces. They will come to appreciate the nature and significance of innovation and recognize how values often influence events. More specifically, they can trace the evolution of Western ideas about such essential matters as nature, humans, authority, the gods, even history itself; that is, they learn how the West developed its distinctive character. And, as historian Reed Dasenbrock has observed, in an age that seeks multicultural understanding there is much to be learned from "the fundamental multiculturalism of Western culture, the fact that it has been constructed out of a fusion of disparate and often conflicting cultural traditions." Of course, the articles collected in this volume cannot deal with all these matters, but by providing an alternative to the summaries of most textbooks, they can help students better understand the diverse traditions and processes that we call Western civilization. As with the last publication of *Annual Editions: Western Civilization, Volumes I and II*, there are World Wide Web sites that can be used to further explore topics that are addressed in the essays. These sites can be hot-linked through the *Annual Editions* home page: http://www.dushkin.com/annualeditions.

This book is like our history—unfinished, always in process. It will be revised biannually. Comments and criticisms are welcome from all who use this book. For that a postpaid article rating form is included at the back of the book. Please feel free to recommend articles that might improve the next edition. With your assistance, this anthology will continue to improve.

Robert L. Lembright
Editor

Contents

UNIT 1
The Earliest Civilizations

These articles discuss some of the attributes of early civilizations. The topics include the deciphering of ancient scripts, a powerful Egyptian pharaoh and several ancient empires.

Unit Overview   **xiv**

The concepts in bold italics are developed in the article. For further expansion, please refer to the Topic Guide and the Index.

UNIT 2
Greece and Rome: The Classical Tradition

These articles focus on Greek and Roman society. Sports, military conquests, women in Hellenic society, the old in Rome, are discussed.

The concepts in bold italics are developed in the article. For further expansion, please refer to the Topic Guide and the Index.

UNIT 3
The Judeo-Christian Heritage

The articles in this section examine Abraham, Jesus and the concepts of evil on the Judeo-Chrisitan heritage.

Unit Overview   70

The concepts in bold italics are developed in the article. For further expansion, please refer to the Topic Guide and the Index.

UNIT 4
Muslims and Byzantines

Three selections discuss the effects of Hellenic and Christian cultures on the development of Muslim and Byzantine worlds.

UNIT 5
The Medieval Period

These selections examine the medieval world. Topics include empire building, military conquests and culture.

The concepts in bold italics are developed in the article. For further expansion, please refer to the Topic Guide and the Index.

The concepts in bold italics are developed in the article. For further expansion, please refer to the Topic Guide and the Index.

UNIT 6
Renaissance and Reformation

The following articles discuss Byzantium, the role of art in the Renaissance, politics, culture, and the importance of religion in Western Europe.

The concepts in bold italics are developed in the article. For further expansion, please refer to the Topic Guide and the Index.

The concepts in bold italics are developed in the article. For further expansion, please refer to the Topic Guide and the Index.

Topic Guide

This topic guide suggests how the selections in this book relate to the subjects covered in your course. You may want to use the topics listed on these pages to search the Web more easily.

On the following pages a number of Web sites have been gathered specifically for this book. They are arranged to reflect the units of this *Annual Edition*. You can link to these sites by going to the DUSHKIN ONLINE support site at *http://www.dushkin.com/online/*.

ALL THE ARTICLES THAT RELATE TO EACH TOPIC ARE LISTED BELOW THE BOLD-FACED TERM.

Archaeology
1. Deciphering History
3. Past, Present, Future: Perceptions of Time Through the Ages

Art
35. Virtue and Beauty: The Renaissance Image of the Ideal Woman

Assyria
5. Grisly Assyrian Record of Torture and Death

Bible
6. Fact or Fiction?
15. The Legacy of Abraham
16. The Other Jesus
17. Mary Magdalene: Saint or Sinner
18. Who the Devil Is the Devil?
21. In the Beginning, There Were the Holy Books

Byzantium
19. The Emperor's State of Grace
20. The Survival of the Eastern Roman Empire
33. The Fall of Constantinople

Christianity
16. The Other Jesus
17. Mary Magdalene: Saint or Sinner
18. Who the Devil Is the Devil?
19. The Emperor's State of Grace
27. The Emergence of the Christian Witch
30. Spreading the Gospel in the Middle Ages

Culture
7. Olympic Self-Sacrifice
8. To Die For?
9. Love and Death in Ancient Greece
11. The Year One
12. Old Age in Ancient Rome
20. The Survival of the Eastern Roman Empire
22. The Ideal of Unity
24. An Iberian Chemistry
26. Doctor, Philosopher, Renaissance Man
34. Machiavelli
35. Virtue and Beauty: The Renaissance Image of the Ideal Woman

Disease
32. How a Mysterious Disease Laid Low Europe's Masses

Egypt
2. Hatshepsut: The Female Pharaoh
10. Cleopatra: What Kind of a Woman Was She, Anyway?

England
13. Celtic War Queen Who Challenged Rome
23. The Most Perfect Man in History?
28. Lackland: The Loss of Normandy in 1204
41. Reign On!

Europe
22. The Ideal of Unity
27. The Emergence of the Christian Witch
31. Saints or Sinners? The Knights Templar in Medieval Europe
32. How a Mysterious Disease Laid Low Europe's Masses
34. Machiavelli
35. Virtue and Beauty: The Renaissance Image of the Ideal Woman
36. Martin Luther's Ninety-Five Theses
37. Explaining John Calvin
38. The Development of Protestantism in 16th Century France

Greece, ancient
7. Olympic Self-Sacrifice
8. To Die For?
9. Love and Death in Ancient Greece

Islam
18. Who the Devil Is the Devil?
21. In the Beginning, There Were the Holy Books
24. An Iberian Chemistry
25. The Capture of Jerusalem
26. Doctor, Philosopher, Renaissance Man
33. The Fall of Constantinople
39. Siege of the Moles
40. The Muslim Expulsion from Spain

Italy
34. Machiavelli
35. Virtue and Beauty: The Renaissance Image of the Ideal Woman

Jews and Judaism
6. Fact or Fiction?
14. The Great Jewish Revolt Against Rome, 66-73 CE
15. The Legacy of Abraham
18. Who the Devil Is the Devil?

Medieval society
22. The Ideal of Unity
27. The Emergence of the Christian Witch
30. Spreading the Gospel in the Middle Ages
32. How a Mysterious Disease Laid Low Europe's Masses

Middle East
25. The Capture of Jerusalem
33. The Fall of Constantinople
39. Siege of the Moles

Military
4. The Coming of the Sea Peoples
5. Grisly Assyrian Record of Torture and Death
9. Love and Death in Ancient Greece
13. Celtic War Queen Who Challenged Rome
14. The Great Jewish Revolt Against Rome, 66-73 CE
25. The Capture of Jerusalem
29. Hero of the Neva and Lake Peipus
31. Saints or Sinners? The Knights Templar in Medieval Europe
33. The Fall of Constantinople
39. Siege of the Moles

UNIT 1

The Earliest Civilizations

Unit Selections

1. **Deciphering History**, Andrew Robinson
2. **Hatshepsut: The Female Pharaoh**, John Ray
3. **Past, Present, Future: Perceptions of Time Through the Ages**, Dan Falk
4. **The Coming of the Sea Peoples**, Neil Asher Silberman
5. **Grisly Assyrian Record of Torture and Death**, Erika Bleibtreu
6. **Fact or Fiction?**, Stephen Goode

Key Points to Consider

- How does the author believe that Stonehenge was built? How does this differ from some of the other theories?

- How was Hatshepsut such an unusual pharaoh in Egypt? Why did Hatshepsut not have many military adventures?

- Why was the introduction of money important for the Mesopotamian civilizations? What did the Mesopotamians use for money?

- Who were the "sea peoples," and how did their weapons and tactics launch a military revolution in the ancient world?

- How did the Assyrian kings maintain control over their subject peoples?

- Why were the Scythians regarded as some of the fiercest warriors of the ancient world?

 **Links: www.dushkin.com/online/**
These sites are annotated in the World Wide Web pages.

Hypertext and Ethnography
http://www.umanitoba.ca/anthropology/tutor/aaa_presentation.html
NOVA Online/Pyramids—The Inside Story
http://www.pbs.org/wgbh/nova/pyramid/
The Oriental Institute/University of Chicago
http://www.oi.uchicago.edu/OI/default.html

Civilization is a relatively recent phenomenon in human experience. But what exactly is civilization? How do civilized people differ from those who are not civilized? How is civilization transmitted?

Civilization, in its contemporary meaning, describes a condition of human society marked by an advanced stage of artistic and technological development and by corresponding social and political complexities. Thus, civilized societies have developed formal institutions for commerce, government, education, and religion—activities that are carried out informally by pre-civilized societies. In addition, civilized people make much more extensive use of symbols. The greater complexity of civilized life requires a much wider range of specialized activities.

Symbolizations, specialization, and organization enable civilized societies to extend greater control over their environments. Because they are less dependent than pre-civilized societies upon a simple adaptation to a particular habitat, civilized societies are more dynamic. Indeed, civilization institutionalizes change. In sum, civilization provides us with a wider range of concepts, techniques, and options to shape our destinies.

In the West, the necessary preconditions for civilization first emerged in the great river valleys of Mesopotamia and Egypt. There we find the development of irrigation, new staple crops, the introduction of the plow, the invention of the wheel, mathematics, science, improved sailing vessels, and metallurgy. These developments revolutionized society. Population increased and became more concentrated and more complex. The emergence of cities or "urban revolution" marked the beginning of civilization.

Civilization combines complex social, economic, religious, and political structures with a corresponding network of ideas and values. The Sumerians organized themselves in city-states, headed by kings who acted in the name of the local patron deity. The Egyptians developed the first centralized and authoritarian system based on loyalty to divine pharaohs. The Assyrians used force and intimidation to shape an international empire.

These early civilizations allowed for little individualism or freedom of expression. As historian Nels M. Bailkey notes in *Readings in Ancient History: Thought and Experience from Gilgamesh to St. Augustine* (2002), "their thought remained closely tied to religion and found expression predominantly in religious forms." Elaborate myths recounted the deeds of heroes, defined relations between humans and the gods, and generally justified the prevailing order of things. Thus, myths reveal something of the relationship between values and the social order in ancient civilizations. The link between beliefs and authority, particularly in Egypt, is treated in the article "Hatshepsut: the Female Pharaoh."

We are inclined to make much of limitations of ancient systems of thought and authority. Yet the record of the Mesopotamians and Egyptians demonstrates, from the beginning,

civilization's potential for innovation and collective accomplishment. They developed mathematics, monumental architecture, law, astronomy, art, timekeeping (see the article "Past, Present, Future: Perception of Time Through the Ages") and monetary systems, and literatures rich with diversity and imagination. The record of ancient civilizations is full of cruelty and destruction, they also include an awakening concern for justice and moral righteousness. These early civilizations are notable for their heroic efforts to bring nature under human control.

For a time the great river valleys remained islands of civilization in a sea of barbarism. The spread of civilization to rain-watered lands required that outlying areas find the means to produce a food surplus and to develop the social mechanisms for transferring the surplus from farmers to specialists. The first condition was met by the diffusion of plow agriculture; the second by cultural contacts that came through conquest, trade, and migration.

Several satellite civilizations evolved into great empires. Such enterprises grew out of conquest; their initial success and later survival typically depended upon their relative capacity to wage war. "The Coming of the Sea Peoples" describes how an ancient military revolution affected the balance of power in the Near East and furthered cultural exchange between diverse and dispersed societies. The problem of governing scattered and often hostile subjects required that conquerors create new patterns of authority. The growth of the Assyrian and Persian empires was not mere acts of conquest; it was innovations in government and administration. The earliest efforts to impose and maintain imperial hegemony could be both crude and cruel, as the report "Grisly Assyrian Record of Torture and Death" attests.

Deciphering History

Andrew Robinson *looks at some linguistic puzzles still facing historians.*

by Andrew Robinson

WRITING IS, AMONG the greatest inventions in human history, perhaps *the* greatest invention, since it made history possible. Yet it is a skill most writers take for granted. Looking at a page in a foreign script that is totally incomprehensible to us—perhaps Arabic or Japanese—reminds us forcibly of the nature of our achievement. An extinct script, such as Egyptian hieroglyphs, Babylonian cuneiform or the glyphs of the ancient Maya of Central America, may strike us as little short of miraculous and bizarrely different from our own alphabetic scripts. We want to know what kind of people the early writers were, and what kind of information, ideas and feelings they chose to make permanent. But to obtain such insights it is first necessary to decipher the ancient scripts: to understand not only the sign system but also the spoken language the signs encoded.

Deciphering has its roots in the Renaissance fascination with ancient Egypt, although the actual word was not coined until 1677, when an Englishman, Thomas Herbert, referring to the mysterious cuneiform inscriptions of the Persian king Darius at Persepolis, called them:

> well worthy of the scrutiny of those ingenious persons that delight themselves in the dark and difficult Art or Exercise of deciphering.

Some groundwork in deciphering was laid in the eighteenth century, but it was not until the 1820s that there was a great breakthrough, with Jean-Francois Champollion's 'cracking' of the Egyptian hieroglyphs, aided by the Rosetta stone. In the 1850s, the several cuneiform scripts of Mesopotamia started to reveal their secrets; in the first half of the twentieth century, the Hittite (Luvian) hieroglyphs of Anatolia were deciphered; in the 1950s, the Linear B script of the Mycenaeans and Minoans was understood; and in the final decades of the last century, the Mayan glyphs began to make sense to scholars—to mention only the most famous decipherments.

However some ancient scripts still defy decipherment. Although elements of them are understood by scholars, we can only guess at the meanings of particular inscriptions. There are at least eight major examples—though many more if we count the scripts of which there are only tantalising fragments. These include the proto-Sinaitic script dated to *c.*1500 BC and found a century ago on sphinxes and rocks in the ancient Egyptian mines of Sinai, which was once thought to be a precursor of the first alphabet; and the unique, punched disc found in 1908 in Phaistos in Crete, the date of which, *c.*1700 BC, means that it has a claim to be the world's first printed document.

The most important undeciphered script is that of the Indus Valley in what is now Pakistan and northwestern India, since it is the writing of a great civilisation, that of ancient India, *c.*2500-1800 BC, one of the four 'first' civilisations along with those of Mesopotamia, Egypt and China. Other undeciphered scripts include Linear A from Crete and the Aegean, which is older than Linear B and probably was the script of King Minos; the Etruscan script of Italy, which is essentially the Greek alphabet but with an underlying language that seems to be unrelated to any other European language; the Zapotec script of Mexico, which predates Mayan and appears to be the oldest writing in the Americas; the Meroitic script of the African kingdom of Meroe (Kush) in today's Nubia, which has at least some resemblance to the hieroglyphs of its northern neighbour Egypt; and the *rongorongo* script of isolated Easter Island, the only writing from pre-colonial Oceania (assuming its origin really does predate the arrival of Europeans on Easter Island, which is disputed). If it could be proved that *rongorongo* was invented on the island independently of outsiders, this would be extremely powerful evidence that writing has had multiple origins rather than a single origin, apparently in Mesopotamia in the fourth millennium BC.

Before taking a closer look at three of these 'lost' languages/scripts—Etruscan, *rongorongo* and the Indus script—it is worth briefly surveying the deciphered scripts to extract an answer to the question posed above: what kind of information did the ancient writers record? For it is surely likely that broadly similar information is recorded in the undeciphered scripts—not something totally unexpected (such as a record of visitations by extraterrestrial beings, as claimed by at least one 'decipherer' of *rongorongo*).

Political leaders, especially autocrats and dictators, have always used writing for propaganda purposes. Nearly 4,000 years and a totally different script separate the famous law code inscribed in black basalt of Hammurabi of Babylon (1792-1750 BC) from the slogans and billboards of its modern equivalent in much the same location in Iraq at the beginning of the third millennium AD—but the messages are (regrettably) similar. Hammurabi called himself, in purest Babylonian cuneiform, 'King, King of Babylon, King of the whole country of Amurru, King of Sumer, King of the Four Quarters of the World'; and he promised that if his laws were obeyed, then all of his people would benefit. Yet it is unlikely that such propaganda will be found in any of the undeciphered scripts, since the surviving inscriptions are not monumental—with the exception of a few Meroitic ones and a single, challenging inscribed stone, the La Mojarra stela, written in the Isthmian script of the Mexican Isthmus of Tehuantepec in the second century AD.

The urge for immortality, too, has often been of the first importance to writers. Egyptian hieroglyphic inscriptions in tombs and associated with mummies epitomise the idea that the voices of the dead can be heard again through the written word. Most of the thousands of known fragments written by the Etruscans are funerary inscriptions. We can read the names of the deceased and of his or her relations, and often the age of death, because the signs are a simple adaptation of the Greek alphabet; but that is almost all we know of the language of this important people who borrowed the alphabet from Greece and handed it on to the Romans, who in turn gave it to the rest of Europe.

Another common purpose for writing was to predict the future. All ancient societies were obsessed with what was to come. Among the Maya, prognostication took the form of bark-paper books elaborately painted in colour and bound in jaguar skin; it was based on a written calendrical system so sophisticated it extended as far back as five billion years ago, more than our presently scientifically estimated age for the Earth. A lunar 'calendar' in a *rongorongo* inscription was presumably used for prognostication, and is one of the very few generally accepted decipherments of this enigmatic script.

But most ancient writing was probably comparatively mundane, destroyed, like last year's newspapers, by the ravages of time. It provided, for example, the equivalent of an identity card or a property marker. The cartouche or oval ring enclosing the name of Tutankhamun was found on objects throughout his tomb. Any significant ancient ruler required a personal seal for signing clay tablets and other inscriptions. Such name-tagging has been found as far apart as Mesopotamia, China, Central America and the Indus Valley, although in the latter case we cannot be sure of the purpose of the exquisite symbols engraved on the large numbers of Indus seal stones, as the script is undeciphered.

Much more common than name-tagging was writing used for accountancy. The earliest writing of all, on clay tablets from ancient Sumer in Mesopotamia, and the slightly later tablets from neighbouring Iran (ancient Elam)—a partially undeciphered script known as proto-Elamite—concerns lists of raw materials and products, such as barley and beer, lists of labourers and their tasks, lists of field areas and their owners, the income and outgoing of temples, and so forth: all with calculations concerning production levels, delivery dates, locations, payments and debts. The same is true, generally speaking, of Linear B—and probably, too, of the earlier Linear A, at least judging from the similarity of its context and appearance with Linear B. The tablet found at the 'Palace of Nestor' in Greece that clinched the decipherment of Linear B in 1953 was simply an inventory of tripod cauldrons—one of them with its legs burnt off—and of goblets of varying sizes and numbers of handles. Such a goblet is described in Homer's *Iliad*, before Nestor sets off for the Trojan war; but Linear B tablets, being palace archives, contain no poetry or literature.

IT IS KNOWN THAT THE ETRUSCANS borrowed the Greek alphabet to write their own language from Greek colonists who had settled in Italy around 775 BC at Pithekoussai (modern Ischia). There are many examples of a 'model' alphabet clearly copied from the Greek alphabet written on objects from aristocratic Etruscan graves. But though the actual Etruscan alphabet strongly resembles this 'model' alphabet, it differs significantly too.

For a start, the letters generally point in the opposite direction to the Greek ones, because Etruscan was written from right to left, whereas classical Greek was written from left to right. And the Etruscans based their signs on the early Greek alphabet (eighth century BC), not on the classical Greek alphabet (fifth century BC and after), and thus the Etruscan alphabet includes, for example, four distinct signs for 's'—the last three of which had been inherited by the early Greeks from the Phoenician alphabet but were later reduced by the classical Greeks to two signs. Then again, there are letters in the 'model' alphabet, such as beta, delta and omicron, which were never used by the Etruscans because their language did not include the particular sounds for which those letters stood in Greek. (A similar situation pertains today in Italy, where schoolchildren learn the roman letters 'k', 'j', 'w' and 'y', which never appear in Italian words.)

As for the Etruscan language, throughout the nineteenth and well into the twentieth century, scholars and amateurs persisted with efforts to relate it to other European languages (even Basque, another 'isolate') by comparing what little could be understood of Etruscan vocabulary from the inscriptions with equivalent words in other languages. But eventually it became clear that the attempt was hopeless. Etruscan was obviously not an Indo-European language and was unrelated to Basque.

Despite the mystery of the language, scholars have long been able to read hundreds, if not thousands of Etruscan words which must from their contexts in the inscriptions be names, such as Ruma (Rome), Clevsina (Chiusi, a city), Fufluns (the god Dionysus), Seianti Hanunia Tlesnasa (the name of a woman on a sarcophagus) and Laris Celatina Lausa (the name of a man). The problem has been to find the meanings of the many words that are not obviously names—to devise techniques that will give information about the language other than by trying to identify it with known language families. Over a long period, since the nineteenth century, it has proved possible to deduce a considerable amount of Etruscan vocabulary (about 250 words) and grammar from a range of clues.

A good example is the Tabula Cortonensis, the third-longest Etruscan inscription. Its discovery in the 1990s, apparently on a building site in the Cortona area, caused a flurry of excitement—and led to a court case in Italy in which the discoverer was accused of theft against the state because one of the pieces of the tablet was missing. Seven remain, which can be fitted together with only small gaps. That the tablet was broken in antiquity can be proved from a scientific analysis of the lines of fracture; maybe someone in ancient times intended to melt it down and reuse the bronze. Its size, 28.5 x 45.8 cm (11.2 x 18 in), is roughly that of two sheets of office paper. At the top, there is a handle, so perhaps the tablet once hung in a public place, such as an archive. Its date of manufacture lies between 225 and 150 BC.

The letters run from right to left, as usual with Etruscan inscriptions. They have been beautifully inscribed on both sides of the tablet, either from a mould using the *cire perdue* (lost wax) technique or, more probably, by direct engraving on the bronze. They cover all of one side (shown here) but only eight lines of the other. Important observations can be made without actually reading the inscription. To begin with, it is clear that one scribe wrote both sides of the tablet except for the last six lines of side A, which are engraved more deeply and therefore with an accentuated curvature. (Why there were two scribes, we can only speculate.) Secondly, there are four unusual marks as in ꟼꟼ which look remarkably like the 'insert paragraph' marks of a modern proofreader; and this is exactly what their function appears to have been. Finally, we can note that the sign standing for e, Ⅎ, which the Etruscans borrowed from the Greek epsilon, appears in *two* versions in the Tabula Cortonensis, facing in opposite directions Ⅎ and Ⅎ. This variant is known from other inscriptions to be local to the Cortona area, and is virtual proof that the

tablet is from Cortona; and this inference is reinforced by the occurrence, twice on the tablet, of the name Velara, an ancestral (or family) name characteristic of Cortona. It is spelt with the local form of the epsilon: ꟼꟼꟼꟼ

The tablet was quickly read by applying the Etruscan alphabet. Word divisions were easily recognised from dots inscribed in the bronze and from the familiarity of many of the sign groups as proper names and other known words such as *cel* (earth, land), *vina* (vineyard) [related to Latin *vinum* (wine)], *puia* (wife), *clan* (son), *rasna* (Etruscans, people) and the numerals *zal* (2), *sa* (4) and *sar* (10). But there were so many names (more than two thirds of the words) and a relatively high proportion of unknown words among the remaining words, that it was not possible fully to translate the document, even though we can be sure of its general content. According to Luciano Agostiniani of the University of Perugia, who published the Tabula Cortonensis in 2000, the tablet is almost certainly a record of a contract between the Cusu family, to which Petru Scevas and his wife Arntlei belong together with fifteen other people, witnessed by a third group of names, including some of their children and grandchildren. It relates to a sale, or lease, of land including a vineyard, in the plain of Lake Trasimeno, a place apparently spelt (on the reverse side) *celtinêitiss tarsiminass*:

ꟼꟼꟼꟼꟼꟼꟼꟼꟼꟼꟼꟼꟼꟼꟼꟼꟼꟼꟼꟼ

The first part of the first word, celtinei, is known to be related to cel (earth, land), so tiss is likely to mean 'lake': a reasonable deduction which was exciting for Agostiniani since it added a new word to the Etruscan vocabulary.

RONGORONGO—which means 'chants' or 'recitations' in the language of Rapanui, the modern name for Easter Island—is a tougher proposition than Etruscan to decipher. Although the language of the inscriptions is probably similar to Rapanui, a Polynesian language, the signs are complex and baffling; there are only some twenty-five surviving inscriptions (though some are quite long), written on wood with a shark's tooth or obsidian flake; and there are no contiguous historical cultures, like

that of ancient Greece and Rome, to provide helpful clues.

The age of *rongorongo* is also puzzling. Rapanui legend has it that the writing was brought to the island by boat from Polynesia when the island was settled, but it could be as recent as the late eighteenth century. The first European visitors to the island, a Dutch fleet which landed in 1722, saw no evidence of writing. When two Spanish ships arrived in 1770 and made a 'treaty' with the islanders claiming Easter Island for Spain, the islanders 'signed' the document with characters that could be writing; but these signatures do not resemble *rongorongo*, though two of the signs do resemble petroglyphs (rock carvings) on the island that almost certainly predate European contact. James Cook, landing in 1774, saw no writing. Indeed the first definite sighting of *rongorongo* does not occur until nearly a century later, recorded in 1864 by a French missionary who noted that knowledge of the signs was already dying out among the islanders. Despite the efforts of the bishop of Tahiti in the 1870s, no islander could be found to read the writing meaningfully; and ever since then scholars have been at odds on how to interpret the inscriptions.

One thing is sure: the direction of reading of *rongorongo* is unusual, known as reverse-boustrophedon (the word comes from the Greek for 'as the ox turns', when ploughing). To read a *rongorongo* tablet, one starts at the bottom left-hand corner and reads along to the right-hand corner. Then one turns the tablet through 180 degrees (hence 're-verse') and begins reading from left to right again. At the end of the second line, one repeats the 180-degree turn so that the tablet is in the same orientation as at the beginning, and reads the third line from left to right, and so on.

In the *rongorongo* tablet known as Mamari, for example, even-numbered lines are upside-down. Four lines of this tablet contain frequent symbols of the crescent moon and show what are almost certainly the nights of the well-known traditional Rapanui lunar calendar, as marked 1-30 in the diagram above by the *rongorongo* scholar Jacques Guy. The last two moon symbols, marked 29 and 30, named Hotu and Hiro, appear to be intercalary nights, inserted as needed to maintain the accuracy of the calendar, which alternated 29-day and 30-day months (a lunar month is actually 29.52 days long). Many of the other symbols have been plausibly interpreted by Guy, for example the ﹖ symbol, representing the waxing moon, and the symbol ﹖ the waning moon. Symbol 15, standing for the full moon, is a picture of the 'Cook-in-the-Moon' (a homunculus with cooking stones as oven), common to Polynesian and most Melanesian mythologies.

WITH THE INDUS VALLEY SCRIPT, decipherers face a situation even more challenging than Etruscan and rongorongo. Neither the signs of the script nor the language of the Indus civilisation is understood, and since it ceased to exist in the early second millennium BC, its connection with the later civilisations of India is likely to be obscure. It covers a large area, approximately a quarter the size of Europe, bigger than the ancient Egyptian and Mesopotamian empires of the third millennium; over 1,500 sites have been discovered, including two major cities, Mohenjodaro and Harappa, and more material continues to be unearthed almost every year, including inscriptions.

About 3,700 inscribed objects are known, 60 per cent of them small seals. In addition to the signs of the script, many of the seal stones are engraved with an often-detailed intaglio of animals, such as rhinoceroses, elephants, tigers, buffaloes and zebus (though curiously no monkeys, peacocks or cobras), some of which are fantastic or chimerical, including a one-horned animal which the early excavators in the 1920s promptly dubbed a 'unicorn' (a creature legendarily originating in India). Once seen, the seals are never forgotten, so exquisite are they. 'At their best, it would be no exaggeration to describe them as little masterpieces of controlled realism, with a monumental strength in one sense out of all proportion to their size and in another entirely related to it', wrote Sir Mortimer Wheeler in the 1950s.

There appear to be three major possibilities for the language of the Indus civilisation. It could be related to Sanskrit, the language of northern India in classical times, which flourished more than 1,500 years after the disappearance of the Indus Valley civilisation; or to the Dravidian languages of southern India, such as Tamil and Malayalam, which were also classical Indian languages; or it could be an 'isolate', like Etruscan. For a number of reasons, archaeological and linguistic, Dravidian languages are favoured by a large majority of scholars, Sanskrit by a handful of nationalistic Indian scholars, who wish to perceive a continuity between an indigenous first Indian language and the mother language of the Hindu heartland. But such is the time gap between the Indus and classical Indian civilisation that no one can do more than speculate intelligently on the Indus language.

In the 1950s, it was suggested that the very common sign in the script that looks like a fish might have been pronounced *min*, which means 'fish' in almost all Dravidian languages. But in many of these languages, *min* also means 'star'. (Compare 'son' and 'sun' in English.) A star, in Indian iconography, is an emblem of divinity and can thus stand for 'god'. The 'fish' sign could then be a rebus forming part of a theophoric name—a very common occurrence in Indian culture, where people are often named after gods and goddesses (e.g. Rama, Krishna, Ganesh, Indira, Lakshmi, Arundhati). Seals with 'fish' signs together with other signs might therefore be identity markers engraved with the names of their owners or institutions. The leading Indus script scholar, Asko Parpola of the University of Helsinki, goes further and speculates that: a beautiful seal from Harappa with a 'fish' sign and seven vertical strokes can be read as *elu min*, 'seven stars', i.e. the constellation Ursa Major.

Like so many interpretations of undeciphered scripts—especially the Indus inscriptions, which have generated as many as 100 serious but conflicting 'decipherments' since 1925—Parpola's reading is contested. But lack of concrete evidence will not stop would-be decipherers from advancing theories and interpretations. A fact of archaeological decipherment is that it attracts both geniuses and cranks; and it is not always easy to tell the two apart.

FURTHER READING

Andrew Robinson, *Lost Languages: The Enigma of the World's Undeciphered Scripts* (McGraw-Hill, 2002); Maurice Pope, *The Story of Decipherment: From Egyptian Hieroglyphs to Maya Script* (2nd edn, Thames and Hudson, 1999); John Chadwick, *The Decipherment of Linear B* (3rd edn, Cambridge UP, 1992); Andrew Robinson, *The Man Who Deciphered Linear B: The Story of Michael Ventris* (Thames and Hudson, 2002); Michael D. Coe, *Breaking the Maya Code* (Thames and Hudson, 1992); J. T. Hooker et al, *Reading the Past: Ancient Writing from Cuneiform to the Alphabet* (British Museum Press, 1990); Asko Parpola, *Deciphering the Indus Script* (Cambridge UP, 1994); Hans J. Nissen, Peter Damerow and Robert K. Englund, *Archaic Bookkeeping: Writing and Techniques of Economic Administration in the Ancient Near East* (University of Chicago Press, 1993).

ANDREW ROBINSON is literary editor of *The Times Higher Education Supplement.*

Hatshepsut

The Female Pharaoh

Continuing our look at women in ancient Egypt, John Ray considers the triumphs and monuments of Queen Hatshepsut, the only female Pharaoh.

John Ray

The Pharaoh of ancient Egypt is normally described as the typical example of a divine ruler. The reality was more complex than this, since the Pharaoh seems to have been a combination of a human element and a divine counterpart. This duality is expressed not only in the ruler's titles, which often have a double aspect to them, but also in the king's names. Every Pharaoh had a human name, given to him at birth and used in intimate contexts throughout his life. These names are the ones by which we know them. Since such names tended to repeat themselves in families, we now need to distinguish kings with the same name by numbers. In addition, there was a throne-name, conferred at the accession and containing the immortal form of the ruler's divinity. The king was an embodiment of the sungod, an eternal prototype, and the human frailties of the individual ruler did not affect this embodiment: a convenient system, surely, for having the best of both worlds when it comes to government. The Pharaoh was essentially an icon, much as the imperial Tsar was an icon, and even the president of the United States sometimes appears to be.

How far can icons be stretched? Pharaoh was the manifestation of the sun in time and place: he could be old, young, athletic, gay, incompetent, boring, alcoholic or insane, but he would still be Pharaoh. Examples of all these types are known, or hinted at in the sources. But could he be female? The theoretical answer to this question may have been 'yes', since there are several ancient Egyptian texts describing creator-gods with both male and female attributes, but it was one thing to concede an abstract possibility and another to welcome its embodiment. Female rulers are attested in the long history of dynastic Egypt, and later tradition puts the names of queens at or near the end of both the Old Kingdom (*c.* 2200 BC) and the Middle Kingdom, some five centuries later. (The Old Kingdom one, Nitocris, later

attracted considerable legends, and appears prominently in Herodotus). However, the important point was that tradition placed these queens at the end of their particular dynasties: female Pharaohs were unnatural, and meant decline and retribution. Egyptian society gave remarkable freedoms and legal rights to women—far more than in the rest of the Near East or in the classical world—but limits were limits, even by the Nile.

Egypt was, and is, a Mediterranean country, where the most powerful man can frequently be reduced to confusion and paralysis by a remark from his mother, but women were limited to their sphere: if they had no other title, they could always be honoured as 'lady of the house'. If they stayed within this domain, they could expect to retain status and protection. Agriculture beside the Nile was intensive, and this meant that women's contributions were essential, as opposed to the more nomadic societies of the Near East, where females were often seen as an encumbrance. Many Egyptian women may not have thought their position a bad bargain; pregnancy and childbirth were expected but dangerous, and support outside the family was unknown and perhaps impossible. Security, and the real possibility of influence over the holders of power, may not have seemed so poor a prospect, especially if a woman produced a son or two, while divorce and inheritance rules for females were relatively favourable. Why break the mould?

The early part of the Eighteenth Dynasty is often known as the Tuthmosid period, after the name of its principal rulers. Tuthmosis I (*c.* 1525–512 BC, although another reckoning would lower these dates by twenty-five years) was a warrior ruler, who took on the scattered principalities of Lebanon and Syria and carried his arms far beyond the Euphrates, setting up a victory stela on the banks of what the Egyptians described as the 'topsy-turvy' river, since it flowed the opposite way to the Nile. In ret-

A granite head of Tuthmosis III, the sidelined young Pharaoh who took revenge on his over-assertive aunt by erasing her inscriptions after her death.

rospect, this is the beginning of something resembling an Egyptian empire in Asia, a subject which was to preoccupy foreign policy throughout the next two dynasties. However, retrospect is a one-way street, and contemporaries may have thought that one show of force was enough. It may equally be that the modern concept of empire is an anachronism for the period: 'sphere of influence' might be a closer guide to Egyptian thinking. Tuthmosis I was followed by another Tuthmosis, a Pharaoh of whom little is known and arguably little worth knowing. However, he was married to Hatshepsut.

Hatshepsut was Tuthmosis II's half-sister (marriage to close relatives was not a problem in the Tuthmosid royal family, and this may explain the prominence given to queens in the early years of the dynasty; all were equally descended from the dynasty's heroic founder). However, it is likely that the king was worried about his wife's ambitions; her name, after all, meant 'Foremost of the noble ladies'. On his premature death (*c.* 1504 BC) he and Hatshepsut had produced only a daughter, Nefrure, and the official successor was Tuthmosis III, a young son by one of the king's minor wives. Clearly the boy was in need of a regent. His aunt thought herself qualified for the job; more importantly, she had convinced enough others of the same truth that she was able to stage a coup. She and Tuthmosis III were declared joint Pharaohs. There were precedents for this in earlier dynasties, and this may have gone some way towards blurring the innovatory fact that one of the co-regents was not male. In a few early scenes she is shown dutifully following her partner, but this soon changes. This was to be a co-regency that was far from equal. For the next twenty-two years it would be 'goodnight from her, and goodnight from her'. The reign of Hatshepsut had begun, and her throne-name was Maatkare, 'Truth (a female principle which also embodies the ideas of justice and harmony) is the genius of the sungod'.

There is a sense in which all history is about the meanings of words, and it is certainly true that to change history involves colliding with the language in which it is expressed. Hatshepsut does this. Traditional Pharaohs were the embodiment of the god Horus; Hatshepsut is also Horus, but the epithets she adds in hieroglyphs are grammatically in the feminine forms. Furthermore, she describes herself as 'The she-Horus of fine gold', fine gold (electrum) being an amalgam of this metal with the rarer and more valuable silver. It is as if she were to style herself the platinum goddess. Like other Pharaohs, she regularly refers to herself as 'His Majesty' (a closer rendering might be 'His Person'). However, the word for majesty is turned into a new feminine equivalent. One is reminded of Elizabeth I of England, with her doctrine of the dual body of the monarch, one of which happens to be female. Rewriting language in the light of gender is not a twentieth-century discovery. It did not work in ancient Egypt (and it might not work now), but the attempt was none the less made. The changes either originated with the queen, or were approved by her, and they must correspond with her thinking. In conventional temple scenes, where the icon of a traditional Pharaoh is necessary, she appears as a male ruler. In sculpture, on the other hand, she is shown as female but imperial, with the typical Tuthmosid face and arched profile. Her portraits are unmistakable.

Hatshepsut's standard bearer is followed by men carrying herbs and spices from the Punt expedition, underlining the possibility that its motive was economic.

(Below) Loading up the Egyptian ships at Punt (from Howard Carter's drawings at the turn-of-the-century of the Deir el-Bahri reliefs): among the `booty' were the frankincense trees that stood in front of Hatshepsut's temple.

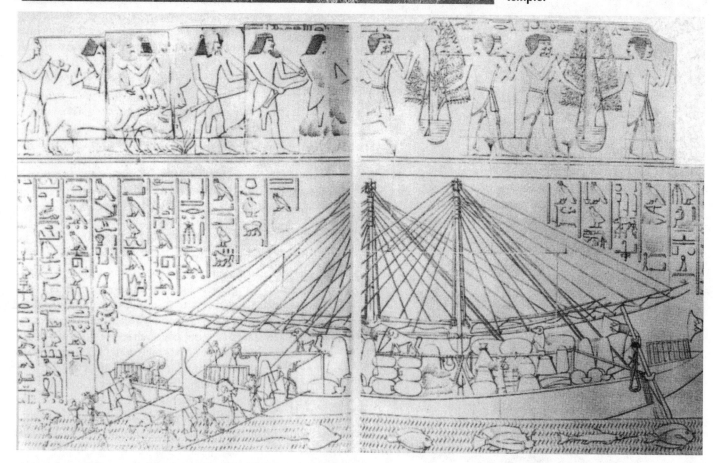

A characteristic of Hatshepsut is her preoccupation with historical context. It is as if she is trying to define her own role in events, to justify her intervention on to the stage and to issue a challenge at the same time. In a deserted valley in Middle Egypt, in the eastern cliffs about 175 miles south of modern Cairo, is an unusual rock-cut temple known by its classical name of Speos Artemidos, the grotto of Artemis. The goddess in question was known to the Egyptians as Pakhet, an obscure deity with the attributes of a lioness. On the facade of this temple is a long dedication, put there by Hatshepsut and her artists, designed, as she tells us, to 'record the annals of her supremacy for ever'. In this text she announced the theme of her reign, which is no less than a complete rebuilding of the land of Egypt. Solar imagery abounds in the text, and Hatshepsut is described without any attempt at modesty as the one predestined since the moment of creation to restore the ritual purity of the temples, to recapture the perfection of the world's origins:

A touch of the exotic—the 'fat lady' of Punt and her husband—one of the observations of Hatshepsut's artists from the walls of her temple on the expedition sponsored by the queen in years 8-9 of her reign.

> I raised up what was dismembered, even from the time when the Asiatics were in the midst of (the Delta), overthrowing what had been created. They ruled in ignorance of Re (the sun-god), and acted not by divine command, until my august person.

This is a reference both to the resurrection of the god Osiris and to the occupation of Egypt by the alien Hyksos, which had preceded the Eighteenth Dynasty: an episode which was shameful, but by no means as barbaric as Hatshepsut makes out. Nor did it last as long as she pretended. This combination of historical perspective and return to religious purity is characteristic of Hatshepsut. Since her position as Pharaoh was unorthodox, an appeal to fundamentalism was necessary to correct the balance. This may well have corresponded to her own thinking, and need not be merely cynical.

Determination to rewrite history is also seen in the official version of the queens proclamation and accession, where the choice of her as ruler is made, not by inheritance or acclamation, but by the oracle of the god Amun, leader of the Egyptian pantheon and ruler of the royal city of Thebes. An oracle of this sort probably happened, since it is suspiciously convenient and could easily have been arranged by the queen's followers after her seizure of power. What is more important is that the queen

is cutting out any human medium, and going straight for an identification with the divine. As Pharaoh, she had this identification automatically, and there would normally be no need to labour the point. Hatshepsut is not normal, and she labours the point for all it contains, here and in her other inscriptions. The platinum goddess can be seen as the Egyptian equivalent of Gloriana, the mythical transformation of Elizabeth I. This is a comparison to which we will return.

One feature of Hatshepsut's reign is often noted: the apparent lack of military activity. There is evidence for minor campaigns in Nubia, and the period is not a complete blank, but the frantic action of the previous reign is lacking. This is sometimes explained as a deliberate attempt by Hatshepsut to adopt a pacifist and feminine approach to politics. This is so completely out of line with what can be deduced about her character that it cannot convince. Female rulers can be as warlike as any man, especially if they feel that they have something to prove. A more likely reason is that Hatshepsut could not trust the army. If she led a campaign herself, even if this were politically acceptable, what would happen if she lost? A female commander would be the natural thing to blame for defeat. If the army won, it might start agitating for more victories, and for a greater role for the queen's nephew, who would gain status as he grew in years. The whole subject was best avoided, especially if Tuthmosis I had already made the point that Egypt was the leading power in Asia. Some things could be left as they were.

If the army could not be used on a large scale, an outlet must be found elsewhere. This is one of the purposes behind the famous expedition to the land of Punt, which occupied the eighth and ninth years of her reign. The location of Punt is unknown, though it may have been Eritrea or part of Somalia, or somewhere further south, but it was the home of the frankincense-tree. The adventure is recorded on the walls of the queen's masterpiece, the great temple in the cliffs of Deir el-Bahri in western Thebes, the modern Luxor. Exquisite reliefs show the departure of the expedition, the arrival at the exotic land beyond the sea, the lading of Hatshepsut's ships with the produce of Punt, and the preparations for the voyage home.

The event was not simply a foraging mission, since it was accompanied by artists to record the flora and fauna of the Red Sea and of the African coast. It can almost be described as the beginning of comparative anthropology, even if the climax—the appearance of the grossly overweight queen of Punt accompanied by a donkey—has an element of the ridiculous about it. Part of the expedition found its way back to Egypt by way of the upper Nile, while five shiploads, including incense-trees, returned by sea. Walter Raleigh would probably have enjoyed Punt, although the reasons for the voyage are not entirely clear. It may have been imperial prospecting, although this is unlikely at this early stage in the dynasty. Perhaps it was economic, an attempt to corner part of the lucrative incense-trade for Egypt. It was certainly an exercise for an underemployed army, and it was propaganda for the queen as provider of the exotic. Perhaps it was also fun.

The roots of the incense-trees can still be seen before the Deir el-Bahri temple, where they were planted and where they perfumed the night air. The temple has been excavated slowly over

Careful courtier: Senenmut, Hatshepsut's steward and one of the queen's closest advisers, shown here as a tutor cradling her daughter, the princess Nefrure.

showing the slightly austere elegance that is common to Tuthmosid art, the balance between light and shade which is necessary in such an exposed site, and the originality of its design make the building unique. Perhaps to contemporaries it was too unique; certainly the concept was never recreated. Manuals of classical architecture tell us that the Doric column was developed in Greece around the seventh century BC. The north colonnade of Deir el-Bahri was composed of them, eight centuries earlier.

Part of the temple was devoted to the divine birth of Hatshepsut, another piece of mythology which normal Pharaohs did not need to use. The god Amun himself desired to create his living image on earth, to reveal his greatness and to carry out his plans. He disguised himself as Tuthmosis I, went one day to see the queen, and the result, in due course, was Hatshepsut. Amun did not mind that his image was female, so why should anyone else?

Similar themes are explored in a rather strange medium, an inscribed pair of granite obelisks which the queen set up in her sixteenth year before the temple of Amun at Karnak opposite Deir el-Bahri. The entire work, she tells us, took seven months. Obelisks in Egyptian thinking were a representation of the first ray of light which inaugurated the creation, or what we would now call the Big Bang. In the text Hatshepsut knows the mind of God: she was present with the creator at the beginning, she is the luminous seed of the almighty one, and she is 'the fine gold of kings'—another reference to electrum. This metal was even used to coat the obelisks, to make her splendour visible. Her sense of posterity, and the force of her personality, are clear from the words she uses:

> Those who shall see my monument in future years, and shall speak of what I have done, beware of saying, 'I know not, I know not how this has been done, fashioning a mountain of gold throughout, like something of nature'... Nor shall he who hears this say it was a boast, but rather, 'How like her this is, how worthy of her father'.

She also tells us that her obelisks were situated by the gateway of Tuthmosis I, since it was he who began the obelisk habit. This preoccupation with the father is not accidental. Pharaoh was Pharaoh because his father had been Pharaoh; in Egyptian mythology, he was Horus to his predecessor's Osiris, one god ruling on earth while the other reigned over the netherworld. However, this was conventional, and orthodox Pharaohs did not need to make it explicit. Hatshepsut, the female Horus, was not orthodox. Her kingship depended on mythological props, and also on political ones; in fact, she would not have made a distinction between the two. But there may well be a third element at work, a personal one.

Tuthmosis I is prominent in many of her inscriptions, far more than is necessary. His sarcophagus was even discovered in his daughter's tomb, where it had been transferred from his own. Clearly she intended to spend eternity with the man who had been her father on earth. She left her husband, Tuthmosis II, where he was lying in the Valley of the Kings, and her inscrip-

the past century (its scenes were first copied by a young draughtsman named Howard Carter), and its plan is now clear. No one who walks the path over the mountain from the Valley of the Kings and looks down at the other side can ignore the series of terraces below, built into the western cliffs. It is one of the most dramatic sights in Egypt. The variety of its scenes, all

tions never mention him, even though he was presumably the parent of her child. This is a trait which prominent females sometimes show. Anna Freud turned herself into Sigmund's intellectual heir, Benazir Bhutto makes a political platform out of her father's memory, and one is reminded of a recent British prime minister whose entry in *Who's Who* included a father but no mother. Did Tuthmosis I ever call his daughter 'the best man in the dynasty', and is this why Hatshepsut shows no identification with other women? This is not entirely hypothetical: among Hatshepsut's inscriptions is an imaginative reworking of an episode when she was young, in which her father proclaims her his heir before the entire palace. Such a text could have been based on a coming-of-age ceremony, or even a chance remark to an impressionable child.

Hatshepsut was determined to hold on to power, and the way she achieved this is clear. After the gradual disappearance of her father's advisers, almost all her supporters are new men (women she could not have appointed, even if she had had a mind to). They owed nothing to the traditional aristocracy, little to conventional patronage: they were 'one of us'. They were hers, and if she fell, they would fall also. Their tombs are still visible in the cliffs above Deir el-Bahri. They are easily distinguished by the terraced effect of their facades, which resemble the royal temple; even in their architecture they showed whose men they were. This must have been a court where many lesser lights danced attendance on the sun-queen.

The most prominent courtier of Hatshepsut's reign is Senenmut. He dominates the temple of Deir el-Bahri, where he seems to be an overall but ill-defined master of works. His figure even appears in small niches in some of its chapels, worshipping the god Amun and his royal mistress. These niches are hidden behind the doors, but the gods would have known what was in them, and so probably did Hatshepsut. This must have been done with her approval. Senenmut's place in the royal household is confirmed by his position as tutor to the queen's daughter Nefrure, and statues survive showing Senenmut crouching in the guise of a patient client, while the head of the royal infant peeps out from between his knees. Senenmut was given permission to be buried within the precincts of the great temple, an unprecedented honour.

Around the seventh year of the reign Senenmut's mother died, and she too was interred in the temple. Senenmut exhumed the body of his father at the same time, and reburied him in splendour alongside her and other members of his family. The father had no title (otherwise the Egyptians, who were obsessed with titles, would have not failed to mention it), and his original burial was tantamount to a pauper's. Senenmut must have come from a small town along the Nile, and rose to prominence entirely through merit and the queen's patronage. This sheds unexpected light on what could happen in ancient Egypt. Senenmut seems never to have married. Perhaps he did not dare

to; did not Walter Raleigh fall from grace as soon as he married one of Gloriana's maids?

Recently evidence has emerged that the reign of Hatshepsut could inspire distinctly tabloid reactions. Some years ago, in an unfinished tomb above the Deir el-Bahri temple, a series of graffiti were found. One of these is a feeble drawing of Senenmut, but on another wall there is a sketch showing a female Pharaoh undergoing the attentions of a male figure, in a way that implies her passive submission. This may be a contemporary comment on the relationship between Senenmut and the queen, or it may be a later satire on the notion of an impotent female Pharaoh, or it may simply be the fantasy of a little man for something he could never attain, rather on the lines of the stories which later circulated about Cleopatra or Catherine the Great. If the scene is genuine, it is extremely interesting, even if its meaning is less explicit than its drawing.

The queen died on the tenth day of the sixth month of the twenty-second year of her reign (early February 1482 BC). She was perhaps fifty. Tuthmosis III, so long cooped up, became sole Pharaoh and immediately led his army into Syria, where in seventeen campaigns he restored Egyptian overlordship of the Near East. At some point, though not for some years, he began a proscription of his aunt's memory. Probably he chose to wait until Senenmut and her other supporters had passed away. Perhaps he remained in awe of her. Her inscriptions were erased, her obelisks surrounded by a wall, and her monuments forgotten. Her name does not appear in later annals, which is why we refer to Tuthmosis by a Greek transcription, while hers is missing. The bodies of many of the New Kingdom Pharaohs survive, and are now in the Cairo Museum. As far as we know, hers is not among them. What we do know about her has been gained by excavation and careful epigraphy over the past hundred years. Perhaps this is as it should be, since the late twentieth century is a better time than most to think about the meaning of her reign. Will the feminist movement rediscover her, or will she be uncomfortable for us, as she was for some of her contemporaries?

FOR FURTHER READING:

Cambridge Ancient History (3 edn., vol. II, 1973, ch. 9); Peter F. Dorman, *The Monuments of Senenmut* (Kegan Paul International, 1988); Miriam Lichtheim, *Ancient Egyptian Literature II* (California, 1976); Donald B. Redford, *History and Chronology of the Eighteenth Dynasty of Egypt* (Toronto, 1967) and the same author's *Egypt, Canaan, and Israel in Ancient Times* (Princeton, 1992); John Romer, *Romer's Egypt* (Rainbird, 1982); Edward F. Wente, 'Some Graffiti from the Reign of Hatshepsut', *Journal of Near Eastern Studies 43* (1984).

John Ray is Herbert Thompson Reader in Egyptology at Cambridge University.

Past, Present, Future

Perceptions of Time Through the Ages

by DAN FALK

TIME ENVELOPS AND DEFINES OUR WORLD. We try to save time; we hate to waste time; we say we'll make time for some favorite activity. We say that time flies when we're having fun and slows to a crawl when we're not. Many of us are paid by the hour; Internet and phone companies bill by the minute; advertising time is sold by the second. Yet just a few centuries ago, our ancestors would have worried little about minutes and not at all about seconds. The way we conceive of time has varied greatly across the millennia and from one ancient culture to another—from those who tracked the sun and stars with stunning accuracy to those who barely acknowledged the existence of past and future. In some cases, time's fingerprints can be seen in the archaeological record—in clocks and calendars, observatories, and monuments. But it is also reflected in more subtle ways—in the religions we practice, the rituals we follow, and even the words we speak. Perceptions of time have shaped the lives and minds of everyone who has lived on this planet, in every culture and in every age.

AWARENESS OF TIME has been a fundamental part of the human experience. Even the earliest hominids must have been aware of time's passage, says Paleolithic archaeologist John Shea of the State University of New York at Stony Brook. Those early human ancestors, he says, "probably had a rudimentary conception of time similar to our own—an understanding of the past, an understanding of the future—and the ability to perceive the future in terms of contingencies, in terms of 'if this, then that.'" Paleolithic peoples may have even used tools to track time: A carved bone tablet from the Dordogne Valley in France, dating back some thirty thousand years, has a series of notches scratched in it, set down in rows of fourteen or fifteen—roughly the number of days from new moon to full moon. It may have been a primitive lunar calendar—or, as skeptics have pointed out, a way for a woman to track her menstrual cycle, or simply a knife-sharpening tool. Signs of ritual burial, including grave goods that hint at a conception of eternity, go back nearly as far.

By the time the first civilizations emerged from the shadows of prehistory some five thousand years ago, our species had developed a fascination with time's most visible natural cycles. All of the great ancient civilizations boasted intricate calendars inspired by the regularity of the heavens—the daily motion of the sun, the monthly waxing and waning of the moon, the annual parade of the seasons.

The Neolithic peoples of northern Europe, who lacked a written language, may have been careful observers of those heavenly patterns. The great stone circles found in the British Isles and northern Europe (Stonehenge, built beginning around 2700 B.C., being the most famous) have often been interpreted as observatories and planetariums. At Stonehenge, a person standing at the center of the array who gazed through two pairs of giant vertical megaliths and past the "heel stone" would be able to watch the the summer solstice sunrise. The so-called "German Stonehenge," recently unearthed near the town of Goseck in eastern Germany, may be even older. Further evidence for ancient German astronomy comes from the Nebra disk, touted as the world's oldest star map. The 3,600-year-old bronze and gold disk, twelve inches across, has images of the sun, moon, and thirty-two stars.

Ancient sky watchers dissected the day as well. The Egyptians may have been the first to use sundials (though ancient Chinese devices are a close contender). A fragment of an Egyptian sundial dating from about 3000 B.C. can be seen in the Metropolitan Museum of Art in New York; the largest surviving ancient sundial is the ninety-seven-foot obelisk at Karnak, Egypt, erected around 1470 B.C., which casts its shadow on a temple of the sun god Amun Ra.

The Egyptians had portable timekeepers as well. "Shadow clocks" were T-shaped devices that were pointed toward the sun, the shadow of the crossbar falling on the ruled perpendicular bar. They were in use by around 1500 B.C.; an example from the eighth century B.C. is found in the Museum of the Ancient Agora in Athens.

The Egyptians used sundials to track twelve hours of daylight, with twelve more passing at night—a tradition that we've kept, but with one important change: The length of the Egyptian hour varied with the seasons, while we fix the hour at sixty minutes. By the time of the Roman Empire, sundials had become both sophisticated and common, allowing the day to be mapped out into hours and the hour cut into halves and quarters.

The Roman Playwright Plautus griped, "Confound him, who in this place set up a sundial, to cut and hack my days so wretchedly into small pieces!"

Not everyone was pleased with the growing tyranny of timekeeping. "The gods confound the man who first found out how to distinguish the hours," the Roman playwright Plautus griped in the second century B.C. "Confound him, too, who in this place set up a sundial, to cut and hack my days so wretchedly into small pieces!"

The Romans, borrowing elements from the Egyptians and the Babylonians, also gave us our 365-day calendar—365 and a quarter with the introduction of the leap year under Julius Caesar, later modified into its present form by Pope Gregory XIII. Ever wonder why December is the twelfth month and not the tenth, as its name suggests? Because in Roman times it was indeed tenth, the year having begun in March. When the New Year begins is, after all, an arbitrary marker—and many cultures adopted spring, with its suggestion of rebirth and renewal, as the starting point.

For the ancient Egyptians, the key annual event happened in midsummer, and it involved not only the sun but also the bright star Sirius (which they equated with the astral god Sothis). Every spring Sirius disappears for several weeks, hidden by the sun's glare; the New Year began when Sirius first became visible again in the predawn sky, heralding the flooding of the Nile.

Islam's quest for accurate timekeeping, a requirement for its strict regimen of prayer, led Muslims to become expert astronomers.

Sirius, which has its roots in the Greek word for "scorching," is the brightest star in the constellation Canis Major (the Big Dog); because in ancient Rome the star rose and set with the sun during the hottest time of the year, those were called the "dog days" of summer—a colloquialism that survives to this day.

Many South American cultures used the Pleiades star cluster (the "Seven Sisters") to track important events; in many native languages, the word for "year" and "Pleiades" is the same. The key role played by the Pleiades and other celestial bodies can be seen in some of the surviving ancient structures of the region, especially those of the Incas. At Machu Picchu, for example, an oval-shaped stone building, known as the Torreon, has one of its windows aligned with the point on the horizon where the Pleiades rises. In Cuzco, the ancient capital, the Coricancha, or Temple of the Sun, was an observatory from which astronomers tracked celestial cycles such as equinoxes, solstices, and eclipses. From these observations the rulers of the vast empire were able to "regulate time in order to fix civil, agricultural, and religious dates over a wide area," writes archaeoastronomy expert Anthony Aveni in *Empires of Time*, one of the best popular accounts of timekeeping and ancient cultures.

THE MONTH—the period from one new (or full) moon to the next—is perhaps an even more obvious cycle. Islamic cultures have based their calendar on the moon exclusively; notice how the flags of many Muslim nations feature the crescent moon. Islam's quest for accurate timekeeping, a requirement for its strict regimen of prayer, led Muslims to become expert astronomers. By the turn of the first millennium A.D., Arab and Muslim scientists had perfected astronomical instruments like the astrolabe and established great observatories across the Middle East. The oldest surviving one is the recently renovated thirteenth-century observatory at Maragha (present-day Maragheh) in northern Iran. Because the Muslim year consists of twelve cycles of the moon, it is 354 days long—some eleven days short of a solar year. For that reason, the Muslim calendar year "drifts" relative to the seasons.

Some cultures, meanwhile, piled cycles on top of cycles. The Maya of ancient Mexico and Central America offer one of the most impressive examples. They marked not only the (approximately) 356-day cycle of the seasons, but also a 260-day "sacred round" (variously interpreted as relating to the planet Venus, eclipses, and pregnancy), a longer cycle of 360 days known as the *tun*, and a 584-day cycle associated with the movement of Venus. Their calculation of the solar year, in fact, was more accurate than our Gregorian calendar.

What most distinguishes the Maya conception of time from the Western view, however, is not the counting system but the imagined nature of time itself. For us, time is inanimate: We feel that it "flows" by at a constant rate, with no heed paid to human or machine. We can neither give it a boost nor slow it down. For the Maya, however, time is organic—it can be stretched, shrunk, or even stopped by human activity; people are seen to be intimately involved in time's passage. For starters, each of the twenty named days in the Maya calendar was essentially deified and said to have a distinct personality; certain days were deemed good for some tasks and bad for others. A child born on a particular day would be expected to have certain character traits associated with the day and its god. (Our modern-day astrology charts, based on the constellations of the zodiac, claim to do the same thing.) Keeping time on its course was a community effort; everyone had to pitch in. The king, however, had the greatest responsibility. As divinely ordained ruler, he was seen as the embodiment of time, and it was his duty to use time to maintain the social, political, and cosmological order.

A Maya king was seen as the embodiment of time, and it was his duty to use time to maintain the social, political, and cosmological order.

The burden of that temporal responsibility comes to life in one of the most striking exhibits at Harvard University's Peabody Museum—a cast of a stone monument from the Maya city of Copan, in Honduras, known as Altar Q. The square stele is carved with the figures of sixteen kings—four to a side—spanning nearly four hundred years of history. Time wraps around this monument, so that the sixteenth monarch is face to face with the first. The old king is passing what looks like a torch to the new king.

"This is the guy who actually dedicated the stone," says David Stuart, a curator of Maya hieroglyphics at the Peabody and a lecturer in anthropology at Harvard, referring to the sixteenth king. "He's the living king. His name was Yax Pasaj." Beside the king are glyphs indicating the date of his inauguration and commemorating the symbolic passing of the throne from the founding king.

Imagine a train bound for Chicago that departs when the people are on board rather than at, say, 5:15 p.m.

Yax Pasaj was the last king; the regime soon collapsed. Perhaps it was the result of the droughts, famine, and warfare that were swirling around Copan in the eighth century A.D., but Stuart can't help wondering if the calendar played a role: The king began his reign just as the *baktun*, a 394-year cycle, was drawing to a close. "It would have been hard for any king who came after this to really put himself into this cosmological scheme," suggests Stuart. The Maya of Copan, he says, "may have seen it as a time when change was necessary."

THE MAYA WERE HARDLY ALONE in seeing time as an organic, animate entity. In many cultures the organic nature of time is reflected in the relative importance of events and sequences rather than the time marked by the clock or calendar. In parts of Africa, there is a prevalence of "event time" over "clock time." The semino-madic Nuer of the southern Sudan divide the year into wet and dry months; the seasons are recognized by changes in rainfall and wind patterns. Ask a Nuer in May what time of the year it is, and he'll say "the old people are returning to the villages." Ask again in January and you'll be told "everyone is returning to the dry-season camps." Aveni writes in *Empires of Time*, "The temporal logic [for the Nuer] seems to be: if I'm going to church this must be Sunday; or *since* people are on the move going between camp and village, *then it must be* [the month of] *dwat*.... Activity supercedes time in the sense that we know it." Try to imagine a Wall Street brokerage that begins the trading day when the employees have begun trading rather than at 9:30 A.M., or a train bound for Chicago that departs when the people are on board rather than at, say; 5: 15 P.M.

When time is marked by events rather than clocks and calendars, the order of those events becomes paramount. For the Luo people of western Kenya, time is literally felt to stand still unless certain events take place in their prescribed order. "The role played by the first wife, in a polygamous Luo household, is very, very clear," says Chap Kusimba, an archaeologist and tribal African culture authority at the Field Museum in Chicago. "The first wife must be the first one to plant her crops, to prepare her farm, before all the other women. She must be the first one to weed, the first to eat," he says. Similarly, the first-born son "must be the one to marry first, whether he likes it or not.... Things are done in a particular way. You can't break that rule."

In some cultures, time as we think of it in the West barely seems to exist. For many Native American cultures, Australian Aboriginals, and a number of African and Pacific island societies, there is no single word for "time." Evan T. Pritchard, a descendant of the Miramichi branch of the Micmac Nation of eastern Canada, spent many years observing the elders of his tribe. The Micmacs have words for day, night, sunrise, sunset, youth, adulthood, and old age—but not for time itself, he notes in his aptly titled book *No Word for Time*. "There is no concept of time outside its embodiment of things in nature," he writes. In parts of Asia where Hinduism and Buddhism are the dominant religions, cyclical time guarantees that everything will return to a former state; history is an illusion. Nothing is permanent, and even death is merely a passageway to birth and renewal.

The Micmacs have words for day, night, sunrise, sunset, youth, adult, and old age—but not for time itself.

Perhaps no ancient culture had as complex a view of time as China. The Chinese tracked the motions of the night sky in minute detail. Oracle bones from the Shang Dynasty (thirteenth century B.C.) describe a lunar eclipse and constitute one of the oldest surviving records of a specific astronomical event. But the cosmos was viewed as having terrestrial influence, with the appearance of each comet, eclipse, or planetary alignment seen as a divine commentary on earthly events.

Time, for the Chinese, was in part cyclic; political dynasties were seen to rise and fall, mirroring celestial cycles. The fifth-century B.C. sage Confucius compared the ideal ruler to the North Star, around which the entire cosmos revolved. Yet superimposed on this was a deep sense of linear time on both short and long scales. China's mechanical water clocks predate Europe's first weight-driven clocks by several centuries. The best known was the so-called "heavenly clockwork" of Su Sung, begun in A.D. 1077. This elaborate instrument used flowing water to turn a giant wheel at a precise, steady rate. By the time it was completed in 1090, it was nearly thirty feet tall, employing dozens of wheels, bells, and gongs; it was housed in a pagoda five stories high.

Intriguingly, such temporal sophistication was coupled with what would seem to a Western sensibility to be a highly counterintuitive view of causality. In ancient China, says David Pankenier, an authority on Chinese history, language, and culture at Lehigh University in Pennsylvania, time is "woven together as if in a large fabric." Events in one part of the empire are seen to impact events elsewhere, regardless of their sequence in time—just as a fabric pulled in one spot causes ripples to be felt across its breadth. When a dynasty is in decline—imagine an Asian cousin of the unfortunate Yax Pasaj of Copan—the malaise is felt throughout the empire. "It's the whole tenor of the moment," says Pankenier. "It's [like] listening to the keynote of a musical piece that is off-key." For the Chinese, the goal is "temporal harmony within the person, among individuals, and between society and nature," according to J.T. Fraser, the founder of the International Society for the Study of Time.

Time, for the Chinese, was in part cyclic; political dynasties were seen to rise and fall, mirroring the celestial cycles of the sun, moon, and stars.

HERE IN THE WEST it was a different story. Judeo-Christian theology described history as a unique sequence of events that unfold under God's watchful eye, from a singular Creation toward an eventual Day of Judgment—a decidedly linear view of time.

The conception of linear time, historians have argued, became a cornerstone of the Western worldview, along-

side science, reason, and a sense of progress, paving the way for the Scientific Revolution and the Industrial Revolution. By the end of the seventeenth century, Europeans viewed time as an abstract entity wholly independent of human activity.

In the Western view, the ability to dissect time is limited only by technology. Europe's first mechanical clocks, dating to the late thirteenth or early fourteenth century, were found in the cathedrals; monks needed timely reminders for their seven rounds of daily prayer. One of the earliest of these weight-driven clocks can still be seen today: Dating from the 1380s, the wood-and-iron clock in Salisbury Cathedral in England may be the world's oldest surviving mechanical timepiece.

Before long, the bells were ringing out over the marketplace as well. Industrialization would eventually bring the factory whistle, the steamship, the locomotive, and, by the nineteenth century, the telegraph and the telephone, creating a more scheduled world. It was also a world in which time had become a commodity. If time is money, then every second counts. In today's world, many of us try to squeeze as much as we can into each minute, each day, each year.

Judeo-Christian theology described history as a unique sequence of events that unfolds under God's watchful eye.

Knowing how the passage of time was viewed, used, and tracked by ancient civilizations helps archaeologists understand how those cultures organized their lives. Our ancestors began measuring time out of necessity: Agriculture demanded attention to the seasons, and reaping the largest harvests demanded knowledge of the sun and stars and their endless cycles. But time's grasp reached further, influencing every facet of public and private life. A ruler used time to maintain the political order in his empire; a monk, rabbi, or imam to schedule his prayers; a shaman to determine the sequence of rituals; a merchant to run his business; a tribesman to determine when to marry. For some, time was organic and flexible; for others, it ran in cycles, mirroring those seen in nature. For still others, including ourselves, time was inanimate, linear, and relentless. No one—king or queen, farmer or trader, priest or peasant—escapes time's shadow.

DAN FALK is a science journalist based in Toronto. His first book, *UNIVERSE ON A T-SHIRT: THE QUEST FOR THE THEORY OF EVERYTHING*, was published this winter by Arcade Publishing.

The Coming of the Sea Peoples

*A low-tech revolution in Bronze Age battlefield tactics
changed the history of the Western world.*

by Neil Asher Silberman

In the long annals of Western military history, one important group of battlefield innovators—whose archaeological traces have been uncovered from mainland Greece to the coasts of Lebanon and Israel—has often been overlooked. Around 1200 B.C., a wave of sword-wielding warriors streamed southward across the Aegean and eastward toward Asia Minor, Cyprus, and Canaan. By around 1175, some of them had reached the borders of Egypt, where they were finally repulsed by the land and sea forces of Pharaoh Ramesses III. Yet in their stunning military successes throughout the region, these warriors exerted an enormous impact on the development of ancient warfare and proved instrumental in the transformation of Mediterranean society. In subsequent centuries, the rising kingdoms of Israel and Phoenicia and the city-states of Classical Greece all adopted their tactics, arms, and strategic mentality.

Who were these invading forces and where did they come from? What was it about their weapons and tactics that proved to be so deadly to the great Late Bronze Age empires—and so influential in shaping the societies that succeeded them? For the past 150 years, historians have recognized that the twelfth century B.C. was a time of great upheaval, in which ancient empires were toppled and new societies were born. They have as-cribed this dramatic transformation not to innovations in warfare but to vast population movements, spearheaded by a coalition of northern tribes and ethnic groups who are mentioned repeatedly in ancient Egyptian inscriptions—and whom nineteenth-century scholars dubbed the "Sea Peoples" or the "Peoples of the Sea." These Sea Peoples were not simply Bronze Age Vikings but were a haphazard collection of farmers, warriors, and craftspeople, as well as sailors who originated in the highlands of the Balkans and the coastlands of Asia Minor. Their only common trait seems to have been their movement across the Mediterranean toward the centers of trade and agriculture of the Near East.

Their impact on the Near Eastern empires was dramatic, though scholars are deeply divided on the reasons. Some maintain that the Sea Peoples were displaced from their homelands by famine, natural disasters, or political breakdown and were able to overcome the sophisticated, cosmopolitan empires of the Mediterranean by their sheer barbarian savagery. Others suggest that a closer analysis of the historical records and archaeological remains from this period can pinpoint a more specific agent of change connected to the era's vast population movements. There is reason to believe that only a small, specialized class of professional warriors, in the midst of the much more massive migratory waves, was responsible for the military attacks of the Sea Peoples. As a skilled caste of mercenary foot soldiers who drifted southward to find employment in kingdoms throughout the region, this group of Sea Peoples had both the tactical know-how and the weaponry to recognize—and demonstrate—just how pitifully vulnerable the great Late Bronze Age powers had become. The civilization of the Late Bronze Age (c. 1550 to c. 1200 B.C.), to which these northern mercenary contingents gravitated, was typified by grand monuments, opulent palace cultures, and some of the most complex administrative and accounting systems the Mediterranean world had ever seen. In Egypt, the powerful pharaohs of the New Kingdom resided amid the splendor of Thebes in Upper Egypt. There they prospered from the rich agricultural produce of the Nile valley and enjoyed the luxury goods acquired from a far-flung trade network reaching from Africa and the southern coast of Arabia to the islands of the Aegean Sea. To the north of Egypt, in the city-states of Canaan, on the island of Cyprus, and at the cosmopolitan port of Ugarit, local dynasties ruled over docile peasant populations and vied with one another for diplomatic or commercial advantage. In the vast continental expanse of Asia Minor, the Hittite empire

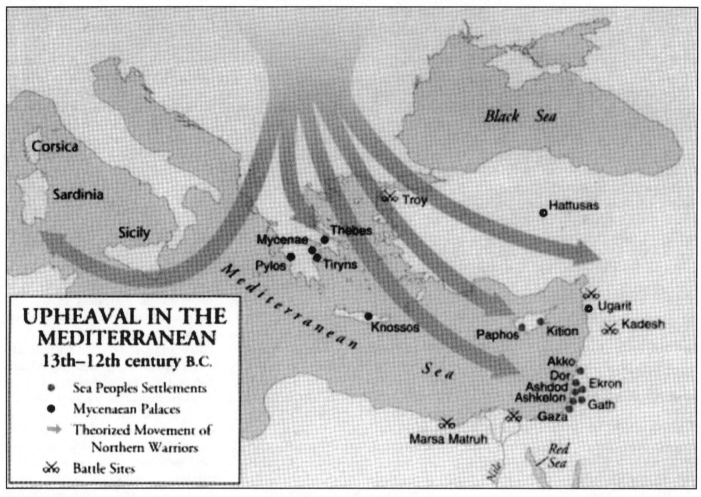

GEOSYSTEMS, COLUMBIA, MD

Not long after appearing in Egypt, Sea People warriors fought for the Egyptians at Kadesh (c. 1275 B.C.). They would become agents of radical change, likely bringing down Mycenaean civilization and enfeebling the great empires of the ancient world.

maintained its feudal rule from the stronghold of Hattusas. And across the Aegean Sea, on mainland Greece, Crete, and the islands, a unique palace-based civilization of regional rulers, with their coteries of servants, craftsmen, priests, and mercenary forces, comprised the chivalric society that was at least partially reflected in the physical details of Homer's *Iliad*.

Despite these differences in styles and traditions, all the empires of the Late Bronze Age were united in their dependence on a single military technology. No self-respecting kingdom could exist for long without attack forces based on the light battle chariot, which was then the most sophisticated and reliable vehicle of war. The chariots of this period were constructed with considerable skill—and at considerable cost—from

sturdy yet highly flexible laminates of wood and bone that enabled them to travel at high speed and with great maneuverability. Propelled by a specially bred and trained two-horse team, the chariot was manned by a professional driver and a combat archer, whose composite bow, also constructed of laminated materials, could launch arrows with extraordinary accuracy and force. These factors all added up to make the light chariot a high-powered, highly mobile weapons delivery system that could swoop down on static infantry forces with frightening speed and velocity.

The figure of the charioteer—as an embodiment of individual skill and courage—became, in many respects, a symbol for the age. The firepower of the new-style chariots was so overwhelming on the battlefield that no ruler who hoped

to maintain his throne against his local or regional rivals could afford to be without them—any more than any truly modern nation can afford to be without an effective air force. As a result, Bronze Age kings, pharaohs, and princes scrambled to assemble chariot forces. And just as the kings and potentates of other eras strutted in the guise of knights-errant, cavalry officers, or naval commanders, Late Bronze Age Egyptian pharaohs and Mycenaean, Hittite, and Canaanite kings were all grandly depicted on their monuments in the pose of triumphant charioteers. Yet as the chariot buildup continued through the fourteenth and thirteenth centuries B.C., and as chariot formations gradually rendered infantry battles obsolete in conflicts between rival city-states or empires, a costly arms race began to get out of control.

By the time of the Hittite-Egyptian confrontation at the battle of Kadesh in Syria in 1275 B.C., relatively modest chariot corps of a few dozen vehicles had expanded to enormous contingents. At Kadesh, the Hittite chariot corps alone numbered at least 3,500 vehicles. This placed a strain on even the wealthiest kingdoms. The cost of chariots and horses was substantial. And the skilled craftsmen, chariot drivers, archers, and horse trainers required to maintain the battle-readiness of a kingdom's chariot force could—and did—demand lavish personal support, generous land grants, and conspicuously privileged status at each court they served. Thus, at times of shortage brought about by drought, flood, disease, or poor crop yields, the demands of the charioteers and their staffs could force individual kingdoms toward the breaking point. And yet the Late Bronze Age powers had all become dangerously dependent on this method of warfare. Little wonder, then, that when its tactical vulnerability was discovered, the whole edifice came tumbling down. The result was one of the great turning points in history dubbed by some the Great Catastrophe. Within the span of just a few decades before and after 1200 B.C., the Bronze Age civilizations of Greece and Asia Minor were shattered, and Egypt gradually lost its role as a regional superpower. At the same time, the sudden arrival and settlement of new peoples on Cyprus and along the coast of Canaan ushered in a new era of small kingdoms and city-states.

Just beyond the confines of the civilized regions of the Mediterranean world, in the mountainous areas of the Balkan peninsula and in the rugged hinterlands of western and southern Asia Minor, the chariot had no power. It was suited only to action on the relatively level battlefields of the lowlands and the plains. On the occasions when the great empires felt the need to mount punitive expeditions against the inhabitants of the highlands, they dispatched infantry forces for brief, brutal demonstrations of force. For the most part, however, the highlanders were left alone as long as

they handed over the demanded tribute and did nothing to interfere with the main routes of trade. Among the tribal societies of these regions, internal disputes were settled in contests of single combat between experienced professional warriors. Archaeological finds from warriors' tombs across western and central Europe, from Scandinavia to the Black Sea, have provided evidence of this mobile, deadly kind of hand-to-hand warfare, waged with long, two-edged swords that could be swung with enough momentum to decapitate an opponent or cut off a limb. Small round shields seem also to have been used to deflect rapid parries. Helmets of various designs and light body armor of many shapes and materials were also common in this individualistic style of war. In terms of weaponry and personal aggressiveness, the warriors of the frontier areas were much more formidable than the typical infantries of the Mediterranean empires, whose members were usually conscripted from the local peasantry, poorly trained, and armed only with short daggers, spears, or clubs.

The reason for the neglect of the infantry by the Mediterranean empires was the overwhelming importance accorded to chariot forces, which comprised the main tactical elements. Lines of chariots would charge against each other like modern tank forces, and, having penetrated or outflanked the opposing formation, would wheel around quickly and charge against the opposing chariots again. Foot soldiers were used in the decidedly secondary capacities of guard duty, road escort, frontier patrols, and routine police work. The only battlefield function reserved for foot soldiers was as "runners" who raced behind and among the chariots, snatching up fallen enemy booty and finishing off wounded enemy chariot crews. This mopping-up function was of little tactical significance. But by the time of the battle of Kadesh, the appearance of a new kind of runner proved to be an omen of the way that subsequent wars in the Mediterranean region would be waged—and won.

In a provocative new book entitled *The End of the Bronze Age: Changes in Warfare and the Catastrophe, ca. 1200 B.C.*, Robert Drews, a professor of an-

cient history at Vanderbilt University, argues that the arrival of northern-style warriors in the Mediterranean upset the unquestioned domination of the chariot. By so doing, it undermined the foundations of the regimes the chariots were meant to defend. Drews notes that barely ten years before the battle of Kadesh, Egyptian hieroglyphic reliefs recorded the ominous movements of a people named the "Sherden," who had arrived "in their warships from the midst of the sea." Wearing trademark horned helmets and armed with long swords and small round shields, they obviously made a profound impression on the Egyptians. By the time the Egyptian chariot forces moved north to confront the Hittites, contingents of Sherden had been recruited by the Egyptians to serve as bodyguards and particularly deadly "runners" among the chariots.

In contrast to the usual runners, who merely mopped up after the chariot charges, the Sherden apparently became an independent offensive force. They are shown in the reliefs of the battle of Kadesh using their weapons to slash, hack, and dismember enemy charioteers. Their weapons, which were originally designed for individual combat, made Sherden warriors far more mobile and adaptable to changing battlefield conditions than the traditional formations of infantry. And with significant numbers of aggressive, northern-style warriors swarming among the chariots, deflecting arrows with their shields and pouncing on disabled vehicles with long swords swinging, they would have posed a sudden, unexpected threat to the firepower and mobility of even the most impressive concentrations of chariotry. While the traditional Bronze Age foot soldiers marched together in relatively slow-moving formations and used weapons such as clubs and spears, which had only a limited radius of effectiveness, the Sherden seem to have ranged widely, pouncing on vulnerable chariot crews.

No less important, they possessed weapons far more effective in combat than those of standard Bronze Age foot soldiers. Ancient pictorial representations of Sherden runners suggest that they were also skilled in the use of the hunting javelin, commonly used in this period for felling wild game. In combination with the long sword, the hunting javelin would have been especially deadly. Drews makes a persuasive—if admittedly speculative—case for suggesting that these new weapons could transform units of runners into an effective battlefield strike force. "For the 'hunting' of chariot horses the javelin must have been ideal," Drews writes, "although it seldom would have killed the horse that it hit, the javelin would have surely brought it to a stop, thus immobilizing the other horse, the vehicle and the crew."

The battle of Kadesh ended in a stalemate between the Egyptians and the Hittites, ushering in a brief period of military balance between the two powers. But by the middle of the thirteenth century B.C., new groups of northern warriors armed with long swords and javelins were drawn in increasing numbers toward the centers of the Late Bronze Age empires, where they were destined to upset the delicate geopolitical balance. Initially, they found employment as mercenaries just as the Sherden had done. Among the names mentioned in Egyptian records and in the archives of Ugarit and the Hittite empire were—in addition to the Sherden—groups known as the Shekelesh, Tursha, Lukka, Shardana, and Ekwesh. Linguistic analysis of these names has enabled scholars to identify them with peoples mentioned in classical and biblical literature: Sicilians, Tyrrhenians, Lycians, and Achaean Greeks. The Sherden have been identified as a group originating on the island of Sardinia, or, according to some scholars, as its eventual conquerors.

It is important to recognize, however, that these Sea Peoples mentioned in the ancient records were not entire nations displaced from their homelands, but a particular military caste represented by warriors from many ethnic groups. Like the pirates and freebooters of the seventeenth-century Caribbean, their many separate nationalities were as conspicuous as the threatening uniformity of their weapons and hand-to-hand fighting techniques.

Archaeologists are generally agreed that the relative tranquility of the Late Bronze Age world following the battle of Kadesh was rocked sometime after 1250 B.C. by a great wave of destructions and upheavals that seems to have begun in the Aegean basin. The Mycenaean palace of Thebes in Boeotia was destroyed and abandoned. The flourishing city of Troy, guarding the trade routes to the Black Sea, was likewise destroyed in a great conflagration, to be succeeded by a much more modest settlement. There is suggestive evidence that these destructions may not have resulted from normal clashes between chariot forces. The hasty construction of a great fortification wall across the Isthmus of Corinth and the strengthening of the defenses around other Mycenaean palace complexes may reflect apprehensions about a far more pervasive danger, perhaps a threat by potential attackers that Bronze Age chariotry would have been unable to withstand. And those apparent fears of attack and conquest seem to have been justified, for by the middle of the next century, the destruction of all the Mycenaean palace complexes was virtually complete.

There may, of course, have been many specific, local reasons for this wave of upheaval. In some places, rivalries between regional centers could have led to the violence. In others, widespread social unrest caused by growing inequalities in late Bronze Age society may have led to local uprisings and the overthrow of the palace elite. Yet in a thought-provoking hypothesis that has already aroused considerable scholarly discussion, Drews pulls together tactical analysis, archaeological evidence, and the colorful testimony of heroic Greek myth to offer a novel reconstruction of the events. He suggests that the legendary accounts of the attacks against Thebes by a coalition of champions (immortalized by Aeschylus in his play *Seven Against Thebes*) and Homer's epic poem about the sack of Troy by Agamemnon's forces preserve memories of the first dramatic triumphs of free-lance northern infantry concentrations, fighting in the new style.

The gradually increasing scope of such encounters may suggest that news of the vulnerability of chariot forces spread among northern mercenary contingents. And in this very period, a wave of northern warriors now made their way southward in search of plunder, not employment. In looking anew at Homer's poetic metaphors about the epic battle between Achaeans and Trojans, it may well be—as Drews suggested—that the repeated description of the Achaean hero Achilles as "fleet-footed," and the characteristic description of the Trojans as "horse-taming," preserve memories of an epic clash between foot soldiers and horse-powered troops. Even though the *Iliad* was set down in writing several centuries later, at a time when chariot warfare had long been abandoned, the vivid image of Achaean soldiers streaming from the Trojan Horse may eloquently express, at least in mythic language, the sudden emergence of a new style of infantrymen—whose hidden power was revealed in an age of horse-based warfare. In their conquest of Troy, the Achaean foot soldiers departed from the empty wooden horse, thereby symbolically leaving behind the horse (and chariot) as the preferred weapons platforms of the age.

The violent events in the Aegean do not seem to have affected the great capitals and emporia of the Near East—at least not immediately. International commerce continued throughout the thirteenth century B.C., and a certain measure of prosperity was enjoyed in the royal courts of the Near East. New Kingdom Egypt (where at least some Sea People had gone to find work as mercenary runners) therefore beckoned as a tempting target for plundering attacks. The aging pharaoh Ramesses II (c. 1279–c. 1212 B.C.), after having emerged from the battle of Kadesh in a military stalemate with the Hittites, still presided over a vast territory and trade network extending from Canaan, south to Nubia, and as far west as Libya. Excavations at Late Bronze Age port cities and recovered cargoes from sunken merchant ships of this period throughout the eastern Mediterranean have emphasized the volume of international trade—and the extent of interaction between nations, cultures, and ethnic groups during this cosmopolitan age. Only recently have excavations uncovered the ruins of a once busy Late Bronze Age trade depot—littered with sherds of pottery from Mycenaean Greece, Egypt, Cyprus, and Canaan—on a sandy island known as Bates's Island off the coast of Egypt's western desert, about 120 miles east of the modern border with Libya.

It was surely no coincidence or accident that the first major attack by northern warriors on Egypt was launched from this direction. Far from being an isolated wilderness, Libya was connected to Egypt by land and sea trade routes. At a time of reported famine, it was a Libyan leader named "Meryre, Son of Did," who instigated the first major operation in which a coalition of northern warriors played a prominent role. Scholars have always puzzled over how and why Libyans forged a coalition with the various Sea Peoples. Yet the archaeological evidence of an offshore trade depot so close to Libya indicates that it was not a cultural backwater but on one of the main routes in the movement of people and goods. It is entirely conceivable that Meryre was aware of events going on elsewhere in the eastern Mediterranean, possibly through the contact his subjects had with the polyglot gangs of sailors, stevedores, and workers who were drawn into the networks of long-distance trade. More important, he seems to have been keenly aware of the recent—one might even say revolutionary—developments in the art of warfare. Indeed if Meryre had heard about recent successes achieved by northern warriors in direct assaults on chariot forces in Greece and Asia Minor, his subsequent actions in recruiting Sea People warriors for his own campaign would suddenly be understandable.

Why else would he contemplate an invasion of Egypt with only foot soldiers? If he were planning a less organized infiltration of the border lands, he would not have needed to form the grand coalition he did. Yet soon after the death of Ramesses II around 1212 B.C., Meryre began to organize a campaign against the western Nile Delta, for which he gained the cooperation of a number of warrior bands. Later Egyptian records note that they came from "the northern lands"—which could indicate an origin in any of the territories along the northern shores of the Mediterranean. The specific men-

tion of Ekwesh, Lukka, Sherden, Shekelesh, and Tursha (identified as Achaeans, Lycians, Sardinians, Sicilians, and Tyrrhenians) suggests that Meryre's appeal attracted recruits from many lands. He promised them a share of the fertile territory and booty to be gained in attacking the forces of the new pharaoh, Merneptah, the long-lived Ramesses' already elderly son. Seen in the context of the times, Meryre thus made an audacious tactical gamble: in recruiting tens of thousands of northern-style foot soldiers along with his own sizable infantry contingents, he was confident that he could overcome the Egyptian chariotry.

As things turned out, Meryre lost his gamble but proved to be a strategist ahead of his time. Merneptah's chariots met the advancing Libyan-Sea People coalition in midsummer 1208 B.C. in the western desert, at a site probably not far from the later and also fateful battlefield of El Alamein. The Egyptian forces reportedly slew 6,000 Libyans and more than 2,200 of the invading Ekwesh, with significant casualties suffered by the other Sea Peoples as well. Yet the list of spoils taken in the battle by the Egyptians gives a clear indication of the novel nature of the encounter: more than 9,000 long swords were captured from the invaders—with only an utterly insignificant twelve Libyan chariots being seized. For the time being, the pharaoh's chariots had prevailed over massed formations of swordsmen and javelineers. But new troubles were not long in coming for the pharaoh. Frontier populations in other regions were growing restless, and Merneptah soon had to undertake a punitive campaign into Canaan, where he was forced to reassert his control over some important cities and pacify the highlands. In typically bombastic prose he reported one of the most gratifying outcomes of the encounter: "Israel is laid waste; his seed is not!" The clear, if mistaken, implication was that this people had been so thoroughly defeated that they or their descendants would never appear on the stage of history again.

The quotation, which comes from Merneptah's so-called Victory Stele at the Temple of Karnak, contains this earliest mention of the people of Israel outside the Bible, and it may also indicate

the extent of the tactical revolution spreading throughout the Mediterranean world. For in the hill country of Canaan at precisely this period, c. 1250–c. 1200 B.C., archaeologists have discovered the sudden establishment of scores of hilltop villages throughout the modern area of the West Bank. Being far from the lowland Canaanite urban centers and outposts of Egyptian presence in fortresses along the coast and major trade routes, they represent the earliest settlements of the Israelites. Their defense against outside powers was not based on chariot warfare but most likely on coordinated militia campaigns. Certainly the biblical books of Joshua and Judges are filled with references to the defeat of the Canaanite kings and the destruction of their chariot forces. Although many historians have come to question the historical reliability of the story of the Israelite Exodus from Egypt, the vivid scriptural account of the drowning in the Red Sea of the pharaoh's pursuing army— and its great chariot corps—might preserve in dreamlike narrative an indelible historical memory of an era of great victories over chariotry.

The threats by northern-style raiders against Egypt and the other great centers of the Bronze Age civilization continued to intensify in this period, with port cities, fortresses, temples, and trade depots throughout the region put to the torch, and in some cases never fully reoccupied again. It is likely that in the spreading chaos, movements of people grew more frequent. Warriors and mercenaries were on the move, of course, but so were other groups formerly serving as craftsmen, servants, or functionaries in the palace centers that had been destroyed by hostile attacks. All of these groups were the "Sea Peoples," both the victims and the perpetrators of the spreading wave of violence. In certain places on Cyprus and along the coast of Canaan, settlers from the Aegean world arrived to establish new communities in the ruins of destroyed Late Bronze Age cities. And the characteristic Mycenaean-style pottery they produced at sites such as Ashkelon, Ekron, and Ashdod in Canaan clearly indicates that whether they themselves were marauders or refugee craftsmen and officials from the destroyed palace-centers of the Aegean, the course of their lives and communities had been disrupted by upheavals throughout the Mediterranean world.

Although it is impossible to follow precisely the sequence of raids, conquests, and refugee colonizations in Greece, Cyprus Egypt, and Canaan, there is suggestive evidence that the use of new weapons and tactics by the invaders continued to play a crucial role. In the rubble of the great trading emporium of Ugarit on the coast of modern Syria, for example, excavators have found a number of hunting javelins scattered in the destruction ruins. And the discovery of several newly cast long swords (one even bearing the royal cartouche of Merneptah!) hidden away in hoards at the time of the city's destruction may reflect a desperate, last-ditch effort by some local commanders to equip their forces with the same deadly weapons borne by the marauding Peoples of the Sea.

The last and greatest of attacks by contingents of northern warriors against the centers of Bronze Age civilization is memorialized in exacting detail on the outer walls of the Egyptian temple of Medinet Habu in Upper Egypt, built by Pharaoh Ramesses III, who ruled from c. 1186 to c. 1155 B.C. The Medinet reliefs depict what was one of the most notable events of Ramesses' reign: thousands of Egyptian foot soldiers, sailors, and archers are shown engaged in battles on land and sea against a bizarrely costumed coalition of invaders, who include—in addition to the Sherden and the Shekelesh of the earlier invasions—people known as the Tjekker, Denyen, Weshesh, and Peleset (whom scholars have identified as the biblical Philistines).

This invasion was apparently different and far more threatening than earlier actions. The tone of Ramesses III's official inscription accompanying the pictorial representations conveys an atmosphere of deep crisis that gripped Egypt when word arrived that seaborne and overland coalitions of northern warriors "who had made a conspiracy in their islands" were approaching. Although the precise origin of these warrior bands has never been pinpointed, the mention of "islands" suggests that the threat came from the direction of the Aegean Sea. Ramesses' chronicle goes on to trace the progress of the invaders across the region, in which many separate actions seem to have been combined for rhetorical purposes to heighten the drama of the events.

"All at once the lands were removed and scattered in the fray," reported the inscription in tracing the path of the invaders southward from the Hittite empire, through the cities of Cilicia, Cyprus, and Syria, toward Canaan, which was also known as Amor. "No land could stand before their arms from Hatti, Kode, Carchemish, Arzawa, Alayshia on, being cut off at one time. A camp was set up in one place in Amor. They desolated its people, and its land was like that which has never come into being. They were coming forward to Egypt, while the flame was being prepared before them," the inscription continued. "They laid their hands upon lands as far as the circuit of the earth, their hearts confident and trusting, 'Our plans will succeed!'"

In retrospect, we can see that Pharaoh Ramesses III was placed in an impossible situation in the Great Land and Sea Battles of 1175 B.C. When this last and greatest wave of Sea Peoples' invasions burst upon Egypt, Ramesses was forced to confront forces that had proved they could successfully overcome chariots—which remained the backbone of the Egyptian defense. In response, he apparently tried to change radically the fighting capabilities of his forces—as many desperate, doomed warlords have attempted to do throughout history. Indeed, as analysis of the Medinet Habu reliefs suggests, the vaunted Egyptian chariotry played almost no role in the fighting. Ramesses III's inscriptions can be seen as a commemoration of the heroism of his own infantry. He boasted that the Egyptian foot soldiers—once scorned as insignificant tactical factors—had fought "like bulls ready on the field of battle" and that the militiamen who engaged the enemy in hand-to-hand fighting aboard their ships "were like lions roaring on the mountaintops." No less significant is the fact that in one scene Ramesses himself is depicted as an unmounted archer—not a charioteer—with his two royal feet firmly planted on the bodies of fallen Sea People enemies.

Yet in discarding the ethos and discipline of chariot warfare on which his empire had become so dependent—and in mobilizing his foot soldiers to fight on the same terms and with the same weapons as the invaders—Ramesses sealed the fate of New Kingdom Egypt as surely as a defeat at the hands of the Sea Peoples would have done. For even though the Sea Peoples' invasion was repulsed, and some of the Sea Peoples, like the Philistines, were permitted to settle peacefully in colonies along the nearby coast of Canaan, Egypt would never regain its former strength. The Egyptian Empire—like all other Late Bronze Age kingdoms—had been built and maintained over hundreds of years as a towering social pyramid in which the king, his court, officers, and chariot forces reserved the pinnacle for themselves. The new method of marshaling units of highly mobile, highly motivated infantry against chariot forces required unprecedentedly large numbers of trained fighters. Egypt was never a society that viewed its general population as much more than beasts of burden; to accord peasant recruits respect and intensive training within the armed forces was something that the highly stratified society of New Kingdom Egypt found extremely difficult to do. The strict hierarchy began to crumble, and the growing power of mercenary units and local infantry bands caused widespread social unrest. By the end of the twelfth century, the power of New Kingdom Egypt was ended, and the country entered a new dark age. In contrast, the new world that unfolded in the centuries after the appearance of the Sea Peoples in Greece, Cyprus, Asia Minor, and Canaan drew its strength from the new cultural pattern, which was based on the solidarity and military might of local levies of foot soldiers, not elite units of courtly charioteers.

Chariot forces would again be used on the field of battle—as in the later campaigns of the Assyrian empire in the ninth and eighth centuries B.C.—but only in a supporting role to the infantry. And with the development of effective tack and stirrups during the subsequent centuries, the chariot could be dispensed with altogether, except perhaps as a battlefield conveyance for generals and kings. The Sea People warriors themselves were eventually assimilated into the general populations of the refugees from the great upheavals. Along the coast of Canaan and on Cyprus, new societies derived from Mycenaean models and led by descendants of refugees were born. Even in the rising kingdoms of Israel, Phoenicia, Aramea, Cilicia, Phrygia, and the city-states of Greece, where new forms of military and social organization emerged after the end of the Bronze Age, the legacy of the Sea Peoples—though dramatically transformed—could still be perceived. Just as the fleet-footed Achaean warrior Achilles became the role model for the citizen soldier of the archaic Greek polis, the image of the young David, surrounded by his band of mighty men of war, remained a cherished biblical symbol of national solidarity. And there were to be even more far-reaching developments in the use of large infantry formations as the kingdoms of Assyria and Babylonia swelled into great empires with enormous populations. Eventually, the massive formations of infantry units evolved into the Macedonian phalanx and the Roman legion.

The sweeping scenario of scattered contingents of Sea People warriors streaming together from their distant islands and hill country homes to overcome the elite chariot forces of the Bronze Age Mediterranean has not been without its critics. Scholars who still favor explanations such as natural disasters, generalized social breakdown, or the gradual cultural shift from Bronze Age chariot empires to Iron Age infantry kingdoms are skeptical of a single military cause. But without minimizing the possibility that natural or economic crises may indeed have undermined the political order and intensified social tensions, there is much to be said for the contention that only something as dramatic as the introduction of new weapons and tactics could have triggered violent upheavals on such a massive scale.

And there is, even beyond the specific questions of this remote period, a far more basic historical point. We must not merely see the episode of the "Sea Peoples" as a bizarre and bloody episode that took place in a far-off region more than 3,000 years ago. The long swords, javelins, and body armor of the invading Sea Peoples may seem quaintly rustic to us in a day of Stealth fighter-bombers and Tomahawk missiles. Yet they offer an important object lesson in the way that complacent dependency by great powers on expensive and complex military technology can suddenly be undermined. The grand catastrophe of the end of the Bronze Age and the role of the Sea Peoples in it should show us how unexpectedly simple weapons in the hands of committed warriors can topple great empires. Societies in any age can become dangerously presumptuous about the invulnerability of their advanced military technologies. Over centuries or even decades the society molds itself, in its religion, political order, and social hierarchy, to conform to the dominant technology. If that technology is undermined by groups with little stake in preserving the existing system, the results can be catastrophic. Today we speak of terrorists with homemade bombs and shoulder-fired missiles, but at the end of the Late Bronze Age in the eastern Mediterranean, it was northern warriors with long swords and hunting javelins who laid the groundwork for a dramatic transformation of society.

Neil Asher Silberman is an author and historian specializing in the ancient history of the Near East. He is a contributing editor to Archaeology *magazine.*

Grisly Assyrian Record of Torture and Death

Erika Bleibtreu

Assyrian national history, as it has been preserved for us in inscriptions and pictures, consists almost solely of military campaigns and battles. It is as gory and bloodcurdling a history as we know.

Assyria emerged as a territorial state in the 14th century B.C. Its territory covered approximately the northern part of modern Iraq. The first capital of Assyria was Assur, located about 150 miles north of modern Baghdad on the west bank of the Tigris River. The city was named for its national god, Assur, from which the name Assyria is also derived.

From the outset, Assyria projected itself as a strong military power bent on conquest. Countries and peoples that opposed Assyrian rule were punished by the destruction of their cites and the devastation of their fields and orchards.

By the ninth century B.C., Assyria had consolidated its hegemony over northern Mesopotamia. It was then that Assyrian armies marched beyond their own borders to expand their empire, seeking booty to finance their plans for still more conquest and power. By the mid-ninth century B.C., the Assyrian menace posed a direct threat to the small Syro-Palestine states to the west, including Israel and Judah.

The period from the ninth century to the end of the seventh century B.C. is known as the Neo-Assyrian period, during which the empire reached its zenith. The Babylonian destruction of their cap-

ital city Nineveh in 612 B.C. marks the end of the Neo-Assyrian empire, although a last Assyrian king, Ashur-uballit II, attempted to rescue the rest of the Assyrian state, by then only a small territory around Harran. However, the Babylonian king Nabopolassar (625–605 B.C.) invaded Harran in 610 B.C. and conquered it. In the following year, a final attempt was made by Ashur-uballit II to regain Harran with the help of troops from Egypt, but he did not succeed. Thereafter, Assyria disappears from history.

We will focus here principally on the records of seven Neo-Assyrian kings, most of whom ruled successively. Because the kings left behind pictorial, as well as written, records, our knowledge of their military activities is unusually well documented:

1. Ashurnasirpal II—883–859 B.C.
2. Shalmaneser III—858–824 B.C.
3. Tiglath-pileser III—744–727 B.C.
4. Sargon II—721–705 B.C.
5. Sennacherib—704–681 B.C.
6. Esarhaddon—680–669 B.C.
7. Ashurbanipal—668–627 B.C.

Incidentally, Assyrian records, as well as the Bible, mention the military contracts between the Neo-Assyrian empire and the small states of Israel and Judah.

An inscription of Shalmaneser III records a clash between his army and a coalition of enemies that included Ahab, king of Israel (c. 859–853 B.C.). Indeed, Ahab, according to Shalmaneser, mustered more chariots (2,000) than any of the other allies arrayed against the Assyrian ruler at the battle of Qarqar on the Orontes (853 B.C.). For a time, at least, the Assyrian advance was checked.

An inscription on a stela from Tell al Rimah in northern Iraq, erected in 806 B.C. by Assyrian king Adad-nirari III, informs us that Jehoahaz, king of Israel (814–793 B.C.), paid tribute to the Assyrian king: "He [Adad-nirari III of Assyria] received the tribute of Ia'asu the Samarian [Jehcahaz, king of Israel], of the Tyrian (ruler) and the Sidonian (ruler)."[1]

From the inscriptions of Tiglath-pileser III and from some representations on the reliefs that decorated the walls of his palace at Nimrud, we learn that he too conducted a military campaign to the west and invaded Israel. Tiglath-pileser III received tribute from Menahem of Samaria (744–738 B.C.), as the Bible tells us; the Assyrian king is there called Pulu (2 Kings 15:19–20).

In another episode recorded in the Bible, Pekah, king of Israel (737–732 B.C.), joined forces with Rezin of Damascus against King Ahaz of Judah (2 Kings 16:5–10). The Assyrian king Tiglath-pileser III successfully intervened against Pekah, who was then deposed. The Assyrian king then placed Hoshea on the Israelite throne. By then Israel's northern provinces were devastated and part of her population was deported to Assyria (2 Kings 15:29).

At one point, Israel, already but a shadow of its former self and crushed by the burden of the annual tribute to Assyria, decided to revolt. Shalmaneser V (726–722 B.C.), who reigned after Tiglath-pileser III, marched into Israel, besieged its capital at Samaria and, after three years of fighting, destroyed it (2 Kings 18:10). This probably occurred in the last year of Shalmaneser V's reign (722 B.C.). However, his successor, Sargon II, later claimed credit for the victory. In any event, this defeat ended the national identity of the northern kingdom of Israel. Sargon II deported, according to his own records, 27,290 Israelites, settling them, according to the Bible, near Harran on the Habur River and in the mountains of eastern Assyria (2 Kings 17:6, 18:11).

Later, in 701 B.C., when King Hezekiah of Judah withheld Assyrian tribute, Sargon II's successor, Sennacherib, marched into Judah, destroying, according to his claim, 46 cities and besieging Jerusalem. Although Sennacherib failed to capture Jerusalem (2 Kings 19:32–36), Hezekiah no doubt continued to pay tribute to Assyria.

The two principal tasks of an Assyrian king were to engage in military exploits and to erect public buildings. Both of these tasks were regarded as religious duties. They were, in effect, acts of obedience toward the principal gods of Assyria.

The historical records of ancient Assyria consist of tablets, prisms and cylinders of clay and alabaster. They bear inscriptions in cuneiform—wedge-shaped impressions representing, for the most part, syllables. In addition, we have inscribed obelisks and stelae as well as inscriptions on stone slabs that lined the walls and covered the floors of Assyrian palaces and temples.

In all of these inscriptions, the king stands at the top of the hierarchy—the most powerful person; he himself represents the state. All public acts are recorded as his achievements. All acts worthy of being recorded are attributed only to the Assyrian king, the focus of the ancient world.

The annals of the kings describe not only their military exploits, but also their building activities. This suggests that the spoil and booty taken during the military campaigns formed the financial foundation for the building activities of palaces, temples, canals and other public structures. The booty—property and people—probably provided not only precious building materials, but also artists and workmen deported from conquered territories.

The inscriptional records are vividly supplemented by pictorial representations. These include reliefs on bronze bands that decorated important gates, reliefs carved on obelisks and some engravings on cylinder seals. But the largest and most informative group of monuments are the reliefs sculpted into the stone slabs that lined the palaces' walls in the empire's capital cities—Nimrud (ancient Kalah), Khorsabad (ancient Dur Sharrukin) and Kuyunjik (ancient Nineveh).

According to the narrative representations on these reliefs, the Assyrians never lost a battle. Indeed, no Assyrian soldier is ever shown wounded or killed. The benevolence of the gods is always bestowed on the Assyrian king and his troops.

Like the official written records, the scenes and figures are selected and arranged to record the kings' heroic deeds and to describe him as "beloved of the gods":

"The king, who acts with the support of the great gods his lords and has conquered all lands, gained dominion over all highlands and received their tribute, captures of hostages, he who is victorious over all countries."[2]

The inscriptions and the pictorial evidence both provide detailed information regarding the Assyrian treatment of conquered peoples, their armies and their rulers. In his official royal inscriptions, Ashurnasirpal II calls himself the "trampler of all enemies... who defeated all his enemies [and] hung the corpses of his enemies on posts."[3] The treatment of captured enemies often depended on their readiness to submit themselves to the will of the Assyrian king:

"The nobles [and] elders of the city came out to me to save their lives. They seized my feet and said: 'If it pleases you, kill! If it pleases you, spare! If it pleases you, do what you will!'"[4]

In one case when a city resisted as long as possible instead of immediately submitting, Ashurnasirpal proudly records his punishment:

"I flayed as many nobles as had rebelled against me [and] draped their skins over the pile [of corpses]; some I spread out within the pile, some I erected on stakes upon the pile... I flayed many right through my land [and] draped their skins over the walls."[5]

The account was probably intended not only to describe what had happened, but also to frighten anyone who might dare to resist. To suppress his enemies was the king's divine task. Supported by the gods, he always had to be victorious in battle and to punish disobedient people:

"I felled 50 of their fighting men with the sword, burnt 200 captives from them, [and] defeated in a battle on the plain 332 troops.... With their blood I dyed the mountain red like red wool, [and] the rest of them the ravines [and] torrents of the mountain swallowed. I carried off captives [and] possessions from them. I cut off the heads of their fighters [and] built [therewith] a tower before their city. I burnt their adolescent boys [and] girls."[6]

A description of another conquest is even worse:

"In strife and conflict I besieged [and] conquered the city. I felled 3,000 of their fighting men with the sword... I captured many troops alive: I cut off of some their arms [and] hands; I cut off of others their noses, ears, [and] extremities. I gouged out the eyes of many troops. I made one pile of the living [and] one of heads. I hung their heads on trees around the city."[7]

The palace of Ashurnasirpal II at Nimrud is the first, so far as we know, in which carved stone slabs were used in addition to the usual wall paintings. These carvings portray many of the scenes described in words in the annals.

From the reign of Shalmaneser III, Ashurnasirpal II's son, we also have some bronze bands that decorated a massive pair of wooden gates of a temple (and possibly a palace) at Balawat, near modern Mosul. These bronze bands display unusually fine examples of bronze repoussé (a relief created by hammering on the opposite side). In a detail, we see an Assyrian soldier grasping the hand and arm of a captured enemy whose other hand and both feet have already been cut off. Dismembered hands and feet fly through the scene. Severed enemy heads hang from the conquered city's walls. Another captive is impaled on a stake, his hands and feet already having been cut off. In another detail, we see three stakes, each driven through eight severed heads, set up outside the conquered city. A third detail shows a row of impaled captives lined up on stakes set up on a hill outside the captured city. In an inscription from Shalmaneser III's father, Ashurnasirpal II, the latter tells us, "I captured soldiers alive [and] erected [them] on stakes before their cities."[8]

Shalmaneser III's written records supplement his pictorial archive: "I filled the wide plain with the corpses of his warriors.... These [rebels] I impaled on stakes.[9]... A pyramid (pillar) of heads I erected in front of the city."[10]

In the eighth century B.C., Tiglath-pileser III held center stage. Of one city he conquered, he says:

"Nabû-ushabshi, their king, I hung up in front of the gate of his city on a stake. His land, his wife, his sons, his daughters, his property, the treasure of his palace, I carried off. Bit-Amukâni, I trampled down like a threshing (sledge). All of its people, (and) its goods, I took to Assyria."[11]

Such actions are illustrated several times in the reliefs at Tiglath-pileser's palace at Nimrud. These reliefs display an individual style in the execution of details that is of special importance in tracing the development of military techniques.

Perhaps realizing what defeat meant, a king of Urartu, threatened by Sargon II, committed suicide: "The splendor of Assur, my lord, overwhelmed him [the king of Urartu] and with his own iron dagger he stabbed himself through the heart, like a pig, and ended his life."[12]

Sargon II started a new Assyrian dynasty that lasted to the end of the empire. Sargon built a new capital named after himself—Dur Sharrukin, meaning "Stronghold of the righteous king." His palace walls were decorated with especially large stone slabs, carved with extraordinarily large figures.

Sargon's son and successor, Sennacherib, again moved the Assyrian capital, this time to Nineveh, where he built his own palace. According to the excavator of Ninneveh, Austen Henry Layard, the reliefs in Sennacherib's palace, if lined up in a row, would stretch almost two miles. If anything, Sennacherib surpassed his predecessors in the grisly detail of his descriptions:

"I cut their throats like lambs. I cut off their precious lives (as one cuts) a string. Like the many waters of a storm, I made (the contents of) their gullets and entrails run down upon the wide earth. My prancing steeds harnessed for my riding, plunged into the streams of their blood as (into) a river. The wheels of my war chariot, which brings low the wicked and the evil, were bespattered with blood and filth. With the bodies of their warriors I filled the plain, like grass. (Their) testicles I cut off, and tore out the privates like the seeds of cucumbers."[13]

In several rooms of Sennacherib's Southwest Palace at Nineveh, severed heads are represented; deportation scenes are frequently depicted. Among the deportees depicted, there are long lines of prisoners from the Judahite city of Lachish; they are shown pulling a rope fastened to a colossal entrance figure for Sennacherib's palace at Nineveh; above this line of deportees is an overseer whose hand holds a truncheon.

Sennacherib was murdered by his own sons. Another son, Esarhaddon, became his successor. As the following examples show, Esarhaddon treated his enemies just as his father and grandfather had treated theirs: "Like a fish I caught him up out of the sea and cut off his head,"[14] he said of the king of Sidon; "Their blood, like a broken dam, I caused to flow down the mountain gullies";[15] and "I hung the heads of Sanduarri [king of the cities of Kundi and Sizu] and Abdimilkutti [king of Sidon] on the shoulders of their nobles and with singing and music I paraded through the public square of Nineveh."[16]

Ashurbanipal, Esarhaddon's son, boasted:

"Their dismembered bodies I fed to the dogs, swine, wolves, and eagles, to the birds of heaven and the fish in the deep.... What was left of the feast of the dogs and swine, of their members which blocked the streets and filled the squares, I ordered them to remove from Babylon, Kutha and Sippar, and to cast them upon heaps."[17]

When Ashurbanipal didn't kill his captives he "pierced the lips (and) took them to Assyria as a spectacle for the people of my land."[18]

The enemy to the southeast of Assyria, the people of Elam, underwent a special punishment that did not spare even their dead:

"The sepulchers of their earlier and later kings, who did not fear Assur and Ishtar, my lords, (and) who) had plagued the kings, my fathers, I destroyed, I devastated, I exposed to the sun. Their bones (members) I carried off to Assyria. I laid restlessness upon their shades. I deprived them of food-offerings and libations of water."[19]

Among the reliefs carved by Ashsurbanipal were pictures of the mass deportation of the Elamites, together with severed heads assembled in heaps. Two Elamites are seen fastened to the ground while their skin is flayed, while others are having their tongues pulled out.

There is no reason to doubt the historical accuracy of these portrayals and descriptions. Such punishments no doubt helped to secure the payment of tribute—silver, gold, tin, copper, bronze, and iron, as well as building materials including wood, all of which was neces-sary for the economic survival of the Assyrian empire.

In our day, these depictions, verbal and visual, give a new reality to the Assyrian conquest of the northern kingdom of Israel in 721 B.C. and to Sennacherib's subsequent campaign into Judah in 701 B.C.

NOTES

1. Stephanie Page, "A Stela of Adad-nirari III and Nergal-eres from Tell al Rimah," *Iraq* 30 (1968), p. 143.
2. Albert Kirk Grayson, *Assyrian Royal Inscriptions*, Part 2: *From Tiglath-pileser I to Ashur-nasir-apli II* (Wiesbaden, Germ.: Otto Harrassowitz, 1976), p. 165.
3. Ibid., p. 120.
4. Ibid., p. 124.
5. Ibid.
6. Ibid., pp. 126–127.
7. Ibid., p. 126.
8. Ibid., p. 143.
9. Daniel David Luckenbill, *Ancient Records of Assyria and Babylonia*, 2 vols. (Chicago: Univ. of Chicago Press, 1926–1927), vol. 1, secs. 584–585.
10. Ibid., vol. 1, sec. 599.
11. Ibid., vol. 1, sec. 783.
12. Ibid., vol. 2, sec. 22.
13. Ibid., vol. 2, sec. 254.
14. Ibid., vol. 2, sec. 511.
15. Ibid., vol. 2, sec. 521.
16. Ibid., vol. 2, sec. 528.
17. Ibid., vol. 2, secs. 795–796.
18. Ibid., vol. 2, sec. 800.
19. Ibid., vol. 2, sec. 810.

Fact or Fiction?

Some archaeologists are challenging the veracity of Old Testament histories such as those of Kings David and Solomon. Can the Bible withstand such challenges?

by Stephen Goode

Bible stories are among the most familiar we know. We've heard them time and again, and the majority of us probably regard them as mostly true and based on events that really happened. Think about one of the most familiar: A young shepherd boy named David slays the Philistine giant Goliath with a slingshot and a stone and later becomes a king of Israel and author of the great religious poetry known as the Psalms—which still are read, sung and chanted by hundreds of millions of devout Christians and Jews worldwide.

David's son, the wise Solomon, succeeds him as king in a magnificent kingdom at the height of its splendor. Solomon plans and builds a great temple, an act beautifully described in I Kings 5:3-6, in a letter Solomon wrote to Hiram, king of Tyre: "You know that my father, David, was not able to build a Temple to honor the name of the Lord his God because of the many wars he waged with surrounding nations. He could not build until the Lord gave him victory over his enemies. But now the Lord my God has given me peace on every side, and I have no enemies and all is well. So I am planning to build a Temple…. Now please command that cedars from Lebanon be cut for me. Let my men work alongside yours, and I will pay your men whatever wages you ask."

These stories excite most of the Old Testament, including I and II Samuel, I and II Kings and I and II Chronicles, and form the very heart of Jewish tradition. But did the events they so eloquently describe actually take place? Were David and Solomon genuine historical figures as, say, George Washington and Thomas Jefferson? Or were they men whose lives have become so distorted by legend that it's difficult to locate the real person, such as Wyatt Earp, or outright mythical inventions, such as Paul Bunyan?

All of this is one of several big issues in biblical archaeology these days, a field so wracked by controversy that few of its scholars agree on anything absolutely. Many of them have major disagreements when it comes to very

important issues such as whether David and Solomon really existed and the importance of their authenticity to history.

The traditional view is that David and Solomon are central to Jewish history, and it's still the view held by many scholars (and supported by some recently discovered archaeological evidence, as we shall see). But a group of highly articulate scholars known as the "new archaeologists"—the most prominent of their group is Israel Finkelstein, the head of the Tel Aviv University Institute of Archaeology—play down the greatness of David and Solomon, claiming that they were, at the most, small-time leaders of local tribes and that the greatness of Israel under their leadership is, well, greatly exaggerated. They strongly doubt that the man the Bible calls Solomon ever built the great temple the Bible describes him as building.

Very aptly these doubters also are called the "minimalists" because they believe in a minimal interpretation of the evidence available about ancient Israel, as opposed to the more traditional "maximalists" whose scholarship accommodates expansive interpretation.

Even more extreme, there is a small number of scholars called the Copenhagen School—some of its members teach at Denmark's University of Copenhagen—who argue that David and Solomon didn't exist but were invented, probably by Jewish writers in the third century B.C., as part of a program to create a great (but fictional) past for the Jews.

In a recent issue of *Biblical Archaeology Review (BAR)*, Neils Peter Lemche, one of the Copenhagen School scholars, is quoted as saying: "From a historian's point of view, ancient Israel is a monstrous creature. It is something sprung out of a fantasy of biblical historiographers and their modern paraphrasers."

David and Solomon invented? Or merely second-rate leaders of little historical significance? To many in the field it seems astonishing but not wholly unexpected. "If

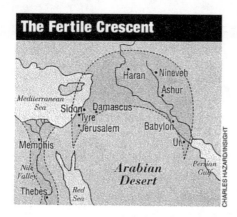

The Fertile Crescent

you look at the history of the last 200 years of biblical interpretation," Hershel Shanks, editor of *BAR* tells **Insight**, "the so-called progress has been limited to the historical value of various parts of the Bible."

Earlier generations of scholars called into question such onetime biblical givens as the Exodus or the Israelite conquest of the Promised Land and decided they probably didn't happen, so why not extend the cloud of historical doubt over David and Solomon, too? To the faithful this smacks of heresy, but P. Kyle McCarter, professor of Near East studies at Johns Hopkins University, cautions **Insight** that, "People make assumptions that archaeologists are trying to prove or disprove the Bible. No serious archaeologist is doing that. If you find one that is, you should be suspicious of that archaeologist."

This, no doubt, is good advice. But McCarter adds, "What archaeologists find is not a threat to anyone's belief. An archaeologist can't confirm or refute anyone's religious beliefs." To which a reply might be, Yes, that's probably true, but in religions based in history as firmly as Judaism and Christianity—both of which are religions attached to specific historical events, such as the Exodus or the Crucifixion—then a rewriting of history that alters the past would seem significant indeed.

Just how controversial the new developments are was underlined last September at a conference at Beit Jala, near Bethlehem, attended by both Israeli and Palestinian archaeologists, and at which the Palestinian archaeologists used the event to declare that present-day Palestinians are descendants of people who inhabited the Near East long before the Jews were there. They based much of their argument on the claims of the new archaeologists that David and Solomon weren't important leaders and that 10th-century Israel was an insignificant entity. The implications were clear: If David's Israel hadn't been great, then Jewish claims to the region weren't as solid as they might be, and Palestinian claims could be advanced.

Probably even more significant than the September conference was an exchange at the ill-fated Camp David meetings between President Clinton and Israeli and Palestinian leaders. A short time before the discussions broke down in July, according to the *Jerusalem Report*, Sa'eb Erekat, a senior Palestinian negotiator, turned to Is-

raeli Minister of Internal Security Shlomo Ben-Ami during an argument about the status of the much-disputed Temple Mount section of Jerusalem and said: "How do you know that your Holy Temple was located there?" It was a challenge based directly on the claims of the new archaeologists that the temple erected by Solomon on Temple Mount never existed and, therefore, there was no reason to regard the spot as more important to Jews than any other. *Jerusalem Report* was told by a member of the Knesset that the archaeological issue was the "hottest topic" at Camp David and that Palestinian leader Yasser Arafat used it to try to delegitimize Israeli claims.

How does Tel Aviv University professor Finkelstein respond? "I don't see a connection between research of the past and the present," he tells **Insight**. "I don't think that there is a jury sitting somewhere and judging the right of people according to a time scale. The only thing I can ask for is that my views will not be manipulated by politicians."

Of course, the historicity of David and Solomon is important to Christians, too, just as it is to Jews. According to Luke, Jesus was the son of Mary, "engaged to a man named Joseph, a descendant of King David." So what is happening in biblical archaeology today? A great deal, but it all comes down to one big question, says Amy Dockser Marcus, author of *The View From Mount Nebo*, a book the former *Wall Street Journal* Near East reporter who now works for *Money* magazine published earlier this year and in which she recorded her many conversations with archaeologists working in Israel. What all the current dispute comes down to, Marcus tells **Insight**, is the question of "how much history there is in the Bible."

It's a big question. For Marcus, who traveled to archaeological digs with Finkelstein and interviewed him at length and was impressed with his findings, it's clear that "the kingdom of David and Solomon was probably not the golden age it was made out to be."

That's pretty much Finkelstein's position. His first work was *Living on the Fringe*, a collection of his monographs published in 1995. His new book is *The Bible Unearthed: Archaeology's New Vision of Ancient Israel and the Origin of Its Sacred Texts*, coauthored with Neil Silberman. Finkelstein is digging at Megiddo--at a site that has 20 layers of archaeological remains covering more than 6,000 years. Megiddo is believed by many to be Armageddon, the location mentioned in the Book of Revelation where the final battle will be fought. It's also a spot visited by about 200,000 Christian pilgrims each year.

But it's Finkelstein's opinions on Jerusalem that matter most in the current debate, and it's his considered judgment that Jerusalem hardly counts as a center of importance in the 10th century B.C.—the century of David and Solomon. How does he reach this conclusion? Because there is very little archaeological evidence, very little indeed, that has been uncovered by archaeologists and can be traced to that century. For him (and for other minimalists) that's proof enough that a great monarchy never ex-

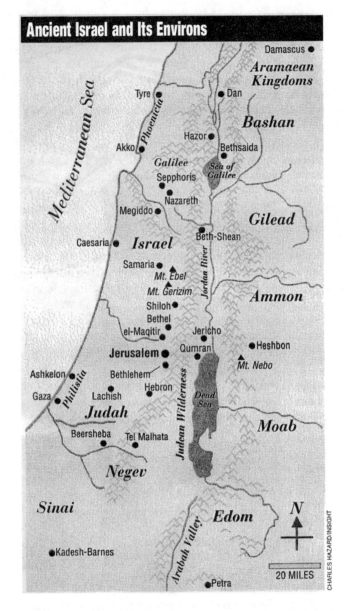

Ancient Israel and Its Environs

CHARLES HAZARD/INSIGHT

ple, who has taught archaeology for 36 years at Ozark Christian College in Joplin, Mo., and participated in many archaeological digs in Israel.

Fields has tried for decades, he tells **Insight**, to discover the name of one of his great-great-grandfathers "who lived before the Civil War and left several orphaned children." He hasn't found the name—and that ancestor lived only a century-and-a-half ago, not 3,000 years ago. Fields is impatient, too, with scholars who approach the Bible with what he calls the "hermeneutics of suspicion." Hermeneutics is the study of the methods used to interpret Scripture, and what Fields means is that too many scholars approach the Bible skeptically and with suspicion, so it isn't surprising that they reach the conclusion that the Bible isn't accurate. For scholars such as Fields, the Bible is "full of the testimony of tradition, which can't be discounted," the testimony of men and women of faith who bore truthful witness.

Bryant Wood is another scholar who doesn't approach the Bible with suspicion. Wood started his professional life as a mechanical engineer, working 13 years for General Electric before his interest in biblical archaeology got the best of him; he left his job and earned a doctorate in Syro-Palestinian archaeology.

These days he's working at a site in Israel called el-Maqitir for the Christian and Maryland-based Associates for Biblical Research. He thinks el-Maqitir might be where the ancient city of Ai was located. Ai is mentioned in the seventh and eighth chapters of the Book of Joshua, a town conquered by the Israelites and left, according to the Old Testament, as "a permanent mound of ruins, desolate to this very day."

Wood tells **Insight** he thinks he may have found the actual Ai, but being a careful and methodical man he's not certain. "In this business [biblical archaeology], you're never 100 percent sure," he says. "It's extremely rare to find a site and to find an inscription there with the name of the site on it." But what's interesting about el-Maqitir, he says, "is that there's a lot of detail in Joshua about Ai, such as that the gate of the city was located on the north side of the fortress, and our site meets the requirements very closely."

That's significant since the Conquest of Canaan by the Children of Israel following the Exodus is one of those events relegated to the realm of fiction by many scholars because there's no archaeological evidence that a conquest took place. Wood's excavation at el-Maqitir, if it turns out to be a likely location for Ai, may be evidence that gives credence to the biblical story of the conquest.

Wood is skeptical of the standard dating of a "fiery destruction" of Jericho, another city attacked by the Israelites during the conquest, according to the Old Testament. Scholarship, based on the dating of pottery shards, puts the fiery destruction at 150 years too early for the conquest. Wood's own investigation of the shards, however, finds them contemporaneous with the conquest—more proof (for Wood, at least) that the conquest took place.

isted, because if it had been a great monarchy, if the age of David and Solomon had been a golden age, then it most surely would have left evidence—and probably a great deal of evidence.

The lack of archaeological evidence in the face of the Bible's claim for David and Solomon's greatness has led the new archaeologists, including Finkelstein, to recommend that where the Bible proves inaccurate it should be chucked as a historical guide in favor of the archaeological record. The "big story here, for us," Finkelstein told reporter Netty C. Gross of the *Jerusalem Report*, "is that biblical text and archaeology are not compatible. And I'm not the first to say so. This has been going on for about 40 years or so."

Yes, that's true, but it's equally true that the new archaeologists haven't converted everyone—not by a long shot. During the last 40 years biblical archaeology has seen advances on other fronts as well. The lack of archaeological evidence doesn't bother Wilbur Fields, for exam-

Wood's background is in science and engineering—whose methods, he says, he brings to his work as an archaeologist—and it's as a scientist that he makes the following observation about biblical archaeology and the way it's done these days: "It's a bizarre situation in this discipline. I find it quite amazing how scholars think in this field." How so? "In engineering, you collect data and analyze it and then reach a conclusion," he says. "In biblical archaeology, you have theories, then you have a piece or two of evidence" and then reach conclusions that seem suspiciously close to the theories started out with—a blatantly unscientific approach. For Wood, it appears that "many of these people [the new archaeologists and others] seem to want to discredit the Bible and go out of their way to discredit it."

There's other evidence, too, that calls into question the theories of the minimalists and that underlines the value of the Bible as history. "From the 14th century B.C., we happen to have an archive from Egypt," notes *BAR* editor Shanks. "It's correspondence exchanged between the Egyptian pharaoh and the King of Jerusalem." At the same time, however, there are very few artifacts from 14th-century excavations (just as there are few from the 10th century, the time of David and Solomon). "We have the literary evidence, but on the basis of no evidence are you going to conclude that there was no Jerusalem in the 14th century," or that it wasn't important?

In addition, Shanks says, there's an Egyptian stela from the 13th century that mentions the people of Israel who live in Canaan—which, he points out, seems to indicate that Israel existed.

Shanks also uses an argument from geography to underline Jerusalem's central importance in Near East history. "If you want to go north and south in Palestine, Canaan, Israel, you've got to stick to the central part of the country and follow the ridge," he tells **Insight**. "If you go to the east or the west you're going to hit the valleys and go up and down and up and down. All the cities are located on this ridge."

Furthermore, Shanks continues, "At Jerusalem, you've got a great water supply, constantly running, which is a blessing. You have a ridge that sticks out and steep valleys on all three sides that are easily defensible. That was important in ancient times. It's not important now." With all these factors taken into consideration, he asks, isn't it reasonable to assume that there must have been a city there continually, and probably a city of significance?

Shanks then offers a general criticism of the minimalist approach to biblical history. "The basic problem of the minimalist is that they usually argue from the absence of evidence, and that is a problem for them logically." Why? "It's not really a valid form of argument," Shanks contends. "You have to be very careful when you so argue, especially when you're talking of something that *didn't happen* thousands of years ago, that it didn't happen because you can't find evidence of it. You have to establish

that you really should be able to find evidence, and that's a hard case to make."

But the biggest find for traditionalists has been a piece of a stela dug up at Tel Dan in 1993 with the Aramaic "House of David" or "Dynasty of David." It dates from about 150 years after David's time but is an early mention, outside the Bible itself, that David did exist and that he wasn't a figment of writers inventing his legend in the third century.

"It came along just when they [the new archaeologists and revisionists] were starting their pitch," says Shanks with obvious glee. It's a find that Finkelstein accepts as genuine. "The translation is reliable," he tells **Insight**. And Marcus, author of *The View From Mount Nebo*, points out that minimalists who first questioned the stone's authenticity now have come around, at least most of them, to accepting it as the real McCoy. "Some have accused archaeologists of salting the mines, but most have since retracted those statements," she says. "There's some question about the exact translation, but the majority believe it says 'House of David.'"

Marcus notes that when she was living in Israel there were stories of new archaeological discoveries almost nightly on the news, a fact that led her to write her book. And everyone **Insight** talked with underlined that we do live in interesting times, archaeologically speaking:

- Explorer Robert Ballard, who found the *Titanic*, for example, recently found evidence of a sunken city on the Black Sea that had experienced a flood. Was this the flood mentioned in the Bible? No one knows, of course, and archaeologist Wood of the Associates for Biblical Research says that a lot of serious work on dating the site scientifically must be conducted before any interpretation can be made.

- In Jerusalem, archaeologists Ronny Reich and Eli Shukron have uncovered a vast underground waterworks system they say dates from the 17th century B.C. They've also discovered a wall from the sixth century B.C., whose date was estimated by Babylonian arrowheads found around it.

- Another recent find in Jerusalem shows how much of the daily lives of ancient peoples archaeology can uncover. It's a toilet that probably dates from 587-586 B.C., the time of Nebuchadnezzer's successful siege of Jerusalem, when the Israelites went into the Babylonian Captivity. An examination of the coprolite residue at the toilet, says Marcus, found that during the siege people were reduced to eating raw meat covered with parasites and weeds.

- Also useful in giving us a picture of life in Christ's time are the Dead Sea scrolls, says Johns Hopkins' professor McCarter, who says "the enrichment they provide is significant be-

	From Ancient Israel to Christianity	
2000-1500 B.C.	Abraham, Issac and Jacob lived	
1260-1250 B.C.	Exodus of Israelites from Egypt	
1200-1000 B.C.	Canaan settled by Israelite tribes	
1001-969 B.C.	David becomes king	
969-931 B.C.	David's son, Solomon, reigns	
931-910 B.C.	Solomon dies. King Rehoboam rules over Judah	
DIVIDED KINGDOM		
931-910 B.C.	King Jeroboam rules Israel	
885-874 B.C.	Omri becomes king of Israel	
874-853 B.C.	Omri's son, Ahab, becomes king of Israel	
723-722 B.C.	Assyrians conquer Sumeria	
605-586 B.C.	Assyrian empire falls as Babylonians take over and burn the first temple	
587-538 B.C.	Babylonians rule Judah	
538 B.C.	Cyrus the Great conquers Babylon	
538-332 B.C.	Persia rules Judah until 336 B.C., when Alexander the Great becomes king of Greece and conquers Judah	
141 B.C.	Writing of the Dead Sea Scrolls begins	
63 B.C.	Romans rule and create Herodian dynasty	
37-4 B.C.	Herod the Great rules Judea	
4 B.C.	Herod dies and a series of appointees govern Judea	
26-36 A.D.	Pontius Pilate governs	

cause they come from the time of the development of Christianity and provide a glimpse into how life was when Jesus walked the earth."

- At Sepphoris, four miles northwest of Nazareth where Jesus grew up, excavators have uncovered a city that may have played a significant role in Christ's life. "There's a debate over how cosmopolitan Sepphoris was," *BAR* editor Shanks says. But "there's a theater there, and they have found some pottery shards associated with the construction of the theater."

"Was that theater there in Jesus' time? The guy who found the shards says they date from the early first century so yes, sir, it was there," Shanks notes. "Imagine a huge theater only four miles from where Jesus was raised!" On the other hand, "there are other archaeologists who say, 'No, no, this is pottery that dates from the late first century, so the theater wasn't there in Christ's time.'"

What, then, can be said about the Bible as historical truth in a time of so much controversy? Wood of the Associates for Biblical Research offers this summation of its authenticity: "A proper interpretation of the archaeological data demonstrates historical accuracy going clear back to Genesis."

That's a long way from the minimalists willing to scrap Scripture when it conflicts, in their view, with the findings of modern archaeology.

It is Shanks who sums up the thinking of a lot of people when he describes the Bible in these words: "It's a theological work in which history is embedded"—a statement that sounds like a very guarded defense of the book as history until he adds: "It is a major source that we have for the ancient history of the Near East."

Timothy W. Maier contributed to this story.

UNIT 2

Greece and Rome: The Classical Tradition

Unit Selections

Key Points to Consider

- How were the ancient Olympic games different from those of today?

- What were the charges brought against Socrates? Was he what we could call a democrat?

- What happened when Alexander died? What is the mystery surrounding Alexander's tomb?

- What was life like for Athenian women? How could the husband make a defense of his actions?

- How did Cleopatra influence Roman history? What were some of the views about Cleopatra?

- What kinds of things did the pirates do that angered the Romans? How were the pirates finally dealt with?

- Who were among the gladiators? Why were they very popular figures in Roman history?

 **Links: www.dushkin.com/online/**
These sites are annotated in the World Wide Web pages.

Diotima/Women and Gender in the Ancient World
   http://www.stoa.org/diotima/
Exploring Ancient World Cultures
   http://eawc.evansville.edu
WWW: Classical Archaeology
   http://www.archaeology.org/wwwarky/classical.html

It has been conventional to say that, for the West, civilization began in Mesopotamia and Egypt, but that civilization became distinctly Western in Greece. These matters no longer go undisputed; witness recent academic debates of Martin Bernal's thesis that Greek civilization derived from the older cultures of Egypt and the eastern Mediterranean.

Those disputes aside, the Greek ideals of order, proportion, harmony, balance, and structure—so pervasive in classical thought and art—inspired Western culture for centuries, even into the modern era. Their humanism, which made humans "the measure of all things," not only liberated Greek citizens from the despotism of the Near East, but also encouraged them, and us, to attain higher levels of creativity and excellence. In "Olympic Self-sacrifice," Paul Cartledge recounts how the games were intertwined with religion.

Though the Greeks did not entirely escape from the ancient traditions of miracle, mystery, and authority, they nevertheless elevated reason and science to new levels of importance in human affairs, and they invented history, as we know it. It was their unique socio-political system—the polis—that provided scope and incentives for Greek culture. Each polis was an experiment in local self-government. But to many moderns the Greek order was tainted because it rested on slavery and excluded women from the political process. Kenneth Cavander discusses the place of Greek women in "Love and Death in Ancient Greece."

Yet for all its greatness and originality, classical Greek civilization flowered only briefly. After the great Athenian victory over the Persians at Marathon, the weaknesses of the polis system surfaced during the Peloponnesian Wars. After the long conflict between Athens and Sparta (see the article "To Die For?"), the polis ceased to fulfill the lives of its citizens as it had in the past. The Greeks' confidence was shaken by the war and subsequent events.

But it was not the war alone that undermined the civic order. The Greek way of life depended upon unique and transitory circumstances—trust, smallness, simplicity, and a willingness to subordinate private interests to public concerns. The postwar period saw the spread of disruptive forms of individualism the privatization of life.

Eventually, Alexander the Great's conquests and the geographical unity of the Mediterranean enabled the non-Greek world to share Greek civilization. Indeed, a distinctive stage of Western civilization, the Hellenistic age, emerged from the fusion of Greek and Oriental elements. At best the Hellenistic period was a time when new cities were built on the Greek model, a time of intellectual ferment and cultural exchange, travel and exploration, scholarship and research. At worst it was an era of amoral opportunism in politics and derivative art styles. It may be

argued that "Cleopatra: What Kind of a Woman Was she, Anyway?" came to represent the best and worst of these ideals.

Later, the Greek idea survived Rome's domination of the Mediterranean. The Romans themselves acknowledged their debt to "conquered Greece." Modern scholars continue that theme, often depicting Roman culture as nothing more than the practical application of Greek ideals to Roman life. In addition, the Roman Republic invented an effective system of imperial government and unique concept of law, which was carried on during the Empire as recounted in the article "The Year One."

The Romans bequeathed their language and law to Europe and preserved and spread Greek thought and values. The Greeks had provided the basis for cultural unity of the Mediterranean; the Romans provided the political unity. Between them they forged and preserved many of the standards and assumptions upon which our tradition of civilization is built—the classical ideal.

Olympic Self-Sacrifice

*With the Sydney Olympics up and running, **Paul Cartledge** explores the radical cultural differences between our present-day interpretation of the Games and their significance in the ancient world.*

The modern Olympics seem so much part and parcel of our modern world—all those accusations of drug-taking and financial chicanery—that it is hard to remember they are only just over a hundred years old. Their founder, Baron Pierre de Coubertin, wished to foster both athletic excellence and international harmony, and as a conventionally educated French aristocrat he looked back to the ancient Greek Olympic Games for inspiration, believing fondly that that was exactly what they too had done, and why they had been founded. In fact, de Coubertin was wildly wrong: not only about the peaceful diplomatic mission of the ancient Games, but also, and more crucially, about their essential nature. The original Olympics, as we shall see, were desperately alien to what we understand by competitive sports today.

First, however, a brief recapitulation of what the ancient Games actually consisted of by the time they were definitively reorganised in the aftermath of the Persian Wars (490–479 BC). They were held then, as always, before and since, at Olympia, in the north-west Peloponnese, a relatively insignificant and inaccessible location. They were under the presidency of the local city-state of Elis, again not one of the major players in the ancient Greek league. So far as the sports component went, there were by then nine main events, all for male competitors only: the *stadion* or one-lap sprint (about

200 metres); *diaulos* or 400 metres; dolichos or 'long' distance (24 laps); *pentathlon*; boxing; four-horse chariot race; *pankration*; horse race; and race-in-armour. But the sports component was only one part, and not the most important, of the five-day festival, held at the second full moon after the summer solstice. The festival began with a swearing-in and oath-taking. It was punctuated by religious rituals and communal singing of victory hymns. And it ended with a religious procession to the Temple of Olympian Zeus, where the victors were crowned, followed by the sacrifice of many animals, feasting and celebrations.

It was indeed the Greeks who invented the idea of competitive games or sports. Their word *agon*, meaning 'competition', gives us our word 'agony', which is a fair indication of the spirit of ancient Greek competitiveness. But they did so within a specifically religious context. We sometimes say today, metaphorically, that for some, sport is a religion. But for the ancient Greeks the sport of the Olympic Games was quite literally a religious exercise—a display of religious devotion and worship. The Olympic Games, the grand-daddy of all the many hundreds of regular and irregular athletic festivals held throughout the Greek world, were in origin part of the worship of Zeus Olympios (Zeus, the mighty overlord of Mt Olympos), far away to the north in Thessaly.

Parallels in this respect can be drawn with the development of the theatre. It was the ancient Greeks, and more especially the Athenians, who invented what is recognisably our idea of theatre, but they did so within the context of religious festivals in honour of the wine-god Dionysos. 'Theatre' at, for example, our Edinburgh 'Festival', bears little obvious trace of its origins in the festivals of Dionysos at Athens (apart perhaps from the consumption of alcohol).

To show how heavily the Games impacted on the Greeks' everyday consciousness, mentality and behaviour, I shall consider four allegedly historical examples, three of them taken from the not (to us) so obviously religious fields of war and politics away from the sanctuary of Zeus at Olympia. It does not matter whether the incidents happened exactly as reported. The point is that the Greeks unquestioningly assumed they could have done, since they fitted in with their established, conventional outlook. They help us to understand the nature of the religious atmosphere and ritual that the Games enshrined, and to answer the question of in what sense and to what extent they remained a religious festival, despite a certain process of secularisation.

The first example concerns a man from the island of Rhodes, who was given the nationalistic name of Dorieus, 'the Dorian'; something akin to our calling a Scottish boy Scott, or an Irish-American girl Erin. This Dorieus came from a family of extraordinarily successful gamesmen. His own speciality was the *pankration*, a notoriously gruelling mixture of judo, boxing and all-in wrestling, with practically no holds barred. In 432, 428 and 424 BC, as we learn from contemporary documents, he won no fewer than three Olympic crowns in a row. These were in addition to eight victories at the Isthmian Games, another Panhellenic (all-Greek) games festival which was held every two years; seven at the Nemean Games (also biennial); and one, by a walkover—the Greek for which was 'without dust'—since no one would challenge him, at the Pythian Games, which were held every four years at Delphi. The fact that he won at all four of the so-called 'Circuit' Games entitled him to claim the special accolade of 'Circuit Victor'.

Dorieus, as his name suggests, was fanatically pro- the Dorian Spartans and anti- the Ionian Athenians. Towards the end of the Peloponnesian War (431–404 BC) between Sparta and Athens, when Athens had almost lost its control of the east Mediterranean, Dorieus fought on the Spartan side with his own ships. But the Athenians captured him and brought him alive to Athens. They were about to put him to death as an enemy, when it became known to the Assembly who he was. Whereupon 'they changed their minds and let him go without doing him the least ungracious action,' as one Athenian source puts it. Would we have treated a captured German athlete in 1944 in quite so gracious a manner, I wonder?

My second example also concerns the Athenian treatment of a successful Olympic competitor, but this time one of its own citizens, the pin-up glamour-boy Alcibiades. In 415 BC he was the leading spirit behind the imperialist gamble of invading and, ideally, conquering all of Sicily. The gamble, we know, ended in total disaster two years later, but at the time, when Alcibiades stood up in the Assembly to speak in its favour, he was on a high and Athens was on a bit of a roll. In addition to the more practical political and military reasons Alcibiades gave for the Athenians to vote in favour

of his proposal, he threw in an extraordinary argument based on his recent success in the Olympic Games.

Can we imagine Tony Blair arguing in favour of war in Kosovo on the grounds that he owned a horse that had won the Derby?

He was, he said, the sort of man who had achieved the unprecedented feat of not only winning the four-horse chariot race at the Olympics, probably in 416, but also of entering no fewer than seven chariot teams in all, which between them gained second, fourth and seventh places as well as the crown itself. Alcibiades had not, of course, personally driven the winning team; as in the Palio, the horse race held at Siena since the Middle Ages, professionals were hired to act as drivers. But he had put up the money—an enormous amount. He even persuaded Euripides to write a commemorative ode about it. Can we imagine Tony Blair or Bill Clinton arguing in favour of war in Kosovo, say, on the grounds that a horse of theirs had won the Epsom or Kentucky Derby?

My third example is not an individual, but rather a city, namely Sparta, which was Athens' major rival or enemy for much of the Classical period. In 480 the Persian Great King Xerxes had led a mighty expedition into Greece by land and sea from the north and east. It was not quite as mighty as Herodotus would have us believe (1,700,000 land troops; 1,207 ships), but it was nevertheless a huge armament to pit against the relatively puny and very disunited Greek resistance. Early in 480 the handful of Greek cities that could actually agree to co-operate, up to a point anyway, decided their first land strategy should be to defend the passes from Thessaly into central Greece. One of these ran through Thermopylai, the 'Hot Gates'. Yet Leonidas, the Spartan king appointed to defend Thermopylai, set off from Sparta with a mere 300 men, champion fighters all, of course, but still only a tiny task

force. Why so? Because the Spartans were an exceptionally religious people, and it happened to be the Dorians' sacred month *Karneios* (in honour of ram-god Apollo), so they felt unable to send out a full force until the *Karneia* festival was over. The other allies found this a completely convincing explanation, since they too had a religious reason for sending out no more than advance forces of their own—as Herodotus put it, 'there was the Olympic festival, which fell in at just the same time as this outbreak of war.' When Herodotus came later to offer a definition of Greekness, it is no surprise to find that central to it was the Greeks' common religious outlook and practice.

Finally, we come to Kleomedes from the tiny Aegean island of Astypalaia, who was victor in the boxing at the Olympics of 484. Let me quote the relevant passage of Pausanias, a religious travel-writer of the second century AD, but one who used much earlier sources:

They say Kleomedes of Astypalaia killed a man called Hikkos of Epidauros; he was condemned by the judges and lost his victory, and went out of his mind from grief. He went home to Astypalaia and attacked a school there where there were sixty boys. He overturned the pillar that held up the roof, and the roof fell in on them. The people stoned him and he took refuge in the sanctuary of Athene, where he climbed inside a chest and pulled down the lid. The Astypalaians struggled in vain to get it open, and in the end smashed in its wooden sides. But they found no trace of Kleomedes either alive or dead. So they sent to the Delphic oracle to ask what had become of Kleomedes, and they say the Pythian priestess gave them this oracle: 'Astypalaian Kleomedes is the last of the heroes. Worship him—he is no longer mortal.'

I have listed these four incidents in reverse chronological order, because I want to show the religious content increasing with each instance. For the ancient Greeks, however, religion was so intimately intertwined with every other aspect of their lives that they did not actually have a word corresponding to our 'religion' (which we have taken from Latin). The nearest they got was a circumlocution meaning, literally, 'the things of the gods'.

A victor in the Olympic Games, in other words, whether or not he actually won in person, and whether or not he had to kill his opponent to win, was regarded as having been touched by divinity, as being raised above the station of a mere mortal. He might even, as in the case of the Houdini-like Kleomedes, receive hero-cult, a form of religious worship, after his death. I stress too the gendered 'he'. This was strictly men-only sport. In fact, women, apart from a priestess, were banned even from watching the Olympic sports. A doubtless apocryphal tale had it that a female relative of Dorieus tried to sneak in to watch her male relations carrying off all those crowns. She was forced to go in male disguise, but alas tripped over, her *chiton* (tunic) rode up, and all—or all that mattered—was revealed.

Gender-disguise and bodily revelation offer an appropriate point of departure for our enquiry into the precise religious nature of the Games. They probably did begin, chiefly as a local Peloponnesian festival, some time around their alleged starting date of 776 BC. But their ultimate origins are lost in the mists of time. All athletes competed at Olympia entirely naked, *gumnos*, whence our word 'gymnastics'. Aetiological stories to account for this practice differed; according to one, in 720 the eventual winner of the *stadion* race (hence 'stadium') or 200-metre dash, then still the only event, crossed the finishing line wearing rather less than when he left the starting sill. In other words, his kit unravelled and fell off, but he won, and ever after all competitors, whatever the event, ran or boxed or threw, or whatever, stark naked (apart from a truss).

In reality, this literally gymnastic practice was not adopted because it was ergonomically more efficient, nor because the ancient Greeks were devoted naturists. Nor, I suspect, was it a survival from those far-off Palaeolithic days

when 'Man the Hunter' allegedly hunted in the nude. This was, rather, a case of ritual nudity, marking the sacredness of Olympic space and time, a crucial part of the religious ritual within which the running and (later) other events were enfolded.

The Olympic truce was simply a practical device for ensuring that competitors and spectators could attend the Games in safety.

Another sign that the Olympic Games were religious, and indeed specially religious, was that the prizes awarded were always symbolic tokens—simple crowns made of olive leaves taken from trees growing wild in the Altis, or sacred precinct of Zeus. Olympic competitors did not compete for money nor for other intrinsically valuable objects. (In contrast, bronze tripods were awarded at the games in honour of Hera at Argos, and oil-filled decorated jars donated at the Athenian Panathenaia.) Competitors at Olympia were therefore technically amateurs, although they could earn a fortune at other, value-prize games, so perhaps we should rather say they were shamateurs. At any rate, the ideology of amateurism and religious devotion was crucial to the ancient Games. Pierre de Coubertin was not then completely offbeam in insisting that his new, revived Olympics should be for amateur as opposed to professional athletes ('athletes' comes from Greek *athlon* meaning 'prize').

He was, on the other hand, totally wrong in his interpretation of the spirit in which the ancient Greeks competed. What seems to have especially misled him was the sacred Olympic truce which ran for a month on either side of the five-day festival. This was not a symbol of the amity then reigning among the comity of Greek nations, but a severely practical device for ensuring that the competitors and spectators could get to the Games safely, and that the Games could then be held without interruption from the other-

wise endemic Greek inter-state warfare. This explains the precise name given to the truce: *ekekheiria*—'a staying of hands' or armistice. Actually, even the declaration of the truce was not always foolproof. In 364, warfare spilled over into the Altis itself.

Furthermore, despite the wishful imaginings of the anglophile de Coubertin, the events at the ancient Olympics were not conducted in any 'gentlemanly' British spirit of 'fair play'. They were more like a paramilitary exercise, 'war minus the shooting', as George Orwell once described modern professional sport. From the gender point of view, moreover, they were in the fullest sense a display of *andreia*. This literally meant 'manliness', but it was also the general Greek word for 'courage' in the sense of martial pugnaciousness. The unintended death of Hikkos in 484 at the hands, or rather fists, of Kleomedes was, predictably, not a one-off occurrence.

To conclude, let me focus briefly on why this article is entitled 'Olympic self-sacrifice'. Sacrifice, derived from the Latin, means in general a 'making-sacred'. Specifically, it is a term used by scholars of ancient religions to describe those acts of ritual dedication and devotion whereby something is given up or offered up by mankind to a god or the gods in exchange for an expected return. It refers to an act of communication or communion between human and superhuman, mortal and divine, but also an act that marks the unbridgeable gap between the two. Almost anything could in principle be sacrificed in this way—even bodily sweat, if you believe David Sansone's theory explaining the origins and meaning of the *stadion* race at the Olympics as a ritual expenditure, or sacrifice, of sweat as the runners dashed towards their goal, the altar of Zeus, in a ritual designed to ensure the goodwill of the Father of Gods and Men.

Less fanciful, and historically better attested, is the religious significance of the undoubted climax of the ancient Olympic festival. This was not in fact any of the athletic events, but the concluding grand procession to the altar of Zeus outside his temple by all participants and spectators, led by the winner of the *stadion* race (who gave his name to the whole Games—thus 720 BC was the Games of Orsippos of Megara). This ritual procession was followed by a great blood-sacrifice of a *hekatomb*, 100 oxen, provided by the organising city of Elis. Such was the antiquity of the festival, and so numerous were the cattle slaughtered ritually over the years, that the great altar of Zeus was not built as usual out of stone, but composed simply of the burnt animals' ashes congealed with blood and fat.

That is perhaps not a very enticing thought, but then ancient religion is often desperately alien to our way of thinking. To the Greeks, however, it all seemed the most natural thing in the world. And they had the texts to back them up—above all the poems of Hesiod (*Theogony* and *Works and Days*) in which they had heard, no doubt many times, the origins-myth of how the Titan Prometheus had once tricked the younger (that is, more recently created) god Zeus on behalf of

mankind in the matter of animal blood-sacrifice. Thereafter, the Olympian gods were entitled to receive only the smell of the animal sacrifice, which rose up to them from the burning of the animal bones wrapped in fat, whereas men got to eat the meat and innards, which thanks to Prometheus's theft of fire they were able to cook to a turn. They then ate the cooked meat in a communion meal which reinforced their sense of common identity as sharers in the ritual feast. In the very special case of the Panhellenic Olympics, it also reinforced their sense of national identity as Greeks.

FOR FURTHER READING

Exhibition Catalogues of the Olympic Museum, Lausanne: D. Vanhove (ed.) *Olympism in Antiquity* vols. 1–3 (1993, 1996, 1998); Pausanias (ed. & tr. Peter Levi), *Description of Greece,* 2 vols. (Penguin 1971); Paul Cartledge, *The Greeks* (revised edition OUP, 1997);

M.I. Finley and H.W. Pleket, *The Olympic Games: the first thousand years* (Chatto & Windus 1976); Mark Golden, *Sport and Society in Ancient Greece* (CUP, 1998); Michael Poliakoff, *Combat Sports in the Ancient World* (Yale UP, 1987); David Sansone, *Greek Athletics and the Genesis of Sport* (University of California Press, 1988); Judith Swaddling, *The Ancient Olympic Games*, 2nd edition (British Museum Press, 1999); A. and N. Yalouris, *Olympia: the Museum and the Sanctuary* (Ekdotike Athenon, 1987); CD-Rom: 'Olympia, 2,800 Years of Athletic Games'—Finatec Multimedia (Athens) media@athena.compulink.gr

---

Paul Cartledge is Professor of Greek History at the University of Cambridge and the author of *The Greeks: Crucible of Civilization* (BBC Books, 2001).

TO DIE FOR?

Paul Cartledge sees ancient Spartan society and its fierce code of honour as something still relevant today.

by Paul Cartledge

The events of September 11th, 2001, jolted many of us into rethinking what was distinctive and admirable—or at least defensible—about Western civilisation, values and culture. Some of us were provoked into wondering whether any definition of that civilisation and its cultural values would justify our dying for them, or even maybe killing for them. Those of us who are historians of ancient Greece wondered with especial intensity, since the world of ancient Greece is one of the principal taproots of Western civilisation. As J.S. Mill put it, the battle of Marathon fought in 490 BC between the Athenians with support from Plataea and the invading Persians was more important than the Battle of Hastings, even as an event in English history. So too, arguably, was the battle of Thermopylae of ten years later. Although this was a defeat for the small Spartan-led Greek force at the hands of the Persians, it was none the less glorious or culturally significant for that. Indeed, some would say that Thermopylae was Sparta's finest hour.

The Spartans were the Dorian inhabitants of a Greek city-state in the Peloponnese that for many centuries was one of the greatest of Greek powers. But who were they really, these Spartans? That question was supposedly asked in about 550 BC by the Persian Great King Cyrus, as reported by Herodotus. Three generations later, Cyrus's successor Xerxes found out all too painfully who they were, and what they were made of: a fighting machine strong enough, skilful enough and sufficiently iron-willed to repel his hordes from the attempt to incorporate the mainland Greeks in his oriental empire already stretching from the Aegean in the West to beyond the Hindu Kush.

He discovered these things in person, at Thermopylae. Although this was formally a defeat for the Spartan forces under King Leonidas, the battle constituted a massive morale victory for the Greeks, and the following year the army Xerxes had left behind in Greece was decisively defeated in a pitched battle at Plataea, principally at the hands of the drilled and disciplined Spartan hoplite phalangites (heavy infantry) commanded by the Spartan regent Pausanias.

Thus, one not insignificant reason why today we should care who the ancient Spartans were is that they played a key role—some might say the key role—in defending Greece and so preserving a form of culture or civilisation that constitutes one of the chief roots of our own Western civilisation. That, at any rate, is certainly arguable. It helps to explain why 2002 might be called the Year of Sparta, rather as 2004 is to be the Year of Athens—and by extension of ancient Olympia and the Olympics.

This year there is a remarkable focus of academic and popular interest in the ancient Spartans. Two television series, one to be aired in over 50 countries on the History Channel, one on the UK's Channel 4; two discussion panels at international scholarly conferences, one to be held in the States (the Berkshire Women's History Conference), one in Scotland; and two international colloquia taking place in modern Sparta itself, one organised by Greek scholars, including members of the Greek Archaeological Service, the other by the British School at Athens (which has been involved with research in and on Sparta since 1906 and is currently seeking the funding to establish a research centre in the city). What can there possibly be still to talk about that merits focusing all this attention on ancient Sparta?

To begin with, Sparta, like some other ancient Greek cities or places, has left its mark on our consciousness by way of enriching English vocabulary. The island of Lesbos, for example, has given us 'lesbian', and Corinth 'corinthian'. But Sparta, prodigally, has given us not one but two English adjectives, and a noun besides: 'spartan', of course, 'laconic', and, less obviously, 'helot'.

To choose an illustration almost at random, a recent profile of the British Tory Party leader Ilain Duncan Smith referred casually to his naval public school as 'spartan'—and aptly so, at least in so far as the British public school system, as invented virtually by Thomas Arnold of Rugby in the nineteenth century and continued by, say, Kurt Hahn's Gordonstoun in the twentieth, had been consciously modelled on an idea, or even a utopian vision, of ancient Sparta's military-style communal education.

The Spartan root of 'laconic' is not so immediately transparent, but it comes from one of the ancient adjectival forms derived from the name the Spartans more often called themselves by: Lacedaemonians. Diminutive but perfectly formed discourse can, according to Umberto Eco, be simply irresistible—and so it seemed to the Spartans, who perfected the curt, clipped, military mode of utterance, used in dispatches from the front or in snappy repartee to an insistent teacher, that we call laconic.

As for helot, the word is used to refer to a member of an especially deprived or exploited ethnic or economic underclass, and is a product of the dark underside of the Spartans' achievement. Other Greek cities, not least Athens, were dependent on unfree labour for creating and maintaining a politicised and cultured style of communal life. But the slaves of the Athenians were a polyglot, heterogeneous bunch, mainly 'barbarians' or non-Greek foreigners, and they were mostly owned individually. The unfree subordinate population of Sparta, by contrast, was an entire Greek people, or perhaps two separate peoples united by a common yoke of servitude, whom they conquered during the eighth century and collectively labelled Helots. The word probably meant 'captives', and the Spartans treated them as prisoners of war whose death sentence they had suspended so as to make them work under constant threat of death, in order to provide the economic basis of the Spartan way of life.

These three words are a small token of the fact that English and indeed European or Western culture as a whole have been deeply marked by the Spartan image or myth, what the French scholar Francois Ollier neatly dubbed *'le mirage spartiate'*. That phrase was coined in the 1930s, an era when Sparta—or rather ideas of how Sparta worked as a society exercised a particular fascination for totalitarian or authoritarian rulers, most notoriously Hitler and pseudo-scholarly members of his entourage such as Alfred Rosenberg. Discipline, orderliness, soldierly hierarchy and subordination of individual endeavour to the overriding good of the state were among the Spartan virtues that most attracted them. There are still neo-fascist organisations that are proud to follow along the same shining path.

Yet Sparta's reputation had not always been put to such sinister uses. When Enlightenment intellectuals of the eighteenth century took up the cudgels where the combatants in the recent Swiftian battle of the books between the ancients and the moderns had laid them down, a contest developed between the proclaimed model virtues of Athens and those of Sparta. In the Athens corner was Voltaire, the advocate of learning and luxury. But in the Sparta corner was, most redoubtably if less predictably, the equally progressive thinker Jean-Jacques Rousseau.

Rousseau formed his view of Sparta in the course of a raging polemic on luxury during the years 1749-53. In his prizewinning *First Discourse* (*Discours sur les scientces et les arts*, 1749-50) he offered a celebrated description of Sparta as a city as famous for its *'heureuse ignorance'* as for the *'sagesse de ses lois'*; in short, he presented it as 'a republic of demigods'. Then came fragments of inchoate historical works drafted in 1751-53, which included a parallel drawn between Sparta and the Roman Repub-

lic and also the beginnings of a history of Sparta. Thereafter, in all the major works of his mature political philosophy, from the *Second Discourse* of 1755 (*Discours sur l'origine et les fondemens de l'inégalité parmi les hommes*) onwards, he gave honourable, if rarely extended, mentions to Sparta and its at least semilegendary legislator, Lycurgus.

Most notably, in his *Considérations sur le Gouvernement de Pologne* of 1772, Rousseau counterposed to mere 'lawmakers' the three ancient 'lawgivers', that is, Moses, Lycurgus, and Numa, the second king of Rome; and in Lycurgus (whose ancient dates were variously given) he saw an almost divinely inspired and authoritative legislator, so in tune with the temper and spirit of his people that he laid down laws which they could unswervingly abide by for centuries to come. Rousseau wrote, approvingly, that Lycurgus fixed 'an iron yoke' and tied the Spartans to it by filling up every moment of their lives. This ceaseless constraint was, to Rousseau, ennobled by the purpose it served, that of patriotism, the ideal of which was constantly presented to the Spartans not only in their public laws, but also in their marital and reproductive customs, and in their festivals, feasts and games. In short, Rousseau saw in Lycurgus's Sparta a society devoted to implementing the general will in a collective, self-effacing, law-abiding, thoroughly virtuous way.

Rousseau was by no means the first, or the last, intellectual who deployed an image or vision of Sparta as an integral component and driving force of a programme of social and political reforms. Among the first on record to do so was Plato, and through him Sparta has a good claim to be the fount and origin of all utopian thinking and utopiography. Indeed, it is one of the paradoxes of what Elizabeth Rawson called 'the Spartan tradition in European thought' that some of Sparta's most fervent admirers have been people who—had they actually experienced the real Sparta at first hand—would not have survived it for very long, or whose peculiar genius would have been quickly snuffed out by Sparta's harshly physical educational system and uncultivated social regimen. Although Plato admired Sparta for having an educational system designed to inculcate virtue, it is impossible to imagine an institution as intellectually radical as Plato's Academy being founded in conservative, tradition-worshipping Sparta.

Yet it is not only for what intellectuals or politicians have made of Sparta, through the centuries, that Sparta remains a choice subject of study. It is also for what the Spartans really did achieve, most conspicuously on the battlefields of 480-479. Had it not been for the Spartans' remarkably successful organisation of their society into a well-oiled military machine, and their diplomatic development of a rudimentary multi-state Greek alliance well before the Persians came to Greece, there would have been no core of leadership around which the Greek resistance could coalesce. Had it not been for the Spartans' suicidal but heroic stand at Thermopylae, which showed that the Persians could be resisted, it is unlikely that the small, wavering and uncohesive force of loyalist Greeks would have had the nerve to imagine that they might one day win. But for charismatic Spartan commanders of the character and calibre of Leonidas (r.490-480) and Pausanias (regent, 480-c.471), the Greek land forces would have been critically weakened.

Finally, had the loyalist Greeks lost in 480-479, and the Persians absorbed the Greeks of the mainland as well as of the islands and the western Asiatic seaboard into their farflung empire, the ensuing Greek civilisation would have been immeasurably different from and, most would say, inferior to what actually evolved in the fifth and fourth centuries.

What did the Spartans bring to the Greek cultural feast, beyond playing a vital role in winning the war that made it possible at all? Different interpreters might stress different aspects of the classical Greek cultural achievement, to emphasise either those aspects that they find most admirable and imitable, or the ones that they consider to have been the most influential on subsequent cultures of the European or Western tradition. I would privilege three qualities or characteristics above all: a devotion to competition in all its forms almost for its own sake; a devotion to a concept and ideal of freedom; and a capacity for almost limitless self-criticism.

The first two might be found equally strongly in either of the two exemplars of ancient Greek civilisation, Sparta and Athens. The third, however, was a peculiarly Athenian cultural trait and not a Spartan one at all. Or so contemporary Athenians liked to think and many have subsequently agreed. Demosthenes, for example, stated to an Athenian audience that it was forbidden to Spartans to criticise their laws, and there was undoubtedly no Spartan equivalent of either the tragic or the comic drama competitions which provided the Athenians with two annual state-sponsored opportunities for self-examination. On the other hand, the Spartans were not quite the unhesitatingly obedient automata of Athenian propaganda. On occasion grumbling might turn into open defiance of authority, both individually and collectively. Even Sparta's kings might be brought low, tried and fined—or, worse, exiled under sentence of death. It would be fairer and more accurate to say that the Spartans' culture was not one that favoured, let alone encouraged, open dissent or argument. Let me therefore first expand a little on Greek, and especially Spartan, competitiveness, and then on Greek, and especially Spartan, attitudes to and practices of freedom.

All Greeks, probably, liked a good contest. Their word for competitiveness, agonia, gives us our word 'agony', which well suggests the driven quality of Greek competition. A war was a contest for them, as was competition in athletics (so called because there was a material or symbolic prize at stake, an athlon). But so too was a lawsuit, and any religious festival that involved athletic and other sorts of competition. It was the Greeks who invented our idea of athletic sports, just as they invented the prototype of our idea of the theatre, both of them within a context of religiously-based but significantly secularised competition.

The Spartans yielded to no other Greeks in their passionate attachment to competition: they even made the act of survival at birth a matter of competition (it was decided by the tribal elders, not by the parents, which boy or girl babies should be allowed to survive and be reared, and which ones hurled to their certain death down a ravine). Likewise adult status for males could be achieved only as the outcome of the series of largely physical competitive tests that constituted an education or group socialisation (known as the Agoge or Upbringing). Thucydides's Pericles referred witheringly to the Spartans' 'state-induced' courage, but that was hardly fair to the ancient Greeks' only state-sponsored, compulsory and comprehensive system of public education, which so warmly impressed Plato, Aristotle and Rousseau among many other commentators. Finally, to become a Spartan full adult in terms of political standing and participation, citizenship was dependent on passing an acceptance test—admission by competitive election to a communal dining mess, at the age of twenty. Those who failed any of those educational or citizenship tests were consigned to a limbo of exclusion, of non-belonging, to permanent outsider status.

As for the general Greek passion for freedom, it was said by Critias—an Athenian admirer, admittedly, who was also an extreme authoritarian thinker and politician, leader of the Thirty Tyrants regime (404-403)—that in Sparta there were to be found both the most free people in Greece, and the most unfree. By the most free he meant the Spartans themselves, or more precisely the Spartan masterclass, who were freed by the compulsory labour of their enslaved workforce from the necessity of performing any productive labour apart from warfare. By the most unfree the author meant the Helots. These people were treated as a conquered population. They came to outnumber their Spartan masters manifold, and for that reason among others were constantly a source of fear, even terror, to them. In the 460s a massive Helot revolt, following a major earthquake that hit the town of Sparta directly, caused serious damage, psychological as well as political and economic. But the Spartans outmatched the Helots in terror in return. The first act of the Spartans' chief board of annual officials, the five Ephors, on taking office was to declare war in the name of the Spartan state on the Helots collectively, the enemy within. That meant that any killing of Helots by Spartan citizens, deliberate or otherwise, was officially sanctioned, even perhaps encouraged, and, crucially (the Spartans were hugely pious), was in religious terms free from ritual pollution.

The Helots, and the Spartans' severe treatment of them, at first puzzled and later disturbed the more sensitive Greek observers. Plato, for example, remarked that the helot system was the most controversial example of servitude in Greece. This controversy was heightened in Plato's lifetime, when, in the aftermath of a decisive defeat of Sparta by the Boeotians at Leuktra in 371, the larger portion of them, the Messenians, finally achieved their collective freedom and established themselves as free Greek citizens of the restored (as they saw it) free city of Messene. This autonomy was attained, moreover, after another collective revolt—something which slaves elsewhere in Greece could only dream of.

Those two aspects of Spartan culture and society by themselves make Sparta worthy of our continued study, but they far from exhaust Sparta's fascination. Consider the following more or less well attested social customs or practices: institutionalised pederasty

between a young adult citizen warrior and a teenage youth within the compulsory state-run educational cycle; athletic sports including wrestling practised officially by the teenage girls; marriage by capture of a bride by the prospective groom; polyandry (women with more than one husband); and wifesharing without the opprobrium or legal guilt of adultery.

A common factor runs through much of this: the unusual (indeed, by Greek standards, unique) functions, status and behaviour of the female half of the Spartan citizen population, the women of Sparta, evidence for whom is sufficiently plentiful, but also sufficiently controversial, to provoke and almost justify an entire book on them.

Spartan girls, unlike Athenian girls, underwent a form of state education, separate from the boys but comparably rigorous and physical; this entitled them to equal food rations to enable them to develop physical strength, especially for eugenic reasons. Spartan wives and mothers were not shrinking violets. They openly berated and chastised any hint of cowardice in their sons. They wept tears of pain if their son or husband came back safe but defeated from battle, tears of joy if he died in a winning cause. The laconic admonition 'With your shield, or on it', meaning either come back alive and victorious or come back dead and victorious, was credited to the archetypal Spartan mother. They ritually humiliated men who were thought to have remained unmarried for too long, or showed signs of not wanting to get married at all. They inherited and owned property, including land, in their own right. They slept with men other than their husbands, and got away with it, indeed sometimes were actually encouraged to do so—by their husbands.

So independent-minded were they that Aristotle (admittedly not the most liberated of ancient Greeks in his outlook on women) believed that in Sparta the men, for all their prowess on the battlefield, actually were ruled at home by their women.

In the second book of his *Politics* he devoted considerable space to the defects as he saw them of Lycurgus's arrangements, and no single factor did he reckon up more adversely than the excessively powerful position of the citizen women.

We should take at least some of this with a dose of salt. Our written sources are exclusively male and non-Spartan. Nevertheless, we may safely infer that Sparta was in vital respects seriously different, even alien, to the traditional Greek norms of political and social intercourse. That alone makes Sparta worth studying. Herodotus wrote that he agreed with the Theban poet Pindar that 'custom was king', in the sense that every human group believes that its own customs are not only better than those of others but absolutely the best possible. With Sparta, he was on to a winner. Here is an illustration from the seventh book of his *Histories*.

Shortly before Thermopylae, it was reported to Xerxes that the Spartans were combing and styling their long hair. He had been told, by an exiled Spartan former king in his entourage, that the Spartans feared the Law more even than his Persian subjects feared their Great King and that in obedience to their Law they would never flee in battle, no matter how greatly outnumbered, but stand firm either to conquer or to die. Xerxes had laughed, refusing to believe that men who coiffed their tresses before fighting would make serious opponents in the field. Yet events were soon to confirm the laconic statement reportedly made by the Spartan ex-king: 'This is their custom before risking their lives'.

Modern Sparta is a charming provincial capital; a few miles to the west, in the foothills of the Taygetos range, lie the ruins of Mistra, once capital of the Byzantine Despotate of the Morea. Here in the fifteenth century, as the Ottoman Turks prepared for their final assault on Constantinople, a monk, George Gemistos Plethon, sat composing Platonist nostrums for regulating the ideal state of human co-existence.

That utopianism seems a world away from the down-to-earth and brutally efficient society of ancient Sparta. And yet the ideal encapsulated in the myth of Thermopylae still resonates, if not always with the happiest of consequences. It is the concept that there are values that are worth dying for. Taken in a destructive direction, as by fundamentalist suicide-bombers, that notion can be wholly repellent. Developed in the direction taken by Lycurgus, however, it can generate ideals of communal co-operation and self-sacrifice that qualify properly and justly for the honorific label of utopia.

I end with one of Lycurgus's more long-lasting endeavours, his in- volvement—according to some sources—in the foundation of the Olympic Games (traditionally in 776 BC) and in the swearing of the first Olympic truce. That truce, partly religious and partly a pragmatic device to enable the Games to take place despite chronic inter-city warfare, is usually misunderstood. For once, though, a historical misunderstanding can be constructive today and in the future. Modern sport can too often be a form of war minus the shooting, as George Orwell put it. But it need not be so, and it is possible for individuals to go faster and higher and be stronger without provoking or exploiting international hatred. The modern Olympic movement, including the Olympic Truce organisation based at Olympia itself, offers a mental as well as material space for overcoming the sort of lethal differences that continue to divide peoples and cultures. For that ideal, we have to thank, in part at least, a Spartan.

FOR FURTHER READING:

Paul Cartledge *Spartan Reflections* (2001); *Sparta and Lakonia. A regional history 1300-362 BC* 2nd edn, 2001); L. Fitzhardinge *The Spartans* (1980); Charles Freeman *The Greek Achievement* (2000, paperback 2001); Elizabeth Rawson *The Spartan Tradition in European Thought* (1969, paperback 1991); N. Sekunda & R. Hook *The Spartan Army* (Osprey 1998).

Paul Cartledge is Professor of Greek History and Chairman of the Faculty of Classics, in the University of Cambridge, and a Fellow of Clare College.

Love and Death in Ancient Greece

Catching him in the act, an obscure citizen of Athens slew his wife's lover. But was it a crime of passion—or premeditated murder?

Kenneth Cavander

Euphiletos was tired. He had been out in the country all day attending to business, and now he was home trying to get some sleep, and the baby was crying. His house was on two floors; the baby slept with a maid on the first floor; above, there was a combined living-dining-sleeping area for him and his wife. Euphiletos told his wife to go downstairs and nurse the baby. She protested that she wanted to be with him; she'd missed him while he was in the country—or did he just want to get rid of her so that he could make a pass at the maid, as he had the time he got drunk? Euphiletos laughed at that and at last his wife agreed to go downstairs and hush the child, but she insisted on locking the door to their room. Euphiletos turned over and went back to sleep. It never occurred to him to ask why his wife had gone through the charade of keeping him away from the maid, or why she had spent the rest of the night downstairs. But a few days later something happened that made him ask these questions, and by the end of the month a man was dead, killed in full view of a crowd of neighbors and friends.

This drama took place nearly two thousand five hundred years ago in ancient Athens. The characters were none of the brilliant and celebrated figures of the times—Socrates, Plato, Euripides, Aristophanes, Alcibiades—but members of the Athenian lower-middle class, obscure people who receded into the shadows of history. Their story is a soap opera compared to the grander tragedies being played out at the festivals of Dionysos in the theater cut into the slopes of the Acropolis.

By a quirk of fate and an accident of politics the speech written for the murder trial that climaxes this story was the work of a man named Lysias. As a boy, Lysias sat in the company of Plato and Socrates, who often visited his father's house. As an adult, he was active in politics, and when a coup by the opposition party sent his family into exile, his property was confiscated and he narrowly escaped with his life. But a countercoup soon allowed him to return to Athens, and Lysias, now without a livelihood, had to find a profession.

He found one in the Athenian legal system. Athenian law was complex and attorneys were unknown; every citizen had to prosecute or defend himself in person. As a result, a class of professional legal advisers emerged that made a living supplying litigants with cogent, legally sound briefs. In time, Lysias became one of the most sought-after of these speech writers and several exam-

ples of his elegant and literate Greek style have been preserved, including the speech written for the defendant in this case.

Euphiletos, like many Athenians of modest means, lived in a small house in the city and commuted to the country to attend to his farm or market garden. He cannot have been well-off, for his house had the minimum number of slaves—one. Even a sausage seller or baker had at least one slave. Euphiletos had recently married and he was a trusting husband, so he said, giving his wife anything she asked for, never questioning her movements, trying to please her in every possible way. The most exciting event in the marriage was the birth of their child, whom his wife nursed herself. But the most significant event was the death of his mother: the whole family attended the funeral and, although Euphiletos did not know it at the time, his marriage was laid to rest that day along with his mother.

After the birth of their child Euphiletos and his wife had rearranged their living quarters. It was too dangerous to carry the baby up and down the steep ladder to the upper floor every time the child needed to be washed or changed, so the family was split up. Euphiletos and his wife moved into the upper part of the

43

house, while the baby, with the slave girl to look after it, stayed downstairs.

The arrangement worked well, and Euphiletos's wife often went down in the middle of the night to be with the baby when it was cranky. But on the evening of the day Euphiletos came back tired from the country, two things in addition to the little drama of the locked door struck him as unusual. One was his wife's makeup: it was only a month since her brother had died—yet he noticed that she had put powder on her face. And there were noises in the night that sounded like a hinge creaking. When his wife awakened him by unlocking the bedroom door the next morning, Euphiletos asked her about these sounds. She said she had gone next door to a neighbor's house to borrow some oil for the baby's night light, which had gone out. As for the makeup, when Euphiletos thought about it he remembered his wife saying how much she had missed him and how reluctantly she had left him to go down and take care of the baby. Reassured, he dismissed the whole episode from his mind and thought no more about it—until something happened to shatter this comforting domestic picture and rearrange all the pieces of the puzzle in quite a different way.

One morning, a few days later, Euphiletos was leaving his house when he was stopped in the street by an old woman. She apologized for taking his time. "I'm not trying to make trouble," she said, "but we have an enemy in common." The old woman was a slave. Her mistress, she said, had been having an affair, but her lover had grown tired of her and left her for another woman. The other woman was Euphiletos's wife.

"The man is called Eratosthenes," said the old slave. "Ask your maid about him. He's seduced several women. He's got it down to a fine art."

In the midst of his shock and anger Euphiletos revealed a streak of something methodical, almost detached, in his character. Instead of going straight to his wife or her lover, he proceeded like an accountant investigating an error in the books.

He retraced his steps to his house and ordered the maidservant to come with him to the market. His wife would see

nothing unusual in this, for respectable married women did not go out shopping in fifth-century Athens. That was left to the men and the slaves. Halfway to the market Euphiletos turned aside and marched the girl to the house of a friend, where he confronted her with the old woman's story. The girl denied it. Euphiletos threatened to beat her. She told him to go ahead and do what he liked. He talked of prison. She still denied it. Then Euphiletos mentioned Eratosthenes' name, and she broke down. In return for a promise that she would not be harmed, she told Euphiletos everything.

Her story was bizarre as well as comic and macabre. It began at the funeral of Euphiletos's mother. Eratosthenes had seen Euphiletos's wife among the mourners and had taken a fancy to her. He got in touch with the maid and persuaded her to act as go-between. Whether it was a difficult or an easy seduction we don't know; but, as the old woman had said, Eratosthenes was a practiced hand.

This love affair, first planned at a funeral and then set in motion by proxy, was carried on mostly at Euphileto's house when he was away in the country. On one occasion his wife may have contrived to meet her lover away from the house, for she had gone with Eratosthenes' mother to the festival of the Thesmophoria, one of several festivals celebrated in honor of feminine deities. During these festivals a woman could leave the seclusion of her own house without arousing suspicious comment.

The slave girl also told Euphiletos that on the night he came back tired from the country, her mistress had told her to pinch the baby to make it cry, which gave her an excuse to go downstairs. His wife's parade of jealousy, Euphiletos now realized, was an act, designed to provide her with a reason to lock the door on him. So while he was a temporary prisoner in his own bedroom, his wife was downstairs in the nursery with her lover, and the maid was keeping the baby quiet somewhere else.

In a crisis, a person will often revert to archetypal behavior. For the Greeks of the fifth century B.C. the Homeric poems provided a mythological blueprint for almost any life situation, and it is in-

teresting to see how Euphileto's next move re-created a scene out of the legends. In *The Odyssey* Homer tells the story of what happened when Hephaistos, the god of fire, found out that his wife, Aphrodite, had been sleeping with the war god, Ares. Hephaistos decided not to face Aphrodite with her infidelity; instead, he wove a magical net that was sprung by the two lovers when they climbed into bed together. Then, as they lay there trapped, Hephaistos invited the other Olympians to come and view the guilty pair, "and the unquenchable laughter of the gods rose into the sky." In his own mundane way, but without the magic net, Euphiletos would follow the example of Hephaistos. He made his slave promise to keep everything she had told him a secret; then, pretending to his wife that he suspected nothing, he went about his business as usual and waited for a chance to spring his trap.

The part of cuckold is a mortifying one to play, and it was particularly so in ancient Athens where the relative status of men and women was so unequal. A freeborn Athenian woman was free in little more than name. She could not vote, make contracts, or conduct any business involving more than a certain sum of money; legally she was little more than a medium for the transmission of property from grandfather to grandchildren through the dowry she brought with her to her husband. Her husband, of course, was invariably chosen for her by her father or by the nearest male relative if her father was dead. Almost the only thing she could call her own was her reputation, which depended on good behavior, an unassertive demeanor, a life spent dutifully spinning, weaving, dyeing clothes, cooking, bearing and raising children, and, above all, on not interfering in the serious business of life as conducted by the men. In a famous speech in praise of the Athenian men who died during the Peloponnesian War, Pericles makes only one reference to women: according to Thucydides, who reports the speech in his history of the war, Pericles said that women should never give rise to any comment by a man, favorable or unfavorable. In the tragic dramas, moreover, women who offer their opinions unasked or who go about alone in public usually feel they have to apologize for behaving in such a brazen and immodest way.

Such was the official status of women. Unofficially, the women of ancient Athens found ways, as their sisters have done in every age and culture, to undermine the barriers of male prejudice. In Euripides' play *Iphigeneia at Aulis* (written within a year or two of Euphiletos's marriage), Agamemnon tries to assert his authority over his wife, Clytemnestra, in order to get her out of the way while he sacrifices his own daughter, Iphigeneia, to Artemis. Clytemnestra, with a show of wifely stubbornness that surely came out of the playwright's contemporary observation, refuses to be dismissed and finally cuts the conversation short by sending her husband about his business. In another play by Euripides, *Hippolytos*, there are some lines that might have been written specifically for Euphiletos himself to speak. Hippolytos, told that his stepmother, Phaidra, is in love with him, remarks scathingly: "I would have no servants near a woman, just beasts with teeth and no voice, [for] servants are the agents in the world outside for the wickedness women do."

Drink and sex are the traditional outlets for the oppressed. The comedies of Aristophanes are studded with snide references to the excessive drinking habits of women. According to Aristophanes, festivals such as the Thesmophoria were excuses for massive alcoholic sprees. More likely, these mystery cults were the safety valve for pent-up emotions, a chance to transcend the cruelly narrow boundaries imposed on women by their roles in a rigidly male society.

As for sex, women were the weaker vessel when it came to this human urge. In *Lysistrata* Aristophanes has the women wondering whether they can hold out long enough to bring the men to their knees. And in the legends that canonized popular wisdom on the subject there is a story about Zeus and Hera squabbling over who gets the greater pleasure out of sex—the man or the woman. When they finally appeal to Teiresias, the blind seer and prophet, who, as part man and part woman, ought to be able to settle the question for them, he duly reports that in the sexual act the

woman, in fact, gets nine-tenths of the pleasure, and the man only one-tenth.

These scraps of myth and folklore, however, filtered through male fantasy as they are, reveal a sense of unease about women. In the Orestes myth, for instance, it is Clytemnestra who takes over the reins of government in the absence of Agamemnon, then murders him when he returns; and it is her daughter Electra who pushes a faltering Orestes into taking revenge for the slain king. A whole army of formidable heroines—Electra, Clytemnestra, Antigone, Hecuba, Andromache, Medea—marches through the pages of Greek drama. The Fates, the Muses, and the Furies are all women. None of these female figures is anything like the meek and passive drudge that the Greek woman of the fifth century was expected to be.

But were they real types, these mythological heroines, or were they phantom projections of male fears and desires, mother imagoes, castration anxieties dressed up as gods, embodiments of the part of a man he most wants to repress—his own irrational and emotional side, his moon-bound, lunatic aspects—thrust onto women because he dare not admit them in himself?

It is possible. Every mythologized figure embodies inner and outer worlds. We see what we wish to see, and the picture we perceive turns into a mirror. Were there actual women in Athens capable of organizing a fully functioning communistic state and pushing it through the assembly, like the Praxagora of Aristophanes' play *Ekklesiazousai?* Were there Electras and Clytemnestras and Medeas? If there were, they never reached the pages of the history books. We hear of Aspasia, Pericles' "companion" (the Greek word is *hetaira*, meaning "woman friend"), for whom he divorced his legal wife. But Aspasia was a member of the demimonde of "liberated" women who lived outside the social order, not necessarily slaves, but not full citizens either. They were often prostitutes, but some of them were cultured and educated, better traveled and more interesting to Athenian men than their own wives. Custom permitted one or more relationships with *hetairai* outside the marriage, but a *hetaira* had no legal

claim on a man, and he could sell her or dispose of her any time he liked. Meanwhile, for the trueborn Athenian woman who wanted a more varied life than the one prescribed by convention, what was there? Gossip with the neighbors. The bottle. A festival now and then. A clandestine love affair.

Four or five days passed while Euphiletos brooded over the wrong done to him. Suppose a child was born from this liaison: who could tell whether it was his or Eratosthenes'? All kinds of complications might follow. But whatever he was feeling, Euphiletos managed to hide it from his wife. She never suspected that he knew anything at all.

Euphiletos had a good friend named Sostratos. Less than a week after his interview with the maid Euphiletos met Sostratos coming home from the country, and since it was late Euphiletos invited his friend to his house for supper. This casual meeting was to become important later at the trial. The two men went upstairs, ate and drank well, and had a pleasant evening together. By custom Euphiletos's wife was not present. After Sostratos had gone home Euphiletos went to sleep.

Some time in the middle of the night there was a knock on his door. It was the maid. Eratosthenes had arrived.

Leaving the maid to keep watch, Euphiletos slipped out a back way and went around the neighborhood waking up his friends. Some of them were out of town, but he managed to collect a small group who went to a nearby store and bought torches. Then they all trooped off to Euphiletos's house where they stood outside in the street holding the lighted torches while Euphiletos tapped on the door. Quietly the maid let him into the courtyard. He pushed past her into the room where his wife was supposed to be asleep with the baby. A few of Euphiletos's friends managed to crowd in behind him.

For a split second the scene must have been like a tableau out of Homer: Eratosthenes naked in bed, Euphiletos's wife in his arms, the two lovers trapped in the light of torches held by the neighbors.

Then Eratosthenes, still naked, sprang up. Euphiletos shouted at him, "What are you doing in my house?" and knocked him off the bed, pulled his wrists behind his back, and tied them.

Eratosthenes offered to pay Euphiletos any sum he named. Euphiletos had a choice: he could accept the bribe, or he could take a form of revenge allowed by law—brutalizing and humiliating Eratosthenes by such methods as the insertion of tough thistles up his rectum. There was also a third option open to him under the circumstances: since he had caught Eratosthenes in the act, and there were witnesses present, Euphiletos could kill him.

Euphiletos interrupted the other man's pleas. "I won't kill you," he said, and then, in the kind of logical twist the Greeks loved, he added, "but the law will."

And in the name of the law he killed Eratosthenes.

Athenian homicide law required the dead man's family, not the state, to bring charges of murder. Eratosthenes' family undertook the task, and approximately three months later Euphiletos found himself facing a jury of fifty-one Athenians in the court known as the Delphinion, located in the southeast corner of Athens, where cases of justifiable homicide were tried. Eratosthenes' family charged Euphiletos with premeditated murder on the grounds that he had sent his maid to lure Eratosthenes to the house; they may also have tried to prove that Eratosthenes was dragged into the building by force, or took refuge at the hearth before he was killed. In the speech he writes for Euphiletos, Lysias sets out to rebut all these charges.

Lysias puts into Euphiletos's mouth some ingenious legal arguments. The law (of which a copy is read to the court) says that a seducer caught in the act may be killed. "If you make it a crime to kill a seducer in this way," he argues, "you will have a situation in which a thief, caught burglarizing your house, will pretend that he is an adulterer in order to get away with a lesser crime." Lysias also

refers the jury to the law on rape. Rape carries a lower penalty than seduction. Why? Because, theorizes Lysias, the rapist simply takes the woman's body, while the seducer steals her soul.

Nevertheless, in spite of Lysias's able and sophisticated defense, there is a flaw in Euphiletos's argument. His defense rests on the assumption that his action was unpremeditated, committed in the heat of the moment, under the shock and stress of finding his wife in bed with another man. That is surely the intent of the law, and Euphiletos goes to great lengths to prove he had not planned the encounter. He cites the dinner invitation to Sostratos, which, he says, is not the behavior of a man planning murder. But the rest of his story contradicts this. The signals by which the maid warned him that Eratosthenes had arrived and by which he let her know that he was waiting at the front door; the rounding up of friends to act as witnesses; the presence of the murder weapon on his person—all point to prior preparation. Euphiletos may prove to the jury's satisfaction that he did not lure Eratosthenes deliberately to his house that night, but he fails to prove that he was taken totally by surprise or that he tried to do anything to stop the affair before it reached that point. His action looks suspiciously like cold-blooded revenge executed under color of a law that forgives even violent crimes if they are committed in the heat of passion.

Neither the speech for the prosecution nor the testimony of witnesses has survived, so we do not know if the wife or the maid gave evidence. Though women were not allowed to appear as witnesses in court cases, the rules for murder trials may have been different. A slave could not testify at all, but a deposition could have been taken from her under torture and read to the court. On the other hand, Euphiletos may have wanted to avoid bringing the women into it: after all, they had been in league against him throughout the whole unhappy affair.

There is something touching in the alliance between the slave, an object without rights or status, and the wife, legally a free citizen but in reality a kind of slave too. The maidservant probably accepted a bribe from Eratosthenes, but all the same she had a moment of heroism when, threatened with a beating and prison, she refused to incriminate her mistress. Afterward, when she became Euphiletos's accomplice, there is an eerie reversal of the situation: the slave admits her master to the house in the same stealthy way that she had opened the door for her mistress's lover a few minutes earlier. But still, there was a moment when Euphiletos was the outsider, barred from his own house and his wife's arms, with only his rage and his group of male friends for company.

Finally there is the wife herself, the center of the drama and its most shadowy character. Apart from his grudging admission that she was thrifty and capable and a good housekeeper, Euphiletos tells us little about her. From what we know of Athenian marriage customs, we can guess that she was probably married at fourteen or fifteen to a virtual stranger and expected to keep house for this man who spent much of his time away from home on business. Was she satisfied with the trinkets that Euphiletos says he let her buy, and with all of the household duties and her young baby?

A small fragment survives from a lost play by Aristophanes in which a character says, "A woman needs a lover the way a dinner needs dessert." Euphiletos's wife was no Lysistrata, able to express her frustration and rebellion in some dramatic act of revolutionary will, but she did find a way to rebel all the same. It cost her dear. By Athenian law, if a man discovered that his wife had been raped or seduced, he was expected to divorce her. And from what we know of Euphiletos's character, we can be sure that he obeyed the law.

From *Horizon*, Spring 1974. Reprinted by permission of American Heritage, Inc., 1974.

Cleopatra: What Kind of a Woman Was She, Anyway?

Serpent of the Nile? Learned ruler? Sex kitten? Ambitious mom? African queen? History is still toying with the poor lady's reputation

Barbara Holland

Until now, everyone has had pretty much the same fix on Cleopatra: passion's plaything, sultry queen, a woman so beautiful she turned the very air around her sick with desire, a tragic figure whose bared bosom made an asp gasp when she died for love. Inevitably, the best-known incarnation of her is Hollywood's: Theda Bara, Claudette Colbert, Elizabeth Taylor, telling us what fun it was to be filthy rich in the first century B.C., spending days in enormous bathtubs and nights in scented sheets. Drinking pearls dissolved in vinegar. (Do not try this at home; it doesn't work.) Lounging around on a barge, being waited on hand and foot. Sometimes the asp looks like a small price to pay.

Hollywood's queen rests less on George Bernard Shaw's Cleopatra, who is a clever sex kitten, than on William Shakespeare's; in the Bard's *Antony and Cleopatra* she's a fiercer soul, downright

unhinged by love for Mark Antony. Of course, they both had to leave out her children. Everyone does. It's tough being the world's top tragic lover with four kids underfoot. Even if you can get a sitter, it doesn't look right.

The latest version, part of the current debate about the possible influences of Africa on Greek and Roman culture, suggests that she was black. The last time we looked she was a Macedonian Greek, but the black-Cleopatra advocates like to point out that since nobody knows anything about her paternal grandmother except that she wasn't legally married to Ptolemy IX, it is possible that she was black.

Most classical scholars disagree. Some note that though Ptolemy II, more than a century earlier, had an Egyptian mistress, the Ptolemies were wicked snobs, so proud of their bloodline, not to mention the line of succession to their

throne, that they tended to marry their brothers and sisters to keep it untainted. When they picked mistresses, they customarily chose upper-class Greeks. They felt so superior to the Egyptians, in fact, that after 300 years in Alexandria, they couldn't say much more than "good morning" to the locals in their native tongue; Cleopatra was the first in her family to learn the language.

Nobody should be surprised at such claims, however. For the fact is that for purposes political and otherwise, people have been fooling around with Cleopatra's image to suit themselves for centuries. In *All for Love* John Dryden gives us a traditional Cleo less a queen and a ruler than an addictive substance. Shaw made her stand for everything unBritish and thus deplorable. In the course of his *Caesar and Cleopatra* she evolves from a superstitious, cowardly little girl into a vengeful, bloodthirsty little girl. To underline his point he lops five years off her actual age and leaves her under the thumb of a sturdy Roman governor, forerunner of the wise and kindly British administrators of later colonies full of childish foreigners.

Of course, nearly everyone's story goes back to Plutarch, the first-century Greek biographer, who included two versions of Cleo. He knew the writings and stories of people in her part of the world who remembered her as a scholar in their own refined tradition, so unlike the ignorant, loutish Romans; a mothering goddess; a messiah sent to liberate the East from under the jackboots of Rome. On the other hand, he had the Roman story, largely attributed to her enemy in war, and conqueror, Octavian (who later became the emperor Augustus—portrayed as the clueless husband of the evil Livia in the television series *I, Claudius*). Octavian worked hard to set her up as everything scheming, treacherous, female, foreign and, most of all, sexually rapacious. His Queen Cleopatra was a drunken harlot, the wickedest woman in the world.

Actually, where we can reasonably deduce them, the facts are more interesting than these exotic scenarios.

Cleopatra VII was born in 69 B.C, the third child of Ptolemy XII, called Auletes, known as the Flute Player. Egypt was still rich, then, but its ancient empire had been nibbled away, and the natives, unfond of their Macedonian masters, were restless. The Flute Player kept going to Rome to get help in holding onto his throne. He may have taken Cleopatra along when she was 12; she may have watched the Roman loan sharks charge him 10,000 talents, or nearly twice Egypt's annual revenue, for services to be rendered.

Not only couldn't he control his subjects, he couldn't do a thing with his children. While he was away his eldest daughter, Tryphaena, grabbed the throne. After she got assassinated, second daughter Berenice grabbed it next—until Ptolemy came back with Roman help and executed her. Cleopatra, now the eldest, had cause to ponder. She knew Egypt needed Roman help, but paying cash for help was beggaring the state. She knew she had to watch her

back around her family. I suppose you could call it dysfunctional.

She seems to have found herself an education. Cicero, like most Romans, couldn't stand her, but he grudgingly admits she was literary and involved like him in "things that had to do with learning." The Arab historian Al-Masudi tells us she was the author of learned works, "a princess well versed in the sciences, disposed to the study of philosophy." According to Plutarch she spoke at least seven languages.

Cleopatra's looks are one of the burning issues of the ages.

In 51 B.C., when Cleopatra was 18, the Flute Player died and left the kingdom to her and her 10-year-old brother (and fiancé) Ptolemy XIII. The reign got off on the wrong foot because the Nile refused to flood its banks to irrigate the yearly harvest. A court eunuch named Pothinus reared his ugly head; he'd got himself appointed regent for little Ptolemy, squeezed Cleopatra clear out of town and began giving orders himself.

Rome, meanwhile, was in the process of shedding its republican privileges to become an empire. An early phase involved the uneasy power-sharing device called the First Triumvirate, with Caesar, Pompey and Crassus (a money man) jointly in charge. It wasn't Rome's brightest idea. Caesar and Pompey quarreled, Caesar defeated Pompey in Greece, Pompey took refuge in Egypt. Not wanting to harbor a loser, the Egyptians had him murdered and cut off his head and presented it to victorious Caesar when he sailed into Alexandria to collect the defunct Flute Player's debts. Pothinus had reason to hate and fear Rome. He was very likely plotting to do in Caesar, too, who took over the palace and stayed on with a guard of 3,000 Roman soldiers. He couldn't take his ships and go home; the winds were unfavorable.

Cleopatra needed a secret word with him, so as we've all heard, she got her-

self rolled up in some bedding and had herself delivered to Caesar as merchandise. According to Plutarch, Caesar was first captivated by this proof of Cleopatra's bold wit, and afterward so overcome by the charm of her society that he made a reconciliation between her and her brother. Then he killed Pothinus. So there was Cleopatra, at the price of being briefly half-smothered in bedding, with her throne back. And of course, sleeping with Caesar, who was in his 50s and losing his hair.

How did she do it? Cleopatra's looks are one of the burning issues of the ages. European painters tend to see her as a languishing blue-eyed blonde with nothing to wear but that asp. However, there's a coin in the British Museum with her profile on it, and she looks more like Abraham Lincoln than a voluptuous queen. Most people who have written about her agree that she commissioned the coins herself and, being a woman, was vain of her looks, so even this profile could have been downright flattering. In any case, it launched a lot of cracks about her proboscis. Had Cleopatra's nose been shorter, according to 17th-century French writer Blaise Pascal, the whole face of the world would have been changed. However, there's no evidence that Antony was unhappy with her nose the way it was.

Or maybe it wasn't so long. Maybe she thought more of her kingdom than her vanity and wanted to scare off possible enemies by looking fierce. Considering the speed with which she corrupted Rome's top commanders—both of them widely traveled, experienced married men—it's possible she looked more like a woman and less like Mount Rushmore than she does on the coins. Besides, the second-century Greek historian Dio Cassius says Cleopatra seduced Caesar because she was "brilliant to look upon... with the power to subjugate everyone." (She knew a few things about fixing herself up, too, and wrote a book on cosmetics full of ingredients unknown to Estee Lauder, like burnt mice.) And Plutarch reports that "It was a pleasure merely to hear the sound of her voice, with which, like an instrument of many strings, she could pass from one language to another...."

She bowled Caesar over, anyway, and when reinforcements came he squelched the rebellious Egyptian army for her. In the process he had to burn his own ships, and the fire spread and took out part of Alexandria's famous library, which housed most of what had been learned up to the time—Shaw called it "the memory of mankind." When the smoke cleared they found Ptolemy XIII drowned in the Nile in a full suit of golden armor, but as far as we know, his sister hadn't pushed him. Caesar then married her to her youngest brother, Ptolemy XIV, age 12, whom she ignored. When Caesar left, she was pregnant. Anti-Cleopatrans scoff at the notion that Caesar was the father, claiming he never admitted it himself, but there was plenty he never admitted, including his whole Egyptian fling, and somehow it seems likely. Giving the childless Caesar a son was a much shrewder move than getting pregnant by your 12-year-old brother; as policy it might have done wonders for Egypt. She named her son Ptolemy Caesar, always referred to him as Caesarion, and took him with her to Rome in 46 B.C. Mindful of her father's mistake, she took Ptolemy XIV, too, so she could keep an eye on him.

In Rome she was Caesar's guest. They gave fabulous parties together. He put up a golden statue of her in the temple of Venus Genetrix, causing a scandal that made him more vulnerable to the people who were plotting to kill him, as they did in March of 44. After he got stabbed, it turned out that he hadn't named Caesarion as his heir, but his great-nephew Octavian, so Cleopatra had to pack up and go home. When brother Ptolemy XIV conveniently died, she appointed the toddler Caesarion as coruler.

Here the record loses interest in her for several years, between lovers, but she must have been busy. She'd inherited a country plagued by civil wars, Egypt was broke, and twice more the Nile floods misfired. Somehow, though, by the time the West began to notice her again, peace reigned even in fractious Alexandria. She'd played her cards deftly with Rome and her subjects loved her. According to the first-century A.D. Jewish historian Josephus, she'd negotiated a sweetheart real estate deal with the Arabs and in general managed the economy so well that Egypt was the richest state in the eastern Mediterranean. So rich that Mark Antony came calling in 41 B.C. in search of funds to finance an attack on the Parthians.

By then the Romans were pigheadedly pursuing the triumvirate notion again, this time with Octavian, Lepidus and Antony. If you believe Plutarch, Antony was simple, generous and easygoing, though a bit of a slob. Cicero says his orgies made him "odious," and there's a story that, [after an all-night party, he rose to give a speech and threw up into the skirt of his toga while a kindly friend held it for him. Still, he was doing all right until Cleopatra came along, when he was, as Dryden laments, "unbent, unsinewed, made a woman's toy."

> *...like any Washington lobbyist with a pocketful of Redskins tickets, she was putting her time and money where they mattered most.*

Plutarch's description of their meeting on her barge makes poets and movie producers salivate. Who could resist those silver oars and purple sails, those flutes and harps, the wafting perfumes, the costumed maidens, and the queen herself dressed as Venus under a canopy spangled with gold? Not Antony, certainly. She knew what he'd come for and planned to drive a hard bargain. Naturally, they became lovers; they also sat down to deal; she would pay for his Parthian campaign, he would help fight her enemies and, for good measure, kill her sister Arsinoe, her last ambitious sibling.

Antony came for money and stayed to play. A sound relationship with Rome was tops on the whole world's agenda at the time. So, like a perfect hostess, Cleopatra lowered her standards of decorum and encouraged her guest in rowdy revels that have shocked the ages. The ages feel that all that frivoling means she was a frivolous woman, and not that, like any Washington lobbyist with a pocketful of Redskins tickets, she was putting her time and money where they mattered most.

She drank and gambled and hunted and fished with him. Sometimes they dressed as servants and roamed the town teasing the natives. Plutarch's grandfather knew a man who knew one of her cooks and reported that each night a series of banquets was prepared. If Antony wanted another round of drinks before dinner, the first banquet was thrown out and a second was served up, and so on. Anyone standing outside the kitchen door must have been half-buried in delicacies.

Back in Rome, Antony's third wife, Fulvia, and his brother raised an army against Octavian. (Lepidus, like Crassus, fizzled out early.) She got whipped, and Antony had to bid the fleshpots farewell and go patch things up. Then Fulvia died, and Antony sealed a temporary peace by marrying Octavian's sister, Octavia. Within weeks of that ceremony in Rome, Cleopatra had twins, Alexander Helios and Cleopatra Selene.

At the news of Antony's marriage, Shakespeare's queen has hysterics and tries to stab the messenger, but the Bard is guessing. The real queen probably took it in stride. She could recognize a political move when she saw it; she had Antony's alliance and a son to prove it, and a country to run besides.

SHE HAD NO TIME TO LOLL IN ASS'S MILK

No one suggests that she had a prime minister, and after Ponthinus, who would? No one denies, either, that Egypt was in apple-pie order. So there sits our drunken harlot, with Caesarion and the twins in bed, working late by oil light, signing papyri, meeting with advisers, approving plans for aqueducts, adjusting taxes. Distributing free grain during hard times. Receiving ambassadors and haggling over trade agreements. She may hardly have had time to put eyeliner on, let alone loll in ass's milk, and apparently she slept alone.

Antony finally got it together enough to invade Parthia. He needed help again, so he sent for Cleopatra to meet him at Antioch and she brought the children. Some see this as strictly business, but Plutarch insists his passion had "gathered strength again, and broke out into a flame." Anyway, they were rapturously reunited, and she agreed to build him a Mediterranean fleet and feed his army in exchange for a good deal of what is now Lebanon, Syria, Jordan and southern Turkey.

Did she really love him, or was it pure ambition? Ambition certainly didn't hurt, but it seems she was fond of him, though he probably snored after parties. Sources say she tried to introduce him to the finer things in life and dragged him to learned discussions, which at least sounds affectionate.

After a happy winter in Antioch, he went off to attack Parthia and she was pregnant again. The Parthian campaign was a disaster, ending with the loss or surrender of nearly half his army.

But for Cleopatra it was another boy, Ptolemy Philadelphus. When she'd recovered, she went to Antony's rescue with pay and warm clothes for the survivors. Presently Octavia announced that she, too, was coming to bring supplies. Antony told her to forget it and stay home. Octavian felt his sister had been dissed and suggested to the Romans that Antony was a deserter who planned to move the capital of the empire to Alexandria and rule jointly with his queen from there.

You could see it that way. In a public ceremony in Alexandria, Antony assembled the children, dressed to the teeth and sitting on thrones, and proclaimed Cleopatra "Queen of Kings" and Caesarion "King of Kings." He made his own three kids royalty, too, and gave them considerable realms that weren't, strictly speaking, his to give. Worst of all, he announced that Caesarion, not Octavian, was Julius Caesar's real son and the real heir to Rome.

Then he divorced Octavia.

All hands prepared for war. If the lovers had been quick off the mark, they might have invaded Italy at once and won, but instead they retired to Greece to assemble their forces, including Cleo-

patra's fleet. She insisted on sailing with it, too; her national treasury was stowed in the flagship. The upshot was that in 31 B.C. they found themselves bottled up at Actium, facing Octavian across the Ambracian Gulf. The standard version of the Battle of Actium is that while the fight hung in the balance, Cleopatra took her ships and left, because, being a woman, she was a coward and deserted in battle. The besotted Antony, we're told, followed her like a dog, and the fight turned into a rout.

With battles, the winner gets to tell the tale. Octavian was the winner, and he saw Cleopatra as a threat to Rome, a lascivious creature, and himself as a noble Roman able to resist her Eastern blandishments. All we really know is that it was a bloody mess, from which she managed to retreat with the treasury intact, enough to build another fleet with change left over. Octavian wanted that money to pay his troops. She wanted Egypt for her children. Perhaps deals could be made. Antony even suggested killing himself in trade for Cleopatra's life, but Octavian was bound for Egypt and he wouldn't deal.

...she and her ladies dressed up in their best finery and killed themselves. Octavian did the handsome thing and had her buried with Antony.

Thus threatened, the queen swiftly stuffed a big mausoleum with treasure, along with fuel enough to burn it down if all else failed, and locked herself in with her serving maids. It's unclear whether Antony was told she was dead or he just felt depressed, but anyway he disemboweled himself. He botched the job—it's harder than you'd think—and lingered long enough to be hauled to the mausoleum and hoisted through the upstairs window, where presumably he expired in Cleopatra's arms. Victorious

Octavian marched into town. He sent his henchmen to the queen, and they tricked their way in, snatched away her dagger, taking her—and her treasure—prisoner.

According to Plutarch, at 39 "her old charm, and the boldness of her youthful beauty had not wholly left her and, in spite of her present condition, still sparkled from within." It didn't help, so she and her ladies dressed up in their best finery and killed themselves. Octavian did the handsome thing and had her buried with Antony. Then he tracked down and killed Caesarion and annexed Egypt as his own personal colony.

The best-remembered Cleo story is the asp smuggled in with the basket of figs. Plutarch, who saw the medical record, mentions it as a rumor, wrestles with the evidence and concludes that "what really took place is known to no one, since it was also said that she carried poison in a hollow comb... yet there was not so much as a spot found, or any symptom of poison upon her body, nor was the asp seen within the monument...."

Later it was suggested—probably by Octavian—that she'd tried various substances on her slaves and, so the story usually goes, opted for the asp, but in truth its bite is even less fun than disemboweling. Maybe she used a cobra, whose effects are less visible. But where did it go? Some people claimed there were two faint marks on her arm, but they sound like mosquito bites to me. Others insist they saw a snake's trail on the sand outside; fat chance, with all those guards and soldiers and distressed citizens milling around shouting and trampling the evidence.

It looks likelier that she'd brewed up a little something to keep handy. She was clever that way; remember the second brother. Octavian's men had patted her down—"shook out her dress," Plutarch says—but she was smarter than they were. And why gamble on the availability of snakes and smugglers when you could bring your own stuff in your suitcase? When Octavian led his triumph through Rome, lacking the actual queen, he paraded an effigy of her with her arm wreathed in snakes, and the asp theory slithered into history. Maybe he'd heard the rumor and believed it, or maybe he started it himself. It would have played well in Rome. In Egypt the snake was a symbol of royalty and a pet of the goddess Isis, but in Rome it was strictly a sinuous, sinister reptile, typical of those Easterners, compared with a forthright Roman whacking out his innards.

History has always mixed itself with politics and advertising, and in all three the best story always carries the day. But why did the man who was now undisputed ruler of the known world work so hard to ruin a dead lady's reputation? Maybe she'd been more formidable than any of our surviving stories tell. We do know she was the last great power of the Hellenistic world, "sovereign queen of many nations" and the last major threat to Rome for a long time. She might have ruled half the known world or even, through her children, the whole thing, and ushered in the golden age of peace that she believed the gods had sent her to bring to the Mediterranean.

At least she would have left us her own version of who she was, and maybe it would be closer to the truth than the others. And then again, given the human urge to tell good stories, maybe not.

Barbara Holland, who often writes wryly about history and politics for the magazine, is the author of several books, including Endangered Pleasures *(Little, Brown).*

From *Smithsonian magazine*, February 1997, pp. 57–62, 64. © 1997 by Barbara Holland. Reprinted by permission of the author.

The Year One

Life was nasty, brutish, and short 2,000 years ago, but the issues of the day were surprisingly modern

By Lewis Lord

Two thousand years ago this week, the Year One arrived. But no one knew it, either then or for several centuries thereafter. The 12 months we call A.D. 1 came and went as just another year. To the Romans who ruled what was considered the civilized world—and whose civilization would one day be the basis for our own—the year was 754 A.U.C. (*ab urbe condita*—"from the foundation of the city")—754 being the number of years since Romulus and Remus, the legendary orphans suckled by a she-wolf, were said to have founded Rome. Among Rome's Greek subjects, who marked time in four-year units between Olympic Games, the year was merely the first quarter of the 195th Olympiad. Meanwhile, the Chinese saw it as nothing more than "the second year of the reign period of P'ing-ti," the boy emperor who would die five years later at the age of 13.

But to a sixth-century monk in Rome, the year ranked as the greatest in all history. According to Dionysius Exiguus's reckonings, it was "Anno Domini"—the first full "year of our Lord"—the year that began a week after the birth of Christ. All time prior to A.D. 1 would be counted as so many years B.C., "before Christ." With papal support, Dionysius's chronological system gradually won almost universal acceptance—even though it miscalculated the Nativity by several years: Scholars believe that Jesus was probably 5, 6, or 7 years old in A.D. 1.

Now and then. The people of the Year One shared concerns that exist today—child rearing, social behavior, faith—but did so in ways now impossible to understand. Historian John Evans tells his first-year students at the University of Minnesota they would find it easier to "deal with a star-faring race that showed up from Betelgeuse than to cross the divides of time and space and deal with the Romans on their own terms."

In the political world of 2,000 years ago, Ronald Reagan would never have made it in politics. Romans ranked actors on a level with prostitutes. Nor would Al Gore have won support by kissing Tipper. Men in love were considered laughable, so much so that one senator was stripped of his seat for embracing his wife in public. But George W. Bush would have stood tall. In Rome, every "young nobleman" was dutybound "to avenge any humiliations suffered by his father," wrote historian Florence Dupont in her book *Daily Life in Ancient Rome*. "Not to be avenged was the worst misfortune that could befall a father and the deepest shame that could sully a son's name."

In the Year One, the world's most powerful politician—a man who unintentionally paved the way for Christianity's rise—was a 63-year-old, 5-foot-5 hypochondriac with gallstones, dirty teeth, and a knack for climbing to the top and staying there. The emperor Augustus, grandnephew and adopted son of the murdered Julius Caesar, was in the 27th year of his 41-year reign as the unquestioned leader of the world's biggest empire.

Those years found Augustus pondering very modern issues: law and order, welfare, family values, and moral decay, including sexual transgressions in his own household. Augustus would boast that he found Rome brick and made it marble, but more lasting by far than his monuments was the influence of his reign, which helped shape life and thought in much of the world for the next 2,000 years. The Age of Augustus would create a framework of government and society that would transform Western Europe—and hence America—with Rome's laws, its institutions, its language, and what eventually would become its state religion, Christianity.

Without the good roads and widespread order of the Pax Romana—the two centuries of peace that Augustus introduced—the "good news" of Christ might never have spread. Yet the stability was wafer-thin. In the decades just before A.D. 1, Augustus had conned the Roman people into scrapping their cherished but ultimately unworkable republic and its freedoms for the security and efficiency of an imperial dictatorship. Beneath the grandeur of empire lay a decaying social system peopled overwhelmingly by the poor and the left out. It was there that Christianity, offering hope in a hopeless world, would take root, grow, and eventually flower.

Indeed, the teachings of Christ were spread in a world of unrelenting cruelty. Who today could condone the sight of men and women being fed to beasts as people of all classes shrilled their delight? To the Romans, the spectacle was a just punishment for lawbreakers. What's to be made of a superpower that conquered cities by enslaving the men and killing the women and children? Owning or killing people, Romans believed, was as natural as water running downhill. Who can comprehend a father's tossing an infant into the village dung heap for being female, sick, or a surplus mouth to feed? The Romans were not offended, especially if the father followed the law and invited five neighbors to examine the baby before he left it to die.

Why not? In the Year One, questioning such behavior would have drawn blank stares. "The Romans saw the world as it was," says Sarah Pomeroy, a classics professor at New York's Hunter College who wrote *Goddesses, Whores, Wives, and Slaves: Women in Classical Antiquity*. "They didn't think of whether anything was unjust."

In the world of the Romans, the cure for stomachache was a dose of water in which feet had been washed. Hawkers in the town squares offered amulets conferring power from gods for every need, from giving sight to the blind to raising a child (among the baby gods: Wailer, Breastfeeder, Eater, and Stander). Children, until they walked and talked, were not considered humans. Citizens didn't use soap but cleansed themselves with olive oil and a scraping tool. A stick with a wet sponge on the tip did what toilet paper does today. (Indeed, paper as we know it did not exist until a hundred years later in China.)

Centuries of rough existence had bred a Roman acceptance of savagery and the conviction that life was a series of bleak choices. How, for instance, might a poor family acquire a slave? If it had food to spare, it could pluck a child from the dung heap and raise it in servitude. "Nothing was wasted in the ancient world: not an abandoned baby, not the cloth that kept the ragpicker in business…not even the grains of barley in horse manure on the streets," writes Yale historian Ramsay MacMullen in his book *Roman Social Relations, 50 B.C. to A.D. 284*. "There were always people poor enough to fight over another's leavings."

Political and social influence was reserved for a tiny group: the senators and knights who owned most of the land and the bulk of the wealth. By one estimate, these elites—essentially the guys in togas in the Hollywood epics—made up less than one tenth of 1 percent of the population. Rome's upper-middle class—prosperous but not immensely rich—ranked socially only a notch above the vast citizenry that was poor. Many of the not-rich-enough contented themselves with a few well-cultivated acres where, amid kin and slaves, they lived relatively comfortable lives, going barefoot, sleeping on straw, and eating pork, vegetables, and bread.

The colossally rich, like the patrician who gave his pet eel a jeweled bracelet, retained their unsalaried political offices by treating supporters to gigantic parties. But in the century leading up to the Year One, fewer and fewer politicians could afford the soaring costs of feasts, theater shows, and gladiatorial combats that the public had come to expect. Many officeholders turned to bribes. By the first century A.D., venality was rampant. Even officers in the army expected payoffs from their soldiers.

Home and away. The Romans had a propensity for rewarding the wrong people. In the two centuries before the Year One, a long series of wars kept untold thousands of farmers in the army and away from their farms. To prevent their families from starving, many soldiers sold their neglected land to rich landowners. Once out of the legions, multitudes sought refuge in Rome, swelling the city's population in A.D. 1 to nearly 1 million people. It wasn't a promise of good jobs that drew the dispossessed veterans to Rome, however. Slaves did nearly all the work, not just the menial but also such important tasks as operating stores, delivering mail, practicing medicine, and tutoring the children of the wealthy. What pulled the ex-soldiers to Rome was "bread and circuses," specifically free food and free entertainment financed by taxes and tributes from conquered territories.

The government, since Caesar's rule, had given daily wheat rations to most citizens of Rome, the plebeians who included all adults except foreigners, slaves, and women. Even farmers who still owned land were abandoning it and flocking to the city to live on the dole. Rome's elites scorned the newcomers as rabble—"the bloodsuckers of the treasury," Cicero called them—and Caesar tried belatedly to curb the giveaway. But his welfare reform was short-lived. Augustus, Caesar's successor, reversed the cuts in 5 B.C. and extended the benefits to boys as well as men.

In the Year One, to keep his citizenry happy and grievance-free, Augustus was delivering a lavish array of religious ceremonies, festivals, and *ludi,* "the games in honor of the gods." Chariot races drew crowds of 200,000 or more to the Circus Maximus, where the most popular scene—a mass littering of overturned chariots, squealing horses, and maimed men—was known as a "shipwreck." A day at the Forum often began with fans savoring Augustus's wild-beast matches, although the regulars had a good idea which animals would win. Packs of hounds always beat herds of deer, bears withstood bulls, and lions usually finished off tigers. But not even the ferocious charge of the rhinoceros could penetrate the thick hide of the elephant.

The afternoon brought more variety: animals vs. humans. Some of the men, trained and equipped with spears, lived to fight another day. But for others, the outcome was never in doubt. They were the *bestiarii*—condemned criminals who later would include Christian men and women—thrown into the arena with no training and no weapons. The carnivore often was a quick-killing lion; many fans preferred smaller beasts that did more dragging and tearing.

By the Year One, the *ludi* were part of everyday Roman life. "One might even say that they pervaded life," wrote the French historian Roland Auguet in *Cruelty and Civilization: The Roman Games*. "They imposed their rhythm on existence and provided nourishment for the passions." Augustus, ever a stickler for order, tried to regulate the gore. If two gladiators still stood after dueling long and hard, he decreed, both should receive the palm of victory. But the mob preferred blood. For centuries, *ludi* sponsors would ignore Augustus's law and force the faceless men—helmets hid their features—to fight until one became a corpse in the sand.

A decree telling spectators where to sit was part of Augustus's most ambitious project, his campaign to restore public morality. The best seats went to patrician couples, the Vestal Virgins, soldiers, and married men. Why favor married men? Augustus had the notion that Rome's population was shrinking because too many men were visiting prostitutes, keeping concubines, and avoiding marriage. If more men would take wives, he believed, Rome would have what Cicero termed "less lust and larger families."

To promote family values, Augustus hatched a system of rewards and punishments. Husbands who fathered three children were put on fast tracks for promotions. Mothers of three won a voice in property questions. Bachelors and spinsters, on the other hand, saw their inheritances restricted. Scrapped was an old law that let husbands kill adulterous wives. But any man who refused to divorce such a woman, the emperor decreed, should be prosecuted. Wives could divorce their husbands, but at a risk: Fathers apparently always got the children.

The men of Rome had griped about their women for nearly two centuries, ever since the Senate agreed in 195 B.C. to let ladies wear dyed clothes and ride in carriages. Wives were expected to keep the hearth burning, fetch water, cook, spin, weave, and bear children. They weren't supposed to drink—a sure sign of sexual aberrations. (The reason men kissed their female kin, Cato the Elder reported, was to check for wine on their breath.) Nor, in the presence of males, were they to appear very smart. Wives who discussed history and poetry and used correct grammar, the writer Juvenal observed, were "really annoying."

No romance. Romans married for duty, specifically to preserve family lines and replenish the citizenry. Fathers decided who wed whom. Until Augustus decreed that engaged girls be at least 10, some Roman daughters, including his own, were betrothed in infancy. Teenage boys, like their fathers, could have their way with prostitutes or slaves of either sex. But first-time brides were expected to be virgins. One of Julius Caesar's wives no doubt passed the test: She was only 11. Affection was rarely a factor in Roman engagements. "But it was taken for granted that if the husband and wife treated each other properly, love would develop and emerge, and by the end of their lives it would be a deep, mutual feeling," says David Konstan, a classics professor at Brown University.

Few people, ancient or modern, made a bigger mess of family life than did the family-values leader of Rome. Augustus ditched his first wife, Scribonia, because of a "moral perversity of hers," namely her contempt for his mistress. A year later, the randy emperor fell for Livia, who happened to be six months pregnant and married to another man. Three days after the baby arrived, Augustus and Livia wed. Livia's freshly divorced husband, posing as her father, obligingly gave her away.

Livia kept Augustus content, critics would claim, by sending slave girls to his chamber and looking the other way as he dallied with politicians' wives. Whatever the cause, the emperor would ultimately laud his marriage as 51 years of happiness. But his opinion of his only child, Julia, was less felicitous.

Julia was born just before Augustus divorced her mother, the strait-laced Scribonia. As a newborn, she was betrothed to a son of her father's ally, Mark Antony. When friend turned foe, Augustus had her young fiancé killed. When she was 14, Augustus wed her to his nephew Marcellus, who would die two years later. She then married another cousin's husband, Agrippa, and consequently gave Augustus four grandchildren. But the emperor was not satisfied. When Agrippa died, Augustus matched Julia with Livia's son Tiberius, even though Tiberius was happily married to someone else.

The result was the greatest sex scandal of the Augustan Age. Tiberius, craving the wife he was forced to divorce, withdrew to an island and brooded. The abandoned Julia, meanwhile, took her first stab at enjoying life on her terms. She had lovers—not just a few, it was said, but many. She got drunk in revels at the Forum, informants reported, and offered herself as a prostitute on the street.

In 2 B.C., word of his daughter's transgressions reached Augustus. In a blaze of publicity, he terminated Julia's marriage, wrote the Senate a letter detailing her alleged debaucheries, and banished her, at 37, to an island in the Tyrrhenian Sea.

Ten years later, an identical charge hit Julia's daughter, also named Julia, and she, too, was sent into exile. For good measure, Augustus struck back at one perceived cause of his progeny's lax morals. The emperor had long endured the poems of Ovid, whose *Art of Love* seduction manual flew in the face of the official family-values campaign. For corrupting his kin, the monarch expelled Rome's most popular poet to a Black Sea town so backward that men wore trousers.

Slippery slope. Augustus never understood that a force far more pervasive than Ovid's poems was fueling Rome's moral slide. It was wealth that rotted out the Roman character. With trade and tribute pouring in from the provinces, the rich grew richer, lazier, and more indulgent. Nor did the doles and free spectacles strengthen the moral fiber of the city's idle mob. As time went on, the disparities between the rich and the wretched widened in every respect. Housing costs in the cities soared, chasing the impoverished into attics and one-room hovels with no water and no hearth. In the countryside, land increasingly fell into the hands of a few patrician families that now owned thousands of acres tended by hundreds of disinherited, indigent workers.

By the third century A.D., to meet the rising costs of defending its frontier, Rome was soaking the poor. The Romans never imagined anything like today's graduated income tax, which places the heaviest burden on those best able to bear it. Rome's system was the opposite: The richer and more politically connected a man was, the less he paid.

The fifth-century collapse of the empire that began just before the Year One had many perceived causes, from exhaustion of topsoil to poisonous lead in the pipes of an otherwise splendid plumbing system. No claim has been more controversial than Edward Gibbon's. His five-volume *History of the Decline and Fall of the Roman Empire* (1776–88) blamed Christianity, asserting that it had wrecked the old religions that had sustained the Roman soul and stabilized the Roman state. But Will Durant, the 20th-century philosopher, noted that the old religions were breaking up long before Jesus was born. Romans lost faith in their leaders, Durant wrote in *Caesar and Christ*, "because the state defended wealth against poverty, fought to capture slaves, taxed toil to support luxury, and failed to protect its people from famine, pestilence, invasion, and destitution."

As for the spread of Christianity—now the world's largest religion with roughly 2 billion followers—sources from antiquity suggest an important role by the emperor who reigned during Jesus's childhood. Thanks to Augustus's Pax Romana, Christ's revolutionary message was able to spread from one generation to the next in a world made stable by the hegemony of Rome, developing, as the apostle Paul described it, "in the fullness of time."

"A peace was prevalent which began at the birth of Christ," the Christian teacher Origen wrote in the second century. "For God prepared the nations for his teaching so that they should be under one prince, the king of the Romans, and that it might not...be more difficult for the apostles to carry out the task laid on them by their Master when he said, 'Go and teach all nations.'"

OLD AGE IN ANCIENT ROME

Mary Harlow and Ray Laurence look at what it meant to become a senior citizen in ancient Rome, and how this early model has a bearing on our attitudes towards ageing today.

by Mary Harlow, Ray Laurence

ROME HELD AN EMPIRE stretching across one-sixth of the surface of the globe, with a population of some 60 million—an achievement equalled by the Chinese empire in the east and only surpassed by Russia and the United States in the nineteenth century. Its capital, Rome, was the first ever metropolis, containing one million people and an urban culture that included architectural achievements unsurpassed until the modern period. This picture of an almost modern nation masks another of massive inequality, alongside sickness and disease that have not been experienced in the West for generations. Life expectancy at birth was short: on average roughly twenty-five to thirty years, with 50 percent of those born not passing the age of ten. In other words, the demographic regime was not unlike that experienced in countries today such as Botswana through the causes of AIDS, international debt, poverty and inequality—a far cry from the modern Western world where average life expectancy becomes ever-higher and runs well into the seventies. A key question for understanding Rome is how society viewed those few people who survived into old age and experienced a life-span not unlike our own today.

There was a strong distinction between the elderly and others in Roman society. The old man was the opposite of the young man, whereas the man in his thirties or forties combined the better qualities of old and young. Such thinking, developed in Greece and in Alexandria, was incorporated into Roman society with an emphasis on a set sequence of stages of life from birth until old age. Varro (writing at the end of the last century BC) gave the framework along chronological lines: *puerita*, up to age fifteen; *adulscentia*, from fifteen to thirty; *iuventus*, from thirty to forty-five; *seniores*, from forty-five to sixty; *senectus*, from sixty until death. Other writers, such as Horace, gave a biological and social dimension to such stages: infancy was associated with a lack of teeth and therefore an inability to communicate; childhood with the ability to speak but needing control; youth with the inability to grow a beard and the potential for wild behaviour and excessive spending; the adult strove for consistency of behaviour, sought wealth and friendship; the old man suffered mental and physical degeneration and was capable only of criticising those younger than himself.

These expositions of the stages of life highlight two points: that the adult stage was clearly the prime of life from which old age was seen as a period of decline; that the female life course did not fit this model. Women had a childhood which ended with marriage at somewhere between the ages of fifteen to eighteen. They thus entered adulthood when their brothers were ending 'adolescence'. Men did not normally marry until between the ages of twenty-five and thirty. Women were 'adult' until they reached the age of menopause, about fifty. Within this stage they might move into different social personae: wife, mother, widow. After the age of fifty, once they were considered past childbearing, they entered 'old age'. The female life course was thus much more defined by the biology of reproduction and any social dimension was defined in relation to parents, husband or children.

The Romans had, and voiced—particularly as they got older—ideas about the role of the elderly in society. A concept of retirement from office-holding into a life of well-deserved but intellectually and physically active leisure (otium) existed alongside a fear of being 'put out to grass'. We have some amusing and instructive images of how to spend a productive old age in the works of Cicero and Pliny the Younger—men attempting to negotiate space for themselves in the social and political world of their time. There was no official 'retirement' age as such but there was a consensus among ancient writers that after the age of sixty a man could, if he so chose, retire honourably from public life. At this age men entered the category of senex. There was an expression, sexagenarios de ponte (sixty-year olds over the bridge), which, while it has been given a variety of meanings, most likely referred to the fact that once an individual had reached sixty he was no longer required to vote—the pontes supposedly being the narrow gangways into the voting enclosures. After the age of sixty men were freed from the duty of attending the Senate or their local council and were exempt from the penalties and disadvantages exacted by the law that promoted marriage—if single and unmarried.

In short, once a man had reached the chronological age of sixty, he could step down from his formal obligations as a citizen and lead a life of leisure. This departure from public life was double-edged: it could be seen as a lifestyle that was characterised as productive (or indulgent) leisure but it could also mean social marginalisation. Moving out of public life in effect led to a loss of social

power and status in the eyes of those still in power. Retiring from public life was no easier for individuals in the Roman period than it is for some today—many of whom continue to work after their sixty-fifth birthday. Despite this, and the fact that there was no social marker, no rite of transition to mark this phase, there was pressure for older men to stand down in favour of younger.

The portraits and statues of the first century BC reflect an ideology that venerated maturity of age and experience in politicians and generals. Images of this period are dubbed 'veristic' because they reflect the gravitas of leaders in their mature, lined, wrinkled, and even scarred, realistic faces. There is an almost generic portrait bust type from this period that shows the individual with receding hair, furrowed brow and deeply incised lines around the mouth. A life spent in loyalty to the state was encapsulated in the image of the careworn individual. The essential male attributes of virtue and gravity were depicted in the lines of the mature adult face. These images reflected an ideology that held older men in high esteem and assumed respect and honour to increase as individuals aged. This ideology assumed respect for the older male in society and was underpinned by the institution of paternal power, which gave authority to fathers (the elderly) over their sons and was a defining feature of Roman society. The eldest male in a family held legal power over all those within his household, except his wife. All children remained legally, socially and financially dependent on their father unless freed from these legal obligations by him. In an extreme case, a son aged fifty could still not make independent decisions about his own finances, could not inherit, marry or transact business without the approval of his father. Such a situation was uncommon, as many male children experienced the death of their father before adulthood and most men were unlikely in middle age to still have their father alive.

The characteristic expression of the relationship between sons and their fathers was one of piety and the performance of a reciprocal duty of care and loyalty between parents and children—specifically an obligation on children to repay the care given them in their infancy by providing for their parents in old age. This social idea that the older generation deserved increasing respect and honour as they aged was also expressed in the political cursus honorum (career ladder) which ring-fenced higher offices and honours for those of the upper age groups.

A series of laws stipulated minimum ages for holding particular political offices. As an individual aged he could expect to hold increasingly senior posts: the quaestorship at twenty-seven, praetorship in his late thirties and the consulship at forty-two. There was great competition for the highest offices. Individuals like Cicero were very proud of the fact that they held the office 'in their year', that is, at the earliest legally acceptable age.

There was increasing tension between those who followed the traditional age rankings and order of office holding of the cursus honorum and those who either leap-frogged offices or held them at an apparently very young age. This upset traditional notions of age-related behaviour and hierarchies of respect. This can be seen in the relationship between Cicero and the young Octavian after the murder of his father by adoption—Julius Caesar. When Octavian arrived in Rome to claim his inheritance, he was only nineteen. Cicero clearly regarded him as a youth who could be manipulated, but he seriously misjudged 'this boy'.

The outcome of the events that followed the death of Julius Caesar in 44 BC were to challenge the assumptions of the age restrictions and, indeed, of the age structure of power holding. When the Roman world emerged from a long series of civil wars it found itself with a leader who had held power since the age of nineteen. Octavian was still only thirty-four when he changed his name to Augustus and assumed the title of *Princeps* to mask the establishment of the new monarchy in Rome in 27 BC. The portraits of Augustus reflect this change in the representation of power. He is shown as a young man consistently youthful throughout his life—he died aged seventy-seven. Not surprisingly, his youthful wisdom and ability to defeat his enemies as a young man were simply signs that he was a god on earth—death brought deification.

It is no coincidence that Cicero wrote a philosophical dialogue on the nature of old age in his sixty-second year and dedicated it to his lifetime friend and financial advisor—Atticus (aged sixty-five). It was intended to lighten their 'common burden of old age'. While it may have served that purpose, and certainly followed in a tradition of philosophic writings on the subject, it is clearly a plea from a man who had been sidelined from the central political events of his day. Cicero was appealing for the honour and position he considered his experience entitled him to. The work, *Cato the Elder on old age*, (*Cato maior de senectute*), was written as a dialogue set in the past (150 BC) between Cato, aged eighty-four, and Scipio and Laelius, in their mid-thirties. The sentiments expressed are not reflections of a real lived experience of old age but they encapsulate hopes and anxieties which would have been common to many upper-class Romans, and, indeed, have echoes for today. Cato argued that while old age brought certain physical disadvantages it need not prevent continued mental activity. He recommended memory exercises. Using examples from the past he stated his case that those with experience have much to offer in terms of advice and authority, which, while it could no longer be expressed in positions that require physical prowess, could be used in persuasive public speaking. He maintained that the weakness of old age should be resisted by a seriously undertaken regimen of frugal eating,

moderate exercise and intellectual pursuit. A common complaint, that increasing age brought about reduced sexual activity, should in fact be welcomed. Like the desire to over-indulge in eating and drinking, sexual activity and desire were a part of an earlier stage of life that should be happily laid aside as a detraction from the higher pursuits of the mind. For Cato (Cicero) the only real downside to old age was that its presence signified the approach of death. This, he countered with the typically stoic response, was nothing to fear—after death there would be the pleasure of the afterlife, or no sensation at all. Old age was something to be endured, and was the source of the branch of philosophy known today as stoicism.

The key to the enjoyment of old age was a tough regimen found by Pliny the Younger in the lifestyle of the elderly senator Spurinna. He was seventy-seven and still in excellent physical health which Pliny attributed to the routine he followed every day. This began, an hour after dawn, with a three-mile walk accompanied by friends in conversation or listening to a book being read aloud, thus exercising both mind and body simultaneously. Followed by a rest and then a carriage ride with his wife or friends. When he took a young friend like Pliny with him he, like Cato, talked of great men and their deeds to inspire his company. At the end of the drive, Spurinna walked another mile on foot and then retired to his room to compose verses in Greek and Latin. In the afternoon he exercised without his clothes in the open air by playing ball, an exercise thought to keep old age at bay, then had his bath. There was a short rest before dinner, which was a simple meal. During the meal there was entertainment in the form of a performance or a reading.

Pliny expressed admiration for Spurinna and his lifestyle, seeing him as a person to emulate. Spurinna in his time had had a glittering public career, but had maintained his position and status after his withdrawal

from public life. Moreover, he accepted this retirement gracefully, sharing Pliny's view that 'a certain amount of irregularity and excitement is not unsuitable for the young, but their elders should lead a quiet and orderly existence; their time of public activity is over, and ambition only brings them into disrepute' Pliny was still in the prime of his adult life when he wrote this, still busy with work but anticipated the final withdrawal from that role and a future old age—he died at the age of fifty-one and thus did not experience what it was to be old.

However much comfort philosophy might offer, the Romans were still aware of the drawbacks of getting old. Physical disability was to be feared. The wealthy might fear it from the point of view of discomfort in a world without effective pain relief but also because it increased the individual's dependency on others. Again from Pliny we have an example that is the opposite of Spurinna: Domitius Tullus was so enfeebled by old age that he was practically paralysed. He could do nothing for himself, not even brush his own teeth. He was 'crippled and deformed in every limb' and totally dependent on his wife and slaves. He could, however, still complain. The potential vulnerability of old age was particularly feared by those who were used to being in control. This desire for control of one's fate is expressed by the choice of death by some elderly individuals who developed illnesses: Cicero's old friend Atticus is said to have died at the age of seventy-eight after refusing food on the diagnosis of an intestinal illness and another of Pliny's mentors chose the same method, at the age of sixty-seven, having suffered from the excruciating pain of gout for thirty-six years.

So far all we have discussed applies to the upper-class male. This is because as the writers of the relevant texts they are, for the most part, only interested in themselves. We have to assume that the majority of the population of the Roman world had little choice but to work, in some capacity or other, until they dropped. Those who did not have family or financial resources would find that incapacity brought an early death. A sad little verse from the Palatine Anthology (a collection of epigrammatic poems dating from the seventh century BC to the tenth century AD, found in the palatine library) encapsulates this:

> Worn by age and poverty, no one stretching out his hand to relieve my misery, on my tottering legs I went slowly to my grave, scarce able to reach the end of my wretched life. In my case the law of death was reversed, for I did not die first to be buried, but I died after my funeral.

Other instances along these lines are a feature of metropolitan poetry, with a cast of the poor awaiting their deaths and facing the prospect of their bodies being disposed of in a rudimentary manner or subject to the attention of roaming packs of dogs. For these people, without access to either the philosophy or the regimen of the rich, old age was brutal; their lives were lived out or simply worn out awaiting death.

Women, unlike men, have a biological marker to indicate transition to a new stage of life in the menopause. Fifty was the age given in the laws on marriage after which a widow was not required to seek remarriage. This assumes that after this age she would no longer be able to bear children. In Rome postmenopausal women all but disappear from the texts. When they do appear it is often in highly stereotypical guises—evil hags, wicked stepmothers or outrageous prostitutes. Women, of course, faced similar anxieties as men about growing older, but these were exacerbated by the status of their sex in Roman society.

A woman's life was centred on her family and she was very much defined by her role within the household as wife and/or mother. There was a sentimentality in Roman writing (by men) about couples who grew old together. Even the decrepit Domitius Tullus was considered lucky to have an 'excellent' (second) wife who cared for him (though there is a sense in Pliny's letter that she might have married him for his money). Women of independent wealth might have an enjoyable old age if they retained their health. The differential age at marriage would suggest that there were many more widows than widowers in Roman society. Men expected to die before their wives, just as women foresaw a life after their husband's death in old age. Some of these widows were well provided for: the widow of Domitius Tullus might have led a fine life after his death. She may also have considered marrying again although she risked censure. It was considered inappropriate for women who had borne children and were now past child-bearing age to remarry and Pliny remarked that she had already been severely criticised for so doing. It was generally assumed that if an individual was to marry late in life it was because their suitor was after their money, indeed some elderly people found themselves surrounded by such 'legacy hunters'.

One elderly lady who lived a highly enjoyable and somewhat indulgent old age, according to Pliny, was Ummidia Quadratilla. Described as having a sound constitution and sturdy physique, she passed her time playing draughts and being entertained by her own private troupe of pantomime actors—clearly a woman who could afford and choose her own pleasures and amusements. However, as a respectable lady she did not allow her pleasures to corrupt her grandson, sending him away while the troupe performed. When she died at the age of seventy-nine she demonstrated her good sense of duty by leaving her estate to her grandchildren and not to her sycophantic actors or other legacy hunters.

Widowed female relations may have gravitated back to the family home and fulfilled childcare and domestic roles again at this later stage of their lives. Women without resources had to fall back on their families or patrons. Julius Caesar's mother lived with him and scrutinised every new bride of her son with an aptitude to identify their adulteries or even to fabricate them. Women without such resources might fall back on the one resource that all possessed, their bodies. The aged female body was a topic of the grotesque in Roman literature. Elderly prostitutes were graphically described by the satirists Horace and Juvenal who make great play on make-up caked faces which failed to conceal wrinkles, toothless gums seeking kisses, sagging breasts under jewellery that failed to disguise the ugliness of the body and inappropriateness of behaviour—some writers associate the techniques of the disguise of age in the brothel with those of the undertaker presenting a corpse. Certain behaviour was only acceptable for certain age groups: old prostitutes seeking young lovers transgressed all acceptable customs; old women were ugly and thus not sexually desirable, to actively seek sexual gratification was doubly transgressive. Old women were also stereotyped in comic literature as drunks, brothel keepers and witches. These literary representations illustrated women who had moved outside male control and thus no longer fulfilled any of the roles that Roman society defined for women. A respectable elderly woman should retire within the household, live a quiet and blameless life, leaving her estate to her children.

The old could be revered by family and the state, but for those with little money or surviving younger family there were real anxieties. As individuals they were marginal to the existence of those with greater access to both wealth and family resources. There was no welfare or charity 'safety net' for them. It is ironic that many of the concepts of age in our own democratic society were learnt from Rome, passed on through the Middle Ages, and incorporated into early twentieth-century sociology. That is where the similarity ends. We may recognise texts suggesting the old act in certain ways at Rome, and sympathise with the response of those growing older in the form of lively defences of the stoic endurance of age. However, the silent majority even of the twentieth century, seen in photographs such as those of Dust-Bowl America in the 1930s, may look old in the manner of veristic Roman portrait before they reached thirty-five. These people do not appear in the world of Rome's elite, or if they do they are caricatures.

It is the unusualness of being old that defines the status of the elite of Rome. Their lives could be summarised as a series of achievements as middle-aged men, and recalled and retold to the young once they had left public life. The old were wise if they were wealthy and were insulated from the dangers of poverty and inequality that was such a part of the structure of the Roman empire. They produced a philosophy of survival—Stoicism. The question for us today is, do these attitudes towards the elderly continue to have relevance? We in the West worry about the possibility of financial well-being in old age—will there be enough younger citizens to support an ever growing population over sixty-five living for longer and longer? Elsewhere, particularly in Africa where populations have been affected by the AIDS virus, life expectancy is dropping to averages similar to those experienced in ancient Rome. But those without AIDS can expect to live into their seventies, having witnessed the deaths of the infected generations. Today, the experience of old age is moving away from that of the wealthy leisured elite of Rome to one characterised by inequality and poverty. The inability or unwillingness of the state, the G8 countries or any other national or international body to address the current demographic time-bombs threaten to return us to the broader Roman experience of old age, in which the state offered no care for the elderly leaving the individual only the family or their own wealth as protection against the uncertainties of the final decades of life.

FOR FURTHER READING

K. Cokayne, *Experiencing Old Age in Ancient Rome* (Routledge, 2003); M. Harlow and R. Laurence, *Growing Up and Growing Old: A Life Course Approach* (Routledge, 2002); Tim Parkin, *Old Age and the Aged in the Ancient World* 'Ageing in antiquity: status and participation', in P. Johnson and P. Thane (eds), *Old Age from Antiquity to Post Modernity* (Routledge, 1998).

Mary Harlow lectures in Roman History at the Institute of Archaeology and Antiquity at the University of Birmingham. Ray Laurence lectures in Roman Social History in the Department of Classics at the University of Reading.

Celtic War Queen Who Challenged Rome

It was easy for Emperor Nero to dismiss a woman from a barbarian tribe in faraway Britannia. But when Boudica and her warriors decimated a legion, Rome took her seriously.

By Margaret Donsbach

SHE SLAUGHTERED A ROMAN ARMY. She torched Londinium, leaving a charred layer almost half a meter thick that can still be traced under modern London. According to the Roman historian Cornelius Tacitus, her army killed as many as 70,000 civilians in Londinium, Verulamium and Camulodunum, rushing "to cut throats, hang, burn, and crucify." Who was she? Why was she so angry?

Most of Boudica's life is shrouded in mystery. She was born around AD 25 to a royal family in Celtic Britain, and as a young woman she married Prasutagus, who later became king (a term adopted by the Celts, but as practiced by them, more of an elected chief) of the Iceni tribe. They had two daughters, probably born during the few years immediately after the Roman conquest in AD 43. She may have been Iceni herself, a cousin of Prasutagus, and she may have had druidic training. Even the color of her hair is mysterious. Another Roman historian, Cassius Dio—who wrote long after she died—described it with a word translators have rendered as fair, tawny, and even flaming red, though Dio probably intended his audience to picture it as golden-blonde with perhaps a reddish tinge. Her name meant "victory."

Boudica's people once welcomed the Romans. Nearly 100 years earlier, when Gaius Julius Caesar made the first Roman foray into Britannia in 55 and 54 BC, the Iceni were among six tribes that offered him their allegiance. But this greatest of all Roman generals was unable to cope with either the power of the coastal tides or the guerrilla tactics of the other Britons who fought him. After negotiating a pro forma surrender and payment of tribute, Caesar departed.

For the next 97 years, no Roman military force set foot on British soil. The Iceni watched as their southern neighbors, the Catuvellauni, grew rich from exporting grain, cattle and hides, iron and precious metals, slaves and hunting dogs to Rome. From Rome, they imported luxury goods such as wine and olive oil, fine Italian pottery, and silver and bronze drinking cups, and they minted huge numbers of gold coins at their capital, Camulodunum.

A century of Roman emperors came and went. Then, in 41 Claudius (Tiberius Claudius Nero Germanicus) rose to the imperial purple. There were many practical reasons why he might have thought it useful to add Britannia to the empire, one being that the island was an important source of grain and other supplies needed in quantity by the Roman army. Stories abounded about the mineral wealth there. Outbreaks of unrest in Gaul were stirred up—so the Romans believed—by druid agitators from Britannia.

The most compelling reason for Claudius, however, was political. Born with a limp and a stutter, he had once been regarded as a fool and kept out of public view—although those handicaps were largely responsible for his survival amid the intrigue and murder that befell many members of his noble family. Now the emperor desperately needed a prestige boost of the sort that, in Rome, could be provided only by an important military victory. So when the chief of a minor British tribe turned up in Rome, complaining that he had been deposed and asking the emperor to restore his rule, Claudius must have thought it the perfect excuse to launch an invasion.

Boudica's husband, Prasutagus, was probably established as a client-king of the Iceni by Britannia's Roman governor, Ostorius Scapula. After Prasutagus' death, Rome's oppressive rule ultimately drove her to war.

Boudica would have been about 18 years old in 43, the year Claudius invaded, old enough to be aware of the events that would transform her life. She may already have been married to Prasutagus, but the king of the Iceni was still Antedios, probably an older relative of Prasutagus. Antedios seems to have taken a neutral position toward Rome. Other tribes openly supported the conquest, but most, including the Icenis' neighbor to the south, did not. Caradoc, king of the Catuvellauni (called Caractacus by the Romans), and his brother Togodumnus led an alliance of tribes to repel the invaders.

When the Roman troops landed at the far southeastern tip of Britannia, Caractacus and his allies harried them as they marched inland. Then the Britons retreated to gather into a single force on the other side of the River Medway. There, the Romans won a major battle in which Caractacus' brother was either killed or mortally wounded. At that point, Emperor Claudius himself came to Britannia to seal the conquest with a victory at Camulodunum—now known as Colchester—where he accepted the formal submission of 11 British rulers, including Antedios of the Iceni.

Boudica and the Iceni may well have expected the Romans to sail away as they had in the past. They soon learned otherwise. Claudius built a legionary fortress at Camulodunum, stationed troops there and established other fortresses throughout eastern Britannia. He appointed the invasion forces' commander, Aulus Plautius, as Britannia's first Roman governor. Caractacus retreated westward, recruited fresh troops and continued to fight a guerrilla war against the Romans.

The ham-fisted Ostorius Scapula replaced Plautius in 47. Caractacus timed a series of raids to coincide with the change of governors, so Ostorius arrived to news of fighting. Was it this unpleasant reception that made Ostorius so mistrustful of all the Britons, even those who had surrendered? Or was he short-tempered because he already suffered from the illness from which he would die five years later? For whatever reason Ostorius decided to disarm those subject tribes that he felt he could not fully trust, including the Iceni. Established Roman law forbade subject populations to keep weapons other than those used for hunting game, but that was contrary to Celtic law and custom. The Iceni rebelled, and Ostorius defeated them. Antedios may have been killed in the rebellion. If not, it seems likely that Ostorius removed him immediately afterward and installed Prasutagus as client-king in his place. Boudica was now queen of the Iceni.

Two years later, in 49, Ostorius confiscated land in and around Camulodunum to set up a *colonia*. This was a town for retired legionaries, in which each veteran was granted a homestead. The town gave the veterans a secure retirement and concentrated an experienced reserve force in the new province, on which Rome could call in case of emergency. In theory, it was supposed to provide a model of Roman civilization to which the natives might aspire. Unfortunately, the *colonia* at Camulodunum caused more problems than it solved. As it grew over the next decade, more and more Britons were driven off their land, some enslaved by the veterans, others executed and their heads exhibited on stakes.

The Iceni had once avoided trade with Rome, while the Catuvellauni grew rich from it. Now, the Iceni submitted, while the former king of the Catuvellauni fought Rome, and his people suffered the consequences. Ostorius finally defeated Caractacus in 51 and captured him in 52. That same year, Ostorius died. Rome replaced him with Didius Gallus, who provoked no internal rebellions, though the unconquered western tribes continued to fight.

Emperor Claudius was poisoned in 54, and Nero (Nero Claudius Drusus Germanicus) succeeded him. Perhaps to deflect the suspicion that he had been involved in his uncle's murder, Nero elevated Claudius to the status of a god and ordered a temple to him built at Camulodunum. Now the British chieftains would be obliged not only to worship once a year at the altar of the man who had invaded and occupied their lands, but also to finance the building of the extravagant and costly temple.

Rome further pressed British patience by calling for the repayment of money given or loaned to the tribes. It is possible that Antedios had received some of the money Claudius had handed out, and his successor, Prasutagus, was now expected to repay it. Prasutagus had probably also received an unwanted loan from Lucius Seneca, Roman philosopher and Nero's tutor, who had pressed on the tribal leaders a total of 40 million sesterces, evidently an investment he hoped would bring a healthy return in interest. Now, the procurator—Rome's financial officer, responsible for taxation and other monetary matters in Britannia—insisted the money from Claudius must be repaid. And Seneca, according to Dio,"resorted to severe measures in exacting" repayment of his loans. His agents, backed by force, may have showed up at the royal residence and demanded the money. Boudica would not have forgotten such an insult.

CAIUS SUETONIUS PAULLINUS, a man in the aggressive mold of Ostorius, became governor of Britain in 58. He began his term with a military campaign in Wales. By the spring of 61, he had reached its northwestern limit, the druid stronghold on the Isle of Mona. Tacitus described the forces Suetonius faced: "The enemy lined the shore in a dense armed mass. Among them were black-robed women with disheveled hair like Furies, brandishing torches. Close by stood Druids, raising their hands to heaven and screaming dreadful curses." For a moment, the Romans stood paralyzed by fright. Then, urged by Suetonius and each other "not to fear a horde of fanatical women," they attacked and enveloped the opposing forces "in the flames of their own torches."

When the battle ended in a Roman victory, Suetonius garrisoned the island and cut down its sacred groves—the fearsome site of human sacrifices, according to Tacitus, who claimed it was a Celtic religious practice "to drench their altars in the blood of prisoners and consult their gods by means of human entrails." In view of the routine, organized murder of the Roman gladiatorial games, one might wonder whether a Roman was in a position to criticize. Though the Celts did practice human sacrifice, most of their sacrifices consisted of symbolic deposits of such valuable objects as jewelry and weapons into sacred wells and lakes.

For Boudica and her people, news of the destruction of the druidic center on Mona, the razing of the sacred groves and the slaughter of druids must have been deeply painful. But Boudica suffered a more personal loss during this time. Prasutagus of the Iceni died sometime during the attack on Mona or its aftermath. He left behind a will whose provisions had no legal precedent under either Celtic or Roman law. It named the Roman emperor as co-heir with the two daughters of Prasutagus and Boudica, now in their teens. According to Celtic tradition, chiefs served by the consent of their people, and so could not designate their successors through their wills. And under Roman law, a client-king's death ended the client relationship, effectively making his property and estates the property of the emperor until and unless the emperor put a new client-king into office. Prasutagus' will may have been a desperate attempt to retain a degree of independence for his people and respect for his family. If it was, it did not succeed.

After Prasutagus died, the Roman procurator, Decianus Catus, arrived at the Iceni court with his staff and a military guard. He proceeded to take inventory of the estate. He regarded this as Roman property and probably planned to allocate a generous share for himself, following the habit of most Roman procurators. When Boudica objected, he had her flogged. Her daughters were raped.

At that point, Boudica decided the Romans had ruled in Britannia long enough. The building fury of other tribes, such as the Trinovantes to the south, made them eager recruits to her cause. Despite the Roman ban, they had secretly stockpiled weapons, and they now armed themselves and planned their assault. Dio wrote that before she attacked, Boudica "engaged in a type of divination by releasing a hare from the fold of her tunic." When it ran on the side the Britons believed auspicious, they cheered. "Boudica raised her hand to heaven and said, 'I thank you Andraste.'" This religious demonstration is the reason some historians think she may have had druidic training.

Boudica "mounted a tribunal made in the Roman fashion out of earth," according to Dio, who described her as "very tall and grim in appearance, with a piercing gaze and a harsh voice. She had a mass of very fair hair which she grew down to her hips, and wore a great gold torque and a multi-colored tunic folded round her, over which was a thick cloak fastened with a brooch." Boudica's tunic, cloak and brooch were typical Celtic dress for the time. The torque, the characteristic ornament of the Celtic warrior chieftain, was a metal band, usually of twisted strands of gold that fit closely about the neck, finished in decorative knobs worn at the front of the throat. Such torques may have symbolized a warrior's readiness to sacrifice his life for the good of his tribe. If so, it is significant that Boudica wore one—they were not normally worn by women.

Tacitus, whose father-in-law served as a military tribune in Britain during that time, recounted the rebellion in detail. Boudica moved first against Camulodunum. Before she attacked, rebels inside the *colonia* conspired to unnerve the superstitious Romans. "[F]or no visible reason," Tacitus wrote, "the statue of Victory at Camulodunum fell down—with its back turned as though it were fleeing the enemy. Delirious women chanted of destruction at hand. They cried that in the local senate-house outlandish yells had been heard; the theater had echoed with shrieks; at the mouth of the Thames a phantom settlement had been seen in ruins. A blood-red color in the sea, too, and shapes like human corpses left by the ebb tide, were interpreted hopefully by the Britons—and with terror by the settlers."

Camulodunum pleaded for military assistance from Catus Decianus in Londinium, but he sent only 200 inadequately armed men to reinforce the town's small garrison. In their overconfidence, the Romans had built no wall around Camulodunum. In fact, they had leveled the turf banks around the legionary fortress and built on the leveled areas. Misled by the rebel saboteurs, they did not bother to erect ramparts, dig trenches or even evacuate the women and elderly.

Boudica's army overran the town, and the Roman garrison retreated to the unfinished temple, which had been one of the prime causes of the rebellion. After two days of fighting, it fell. Recent archaeological work shows how thorough the Britons were in their destruction. The buildings in Camulodunum had been made from a framework of timber posts encased in clay and would not have caught fire easily. But they were burned and smashed from one end of town to the other. So hot were the flames, some of the clay walls were fired as though in a pottery kiln and are preserved in that form to the present day.

The only legionary force immediately available to put down the rebellion was a detachment of *Legio* IX Hispania, under the command of Quintus Petilius Cerialis Caesius Rufus, consisting of some 2,000 legionaries and 500 auxiliary cavalry. Cerialis did not wait to gather a larger force, but set out immediately for Camulodunum.

He never got there. Boudica ambushed and slaughtered his infantry. Cerialis escaped with his cavalry and took shelter in his camp at Lindum.

Suetonius, mopping up the operation on Mona, now learned of the revolt and set sail down the River Dee ahead of his army. He reached Londinium before Boudica, but what he found gave no cause for optimism. Like Camulodunum, Londinium was unwalled. About 15 years old, it had been built on undeveloped ground near the Thames River, by means of which supplies and personnel could be shipped to and from Rome. It was a sprawling town, with few large buildings that might be pressed into service as defensive positions—a smattering of government offices, warehouses and the homes of wealthy merchants. Catus Decianus had already fled to Gaul. Suetonius decided to sacrifice Londinium to save the province and ordered the town evacuated. Many of the women and elderly stayed, along with others who were "attached to the place."

BOUDICA KILLED EVERONE SHE found when she reached Londinium. Dio described the savagery of her army: "They hung up naked the noblest and most distinguished women and then cut off their breasts and sewed them to their mouths, in order to make the victims appear to be eating them; afterwards they impaled the women on sharp skewers run lengthwise through the entire body."

Verulamium, the old capital of the Catuvellauni tribe lying northwest of Londinium (outside of present-day St. Albans), met a similar fate. Rome had granted it the status of *municipium*, giving the townsfolk a degree of self-government and making its magistrates eligible for Roman citizenship. Boudica evidently punished the town for its close and willing association with Rome.

By then Suetonius had an army with him amounting to nearly 10,000 men, comprising *Legio* XIV and parts of *Legio* XX, which he had used for the attack on Mona, as well as some auxiliaries gathered from the nearest stations. He also sent an urgent summons to *Legio* II Augusta at Isca Dumnoniorum, present-day Exeter, but its commander, Poenius Posthumus, never responded. Evidently he was unwilling to march through the hostile territory of the Dumnonii, who had thrown their lot in with Boudica, and thereby risk sharing the fate of Cerialis' men. At the head of his hastily summoned force, Suetonius marched to confront Boudica.

Precisely where they met is not known, but the most plausible guesses—based on Tacitus' description of the favorable terrain where Suetonius positioned his force—include Mancetter in Warwickshire or along Old Roman Watling Street (now A5) near Towcaster. According to Tacitus: "[Suetonius] chose a position in a defile with a wood behind him. There could be no enemy, he knew, except at his front, where there was open country without cover for ambushes. Suetonius drew up his regular troops in close order, with the light-armed auxiliaries at their flanks, and the cavalry massed on the wings." Dio wrote that Boudica's troops numbered about 230,000

men. If we can believe this, Boudica's army would have been more than 20 times the size of Suetonius'. Whatever the actual numbers were, it is clear that her forces greatly outnumbered his. But the Britons' arms and training could not compare to the highly evolved arms and fighting techniques of the Roman legions.

"The forces of the Britons," wrote Tacitus, "pranced about far and wide in bands of infantry and cavalry, their numbers without precedent and so confident that they brought their wives with them and set them in carts drawn up around the far edge of the battlefield to witness their victory. Boudica rode in a chariot with her daughters before her, and as she approached each tribe, she declared that the Britons were accustomed to engage in warfare under the leadership of women."

The picture of Boudica riding about the battlefield to encourage her warriors rings true, but it is unlikely that any Roman understood what she said. She would have spoken in the Celtic tongue and had no need to inform her troops of their own customs. Tacitus puts those words in her mouth as a device to educate his Roman readers about a practice that must have struck them as exotic and strange.

The speech Tacitus reports Suetonius gave may be a closer reflection of what he said, appealing to his legions to "disregard the clamor and empty threats of the natives." He told them: "There were more women visible in their ranks than fighting men, and they, unwarlike and poorly armed, routed on so many occasions, would immediately give way when they recognized the steel and courage of those who had always conquered them. Even when many legions were involved, it was a few men who actually decided battles. It would redound to their honor that their small numbers won the glory of a whole army."

Legions and auxiliaries waited in the shelter of the narrow valley until Boudica's troops came within range. Then they hurled their javelins at the Britons and ran forward in wedge formation, supported by the cavalry with their lances. The Roman infantrymen protected themselves with their capacious shields and used their short swords to strike at close range, driving the points into the Britons' bellies, then stepping across the dead to reach the next rank.

The Britons, who fought with long swords designed for slashing rather than stabbing, needed room to swing their blades and could not fight effectively at such close range. Furthermore, the light chariots that gave them an advantage when fighting on a wide plain were similarly ineffective, with the Romans emerging from a narrow, protected valley that prevented the chariots from reaching their flanks.

The result was an overwhelming Roman victory. Those Britons who survived ran, but the circle of the women's wagons blocked their way, causing confusion and delay. The Romans "did not refrain from slaughtering even the womenfolk, while the baggage animals too, transfixed with weapons, added to the piles of bodies,"

Tacitus reported, citing figures of 80,000 British casualties and 400 Roman dead "and a slightly larger number wounded."

According to Tacitus, there were at least two notable casualties in the immediate wake of the battle. Upon learning of the victory, Poenius Posthumus felt so dishonored by the failure of his *Legio* II to have fought its way out to join Suetonius in full force that he committed suicide by falling upon his own sword. Boudica, Tacitus noted, "ended her life with poison."

The rebellion was effectively over, but its initial success had shocked Rome. The overall Roman casualties are suggested by the number of troops Nero sent from Germany as reinforcements, according to Tacitus a total of 7,000, consisting of "two thousand regular troops, which brought the ninth division to full strength, also eight auxiliary infantry battalions and a thousand cavalry." The civilian dead in Camulodunum, Londinium and Verulamium—some 70,000 if Tacitus' figure is accurate—would have multiplied the toll. British unrest seems to have continued even after the decisive battle. Dio wrote that the Britons were regrouping and preparing to fight again at the time Boudica died.

When the Roman reinforcements arrived, Suetonius stationed them in new winter quarters. Tacitus wrote that, rather than turning to diplomacy, Suetonius "ravaged with fire and sword" those he believed to be still "hostile or wavering." His punitive policy, calculated to crush the Britons rather than to reconcile them with Roman rule, was consistent with the policies that had caused the rebellion.

On top of that, a famine broke out. According to Tacitus, the Britons had expected to raid the Roman grain stores, and so had mustered all available men into the army and neglected to plant a crop. It is hard to believe an agricultural society, which both depended on grain for its own sustenance and produced it as a major export, would neglect to sow an entire year's crop. But if they had planted, much of the crop was likely destroyed in Suetonius' campaign of revenge.

To replace Catus Decianus, Rome sent a new procurator, Julius Classicianus. Tacitus heartily disapproved of Classicianus, sniping that he had a grudge against Suetonius and "allowed his personal animosity to stand in the way of the national interest." Classicianus was a Celt from the Roman province of Gaul, and he seems to have done much to calm the angry Britons. He told them "it would be well to await a new governor who would deal gently with those who surrendered." Then he reported to Rome "that they should expect no end to hostilities unless a replacement were found for Suetonius."

Nero dispatched one of his administrators, a freed slave named Polyclitus, to investigate the situation. Evidently, Polyclitus supported Classicianus' report. Soon afterward, when Suetonius lost some ships and their crews to a British raid, he was recalled. The new governor, Petronius Turpilianus, ended the punitive expeditions, following instead a policy of "not provoking the enemy nor being provoked by them." Tacitus sneered at his "slothful inactivity," but he brought peace to Britain.

Of Boudica, Dio wrote, "The Britons mourned her deeply and gave her a costly burial." The Roman conquest had brought to the Iceni misfortune that ripened into disaster after their rebellion failed. But as time passed, Britannia became an orderly and respected part of the Roman empire. It remained so for another three centuries. Boudica's people finally won what it seems they had wanted all along: respect, peace and a government that treated them with justice and honor.

Margaret Donsback is a Portland, Ore., writer whose work has appeared in Art Times *and* Civil War Times Illustrated. *For further reading, she suggests:* Boudica, *by Graham Webster;* and The Boudican Revolt Against Rome, *by Paul R. Sealey.*

The great Jewish revolt against Rome, 66-73 CE

Neil Faulkner sees the destruction of Jerusalem and fall of Masada in the 1st century as the result of a millenarian movement that sought to escape the injustices of an evil empire.

'THIS IS THE MASADA of the Palestinians', an anonymous Israeli general is supposed to have said at the height of the battle for the Jenin refugee camp on the West Bank in April 2002. New recruits to the Israeli Defence Force regularly swear an oath of allegiance at the ancient fortress of Masada, which fell to the Romans in 73 or 74 CE, and conservative Jews pray at the Wailing Wall in Jerusalem for the reconstruction of the Temple destroyed in 70 CE. The conflict in the Middle East today is fought amid the echoes of another war 2,000 years ago, in which an overwhelming military force destroyed a people's aspiration to national self-determination.

Palestine—by which I mean the southern Levant, today comprising Israel, the Occupied Territories and western Jordan—is one of the bloodiest places on earth. In antiquity, it lay on one of history's great routeways. Caravans laden with eastern exotica destined for the Mediterranean market passed through. Waves of nomadic refugees from the desert—including the ancient Hebrews around the twelfth century BCE—were periodically washed up in 'the Land of Canaan'. And two great centres of early civilisation repeatedly met and clashed here: the Egypt of the Pharaohs and successive Mesopotamian empires ruled by Assyrians, Babylonians, Persians and others. Consequently, periods of political independence and national unity for the peoples who inhabited the region in ancient times tended to be brief. Palestine was too much a prey to periodic bouts of imperial conquest ever to remain in local hands for long.

By the first century CE, Rome was the dominant power in the Levant. The nineteenth-century view of Rome as a fount of civilisation and culture is still held in many quarters. Even though historians of latter-day monstrosities—like Hitler's Germany or Stalin's Russia—are not persuaded of their subjects' virtue by architectural monuments, Rome's roads, aqueducts and hypocausts are sometimes allowed to turn an equally monstrous system of exploitation and violence—the Roman Empire—into a model of human achievement and an object of admiration. But 'The Grandeur That Was Rome'—the towns, villas and monumental architecture, the mosaics, frescoes and sculpture, the leisured aristocratic class that enjoyed these things—was made possible only by creaming off agricultural surpluses from thousands of villages across the empire. A Jewish peasant in Palestine in the first century—after the region had been incorporated into the Roman Empire as the province of Judaea in 6 CE—would have experienced the world of Rome not as 'civilisation' but as so many parasites—the tax-gatherer, the landlord, the priest, the debt-collector, the soldier—coming to steal the fruits of his hard labour on a tiny hillside plot.

By the middle of the first century of the Common Era, society in Palestine was deeply divided. On one side stood the ordinary people, most of them Jews, living in the countryside; on the other the Romans, Greeks and the Jewish upper classes. The Romans were few in number but their authority was upheld by the power of the Imperial army. There were just a hundred or so army officers and civil servants on the staff of the procurator of Judaea and perhaps two or three thousand Roman soldiers, but there were more than ten times that number in nearby Syria, a few days' march to the north. Rome, in any case, had many friends among the population of Palestine. There were the Greeks, who occupied numerous cities on the coast and in Transjordan, forming a series of privileged urban enclaves surrounded by the mainly Jewish countryside. These cities were ruled by oligarchs who enjoyed the backing of the Roman authorities. The general population of artisans, petty traders and small farmers had a colonial mentality, jealously guarding the privileges of Greek citizenship, and capable of occasional outbursts of murderous antisemitism. The Jewish upper classes were also predominantly pro-Roman. Some were of royal blood, descendants of the old Hasmonaean kings (164-37 BCE), or of Herod the Great, the puppet king of Judea (37-4 BCE); and the latter's great-grandson, King Herod Agrippa II (50-93 CE) still ruled a string of territories on the borders of the Roman province. Others were members of the Jerusalem-based aristocracy of priests, who controlled both the Temple, supreme focus of Jewish devotion, and the Sanhedrin, a grand council which combined the roles of senate, high court and holy inquisition. The Romans looked to the high priests and the Sanhedrin for help in governing Judaea; and the Jewish elite, who were essentially big landowners living off rents, tithes and the interest on peasant debt, looked to the Romans for the protection of property and rank.

The other Palestine was the world of farms, villages and the eternal routines of life on the land. Usually we know next to nothing of such worlds. How much can we say, for example, about the peasants of eastern Britain in 61 CE, at the time of the Boudiccan Revolt? Palestine is a special case because we have several sources for the life of the people and we can therefore attempt a 'history from below' which puts the Jewish Revolt of 66-73 CE into context.

Our principal sources for the period are the works of Josephus (b. c. 37 CE), a Jewish priest and aristocrat who, as governor of Galilee, became one of the moderate leaders of the revolt in late 66. Defeated and captured some six months later by the Roman general Flavius Vespasian,

Josephus was spared execution and eventually freed, becoming an interpreter and go-between in the service of his country's enemies. After the war he was well received in Rome, where his conqueror, now the emperor Vespasian, rewarded him richly for his treachery with citizenship, a grant of property and the continuing patronage of the Flavian family. Taking the name Flavius Josephus in honour of his patron, Josephus became, in effect, a court historian and propagandist for the new Flavian dynasty.

His first work, *The Jewish War*, provides a narrative outline of the political background to 66 CE and a detailed military history of the war itself. Further detail is provided in the much longer *Jewish Antiquities*, a complete history of the Jews from Adam up to the outbreak of the revolt, and *My Life*, a tendentious autobiographical essay, which deals with aspects of the author's controversial governorship of Galilee in 67. In these works Josephus describes a society in turmoil. His pages are filled with descriptions of rural bandits, sectarian radicals, urban terrorists and would-be messiahs; of riots, pogroms and communal violence; and of clashes between troops and demonstrators. He charts the mounting popular resistance, which, by the early 60s CE, had led to a breakdown in government authority.

Josephus, however, was an aristocrat and a traitor, a man blinded by class prejudice and with a new political allegiance by the time he came to write about the Jewish revolutionary movement. To him the popular leaders were simply deceivers, brigands and tyrants, their followers the victims of self-serving malice and moral depravity. He offers little sociological insight into what was, in fact, one of the most powerful anti-imperialist movements in antiquity.

Fortunately, there are other sources, and in these we seem to hear the authentic voice of revolution some 2,000 years ago. The Dead Sea Scrolls are one such source. Some 400 separate documents—

complete or in fragments—have survived, mainly in the form of leather scrolls which were wrapped in linen bindings, stuffed into ceramic jars and hidden in caves around the Essene monastery at Qumran near the Dead Sea, probably to keep them safe from the Romans. They reveal the Essenes to have been a radical Jewish sect committed to the revolutionary overthrow of the Romans and their upper-class Jewish allies. The Essene vision of liberation revolved around the ancient biblical idea of the Apocalypse, imagined to be a cataclysmic period of disaster and conflict at 'the End of Days', and culminating in the intervention of heavenly armies to reinforce 'the Sons of Righteousness' in their struggle against 'the Sons of Darkness' and 'the Hordes of Belial'. The anticipated outcome was victory for God's holy forces, a cleansing of the world of its corruption, and the beginning of 'the Rule of the Saints' and 'the Kingdom of Heaven on Earth'.

Political movements with similar objectives are known from later historical periods. In his study of medieval Europe *The Pursuit of the Millennium* (1957), Norman Cohn defined a millenarian group as one which viewed salvation as something collective not personal, earthbound not heavenly, imminent not distant in time, all-embracing not limited in scope, and involving supernatural intervention not just human action. Christopher Hill showed in *The World Turned Upside Down* (1972) that similar ideas (derived from the New Testament Apocalypse of St. John) guided the actions of some of the most radical participants in the English Revolution; and more recently, millenarianism of one form or another has sometimes been a feature of resistance to European imperialism by traditional societies. It is in the context of both the Dead Sea Scrolls and a rich body of comparative historiography, therefore, that we must interpret the turbulent society described so unsympathetically by Josephus.

Jewish tradition held that a 'messiah', or prophet-king for the end of time, would herald the coming Apocalypse and give leadership to God's people in the final battles. Josephus reported several would-be messiahs in the course of the first century, each associated with an abortive millenarian flare-up, usually involving a procession through the Wilderness, a fevered searching for signs, and an eventual bloody clash with the forces of authority. Millenarian movements require a charismatic leader to bind together disparate, unconnected people, and, by convincing them of the imminence of the Apocalypse, turn them into a revolutionary force. But the result is something highly unstable: the movement must either go forward in line with expectation, or it collapses in disappointment. So, for example, when his movement reached critical mass, Jesus—one of the several putative messiahs of his day—went to Jerusalem as prophecy required that he should, and his followers began their apocalyptic purge of the wicked, provoking the inevitable—and in this case effective—state repression.

The revolutionary message of sectarian radicals and messiahs was addressed, above all, to the poor. Josephus was explicit about the class basis of the conflict: it was, for him, a struggle between *dunatoi*—men of rank and power, the property-owning upper classes—and *stasiastai*—subversives, revolutionaries, popular leaders whose appeal was to 'the scum of the districts'. The Dead Sea Scrolls were equally explicit, though from the other side of the barricades: whereas 'the princes of Judah ... wallowed in the ways of whoredom and wicked wealth' and 'acted arrogantly for the sake of riches and gain', the Lord would in due time deliver them 'into the hands of the poor', so as to 'humble the mighty of the peoples by the hand of those bent to the dust', and bring them 'the reward of the wicked'. Jesus, too, for whom the poor were 'the salt of the earth', had little patience with the rich:

Beware of the scribes, who like to walk around in long robes; and to be greeted with respect in the market places, and to have the best seats in the synagogues and places of honour at banquets.

Many men had already taken the message to heart and were in revolt by the early 60s CE. Bandits were operating in much of the countryside—'social bandits' in the sense defined by Eric Hobsbawm: men whom poverty and oppression had driven to live outside the law, but who retained links with their villages, preyed only on the better-off, and were regarded by the peasants as champions of the poor. Others had become revolutionary activists—Zealots—and some of these, the *sicarii* or daggermen, were organised in underground cells to carry out selective assassinations of leading public figures. But those in the active resistance—whether millenarian radicals, social bandits or urban terrorists—were a minority, and they could not hope to defeat the Roman occupation forces without a full-scale peasant revolt. In the villages, though, they found a ready audience.

Peasant plots were commonly half or a third the size needed to support a family, and were burdened with rent, debt, tax and tithe. Many peasants must have handed over half or more of their harvest. Those who took it were from the city, rich absentee lords, people who built mansions and monuments there, who aped the manners of pagans, fawned on foreign masters, and scorned God, the Law and the Prophets. Or so it must have seemed in the villages, where men would gather in the synagogue on the Sabbath to hear itinerant preachers and debate the meaning of scripture. There was a dark mood here in the early 60s CE. Scripture, after all, gave no sanction to great estates which made a few men rich and left many with nothing. On the contrary, the peasant found enshrined in scripture ancient tribal practice designed to keep things equal. Had not the land originally been a gift of God to the Israelites—not Greeks or Romans—to

be distributed in small plots for the subsistence of all? Were not debts to be cancelled and bondsmen set free every seventh year? Was not every fiftieth year intended as a Year of Jubilee, when land would be redistributed and freed of burdens? Jesus had certainly thought so. He once said, quoting from *Isaiah*:

The Spirit of the Lord is upon me, because he has anointed me to bring good news to the poor. He has sent me to proclaim release to the captives and recovery of sight to the blind, to let the oppressed go free, to proclaim the year of the Lord's favour.

The popular movement of 66 CE amounted to a fusion of Apocalypse and Jubilee, the radical minority's vision of a revolutionary war to destroy corruption having become inextricably linked with the peasant majority's traditional aspiration for land redistribution and the removal of burdens. This was the potent mixture which exploded in an urban insurrection in Jerusalem in May 66.

The catalyst was the Roman procurator's demand for 100,000 *denarii* from the Temple treasury, probably to make up a shortfall in revenues caused by a tax strike. To enforce this demand, troops were sent into Jerusalem to disperse demonstrators, resulting in a massacre. The whole city then erupted in a fierce street battle and drove the Romans out. Jewish conservatives spent the summer attempting to restore order, first by persuasion and political manoeuvre, subsequently in an armed counter-revolution spearheaded by King Herod Agrippa's troops. With their failure, the stage was set for a full-scale invasion by the Roman army from Syria.

The revolt might have got no further. Cestius Gallus marched his army of 30,000 men all the way from Antioch to the borders of Judaea, and then inland to Jerusalem, leaving the land behind him laid waste by fire and the sword. But the Jews had mainly kept away, retreating into the hills, allowing the enemy to pass by, and watching in anger as their farms were burned. Now they came back in their thousands, closing in on the Roman communications between Jerusalem and the coast, lightly equipped irregulars armed with slings and javelins, preparing to fight not in the Roman way, in the head-on collision of pitched battle, but in the Eastern way, in the manner of skirmishers and guerrillas. Gallus found that the peasants of Judaea had risen *en masse* to his rear, and he had no choice but to call off his attack on Jerusalem and beat a retreat to the coast. Thus was the scene set for the battle of Beth-Horon.

From November 4th to 8th, 66, as the Roman column trudged back through the hills north-west of Jerusalem, it was engulfed in a hail of shot from the slopes above. Every time the Romans counter-attacked, the Jewish light infantry scurried away to safety, easily out-distancing their enemies on such broken ground. And every time, as the Romans fell back on the column, the Jews returned to resume the barrage of javelins and slingshot. Gallus eventually got his army away in the night, but he left behind 6,000 dead and all of his artillery and baggage. It was the greatest Jewish victory for 200 years, and it sounded through the villages of Palestine like a clarion call to holy war. This, surely, was God's work, the beginning of the long-awaited End of Days, the inaugural event of the Rule of the Saints.

Beth-Horon transformed an urban insurrection into a national revolution. A provisional government of high-priestly aristocrats was set up in Jerusalem; military governors were appointed to different parts of the country; coins were issued with the inscriptions 'Shekel of Israel', 'Holy Jerusalem' and 'Year One' (of the liberation, that is); and there were attempts to raise an army to defend the territory of the new Jewish proto-state. But the real strength of the revolutionary movement lay elsewhere, in the plethora of independent armed militias which now

sprang up across the country. Some were established groups of bandits or terrorists, which now swelled into large guerrilla units. Others were newly formed, perhaps on the initiative of local radicals, a charismatic leader, or a would-be messiah. They varied greatly in size and readiness for war, their membership tended to fluctuate over time, and they formed unstable and shifting alliances with other groups. The government was keen either to incorporate the militias into the regular army or, where they proved unruly, to suppress them. The militias—despite the offer of government pay—generally remained aloof, reluctant to surrender their independence, and the relationship between the two parties quickly soured. The roots of this conflict were deep, and it would culminate in the revolutionary overthrow of the aristocratic regime and its replacement by a government of militia leaders in the winter of 67-68.

This revolution within a revolution has been much misunderstood, thanks largely to the almost complete absence of sociological insight in Josephus' account. The aristocratic regime had been looking in two directions. It wanted to win a strong bargaining position on the battlefield and then to negotiate peace with the Romans, perhaps involving the re-establishment of a Jewish-ruled puppet kingdom of the kind that had existed before 6 CE and briefly again in 41-44 (when the Emperor Claudius had experimented with Herodian restoration). In this way, order and the security of property could be quickly restored. For the government was also embroiled in a conflict with the militias, many of whose members were actively working for the Apocalypse and the Jubilee. Yet it was precisely the radical enthusiasm of the militias —men who believed that they were engaged in a holy war to build heaven on earth—that gave the revolution its strength. The peasant-soldiers were fighting not for kings and high priests, but for God, the overthrow of the corrupt, and for the

right to land. To crush these hopes would be to kill the spirit of revolt. At root, the struggle between aristocratic *dunatoi* and popular *stasiastai*—which Josephus describes—was a struggle between those who would halt the revolution to defend property and those who favoured a 'Jacobin' policy of 'public safety', one prepared to sacrifice the interests of the rich to advance the common cause.

The fate of the aristocratic government was sealed by its defeats in 67, above all in Galilee, when Vespasian's massive army of invasion, perhaps 60,000 strong, captured a string of Jewish strongholds, including the lynchpin fortress of Jotapata, which had held out for a month under the leadership of Josephus himself. Many of the defeated were killed or enslaved, and many more slunk away; but some thousands headed for Jerusalem, determined both to settle accounts with treacherous leaders and to continue the fight in defence of the holy city. The Roman siege of Jerusalem was delayed for another two years after the radical seizure of power, however, since Rome was at war with itself over the Imperial succession in 68-69. The victor was Vespasian, so when the Romans finally came for Jerusalem, they were led by his son Titus, to whom fell the task of defeating 25,000 veteran fighters defending some of the strongest fortifications in the world.

The attackers built ramps, employed battering rams to knock down walls, and mounted massed armoured assaults through the breaches. The defenders hurled missiles from the battlements, sallied forth to burn ramps and engines, and rushed to fill the breaches and throw back the enemy's assaults. The struggle descended into an abyss of horror: men fought each other with bitter savagery; hundreds of prisoners were crucified on the hills around the city; the bodies of famine victims were tossed over the walls to rot in the sun; and as the Romans broke into the city there was mayhem and massacre. The siege was a collision of two worlds: on one side, the military imperialism of Rome guarding the power and property of the rich; on the other, the rage of land-starved peasants from whom the wealth to build 'civilisation' was stolen. There was no middle way, no possibility of compromise, and the collision of these worlds was fought with primal ferocity. The siege culminated in a three-month struggle for control of the Temple Mount, ending when, in mid-August 70, as fighting raged on the great concourse all around it, the Temple itself caught fire. In the confusion, Roman troops burst through the gates, and once inside the complex they cut down everyone they caught and looted the vast treasures stored there. Even then, resistance continued for another month in the Upper City, the remaining militiamen opting to fight on rather than surrender themselves and face a life of slavery.

The liquidation of the 'Jewish Commune' was followed by a relentless campaign to exterminate the Zealot bacillus in the province. The network of cisterns and sewers beneath Jerusalem were combed for fugitives. Some who escaped were eventually run down and destroyed as far away as Egypt and Libya. Several years of counter-insurgency drives destroyed the remaining guerrilla bases in the deserts of southern Palestine, culminating in the siege and capture of Masada in 73. Perched on a rock surrounded by cliffs in the depths of the desert, a community of 960 men, women and children had maintained their 'alternative lifestyle' for six or seven years, while the young warriors formed a guerrilla band that continued to fight for national and social liberation after all others had been defeated. Finally, though, the Romans came for them, 15,000 strong, building an impenetrable siege wall to cage the Zealots in, and then a huge siege ramp from which to bring their engines and assault troops into action. Once the walls were breached, neither victory nor flight was possible for the defenders. But when the Romans stormed the fortress, they faced no resistance and were confronted by an eerie emptiness. In a final, chilling act of revolutionary defiance, the Zealots had cheated their conquerors of the fruits of victory by destroying their possessions and committing mass suicide.

So Masada has become some sort of symbol. For some, a symbol of Israel, a nationalist icon in the predatory wars of the present; but for others—and the anonymous Israeli general at Jenin had a sense of this—it is a symbol of the oppressed fighting back, whether they be Jewish, or Arab, or anyone else, against the evils of a world dominated by greed and war.

FOR FURTHER READING

Josephus, *The Jewish War* (trans. G.A. Williamson, Penguin, 1959); G. Vermes, *The Complete Dead Sea Scrolls in English* (Penguin, 1998); J. Campbell, *Deciphering the Dead Sea Scrolls* (Fontana, 1996); H. Maccoby, *Revolution in Judaea: Jesus and the Jewish Resistance* (Ocean, 1973); I. Wilson, *Jesus: the evidence* (Pan, 1985); M. Grant, *The Jews in the Roman World* (Phoenix, 1999); P. Richardson, *Herod, King of the Jews and Friend of the Romans* (T & T Clark, 1999); Y. Yadin, *Masada, Herod's Fortress and the Zealots' Last Stand* (Weidenfeld & Nicolson, 1966).

UNIT 3

The Judeo-Christian Heritage

Unit Selections

Key Points to Consider

- What are some of the differing views about Israel?

- Describe the relationship that existed among Jews, Christians, and pagans during the Roman era.

- How do the Jews, Buddhists, Hindus, and Muslims view Jesus as opposed to the Christian interpretation?

- What happened to the pagan religions when Christianity arose?

- How is the Devil presented in several of the religions discussed?

 **Links: www.dushkin.com/online/**
These sites are annotated in the World Wide Web pages.

Institute for Christian Leadership/ICLnet
http://www.iclnet.org
Introduction to Judaism
http://philo.ucdavis.edu/zope/home/bruce/RST23/rst23homepage.html
Selected Women's Studies Resources/Columbia University
http://www.columbia.edu/cu/libraries/subjects/womenstudies/

Western civilization developed out of the Greco-Roman world, but it is also indebted to the Judeo-Christian traditions. If Western civilization derives humanism and materialism, philosophy, politics, art, literature, and science from the former, it derives its God and forms of worship from the latter. It is difficult to separate these traditions, for Judeo-Christian heritage comes to us through a Hellenistic filter.

On one hand, the history of the Jews seems similar to other small kingdoms of the Near East, closely situated as they were to such powerful empires as the Babylonians, Assyrians, and Persians. Yet of all the ancient peoples, only the Jews had a lasting influence. What appears to differentiate the Jews from all the rest, writes historian Crane Brinton, is: "The will to persist, to be themselves, to be a people." The reappearance of Israel in the modern world, some 2,000 years after the Romans destroyed the Jewish client-state is remarkable.

The legacy of the Jews is a great one. It includes a rich literary tradition found in their sacred texts. They have also bequeathed to Western civilization their unique view of history; a linear and miraculous God, who intervenes in history to guide, reward, or punish his Chosen People. The Jewish religion also gave birth to the morality within the Ten Commandments, the moral wisdom of the prophets and a messianic expectation, which inspired Christianity and other religions. Their monotheism and their god, Yahweh, formed the model for the Christian and Muslim ideas of God. On this latter idea see the article "The Legacy of Abraham."

A brief comparison of Yahweh and the Greek god Zeus illustrates the originality of the Jewish conception. Both gods began as warrior deities of tribal cultures. But Zeus was chiefly concerned with Olympian affairs rather than human ones. Yehweh, on the other hand, was more purposeful and had few interests except for his people. And unlike Zeus, who was not the creator of the universe, Yahweh had created and ordered the universe, with humans to rule over nature.

Certainly Christianity bears the stamp of Judaism. Jesus himself was a Jew. To his early followers, all of them Jews, he satisfied the prophetic messianic messages inherent in Judaism. The New Testament recounts the growth and spread of Christianity for an obscure Jewish sect in Palestine to a new religion with great appeal in the Roman world. Yet Jesus remains shrouded in mystery, for there is a lack of firsthand evidence. The Gospels, the greatest and most familiar sources, contain wide gaps in their accounts of his life. Nonetheless, they remain a profound record of early Christian faith. See the essays "The Other Jesus" which describes the way Jesus is seen by other religions and "Mary Magdalene: Saint or Sinner?" on the misrepresentation of the Magdalene.

As it separated from Judaism, Christianity took on a new dimension, including the promise of private salvation through participation in the sacraments. From the beginning, its theology reflected the teachings of St. Paul, who changed the focus from converting the Jews to spreading the faith among the Gentiles. Then, as it took hold in the Near East, Christianity absorbed some Hellenistic elements, Stoicism, Platonism, and the Roman pantheon. This prepared the way for a fusion of classical philosophy and Christianity. The personal God of the Jews and Christians became the abstract god of the Greek philosophers. Biblical texts were given symbolic meanings that might have confounded an earlier, simpler generation of Christians. The Christian view of sexuality, for instance, became fraught with multiple meanings and complexities. In effect, Christianity was no longer a Jewish sect; it had become Westernized. It would become a principal agent for Westernization of much of the world.

The last essay in this section deals with the Devil. "Who the Devil is the Devil?" by Robert Wernick recounts the origins and influence of the Devil from the ancient religions until the modern day.

The Legacy of Abraham

He is beloved by Jews, Christians and Muslims. Can this bond stop them from hating one another?

By DAVID VAN BIEMA

MY FIRST REAL EXPERIENCE OF the patriarch Abraham's crossover appeal came on the splendid sun-spangled day in June when I took a crosstown cab to arrange my son's circumcision. Jews have circumcised for thousands of years—ever since God (as the Torah tells it), having made a history-altering pact with Abraham, directed him to "cut my Covenant in your flesh." Some biblical commentators suggest that the circumcision was meant as much as a reminder to the Lord as to the Israelites, a kind of divine Post-it not to extirpate these people. My thought as we rolled eastward across Manhattan was, There must be easier ways.

We slowed behind traffic on one of the roads through Central Park, and I found myself tapping my foot. The tune on the cab's stereo was Arabic but with a catchy, bubbling horn section. I asked who was playing. A Moroccan group, said the cabbie. He told me its name. Did I want to know what it was singing? Certainly. It was a plea to Israel from the Arab people. The chorus was, "We have the same father. Why do you treat us this way?" Who might the father be? I asked. "Ibrahim," he said. "The

song is called *Ismail and Isaac,*" after his sons.

We have the same father. Why do you treat us this way? What did that scrap of a song hint at? First of all, it gave witness that a figure beloved by Jews and Christians has a Muslim constituency, suggesting a connection between Islam and the West that might surprise most Americans in this tense season. But second, it acknowledged that despite this apparent bond, there is still turmoil among the sons of Abraham.

It wouldn't do to call Abraham a neglected giant of the Bible; almost everyone knows the outline of his story. But until recently he probably has not received the credit he deserves as a religious innovator. As biblical pioneer of the idea that there is only one God, he is on a par with Moses, St. Paul and Muhammad, responsible for what Thomas Cahill, author of the 1998 history *The Gifts of the Jews,* calls "a complete departure from everything that has gone before in the evolution of culture and sensibility." In other words, Abraham changed the world.

Even less well known to most Americans is the breadth of his fol-

lowing. Jews, who consider him their own, are largely unaware of Abraham's presence in Christianity, which accepts his Torah story as part of the Old Testament and honors him in contexts ranging from the Roman Catholic Mass ("Look with favor on these offerings and accept them as once you accepted ... the sacrifice of Abraham") to a Protestant children's song ("Father Abraham had many sons/And I am one of them and so are you ... ").

And neither Jews nor Christians know very much about Abraham's role in Islam, which acknowledges the Torah narrative but with significant changes and additions. The Koran portrays Abraham as the first man to make full surrender to Allah. Each of the five repetitions of daily prayer ends with a reference to him. The holy book recounts Abraham's building of the Ka'aba, the black cube that is Mecca's central shrine. Several of the rituals performed in that city by pilgrims making the hajj recall episodes from his history. Those who cannot journey still join in celebrating the Festival of Sacrifice, in which a lamb or goat is offered up to commemorate the same near sacrifice of a son that the Jews feature at their

New Year. It is the holiest single day on the Islamic calendar.

In fact, excluding God, Abraham is the only biblical figure who enjoys the unanimous acclaim of all three faiths, the only one (as the song in the cab suggested) referred to by all three as Father. In theory, this remarkable consensus should make him an interfaith superstar, a special resource in these times of anger and mistrust. And since last September, interfaith activists have been scheduling Abraham lectures, Abraham speeches and even "Abraham salons" around the country and overseas. A new book called *Abraham: A Journey to the Heart of Three Faiths* (William Morrow) by Bruce Feiler, author of the best-selling scriptural travelogue *Walking the Bible*, espouses their cause.

Yet they have an uphill battle. For all the commonality Abraham represents, the answer to the song's plaintive query—*Why do you treat us this way?*—is written in anathemas and blood over the centuries. If Abraham is indeed father of three faiths, then he is like a father who left a bitterly disputed will.

Judaism and Islam, for starters, cannot even agree on which son he almost sacrificed. Then there is Abraham's Covenant with God. Many Jews (and some conservative Christians) believe it granted the Jewish people alone the right to the Holy Land. That belief fuels much of the Israeli settler movement and plays an ever greater role in Israel's hostility toward Palestinian nationalist claims. "Our connection to the land goes back to our first ancestor. Arabs have no right to the land of Israel," says Rabbi Haim Druckman, a settler leader and a parliamentarian with the National Religious Party. This argument infuriates Palestinian Muslims—especially since the Koran claims that Abraham was not a Jew but Islam's first believer. "The people who supported Abraham believed in one God and only one God, and that was the Muslims. Only the Muslims," says Sheik Taysir Tamimi, Yasser Arafat's liaison for religious dialogue.

Not exempt from the tripartite rancor, early Christians used their understanding of Abraham, who they claimed found grace outside Jewish law, to prove that the older religion begged for replacement—a contention that helped propel almost two millenniums of anti-Semitism.

Abraham is thus a much more difficult—and more interesting—figure than at first he seems. His history constitutes a kind of multifaith scandal, a case study for monotheism's darker side, the desire of people to define themselves by excluding or demonizing others. The fate of interfaith stalwarts seeking to undo that heritage and locate in the patriarch a true symbol of accord should be meaningful to all of us suddenly interested in the apparent chasm between Islam and the West. Says *Abraham* author Feiler: "I believe he's a flawed vessel for reconciliation, but he's the best figure we've got."

Feiler began *Abraham* after the Sept. 11 attacks, seeking a unifying symbol in a time of strife. Instead, the book records his growth from a dewy-eyed Abrahamic novice to a more realistic observer. As he remarks, "When I set out on this journey, I believed…the Great Abrahamic Hope was an oasis in the deepest deserts of antiquity, and all we had to do was track him down and his descendants would live in perpetual harmony, dancing Kumbaya around the campfire. That oasis, I realized, is just a mirage." The sober understanding Feiler ends up with, however, is a more realistic basis from which to seek reconciliation.

ABRAHAM THE JEW

Abraham was born, according to tradition, into a family that sold idols— a way of emphasizing the polytheism that reigned in the Middle East before his enlightenment. The stirring first words of the 12th chapter in the Torah's *Book of Genesis* are God's to him and are often referred to as the Call: "Go forth from your native land/And from your father's house/And I will make of you a great nation/And I will bless those who bless you/And curse him that curses

you/And all the families of the earth shall bless themselves by you." Abraham would appear ill suited to the job. To make a nation, one must have an heir, and he is a childless 75-year-old whose wife Sarah is past menopause. Yet he complies, and he and Sarah set off for a desert hinterland—Canaan—and a new spiritual epoch.

As they travel, God elaborates on his offer. Abraham's children will be as numerous as grains of dust on the earth and stars in the sky. They will spend 400 years as slaves but ultimately possess the land from the Nile to the Euphrates. The pact is sealed in a mysterious ceremony in a dream, during which the Lord, appearing as a smoking torch, puts himself formally under oath. He requires a different acknowledgment from Abraham: he must inscribe a sign of the Covenant on his body, initiating the Jewish and Muslim customs of circumcision. He is now committed, God notes later, to "keep the way of the Lord to do righteousness and justice."

Abraham's life becomes very eventful. He travels to Egypt and back and alights in Canaanite towns that may correspond to present-day Nablus, Hebron and Jerusalem. He grows rich, distinguishing himself sometimes as a warrior king and sometimes as an arch-diplomat. At one point, three strangers appear at his tent. A model of Middle Eastern hospitality, he lays out a feast. They turn out to be divine messengers bearing word that God intends to destroy Sodom, where his nephew Lot lives. Abraham initiates an extraordinary haggling session, persuading the Lord to spare Sodom if 10 righteous people can be found. They can't.

Meanwhile, the Torah portrays Abraham's domestic life as a soap opera. Convinced she will have no children, Sarah offers him her young Egyptian slave Hagar to produce an heir. It works. The 86-year-old fathers a boy, Ishmael. Yet God insists that Sarah will conceive, and in a wonder confirming Abraham's faith, she bears his second son, Isaac. Jealous of Hagar's and Ishmael's competing claims on her husband and his legacy, Sarah persuades Abraham to send them out into the desert. God saves the duo and promises Hagar that Ishmael will sire a great nation through 12 sons (assumed by tradition to be 12 Arab tribes). But he stipulates that the Covenant will flow only through Isaac's line.

Then, in one last spectacular test of his faith, God directs Abraham to offer up "your son, your only one, whom you love, your Isaac" as a human sacrifice. With an obedience that has troubled modern thinkers from Kierkegaard ("Though Abraham arouses my admiration, he at the same time appalls me") to Bob Dylan ("Abe says, 'Where do you want this killin' done?' God says, 'Out on Highway 61'")—but which seems transcendentally right to traditionalists—the father commences to comply on a mountain called Moriah. Only at the last instant does God stay the father's hand and renew his pledge regarding Abraham's descendants.

At age 175, Abraham dies and is laid out next to Sarah, who preceded him, in a plot he has bought in a town later called Hebron. Both sons attend his funeral.

That is the story. What is its importance? Despite every effort and argument, there is no way to know what century Abraham lived in, or even whether he actually existed as a person. (If he did live, it would have been between 2100 B.C. and 1500 B.C., hundreds of years before the date most historians assign to the actual birth of the religion called Judaism.) But Abraham represents a revolution in thought. While he is not a pure monotheist (he never suggests that other gods do not exist), he is the Ur-monotheist, the first man in the Bible to abandon all he knows in order to choose the Lord and consciously move ever deeper into that choice, until the point of no return on Moriah.

The implications of his breakthrough are almost infinite. To have "one God that counts" instead of a constellation of gods who require occasional ritual appeasement, as Cahill notes in *The Gifts of the Jews*, means that Abraham's relationship

to God "became the matrix of his life," as it would be for millions who followed. A universal God made it easier to imagine a universal code of ethics. Positing a deity intimately involved in the fate of one's children overturned the prevalent image of time as an ever cycling wheel, effectively inventing the idea of a future. Says Eugene Fisher, director of Catholic-Jewish relations for the U.S. Conference of Catholic Bishops: "Whether you call it submission in Muslim terms, conversion in Christian terms or *t'shuva* [turning toward God] for the Jews, monotheism is a radically new understanding, the underlying concept of Western civilization." So linked is Abraham's name with this new path that each of the subsequent two monotheistic religions reached back hungrily to enfold him—and belittle the others' claims on him.

ABRAHAM THE CHRISTIAN

THE CHURCH OF THE HOLY SEPULCHER in Jerusalem is arguably the most Christian place on earth, and the gray rock mass of Golgotha (or Calvary) inside, the most Christian place in the church. Traditions dating back to the 300s A.D. record that Jesus was crucified here. Just above the rock's Plexiglas-protected expanse is a chapel shared by the Greek Orthodox and Roman Catholic churches. The Catholic side boasts three mosaics. In the center is Mary Magdalene; to the left is Christ, removed from the Cross; and to the right is none other than ... Abraham, about to slay Isaac. Notes Feiler: "The image of Jesus sprawled on the unction stone is nearly identical to the image of Isaac on the altar." The New Testament book *Romans* proposes Isaac's binding and release as a prophetic foreshadowing of the Resurrection.

The man credited with that insight is the Apostle Paul. Jesus mentions Abraham in the Gospels, but it was Paul who did the fine mortise work, citing the patriarch in his New Testament epistles more than any other figure except Christ. Perhaps the most strongly self-identifying

Jew among the Apostles, Paul clearly felt an urgency to connect his new movement with the Jewish paterfamilias. He did so primarily through Abraham's original response to God's Call and through the old man's embattled faith, or "hope against hope," as Paul famously put it, that God would bring him a son. Such faith, Paul wrote, made Abraham "the father of all who believe."

Yet Paul's Abrahamic bouquet to his birth religion contained poisoned thorns. One of his themes was that a believer no longer needed to be Jewish or to follow Jewish law to be redeemed—the way now lay through Christ. Abraham's story served these arguments well. His Covenant long predated the Jewish law as brought down from the mountain by Moses, and so, wrote Paul, "the promise to Abraham and his descendants ... did not come through law."

Nor, Paul argued, did it come through tribal inheritance. The God of the Hebrew Bible deemed Abraham to be "righteous" years before his circumcision, he wrote, which meant that his listeners didn't need to become circumcised Jews to be Abraham's inheritors. Baptism in faith would more than suffice. Paul waffled as to whether Christianity rendered Judaism's Abrahamic Covenant null and void. But his successors assumed so. The 2nd century church father Justin Martyr wrote that far from an indication of grace, circumcision marked Jews "so that your land might become desolate, and your cities burned," something of a self-fulfilling prophecy. Bereft of a divine warrant for their well-being, Jews were at the mercy of their neighbors' worst instincts. In a remarkably frank assessment, the Greek Orthodox bishop of Jerusalem tells Feiler, "What the church did with Abraham was bitter and cruel."

ABRAHAM THE MUSLIM

NO FAITH IS AS SELF-CONSCIOUSLY monotheistic as Islam, and its embrace of Abraham is correspondingly joyful. If many Jews know him best as a dynastic grandfather whose grandson Jacob actually found the nation of Israel, Muslims regard him as one of the four most important prophets. So pure is his submission to the One God that Muhammad later says his own message is but a restoration of Abrahamic faith. The Koran includes scenes from Abraham's childhood in which he chides his father for believing in idols and survives, Daniel-like, in a fiery furnace to which he is condemned for his fealty to Allah. And in the Koranic version of Abraham's ultimate test, Abraham tells his son of God's command, and the boy replies, "O my father! Do that which thou art commanded. Allah willing, thou shalt find me of the steadfast." Notes the Koran approvingly: "They had both surrendered," using the verb whose noun form is the word Islam. For passing such trials, Allah tells Abraham, "Lo, I have appointed thee a leader for mankind!"

But not as a Jew. Somewhat like Paul, Islam concluded that God chooses his people on grounds of commitment rather than lineage, meaning that Abraham's only true followers are true believers—i.e., Muslims. Moreover, if Allah ever had a pact with the Jews as a race, they backslid out of it in episodes such as the worship of the golden calf in the Torah's book of *Exodus*. Indeed, the Koran advises Muslims proselytized by either Jews or Christians to answer, "Nay … (we follow) the religion of Abraham."

Then there is the matter of Isaac and Ishmael. Unlike the Torah, the Koran does not specify which son God tells Abraham to sacrifice. Muslim interpreters a generation after Muhammad concluded that the prophet was descended from the slave woman Hagar's boy, Ishmael. Later scholarly opinion determined that Ishmael was also the son who went under the knife. The decision effectively completed the Jewish disenfranchisement. Not only was their genealogical claim void, but their forefather lost his role in the great drama of surrender.

THE CONTESTED PATRIMONY

THINGS DEVOLVED FROM THERE. JEWS, stung, took steps to cement Abraham's

Jewish identity. The Talmud describes him anachronistically as following Mosaic law and speaking Hebrew. And they severely downgraded Ishmael. Initially, says Shaul Magid, professor of Midrash at New York City's Jewish Theological Seminary, Jewish parents named their boys after Abraham's Arab son, but the custom evaporated as they began living under Muslim rule. By the 11th century the great biblical scholar Rashi, citing earlier authorities, described Ishmael as a "thief" whom "everybody hates," an insult that can still be found in his prominently placed commentary in many Torah editions today and that is taught in many Orthodox religious schools. Ibn Kathir, a 13th century Koranic commentator, struck back by claiming the Jews had "dishonestly and slanderously" introduced Isaac into the Torah story: "They forced this understanding because Isaac is their father, while Ishmael is the father of the Arabs." That sentiment too survives today on the Muslim side.

It is enough to make a grown man cry, which Feiler nearly does. "They took a biblical figure open to all," he writes, "tossed out what they wanted to ignore, ginned up what they wanted to stress and ended up with a symbol of their own uniqueness that looked far more like a mirror image of their fantasies than a reflection of the original story." To his horror, he realized that Abraham "is as much a model for fanaticism as he is for moderation."

The Tomb of the Patriarchs, a massive stone structure built by King Herod 2,000 years ago, is the grim living metaphor for dueling Abrahamisms. Despite God's promise that this land would be his people's one day, Abraham in *Genesis* makes a point of paying Ephron the Hittite 400 silver shekels for a cave in Hebron to serve as a burial plot. He and Sarah were laid there, and later, Scripture adds, so were Isaac and his wife Rebecca, his grandson Jacob and his first wife Leah. Herod erected a grandiose monument at what he thought was the site. For most of the past few hundred years, its Muslim owners, who called it the Mosque of Abraham, allowed Jews to pray near the en-

trance. When the Israelis took control in 1967, believers of both faiths worshipped side by side. Then in 1994 a radical Israeli settler, Dr. Baruch Goldstein, mowed down 29 Muslims at prayer in the tomb. Custody shifted to a complex scheme granting each side access to parts or all of the tomb on different days but avoiding their meeting. Since the latest *intifadeh*, the arrangement continues, but the site, hedged about with checkpoints and razor wire in a neighborhood under strict military curfew, presents a message of piety inextricable from violence and mistrust.

There is an eerie effortlessness to the way in which fights picked by scriptural revisionists hundreds of years ago feed today's psychology of mutual victimhood. The Jewish Theological Seminary's Magid describes a 1st century tradition in which Ishmael is a bully and Isaac "becomes the persecuted younger brother." That belief has persisted. "The Muslims are very aggressive, like Ishmael," an Israeli settler tells Feiler. "And the Jews are very passive, like Isaac, who nearly allows himself to be killed without talking back. That's why they are killing us, because we don't fight back." Arafat's religious liaison Sheik Tamimi snaps that any Jewish claims based in Genesis are "pure lies, aimed at achieving political gains, at imposing the sovereignty of Israeli occupation on the holy places."

HOPES FOR RECONCILIATION

IT IS A STAPLE PREMISE OF THE INTERfaith movement, which has been picking at the problem since the late 1800s, that if Muslims, Christians and Jews are ever to respect and understand one another, a key road leads through Abraham. Says Fisher of the Conference of Catholic Bishops: "We can't not talk to each other about him." But identifying a path does not make it passable. Part of the problem, says Jon Levenson, a Harvard Jewish-studies professor who has examined affinities and conflicts in the Abrahamic traditions, is that even before they went to work on him, his story featured a theme of exclusivity. "If you want a symbol for universal humanity, go to Adam," he says. "Don't go to Abraham, because his whole story is about the singling out of one guy to found a new family, a distinct family marked off from the rest of humanity. He was always a particularist." Another stumbling block between Jews and Muslims is that they are working from two different texts.

Nonetheless, moderate Islamic leaders have periodically enlisted Abraham as a bridge builder. In 1977 Egypt's President Anwar Sadat, announcing before the Israeli Knesset the brave initiative that would become the 1979 Camp David peace accords, invoked, "Abraham—peace be upon him—great-grandfather of the Arabs and the Jews." Sadat noted that Abraham had undertaken his great sacrifice" not out of weakness but through free will, prompted by an unshakable belief in the ideals that lend life a profound significance," clearly hoping that both sides would approach Arab-Israeli cohabitation in the same spirit. The accords went through, although this time a sacrifice was completed. Sadat was assassinated in 1981.

More recently, seeking a way to reach out to the U.S. that would pass the scrutiny of his nation's dogmatic clerics, moderate Iranian President Muhammad Khatami proposed a "dialogue of civilizations," with Abraham as common ground, in 1998. (The U.N.'s Kofi Annan subsequently adopted the gesture.) Observers assumed Khatami was crafting a smoke screen for political talks. But the former professor of Eastern and Western philosophy seems to regard Abraham as a mascot for his comparatively humanistic, open-minded brand of Islam.

A more thoroughgoing theological initiative has been undertaken by the Catholic Church. Christianity's position on Abraham had remained depressingly consistent since Justin Martyr's condemnation of the circumcised, but theologians at the Second Vatican Council of 1962-65, shaken by the Holocaust, reread

Paul's letters. They noted that at one point Paul calls the Covenant between God and the Jews irrevocable and that in one passage he compares Christians to a wild olive branch grafted onto the tree of Judaism. "If the Covenant between God and the children of Abraham dies," says Fisher, "the branch withers with the roots. Christians would be orphans." The resulting Vatican II document rolled back centuries of anti-Judaism and began a rehabilitation of the notion of Abraham as a Jew. No one has pursued its spirit more avidly than Pope John Paul II, who in March 2000 pressed a prayer card between blocks of Jerusalem's Western Wall: "God of our fathers, you chose Abraham and his descendants to bring your name to the nations ... we wish to commit ourselves to genuine brotherhood with the people of the Covenant."

THE EFFECT OF SEPT. 11

SUCH RAPPROCHEMENT, ESPECIALLY involving Muslims, has been trickier in the past 12 months. Interfaith advocates say that after the attacks, many plans for Jewish-Muslim conversations fell through. One group that bucked the trend was the Children of Abraham Institute, a Charlottesville, Va., association that organizes intensive three-way scriptural studies modeled on Abraham's hospitality to the strangers at his tent. It has held meetings in Denver and at England's Cambridge University and has sent representatives to lecture in Cape Town, South Africa, and parley with imams in Malaysia. It has the ear of the incoming Archbishop of Canterbury. At one of its gatherings last October, University of Virginia professor of Islamic studies Abdulaziz Sachedina expressed an interfaith ideal when he contended that people of faith can "control" their respective interpretations of Abraham's story "so that

it doesn't become a source of demonization of the other."

As the anniversary of Sept. 11 passed, several new enterprises inaugurated similar efforts. In Portland, Ore., a group called the Abraham Initiative began a two-year, citywide interfaith program. The venerable, Protestant-founded Chautauqua Institution in upstate New York is starting an open-ended Abraham Program involving lectures and trifaith panels. A participant in several such efforts is Feiler. At the end of *Abraham*, its author announces that understanding how each faith, and seemingly each generation, concocts its own Abraham has liberated him to create his own, whom he whimsically calls "Abraham No. 241." This Abraham, he says, "is perceptive enough to know that his children will fight, murder [and] fly planes into buildings." But he also knows that "his children still crave God, still dream of a moment when they stand alongside one another and pray for their lost father and for the legacy of peace among nations that was his initial mandate from heaven."

It is a historical oddity and a hopeful sign that as the three religions battled over Abraham, they continued (without admitting it) to swap Abraham stories. The borrowings and counterborrowings, as old as the conflicts, make far more pleasant reading. The most heartening may be an Islamic tale cited by Feiler whose roots, scholar Reuven Firestone hypothesized, reach into both Judaism and Christianity. It is set after Abraham's near sacrifice of his son, whichever son it was. The moment of truth is just past; the father's hand is stayed. As the boy lies stunned on the altar, God gazes down with pride and compassion and promises to grant his any prayer. "O Lord, I pray this," the boy says. "When any person in any era meets you at the gates of heaven—so long as they believe in one God—I ask that you allow them to enter paradise."

The Other Jesus

To Christians, he is the Son of God. But the world's other great
religions have their own visions of a legendary figure.

By Kenneth L. Woodward

*Christ is absolutely original and absolutely unique. If
He were only a wise man like Socrates, if He were a
prophet like Muhammad, if He were enlightened like
the Buddha, without doubt He would not be what He is.*
— *John Paul II*

Ever since his election, John Paul II has wanted one thing:
to walk where Jesus walked, preach where Jesus taught and pray
where Jesus was crucified, died and was buried. This week the
pope finally gets his chance. Weary in body but ecstatic in spirit,
John Paul makes his long-anticipated pilgrimage to the Holy
Land. For him it is a personal "journey with God"; there will be
no intruding television cameras when, lost in prayer, he com-
munes alone at Christianity's holiest shrines. But the land of his
heart's desire is holy to Jews and Muslims as well. And so the
pope will visit the Western Wall, Judaism's most sacred site, and
the Mosque of El Aqsa atop the Temple Mount. He will also meet
with Muslim and Jewish religious leaders and—in one particularly resonant moment—pause to pray at Yad Vashem, Israel's memorial to victims of the Holocaust.

Like his powerful plea for forgiveness a fortnight ago, the
pope's trip is also an exercise in religious reconciliation. More
than 90 times since he took office, John Paul has acknowledged
past faults of the church and begged pardon from others—Muslims and Jews, as well as Protestant and Orthodox Christians—
for sins committed in the name of Catholicism. Like the sound
of one hand clapping, however, his efforts have brought few
echoing responses. Now, at the high point of this jubilee year
for the church, he comes to Jerusalem, the city of peace, hoping
to erect bridges among the three monotheistic faiths.

There are, of course, important commonalities among these
three religious traditions. All three believe in one God who has
revealed his will through sacred Scriptures. They all look to an
endtimes when God's justice and power will triumph. And they
all recognize the figure of Abraham as a father in faith. What is
often overlooked, however, is another figure common to the
three traditions: Jesus of Nazareth.

The Christ of the Gospels is certainly the best-known Jesus
in the world. For Christians, he is utterly unique—the only Son
of God and, as the pope puts it, the one "mediator between God
and humanity." But alongside this Jesus is another, the Jesus
whom Muslims since Muhammad have regarded as a prophet
and messenger of Allah. And after centuries of silence about
Jesus, many Jews now find him a Jewish teacher and reformer
they can accept on their own terms as "one of us."

Jesus has become a familiar, even beloved, figure to adherents of Asian religions as well. Among many contemporary
Hindus, Jesus has come to be revered as a self-realized saint
who reached the highest level of "God-consciousness." In recent years, Buddhists like the Dalai Lama have recognized in
Jesus a figure of great compassion much like the Buddha. "I
think as the world grows smaller, Jesus as a figure will grow
larger," says Protestant theologian John Cobb, a veteran of interfaith dialogues.

Perhaps. Each of these traditions—Judaism, Islam, Buddhism and Hinduism—is rich in its own right, and each has its
own integrity. As the pope calls for better understanding among
the world's great religions, it is important to recognize that non-
Christian faiths have their own visions of the sacred and their
own views of Jesus.

JUDAISM

That Jesus was a Jew would seem to be self-evident from
Gospels. But before the first Christian century was out, faith in
Jesus as universal Lord and Savior eclipsed his early identity as
a Jewish prophet and wonder worker. For long stretches of
Western history, Jesus was pictured as a Greek, a Roman, a
Dutchman—even, in the Germany of the 1930s, as a blond and
burly Aryan made in the image of Nazi anti-Semitism. But
for most of Jewish history as well, Jesus was also a deracinated
figure: he was *the* apostate, whose name a pious Jew should
never utter.

Indeed, the lack of extra-Biblical evidence for the existence of Jesus has led more than one critic to conclude that he is a Christian fiction created by the early church. There were in fact a half dozen brief passages, later excised from Talmudic texts, that some scholars consider indirect references to Jesus. One alludes to a heresy trial of someone named Yeshu (Jesus) but none of them has any independent value for historians of Jesus. The only significant early text of real historical value is a short passage from Flavius Josephus, the first-century Jewish historian. Josephus describes Jesus as a "wise man," a "doer of startling deeds" and a "teacher" who was crucified and attracted a posthumous following called Christians. In short, argues Biblical scholar John P. Meier of Notre Dame, the historical Jesus was "a marginal Jew in a marginal province of the Roman Empire"—and thus unworthy of serious notice by contemporary Roman chroniclers.

Christian persecution of the Jews made dialogue about Jesus impossible in the Middle Ages. Jews were not inclined to contemplate the cross on the Crusaders' shields, nor did they enjoy the forced theological disputations Christians staged for Jewish conversions. To them, the Christian statues and pictures of Jesus represented the idol worship forbidden by the Torah. Some Jews did compile their own versions of a "History of Jesus" ("Toledoth Yeshu") as a parody of the Gospel story. In it, Jesus is depicted as a seduced Mary's bastard child who later gains magical powers and works sorcery. Eventually, he is hanged, his body hidden for three days and then discovered. It was subversive literature culled from the excised Talmudic texts. "Jews were impotent in force of arms," observes Rabbi Michael Meyer, a professor at Hebrew Union Seminary in Cincinnati, "so they reacted with words."

HIS ROOTS: Christian and Jewish scholars accept that much of what Jesus taught can be found in Jewish Scriptures, but Jews still see Christ as an 'admirable Jew,' not the Son of God

When skeptical scholars began to search for the "historical Jesus" behind the Gospel accounts in the 18th century, few Jewish intellectuals felt secure enough to join the quest. One who did was Abraham Geiger, a German rabbi and early exponent of the Reform Jewish movement. He saw that liberal Protestant intellectuals were anxious to get beyond the supernatural Christ of Christian dogma and find the enlightened teacher of morality hidden behind the Gospel texts. From his own research, Geiger concluded that what Jesus believed and taught was actually the Judaism of liberal Pharisees, an important first-century Jewish sect. "Geiger argued that Jesus was a reformist Pharisee whose teachings had been corrupted by his followers and mixed with pagan elements to produce the dogmas of Christianity," says Susannah Heschel, professor of Jewish studies at Dartmouth. Thus, far from being a unique religious genius—as

the liberal Protestants claimed—Geiger's Jesus was a democratizer of his own inherited tradition. It was, he argued, the Pharisees' opponents, the Sadducees, who became the first Christians and produced the negative picture of the Pharisees as legalistic hypocrites found in the later Gospel texts. In sum, Geiger—and after him, other Jewish scholars—distinguished between the faith *of* Jesus, which they saw as liberal Judaism, and the faith *in* Jesus, which became Christianity.

The implications of this "Jewish Jesus" were obvious, and quickly put to polemical use. Jews who might be attracted by the figure of Jesus needn't convert to Christianity. Rather, they could find his real teachings faithfully recovered in the burgeoning Reform Jewish movement. Christians, on the other hand, could no longer claim that Jesus was a unique religious figure who inspired a new and universal religion. Indeed, if any religion could claim universality, it was monotheistic Judaism as the progenitor of both Christianity and Islam.

A MAN OF LOVE: Buddhists depersonalize the Jesus who walked this earth and transform him into a figure more like Buddha. Some regard him as a bodhisattva, a perfectly enlightened being who vows to help others

The Holocaust occasioned yet another way of imagining Jesus. If some Jews blamed Christians—or God himself—for allowing the ovens of Auschwitz, a few Jewish artists found a different way to deal with the horror of genocide: they applied the theme of the crucified Christ to the Nazis' Jewish victims. This is particularly evident in harrowing paintings of Marc Chagall, where the dying Jesus is marked by Jewish symbols. And in "Night," his haunting stories of the death camps, Elie Wiesel adopted the Crucifixion motif for his wrenching scene of three Jews hanged from a tree, like Jesus and the two thieves on Golgotha. The central figure is an innocent boy dangling in protracted agony because his body is too light to allow the noose its swift reprieve. When Wiesel hears a fellow inmate cry, "Where is God?" the author says to himself; "Here He is. He has been hanged here, on these gallows." "There's no lack of suffering in Judaism," says Alan Segal, professor of Jewish Studies at Barnard College and Columbia University, "and no reason why Jews shouldn't pick up an image central to Christianity."

Today, the Jewishness of Jesus is no longer a question among scholars. That much of what he taught can be found in the Jewish Scriptures is widely accepted by Christian as well as Jewish students of the Bible. At some seminaries, like Hebrew Union, a course in the New Testament is now required of rabbinical candidates. Outside scholarly circles, there is less focus on Jesus, and most Jews will never read the Christian Bible. And, of course, Jews do not accept the Christ of faith. "They see

SOURCES: CENTRAL BUREAU OF STATISTICS, ISRAEL;
NEWS REPORTS. RESEARCH BY FE CONWAY;
GRAPHIC BY KEVIN HAND/NEWSWEEK.

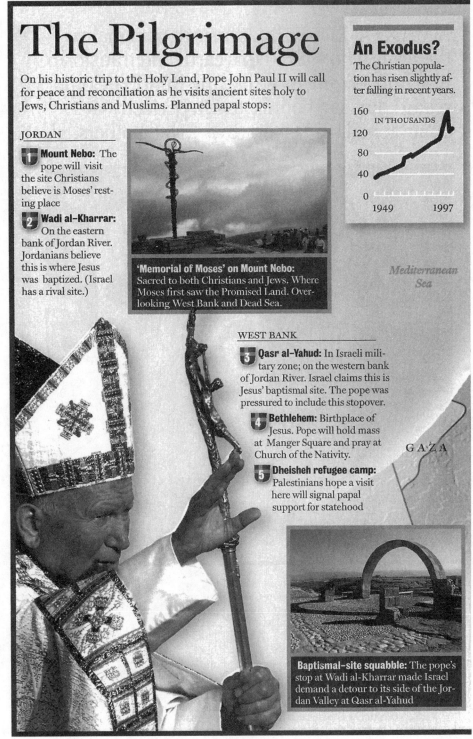

The Pilgrimage

On his historic trip to the Holy Land, Pope John Paul II will call for peace and reconciliation as he visits ancient sites holy to Jews, Christians and Muslims. Planned papal stops:

JORDAN

1 Mount Nebo: The pope will visit the site Christians believe is Moses' resting place

2 Wadi al-Kharrar: On the eastern bank of Jordan River. Jordanians believe this is where Jesus was baptized. (Israel has a rival site.)

'Memorial of Moses' on Mount Nebo: Sacred to both Christians and Jews. Where Moses first saw the Promised Land. Overlooking West Bank and Dead Sea.

An Exodus?

The Christian population has risen slightly after falling in recent years.

IN THOUSANDS

160
120
80
40
0

1949   1997

Mediterranean Sea

WEST BANK

3 Qasr al-Yahud: In Israeli military zone; on the western bank of Jordan River. Israel claims this is Jesus' baptismal site. The pope was pressured to include this stopover.

4 Bethlehem: Birthplace of Jesus. Pope will hold mass at Manger Square and pray at Church of the Nativity.

5 Dheisheh refugee camp: Palestinians hope a visit here will signal papal support for statehood

GAZA

Baptismal-site squabble: The pope's stop at Wadi al-Kharrar made Israel demand a detour to its side of the Jordan Valley at Qasr al-Yahud

Jesus as an admirable Jew," says theologian John Cobb, "but they don't believe that any Jew could be God."

ISLAM

AT THE ONSET OF RAMADAN LAST year, Vatican officials sent greetings to the world's Muslims, inviting them to reflect on Jesus as "a model and permanent message for humanity." But for Muslims, the Prophet Muhammad is the perfect model for humankind and in the Qur'an (in Arabic only), they believe, the very Word of God dwells among us. Even so, Muslims recognize Jesus as a great prophet and revere him as Isa ibn Maryam—Jesus, the son of Mary, the only woman mentioned by name in the Qur'an. At a time when many Christians deny Jesus' birth to a virgin, Muslims find the story in the Qur'an and affirm that it is true. "It's a very strange situation, where Mus-

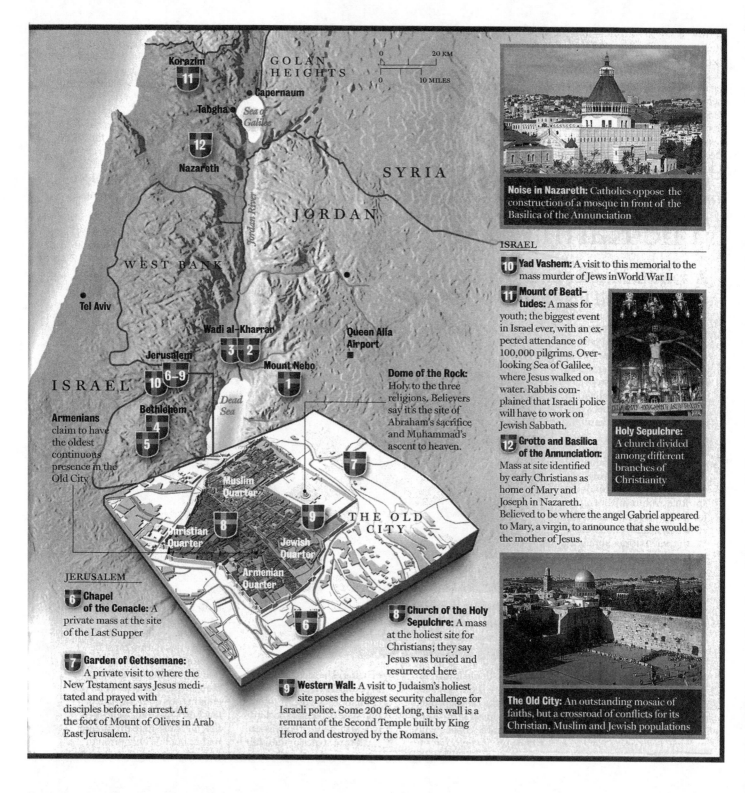

Noise in Nazareth: Catholics oppose the construction of a mosque in front of the Basilica of the Annunciation

ISRAEL

10 Yad Vashem: A visit to this memorial to the mass murder of Jews in World War II

11 Mount of Beatitudes: A mass for youth; the biggest event in Israel ever, with an expected attendance of 100,000 pilgrims. Overlooking Sea of Galilee, where Jesus walked on water. Rabbis complained that Israeli police will have to work on Jewish Sabbath.

Holy Sepulchre: A church divided among different branches of Christianity

12 Grotto and Basilica of the Annunciation: Mass at site identified by early Christians as home of Mary and Joseph in Nazareth. Believed to be where the angel Gabriel appeared to Mary, a virgin, to announce that she would be the mother of Jesus.

Dome of the Rock: Holy to the three religions. Believers say it's the site of Abraham's sacrifice and Muhammad's ascent to heaven.

Armenians claim to have the oldest continuous presence in the Old City

THE OLD CITY

JERUSALEM

6 Chapel of the Cenacle: A private mass at the site of the Last Supper

7 Garden of Gethsemane: A private visit to where the New Testament says Jesus meditated and prayed with disciples before his arrest. At the foot of Mount of Olives in Arab East Jerusalem.

8 Church of the Holy Sepulchre: A mass at the holiest site for Christians; they say Jesus was buried and resurrected here

9 Western Wall: A visit to Judaism's holiest site poses the biggest security challenge for Israeli police. Some 200 feet long, this wall is a remnant of the Second Temple built by King Herod and destroyed by the Romans.

The Old City: An outstanding mosaic of faiths, but a crossroad of conflicts for its Christian, Muslim and Jewish populations

lims are defending the miraculous birth of Jesus against western deniers," says Seyyed Hossein Nasr, professor of Islamic studies at George Washington University. "Many Westerners also do not believe that Jesus ascended into heaven. Muslims do." Indeed, many Muslims see themselves as Christ's true followers.

What Muslims believe about Jesus comes from the Qur'an—not the New Testament, which they consider tainted by human error. They also draw upon their own oral traditions, called *ha-*

dith, and on experts' commentaries. In these sources, Jesus is born of Mary under a palm tree by a direct act of God. From the cradle, the infant Jesus announces that he is God's prophet, though not God's son, since Allah is "above having a son" according to the Qur'an.

Nonetheless, the Muslim Jesus enjoys unique spiritual prerogatives that other prophets, including Muhammad, lack. Only Jesus and his mother were born untouched by Satan. Even Mu-

A Rabbi Argues With Jesus

A noted Talmudic scholar insists that Jews must remain faithful to the words of the Torah.

BY JACOB NEUSNER

Imagine walking on a dusty road in Galilee nearly 2,000 years ago and meeting up with a small band of youngsters, led by a young man. The leader's presence catches your attention: he talks, the others listen, respond, argue, obey—care what he says, follow him. You don't know who the man is, but you know he makes a difference to the people with him and to nearly everyone he meets. People respond, some with anger, some with admiration, a few with genuine faith. But no one walks away uninterested in the man and the things he says and does.

I can see myself meeting this man, and, with courtesy, arguing with him. It is my form of respect, the only compliment I crave from others, the only serious tribute I pay to the people I take seriously. I can see myself not only meeting and arguing with Jesus, challenging him on the basis of our shared Torah, the Scriptures Christians would later adopt as the "Old Testament." I can also imagine myself saying, "Friend, you go your way, I'll go mine, I wish you well—without me. Yours is not the Torah of Moses, and all I have from God, and all I ever need from God, is that one Torah of Moses."

We would meet, we would argue, we would part friends—but we would part, He would have gone his way, to Jerusalem and the place he believed God had prepared for him; I would have gone my way, home to my wife and my children, my dog and my garden. He would have gone his way to glory, I my way to my duties and my responsibilities.

Why? Because the Torah teaches that the kingdom that matters is not in heaven, but the one we find ourselves in now: sustaining life, sanctifying life, in the here and the now of home and family, community and society. God's kingdom is in the humble details of what I eat for breakfast and how I love my neighbor.

Can the Kingdom of God come soon, in our day, to where we are? The Torah not only says yes, it shows how. Do I have then to wait for God's Kingdom? Of course I have to wait. But while waiting, there are things I have to do. Jesus demanded that to enter this Kingdom of Heaven I repudiate family and turn my back on home: "Sell all you have and follow me." That is not what the Torah says.

On Sinai Moses told how to organize a kingdom of priests and a holy people, conduct workday affairs, love God—how to build God's kingdom, accepting the yoke of God's commandments. As a faithful Jew, what I do is simply reaffirm the Torah of Sinai over and against the teachings of Jesus. Moses would expect no less of us. So when I say, if I heard those words, I would have offered an argument, my dispute would have been with a mortal man walking among us and talking with us. Only the Torah is the word of God.

I think Christianity, beginning with Jesus, took a wrong turn in abandoning the Torah. By the truth of the Torah, much that Jesus said is wrong. By the criterion of the Torah, Israel's religion in the time of Jesus was authentic and faithful, not requiring reform or renewal, demanding only faith and loyalty to God and the sanctification of life through carrying out God's will. Jesus and his disciples took one path, and we another. I do not believe God would want it any other way.

NEUSNER *has just been named research professor of religion and theology at Bard College. He is the author of "A Rabbi Talks With Jesus."*

hammad had to be purified by angels before receiving prophethood. Again, in the Qur'an Muhammad is not presented as a miracle worker, but Jesus miraculously heals the blind, cures lepers and "brings forth the dead by [Allah's] leave." In this way Jesus manifests himself as the Messiah, or "the anointed one." Muslims are not supposed to pray to anyone but Allah. But in popular devotions many ask Jesus or Mary or John the Baptist for favors. (According to one recent estimate, visions of Jesus or Mary have occurred some 70 times in Muslim countries since 1985.)

Although Muhammad supersedes Jesus as the last and greatest of the prophets, he still must die. But in the Qur'an, Jesus does not die, nor is he resurrected. Muslims believe that Jesus asked God to save him from crucifixion, as the Gospels record, and that God answered his prayer by taking him directly up to heaven. "God would not allow one of his prophets to be killed," says Martin Palmer, director of the International Con-

sultancy on Religion, Education and Culture in Manchester, England. "If Jesus had been crucified, it would have meant that God had failed his prophet."

A VIRTUOUS MAN: Many Hindus are drawn to Jesus because of his compassion and his devotion to nonviolence, but they find the notion of a single god unnecessarily restrictive.

When the end of the world approaches, Muslims believe that Jesus will descend to defeat the antichrist—and, incidentally, to set the record straight. His presence will prove the Crucifixion

The Karma of the Gospel

A spiritual leader finds connections between Christian teachings and his own traditions.

BY THE DALAI LAMA

As a buddhist, my attitude toward Jesus Christ is that he was either a fully enlightened being, or a bodhisattva of a very high spiritual realization. I see common notes between Buddhism and Christianity. Here are a few:

Transfiguration. In Buddhism, when an individual practitioner reaches a high degree of realization in his or her spiritual evolution, the transformation can manifest itself at the physical level, as well. We find such stories about the Buddha in the sutras. They begin when Buddha's disciples notice a physical change in his appearance. A radiance shines from his body. Then one of the disciples asks the Buddha, "I see these changes in you. Why are these changes taking place?" These parables are similar to the Gospel passages on the Transfiguration when Jesus' face is suddenly glowing.

Karma. In another Gospel passage, Jesus says: "I have not come to judge the world but to save it.... The word I have spoken will be his judge on the last day." I feel this closely reflects the Buddhist idea of karma. There is not an autonomous being (God) "out there" who arbitrates what you should experience and what you should know; instead, there is the truth contained in the casual principle itself. If you act in an ethical way, desirable consequences will result; if you act in a negative way, then you must face the consequences of that action as well.

Faith. In the Buddhist tradition, we speak of three different types of faith. The first is faith in the form of admiration that you have toward a particular person or a particular state of being. The second is aspiring faith. There is a sense of emulation: you aspire to attain that state of being. The third type is the faith of conviction.

All three types of faith can be explained in the Christian context as well. A practicing Christian can have a very strong devotion to and admiration for Jesus by reading the Gospel. That is the first level of faith, the faith of admiration and devotion. After that, as you strengthen your admiration and faith, it is possible to progress to the second level, which is the faith of aspiration. In the Buddhist tradition, you would aspire to Buddhahood. In the Christian context you may not use the same language, but you can say that you aspire to attain the full perfection of the divine nature, or union with God. Then, once you have developed that sense of aspiration, you can develop the third level of faith, a deep conviction that it is possible to perfect such a state of being.

Empathy. One of the grounds on which the presence of Buddha-nature in all people is argued is the human capacity for empathy. Some people may have a stronger force, others less; but all of us share this natural capacity to empathize. This Buddha-nature, this seed of enlightenment, of perfection, is inherent in all of us. To attain perfection, however, it is not enough that a spiritual practitioner merely possess such a nature; this nature must be developed to its fullest potential. In Buddhist practice, you require the assistance of an enlightened guide, a guru or teacher. Christians believe that all of us share this divine nature but it is only through Jesus that one perfects it. Through Jesus it comes into full bloom and becomes unified, one, with the Father.

THE DALAI LAMA *is the author of "The Good Heart"* (Wisdom Publications, Boston), *from which this is excerpted.*

was a myth and eventually he will die a natural death. "Jesus will return as a Muslim," says Nasr, "in the sense that he will unite all believers in total submission to the one God."

HINDUISM

THE GOSPELS ARE SILENT ABOUT the life of Jesus between his boyhood visit to the Jerusalem Temple with his parents, and the beginning of his public ministry at the age of 30. But in India there is a strong tradition that the teenage Jesus slipped away from his parents, journeyed across Southeast Asia learning yogic meditation and returned home to become a guru to the Jews. This legend reveals just how easily Hinduism absorbs any figure whom others worship as divine. To Hindus, India is the Holy Land, its sacred mountains and rivers enlivened by more

than 300,000 local deities. It is only natural, then, that Jesus would come to India to learn the secrets of unlocking his own inherent divinity.

As Gandhi was, many Hindus are drawn to the figure of Jesus by his compassion and nonviolence—virtues taught in their own sacred Scriptures. But also like Gandhi, Hindus find the notion of a single god unnecessarily restrictive. In their perspective, all human beings are sons of God with the innate ability to become divine themselves. Those Hindus who read the Gospels are drawn to the passage in John in which Jesus proclaims that "the Father and I are one." This confirms the basic Hindu belief that everyone is capable through rigorous spiritual practice of realizing his or her own universal "god-consciousness." The great modern Hindu saint Ramakrishna recorded that he meditated on a picture of the Madonna with child and was transported into a state of *samadhi*, a consciousness in which the divine is all that really exists. For that kind of spiritual experience, appeal to any god will do. "Christ-consciousness, God-consciousness, Krishna-consciousness, Buddha-consciousness—it's all the same thing," says Deepak Chopra, an Indian popularizer of Hindu philosophy for New Age Westerners. "Rather than 'love thy neighbor,' this consciousness says, 'You and I are the same beings.'"

BUDDHISM

THE LIFE STORIES OF JESUS AND THE Buddha are strikingly similar. Both are conceived without sexual intercourse and born to chaste women. Both leave home for the wilderness where each is tempted by a Satan figure. Both return enlightened, work miracles and challenge the religious establishment by their teachings. Both attract disciples and both are betrayed by one of them. Both preach compassion, unselfishness and altruism and each creates a movement that bears the founder's name. Thich Nhat Hanh, a Vietnamese Zen Buddhist monk with a large Western following, sees Jesus and Buddha as "brothers" who taught that the highest form of human understanding is "universal love." But there is at least one unbridgeable difference: a Christian can never become Christ, while the aim of every serious Buddhist is to achieve Buddhahood himself.

Thus when Buddhists encounter Christianity they depersonalize the Jesus who walked this earth and transform him into a figure more like Buddha. "Buddhists can think of Jesus Christ as an emanation or 'truth body' [*dharmakaya*] of the Buddha," says Buddhist scholar Robert Thurman of Columbia University. For Tibetan Buddhists, Jesus strongly resembles a bodhisattva—a perfectly enlightened being who vows to help others attain enlightenment. But to reconfigure Jesus as a Buddhist is to turn him into something he was not. Jesus, after all, believed in God, the creator and sustainer of the universe, which Buddhists do not. He believed in sin, which is not a Buddhist concept. Jesus did not teach compassion as a way of removing bad karma, nor did he see life as a cycle of death and rebirth. In short, says the Dalai Lama, trying to meld Jesus into Buddha "is like putting a yak's head on a sheep's body." It doesn't work.

Indeed, nothing shows the difference between the Jesus and the Buddha better than the way that each died. The Buddha's death was serene and controlled—a calm passing out of his final rebirth, like the extinction of a flame. Jesus, on the other hand, suffers an agonizing death on the cross, abandoned by God but obedient to his will.

A TRUE SAVIOR: The Christ of the Gospel is the best-known Jesus in the world. For Christians, he is unique— the only son of God.

Clearly, the cross is what separates the Christ of Christianity from every other Jesus. In Judaism there is no precedent for a Messiah who dies, much less as a criminal as Jesus did. In Islam, the story of Jesus' death is rejected as an affront to Allah himself. Hindus can accept only a Jesus who passes into peaceful samadhi, a yogi who escapes the degradation of death. The figure of the crucified Christ, says Buddhist Thich Nhat Hanh, "is a very painful image to me. It does not contain joy or peace, and this does not do justice to Jesus." There is, in short, no room in other religions for a Christ who experiences the full burden of mortal existence—and hence there is no reason to believe in him as the divine Son whom the Father resurrects from the dead.

Even so, there are lessons all believers can savor by observing Jesus in the mirrors of Jews and Muslims, Hindus and Buddhists. That the image of a benign Jesus has universal appeal should come as no surprise. That most of the world cannot accept the Jesus of the cross should not surprise, either. Thus the idea that Jesus can serve as a bridge uniting the world's religions is inviting but may be ultimately impossible. A mystery to Christians themselves, Jesus remains what he has always been, a sign of contradiction.

With ANNE UNDERWOOD *and* HEATHER WON TESORIERO

Mary Magdalene
Saint or Sinner?

A new wave of literature is cleaning up her reputation.
How a woman of substance was 'harlotized'

By DAVID VAN BIEMA

THE GORGEOUS FEMALE CRYPTOG-rapher and the hunky college professor are fleeing the scene of a ghastly murder they did not commit. In the midst of their escape, which will eventually utilize an armored car, a private jet, electronic surveillance devices and just enough unavoidable violence to keep things interesting, our heroes seek out the one man who holds the key not only to their exoneration but also to a mystery that could change the world. To help explain it to them, crippled, jovial, fabulously wealthy historian Sir Leigh Teabing points out a figure in a famous painting.

"'Who is she?' Sophie asked.

"'That, my dear,' Teabing replied, 'is Mary Magdalene.'

"Sophie turned. 'The prostitute?'

"Teabing drew a short breath, as if the word had injured him personally. 'Magdalene was no such thing. That unfortunate misconception is the legacy of a smear campaign launched by the early Church.'"

Summer page turners tend to sidestep the finer points of 6th century church history. Perhaps that is their loss. *The Da Vinci Code*, by Dan Brown, now in its 18th week on the New York Times hard-cover fiction best-seller list, is one of those hyper-caffeinated conspiracy specials with two-page chapters and people's hair described as "burgundy." But Brown, who by book's end has woven

Magdalene intricately and rather outrageously into his plot, has picked his MacGuffin cannily. Not only has he enlisted one of the few New Testament personages whom a reader might arguably imagine in a bathing suit (generations of Old Masters, after all, painted her topless). He has chosen a character whose actual identity is in play, both in theology and pop culture.

Three decades ago, the Roman Catholic Church quietly admitted what critics had been saying for centuries: Magdalene's standard image as a reformed prostitute is not supported by the text of the Bible. Freed of this lurid, limiting premise and employing varying ratios of scholarship and whimsy, academics and enthusiasts have posited various other Magdalenes: a rich and honored patron of Jesus, an Apostle in her own right, the mother of the Messiah's child and even his prophetic successor. The wealth of possibilities has inspired a wave of literature, both academic and popular, including Margaret George's 2002 best-selling historical novel *Mary, Called Magdalene*. And it has gained Magdalene a new following among Catholics who see in her a potent female role model and a possible argument against the all-male priesthood. The woman who three Gospels agree was the first witness to Christ's Resurrection is having

her own kind of rebirth. Says Ellen Turner, who played host to an alternative celebration for the saint on her traditional feast day on July 22: "Mary [Magdalene] got worked over by the church, but she is still there for us. If we can bring her story forward, we can get back to what Jesus was really about."

IN 1988, THE BOOK MARY Magdalene: *A Woman Who Showed Her Gratitude*, part of a children's biblical-women series and a fairly typical product of its time, explained that its subject "was not famous for the great things she did or said, but she goes down in history as a woman who truly loved Jesus with all her heart and was not embarrassed to show it despite criticism from others." That is certainly part of her traditional resume. Many Christian churches would add her importance as an example of the power of Christ's love to save even the most fallen humanity, and of repentance. (The word maudlin derives from her reputation as a tearful penitent.) Centuries of Catholic teaching also established her colloquial identity as the bad girl who became the hope of all bad girls, the saved siren active not only in the overheated imaginations of parochial-school students but also as the patron of institutions for wayward women such as the grim nun-run laundries featured in the new movie *The Magdalene Sisters*. In the culture at large, writer Kathy Shaidle has suggested, Magdalene is "the Jessica Rabbit of the Gospels, the gold-hearted town tramp belting out *I Don't Know How to Love Him*."

The only problem is that it turns out that she wasn't bad, just interpreted that way. Mary Magdalene (her name refers to Magdala, a city in Galilee) first appears in the *Gospel of Luke* as one of several apparently wealthy women Jesus cures of possession (seven demons are cast from her), who join him and the Apostles and "provided for them out of their means." Her name does not come up again until the Crucifixion, which she and other women witness from the foot of the Cross, the male disciples having fled. On Easter Sunday morning, she visits Jesus' sepulcher, either alone or with other women, and discovers it empty. She learns—in three Gospels from angels and in one from Jesus himself—that he is risen. John's recounting is the most dramatic. She is solo at the empty tomb. She alerts Peter and an unnamed disciple; only the latter seems to grasp the Resurrection, and they leave. Lingering, Magdalene encounters Jesus, who asks her not to cling to him, "but go to my brethren and say unto them, I ascend unto my Father … and my God." In Luke's and Mark's versions, this plays out as a bit of a farce: Magdalene and other women try to alert the men, but "these words seemed to them an idle tale, and they did not believe them." Eventually they came around.

Discrepancies notwithstanding, the net impression is of a woman of substance, brave and smart and devoted, who plays a crucial—perhaps irreplaceable—role in Christianity's defining moment. So where did all the juicy stuff come from? Mary Magdalene's image became distorted when early church leaders bundled into her story those of several less distinguished women whom the Bible did not name or referred to without a last name. One is the "sinner" in *Luke* who bathes Jesus' feet with her tears, dries them with her hair, kisses them and anoints them with ointment. "Her many sins have been forgiven, for she loved much," he says. Others include *Luke's* Mary of

Bethany and a third, unnamed woman, both of whom anointed Jesus in one form or another. The mix-up was made official by Pope Gregory the Great in 591: "She whom Luke calls the sinful woman, whom John calls Mary [of Bethany], we believe to be the Mary from whom seven devils were ejected according to Mark," Gregory declared in a sermon. That position became church teaching, although it was not adopted by Orthodoxy or Protestantism when each later split from Catholicism.

What prompted Gregory? One theory suggests an attempt to reduce the number of Marys—there was a similar merging of characters named John. Another submits that the sinning woman was appended simply to provide missing backstory for a figure of obvious importance. Others blame misogyny. Whatever the motivation, the effect of the process was drastic and, from a feminist perspective, tragic. Magdalene's witness to the Resurrection, rather than being acclaimed as an act of discipleship in some ways greater than the men's, was reduced to the final stage in a moving but far less central tale about the redemption of a repentant sinner. "The pattern is a common one," writes Jane Schaberg, a professor of religious and women's studies at the University of Detroit Mercy and author of last year's *The Resurrection of Mary Magdalene*: "the powerful woman disempowered, remembered as a whore or whorish." As shorthand, Schaberg coined the term "harlotization."

In 1969, in the liturgical equivalent of fine print, the Catholic Church officially separated *Luke's* sinful woman, Mary of Bethany and Mary Magdalene as part of a general revision of its missal. Word has been slow in filtering down into the pews, however. (It hasn't helped that Magdalene's heroics at the tomb are still omitted from the Easter Sunday liturgy, relegated instead to midweek.) And in the meantime, more scholarship has stoked the fires of those who see her eclipse as a chauvinist conspiracy. Historians of Christianity are increasingly fascinated with a group of early followers of Christ known broadly as the Gnostics, some of whose writings were unearthed only 55 years ago. And the Gnostics were fascinated by

Magdalene. The so-called *Gospel of Mary* [Magdalene], which may date from as early as A.D. 125 (or about 40 years after John's Gospel), describes her as having received a private vision from Jesus, which she passes on to the male disciples. This role is a usurpation of the go-between status the standard Gospels normally accord to Peter, and *Mary* depicts him as mightily peeved, asking, "Did [Jesus] really speak with a woman without our knowledge?" The disciple Levi comes to her defense, saying, "Peter, you have always been hot-tempered … If the Savior made her worthy, who are you to reject her? Surely, the Savior loves her very well. That is why he loved her more than us."

Them's fightin' words, especially when one remembers that the papacy traces its authority back to Peter. Of course, the Gnostic Gospels are not the Bible. In fact, there is evidence that the Bible was standardized and canonized precisely to exclude such books, which the early church leaders regarded as heretical for many non-Magdalene reasons. Nonetheless, feminists have been quick to cite *Mary* as evidence both of Magdalene's early importance, at least in some communities, and as the virtual play-by-play of a forgotten gender battle, in which church fathers eventually prevailed over the people who never got the chance to be known as church mothers. "I think it was a power struggle," says Schaberg, "And the canonical texts that we have [today] come from the winners."

Schaberg goes further. In her book, she returns to *John* in light of the Gnostic writings and purports to find "fragments of a claim" that Jesus may have seen Magdalene as his prophetic successor. The position is thus far quite lonely. But it serves nicely to illustrate the way in which any retrieval of Magdalene as a "winner" inevitably shakes up current assumptions about male church leadership. After Pope John Paul II prohibited even the discussion of female priests in 1995, he cited "the example recorded in the Sacred Scriptures of Christ choosing his Apostles only from among men …" That argument would seem weakened in light of the "new" Magdalene, whom the Pope himself has acknowledged by the once unfashionable title

"from the beginning, her view has been ignored, unappreciated. yet she remains. she cannot be silenced."

"Apostle to the Apostles." Chester Gillis, chair of the department of theology at Georgetown University, says conventional Catholics still feel that Mary Magdalene's absence from many biblical scenes involving the male disciples, and specifically from the ordination-like ritual of the Last Supper, rule her out as a priest precedent. Gillis agrees, however, that her recalibration "certainly makes a case for a stronger role for women in the church."

MEANWHILE, THE COMBINATION OF catholic rethinking and Gnostic revelations have reanimated wilder Magdalene speculations, like that of a Jesus-Magdalene marriage. ("No other biblical figure," Schaberg notes, "has had such a vivid and bizarre postbiblical life.") The Gnostic *Gospel of Philip* describes Magdalene as "the one who was called [Jesus'] companion," claiming that he "used to kiss her on her [mouth]." Most scholars discount a Jesus-Magdalene match because it finds little echo in the canonical Gospels once the false Magdalenes are removed. But it fulfills a deep narrative expectation: for the alpha male to take a mate, for a yin to Jesus' yang or, as some neopagans have suggested, for a goddess to his god. Martin Luther believed that Jesus and Magdalene were married, as did Mormon patriarch Brigham Young.

The notion that Magdalene was pregnant by Jesus at his Crucifixion became especially entrenched in France, which already had a tradition of her immigration in a rudderless boat, bearing the Holy Grail, his chalice at the Last Supper into which his blood later fell. Several French kings promoted the legend that descendants of Magdalene's child founded the Merovingian line of European royalty, a story revived by Richard Wagner in his opera *Parsifal* and again in connection with Diana, Princess of Wales, who reportedly had some Merovingian blood. (The Wachowski brothers, those cultural magpies, named a villain in *The Matrix Reloaded* Merovingian, filming him surrounded by Grail-like chalices. His wife in that film was played by Italian actress Monica Bellucci, who will also play Magdalene in Mel Gibson's upcoming Jesus film ... Sorry, this stuff is addictive.) The idea that Magdalene herself was the Holy Grail—the human receptacle for Jesus' blood line—popped up in a 1986 best seller, *Holy Blood, Holy Grail*, which inspired Brown's *Da Vinci Code*. When Brown said recently, "Mary Magdalene is a historical figure whose time has come," he meant a figure with a lot of mythic filagree.

ELLEN TURNER WAS 48 YEARS OLD when she first learned that Mary Magdalene was not a whore. Through Catholic school and a Catholic college, she attests, "I thought about her in the traditional way, as a sinner." But eight years ago, the 56-year-old technical writer tapped into a network of neo-Magdalenites through her connection with the liberal Catholic groups Call to Action and Futurechurch. The discovery that, as Turner puts it, Magdalene "got the shaft" started her thinking about how to change the situation. She was happy to find that the two organizations, which see Magdalene's recovered image as an argument for their goal of a priesthood open to all those who feel called, coordinate celebrations around the world on her feast day.

Last month Turner and her husband Ray played host to such a celebration at their home in San Jose, Calif. About 30 participants drove in from as far away as Oakland. After meeting and greeting and strolling the meditation labyrinth in Turner's backyard, the group held something resembling a church service, with an opening hymn, a blessing over the bread and wine and readings about Magdalene from the four Gospels. There was no priest, but Turner herself read what, if this were a Mass, might be a homily. "From the beginning," she intoned as the sun sank over Silicon Valley, "her view has been ignored, unappreciated. The first to see the risen Lord—those with more power have sought to marginalize her. Yet she is faithful. She remains. She cannot be silenced."

Who the Devil Is the
Devil?

BY ROBERT WERNICK

WITH THE RAPID APPROACH of the third millennium, many people can't help wondering what role the Devil will be playing in it. But a cursory examination of the mainstream press of America reveals almost no mention of him, and even using the Internet services that promise to keep track of everything, it's much easier to find information on Monica Lewinsky than on the Devil.

What a humiliating comedown for one the mere mention of whose name was once enough to make the hair of kings stand up in terror; of whom Saint Augustine said, "The human race is the Devil's fruit tree, his own property, from which he may pick his fruit."

To appreciate the full extent of that downfall, try to put yourself someplace in Western Europe in the year 999, as the second millennium was about to bow in.

In the tenth century and for at least half a millennium thereafter, the Devil was everywhere. He leered out of every church door, he capered through castle and church and cottage, and his plots and pranks and temptings of humans were spelled out in sermons, on the stage, in paintings, in pious books, and in stories told in taverns or in homes at bedtime.

No corner or cranny of daily life escaped him. He lurked outside every orifice of the human body, waiting for the chance to get at the human soul inside—one reason why to this day we say "God bless you" when we hear someone sneeze.

The Devil fathered children on sleeping women, he stirred up conspiracies and treasons, he led travelers astray. He caused boils, plagues, tempests, shipwrecks, heresies, barbarian invasions. Whatever he did, his name was on everyone's tongue, and he went by many names: Satan, Lucifer, Beelzebub, Belial, Mastema, the Prince of Darkness, the Lord of Lies. In the Bible he was the Accuser, the Evil One, the Prince of this World.

This suave, sardonic Devil is actually a new kid on the block.

Today, a few scant hundred years later, he has dropped so far out of sight that some believe he is gone for good. It may be true that 48 percent of Americans tell the pollsters they believe in the existence of the Devil and another 20 percent find his existence probable. But though they use him often enough in common lighthearted expressions (give the devil his due, the devil is in the details) and in the privacy of their hearts may put the blame on him when they covet their neighbor's wife or cheat on their income tax, they do very little talking about him out loud. Reported physical appearances of the Devil are far rarer than sightings of UFOs. In practical terms, people have banished him from public life.

Yet most everyone who discusses moral standards in pulpits or on television talk shows or in the *New York Times* is agreed that morals are lower than ever before. The Devil should be out in the streets and on the airwaves, roaring like a lion about his triumphs. Where has he gone? It all depends on precisely what you mean by "the Devil."

Theologians have been arguing for centuries (and sometimes have gone to the stake for expressing the wrong opinion) to achieve a satisfactory definition. But today the average person with no theological axe to grind is apt to envisage the Devil as a sleek, dark-complexioned male figure, with black chin-whiskers, little horns and cloven hooves, perhaps with a foxy glint in his eye and a trace of a foreign accent, but on the whole handsome, worldly-wise, a persuasive talker, a friendly sort of customer. He may tell you anything, try to talk you into something too good to be true. Only later, when you've taken that risky bet or signed the shady contract, and he comes to collect his due, do you realize you have signed away your immortal soul. He is unquestionably the Lord of Lies.

This suave, sardonic Devil is actually a new kid on the block; he has been around for barely a few hundred years, a mere stutter in the long swell of human misery and woe. And the Devil in general, the Devil with a capital *D*, as opposed to the legions of lowercase devils, demons, imps, satyrs, fiends and so on, first entered human history less than 3,000 years ago.

But humans indistinguishable from us have been around for many thousands of years, and it seems fair to assume that from the very beginning they were all aware of unseen powerful presences affecting their lives and everything around them. Every ancient religion that we know of, as well as many modern religions with hundreds of millions of followers, perceives a bewildering array of such spirits: gods, demigods, angels, devils, demons, sprites, imps, goblins, ghosts, fairies, fauns, nymphs, jinns, poltergeists. Some of them are benevolent, some are malignant, though most of them alternate between the two extremes. The gods of ancient Greece are typical: Zeus was a wise ruler up on Mount Olympus, but he became a serial rapist when he came down to the lowlands; Persephone was goddess of life in spring and goddess of death in autumn. None of these ancient religions ever developed a single Devil concentrating all the essence of evil, any more than they ever concentrated the essence of good in a single God.

The Old Testament, which was composed between the tenth and third centuries B.C., has little trace of the Devil with a capital *D*, and in its earlier books, none at all. God, speaking through the mouth of the prophet Isaiah, says, "I form the light and create darkness, I make peace and create evil, I the LORD do all these things." The serpent who tempted Adam and Eve in the Garden of Eden was later identified by Jewish rabbis and Christian church fathers with the Devil, the principle of Evil; but in the third chapter of Genesis as written, he is only a snake. It took another few hundred years before both snake and Devil were identified with Lucifer ("light-bearer," the Latin translation of the Hebrew and Greek words for the morning star, the planet Venus) who in Isaiah is thrown down from Heaven for having presumed to set his throne high above the stars of God.

Ancient Hebrew had a noun, *satan*, meaning "obstructor" or "accuser," and several satans appear in the Old Testament being sent by God on different errands, such as blocking the path of Balaam's ass or giving King Saul a fit of depression. When the Old Testament was translated into Greek beginning in the third century B.C., *satan* was rendered *diabolos*, "adversary," from which come the Latin *diabolus*, French *diable*, German *Teufel*, English "devil." The first time the word appears with a capital *S*, defining a particular person, is in the Book of Job, where Satan is a sort of celestial J. Edgar Hoover, sent by the Lord to check up on the loyalty of the folks down on earth.

The first Devil, the first concentration of all evil in a single personal form, appears in history some time before the sixth century B.C., in Persia. His name is Ahriman, described by the prophet Zoroaster (Zarathustra) as the Principle of Darkness (evil) engaged in ceaseless conflict for control of the world with Ormazd or Mazda, the Principle of Light (good).

Satan was once an angel who had led a rebellion in Heaven.

The Jews were under Persian domination for almost two centuries, and it is likely that Ahriman had some influence on the formation of the figure of their Satan. He appears for the first time acting independently in the third-century Book of Chronicles, where the text of the much older Book of Samuel is changed from "The LORD incited David," to read "Satan incited David." In the next few centuries of the so-called Intertestamentary Period between the compilation of the Old and New Testaments, when a major subject of theological speculation and literature was the apocalypse—the final struggle between good and evil at the imminent end of the world—this Satan grew in stature as the leader and embodiment of the forces of evil. The Jewish rabbis soon lost interest in him, and though he runs wild through folklore, he

is a very minor figure in modern Judaism. He would be a major figure, however, as the Satan or Lucifer of the Christians or the Iblis or Shaytan of the Muslims. Whatever he does, and however powerful he may be at times, none of these religions have ever followed Zoroaster in allowing the Devil an independent existence apart from God. He is always separate but far from equal, though exactly to what extent separate and unequal has been the subject of perpetual debate on the questions that the postulation of a Devil naturally calls up: Why did a good God create an evil Devil in the first place? And if he had to, why did he give him so much power and let him reign so long? Or, as Friday asked Robinson Crusoe, "If God much strong, much might as the Devil, why God no kill the devil, no make him no more do wicked?" Such questions were being debated in Latin by 12th-century scholars in Paris in almost the same terms as by 12th-century scholars in Baghdad, and they are still being debated by scholars all over the world today.

The Christian Devil, who is the one most familiar in today's literature and art, appears often, but with only sketchy details, in the New Testament. It took three or four centuries of debate and speculation for the church to settle on a unified but not quite consistent picture of his history and functions. He was once an angel—some said the firstborn and chief of all the angels—who had led a rebellion in Heaven (some said out of pride; some said out of envy either of God himself or of the man, Adam, created in God's image; some said out of sexual lust for pretty women) and had been cast down to Hell (some said on the very first day or hour of the creation of the world, others after the creation of Adam, others after the Fall of Man, others during the time of Noah), had tempted humankind into sin, which allowed him to rule the world until the coming of Christ (or until the Second Coming), and would on the Day of Judgment be condemned to perpetual torment along with all the sinners of the race of Adam.

At the beginning there was curiously little interest in the particular features of this Devil, who does not appear at all in the first six or seven centuries of Christian art. Perhaps the early Christians, members of a small persecuted sect faced with the daily possibility of meeting the representatives of the Roman state in the form of gladiators, lions and howling mobs in arenas, did not need to dream up faces for the Devil. After Christianity became the state religion of Rome in the early fourth century, the fight against the enemy changed in character. The heroes were not martyrs in an arena: they were monks who went out into the deserts to meet Satan face-to-face. Satan appeared to all of them to tempt them, and it was then that Satan first acquired a recognizable physical form, appearing variously as lion, bear, leopard, bull, serpent, hyena, scorpion and wolf.

Around the tenth century, the Devil began to assume monstrous forms.

Still, for hundreds of years no one thought of putting an image of the Devil on paper or a church wall. There is a sixth-century manuscript of the Gospels in Syriac that shows a couple of little black-winged creatures fleeing from the mouth of a man being exorcized. Not till the ninth century, in an illustrated manuscript known as the *Utrecht Psalter*, does a recognizable Devil appear, as a half-naked man holding a three-pronged pitchfork. The Devil would appear often like this in the next couple of centuries, human or at least humanoid in form, sometimes wearing the halo of his old angelic days in Heaven.

Then, some time around the pre-millennial tenth century, the Devil began, all over the Western world, to assume monstrous forms. He appeared on the illustrated pages of books now written for the first time in the vernacular languages, and on the painted walls and ceilings and the carved doors and columns and waterspouts of churches and cathedrals. Everywhere there were scenes from sacred history intended to teach the illiterate

masses the way to salvation, and the Devil played a prominent, sometimes predominant, role in these scenes.

He appeared in a thousand grotesque and horrible guises. His features might be derived from those of old gods of Greece and Rome whose broken images still cluttered the soil of Europe, or the newer gods of the barbarian Germans and Scandinavians, or more ancient supernatural beings from Mesopotamia, Egypt, Persia, even China, who spread their wings on imported silks and tapestries. He borrowed horns and hairy legs with cloven hooves from the Greek god Pan, a hooked nose and grimacing lips from the Etruscan death god Charun, a pitchfork from the Roman sea god Neptune, an animal head from the Egyptian god Anubis. Sometimes he was a furry black monkey with great black bat's wings. Sometimes he was a snake, a wolf, a frog, a bear, a mouse, an owl, a raven, a tortoise, a worm. Often he appeared as a combination of human and animal forms, with a tail, spiky flamelike hair, an apish body, a goat's hairy thighs, an ass's feet, a boar's tusks, a wolfish mouth, an eagle's claws, a monkey's paws, a lizard's skin, a snake's tongue. When he led the revolt of the angels in Heaven, fighting Saint Michael, he was a scaly dragon. Enthroned in Hell, he was a potbellied imbecilic old man, with snakes growing out of his head and limbs, mindlessly chewing on the sterile souls of naked sinners as they dropped down to him on Judgment Day.

He was meant to be both frightening and disgusting, to demonstrate both the horror and the folly of sin. The fright was all the greater because the devices like bone-vices, spine-rollers and red-hot prongs being used to torture sinners down in Hell were copied from those being used to torture heretics in public up on earth.

The static visions on the church walls were regularly brought to life in plays staged in front of churches or in public squares. Surrounded by elaborate scenery and firecrackers, the Devil was always a popular performer when, clothed in snakeskin and with a woman's face, he dangled an apple before our First Parents in Eden, or with fanged mask and hairy goat's body, he grimaced and

grunted and growled as he prodded wailing sinners into a Mouth of Hell that could open and shut and spit flames.

One of the most popular stories throughout the Middle Ages, retold hundreds of times in many European languages, was that of Theophilus of Cilicia, a sixth-century ecclesiastic who signed a pact with the Devil, exchanging his soul for a powerful and profitable position in the church. He was then able to lead a life of unbridled pride and corruption till one day the Devil reappeared and demanded his payment. In terror, Theophilus repented and threw himself on the mercy of the Virgin Mary, who took pity on him, descended into Hell, grabbed the pact from Satan, then interceded for the sinner at the throne of God. He was pardoned, and the Devil was cheated of his due.

Ben Jonson summed it up in one of his plays, The Devil is an Ass.

This tale played a major role in establishing the cult of the Virgin in Catholic Europe. It had the subsidiary effect of familiarizing everyone with the idea of diabolical pacts. The authorities of church and state took advantage of this when sometime in the 15th century they claimed to discover a vast conspiracy by a confederation of witches dedicated to the subversion of all order. There were, of course, plenty of supposed witches around, mostly old countrywomen who knew the traditional herbs and chants and charms that would attract a handsome lover or stop an unwanted pregnancy or blast the crops in an unfriendly neighbor's field. But for the space of two or three centuries, tens of thousands of accused witches, most of them women, most of them poor illiterates, were hanged or burned after being forced to confess to taking part in secret midnight meetings at which they ate babies, copulated with the Devil and signed blood compacts with him.

The Salem witch trials of 1692 are the most familiar to Americans, having left an indelible stain on the name of our Puritan forebears. Perhaps the most interesting thing about them is that, compared with what had been going on in Europe for the previous three centuries, they were on such a very small scale: 18 women, one man and two dogs put to death in obedience to the biblical command "Thou shalt not suffer a witch to live." And there were no more witch trials in the Colonies after Salem.

For by the year 1700 few educated people really believed in witches anymore, and increasingly they were coming not to believe in the Devil himself. The reason was that Western Europe, followed in more or less short order by the rest of the world, was entering the modern era, the world of exploration, discovery, science, technology, individualism, capitalism, rationalism, materialism, democracy, progress. In such a world the old Devil was getting to seem both embarrassing and superfluous. When he appeared on the stage with his monkey suits and his conjuring tricks, he was only an unsightly clown—Ben Jonson summed it up in the title of one of his plays, *The Devil is an Ass*. And when you got down to the business of explaining what was going on around you, the Devil only got in the way. When Shakespeare's Othello learns too late how he has been tricked into murdering his wife and losing his soul, his first, medieval instinct is to look down at Iago's feet; then he pulls himself together and says, "But that's a fable." Iago doesn't need supernatural cloven hooves; he has all the wickedness he needs stored up in his own human heart. Bit by bit, the Devil's possessions and prerogatives were stripped from him.

When Benjamin Franklin called down a great spark from Heaven with a mere key hanging on a kite, all the army of infernal spirits that had been swarming through the air vanished, and the atmosphere became nothing but a mass of nitrogen and oxygen and other atoms, whirling around according to laws that Satan had never heard of.

Where the 13th-century Cistercian abbot Richalm blamed the Devil for the "wondrous sound that would seem to proceed from some distemper" of his stomach or bowels, a modern monk sends for a gastroenterologist. Great storms are no longer conjured up by the Devil, but by El Niño currents, and no one blames the wreck of the *Titanic* on anything but errors of judgment and faults of design. People are still possessed by devils, and the Roman Catholic church among others provides means of exorcizing them. But their numbers are infinitesimal compared with the number of people who are daily put under the care of psychiatrists.

The old-fashioned horror-show Devil virtually disappeared from the fine arts with the coming of the Renaissance. In 1505 Raphael painted a traditional picture of Saint Michael beating the Devil out of Heaven; the Devil is a kind of outsize science-fiction insect with horns and wings and a madman's gasping face. Thirteen years later he did another painting on the identical theme, but the Devil this time, though a pair of bat wings grows out of his shoulders, is otherwise wholly human, a young man writhing in the despair of defeat, a much more arresting and moving figure than the bland self-satisfied saint who is poking him with a spear.

> *To adjust to this modern world, the Devil has had to change his ways.*

The real gravedigger of the old brutal, terrifying, physically threatening Devil was John Milton, whose *Paradise Lost* was to influence the world's conception of Satan in a way no other work of art has ever done, though not at all in the way the author intended. It was designed to be an epic poem like those of Homer or Virgil, but told to "justify God's ways to Man," and dealing with creation, sin and salvation. In outline, it is a very orthodox story of pride and sin eventually humbled and destroyed by the infinite wisdom and goodness of God. Milton's Satan follows the theologically correct process of transformation from the most radiant of angels to the loathsome crawling serpent of Book Ten. Few readers, however, get to Book Ten of *Paradise Lost*. They are more apt to let themselves be lost in fascination with the Satan of the first books, a heroic figure of the first order, young, proud, self-confident, self-reliant, inventive, ingenious, yielding to no obstacle, defiant, who will not accept defeat even if defeat is inevitable, who values his own freedom more than happiness, who would rather "reign in Hell than serve in Heaven." These might be considered features of the tireless visionary entrepreneurs from Columbus to Bill Gates whose dreams and exploits have shaped so much of modern history, and provided the heroes for so many modern movies and novels.

But to the modern Devil, even more galling than his loss of physical power, his control of earthquakes and unholy wars, must be his loss of respect. The Prince of Darkness has become, in the view of Prof. Andrew Delbanco of Columbia University, in a book called *The Death of Satan*, a superannuated athlete who has gone on the lecture circuit.

He can always get a supporting role in a horror movie like *Rosemary's Baby* or a science-fiction thriller about a professor of comparative literature who carves up and cooks his more attractive students. But no one takes him really seriously. He is toned down, domesticated. Bowdlerized, he has become politically correct. As one of the title characters in John Updike's *Witches of Eastwick* remarks, "Evil is not a word that we like to use. We prefer to say 'unfortunate' or 'lacking' or 'misguided' or 'disadvantaged.'" Even hellfire preachers who make a speciality of describing in detail the horrors of the afterlife no longer say, as the church fathers of a more robust age used to do, that one of the joys of being in Heaven will be to watch sinners writhing in the hands of the Devil.

To adjust to this pallid modern world, the Devil has had to change his ways. Always an expert shape-changer, he now comes on most often in the form of Mephistopheles. The name was made up in a 15th-century German updating of the old Theophilus legend, which has Mephistopheles signing a pact with Dr. Johann Faustus, a professor-turned-magician who is more than willing to trade his soul for 24 years of unbounded knowledge, power and sex. Christopher Marlowe's play of *Doctor Faustus* would launch both the Faust story and the character of Mephistopheles on a fabulously successful career. He was followed two centuries later by Goethe with his epic drama *Faust*. Between them they created the modern Devil, witty, ironic, disillusioned, a much more complex and interesting character than Doctor Faustus himself. Unlike Faust, however, Mephistopheles never *does* anything; he just talks.

He talks very well, of course. He talks very wittily and convincingly in Dostoyevsky's *Brothers Karamazov* and in George Bernard Shaw's *Man and Superman*. He is funny in a sinister kind of way when in C. S. Lewis' *Screwtape Letters* he becomes a conscientious bureaucrat filling reams of paper with instructions to an Englishman on how to get on his mother's nerves. He looks very handsome and winning when he is played by Al Pacino in the movies. But out in the world of commerce, politics, wars and gross national product, he is little more than a joke.

For some observers like Professor Delbanco and Prof. Jeffrey Burton Russell, of the University of California, Santa Barbara, whose five-volume biography of the Devil is the most authoritative, this is a tragic situation; it means that America, like the modern world generally, has lost its sense of evil, and without a sense of evil a civilization must go straight to Hell.

Perhaps, however, he is not dead after all; he may only be in hiding. A 17th-century Englishman, Richard Greenham, was apparently the first to coin the phrase, later borrowed or reinvented by Baudelaire, Dostoyevsky, G. K. Chesterton and Whittaker Chambers, "it is the policy of the Devil to persuade us that there is no Devil." The Devil, after all, if he is anything, is the personification of evil, and no one can deny that there is plenty of evil around even in today's comparative peace and prosperity.

Common sense tells us that we will go on performing wicked deeds.

The psychiatrist Viktor Frankl was a young doctor in Vienna in 1940 when he and his wife were picked up by Nazi thugs and sent off to concentration camps. She was soon murdered, but he managed to survive through all five years of the war. One night, as he climbed up to his wooden bunk, he found the man next to him moaning and roaring and thrashing, in prey to the worst nightmare Frankl had ever seen in his years of medical practice. His every humane instinct as a doctor told him to wake the man up before he hurt himself, but as he reached out to shake him he suddenly remembered that the reality he would be waking the man up to was Auschwitz, with all its stenches and screams and heavy thudding blows, and that was a hundred times worse than anything the mere human imagination could make up in the confines of a narrow human skull. So he let the nightmare gallop on.

There were no devils running Auschwitz, only human beings doing an ill-paid job that they must have found unpleasant at times but which was clearly preferable to being sent to die in the hell of the Russian front. That does not mean the Devil was not there.

Most everyone these days has taken the pledge that there will be no more Auschwitzes. But such pledges have been taken before. Common sense tells us that we will go on performing wicked deeds of one sort or another till an automated virtue machine is patented or (more likely) till the end of the world.

Madame Carmelita, a psychic on the Upper East Side of Manhattan, has assured me that the world will end on or about my 100th birthday, February 18, 2018. And a science-fiction scenario might have the world (meaning human life) come to an end when a giant comet hits the earth, clearing the ground for little polyps that will evolve into creatures much nicer and more spiritual than us mere mammals. A scientist has assured me that the world (meaning life on earth) will come to an end when our sun becomes a red giant in the year 4,000,001,999. If in the meanwhile a sleek gentleman dressed as a prosperous options-and-derivatives salesman offers you fantastic odds on a bet that he will not be around right up to the last second on any or all of those occasions, and you take him up on it, you will probably be making a bad bet.

Robert Wernick reports that he has received many offers from the Devil but thus far has resisted his blandishments.

Originally appeared in *Smithsonian*, October 1999, pp. 112-123. © 1999 by Robert Wernick. Reprinted by permission.

UNIT 4
Muslims and Byzantines

Unit Selections

19. **The Emperor's State of Grace**, Charles Freeman
20. **The Survival of the Eastern Roman Empire**, Stephen Williams and Gerard Friell
21. **In the Beginning, There Were the Holy Books**, Kenneth L. Woodward

Key Points to Consider

• What were some of the accomplishments of Constantine?

• Why was the Eastern Roman Empire able to survive after the West had fallen? Was this Byzantine civilization merely an extension of late Roman culture, or was it a new departure?

• What are some of the main events in the life of Muhammad? What are the problems today?

 **Links: www.dushkin.com/online/**
These sites are annotated in the World Wide Web pages.

ByzNet: Byzantine Studies on the Net
http://www.thoughtline.com/byznet/

Islam: A Global Civilization
http://www.templemount.org/islamiad.html

Middle East Network Information Center
http://menic.utexas.edu/menic/religion.html

After the western collapse of the Roman Empire, three ethnic/religious entities emerged to fill the vacuum. Germanic kingdoms arose in central and western Europe. In the Balkans and Asia Minor, the eastern remnants of Rome evolved into Byzantine Empire. The Near East, North Africa, and much of Spain fell under the control of the Arabs. Each area developed a unique civilization, based in each instance upon a distinctive form of religion—Roman Catholicism in most of Europe, Orthodox Christianity in the Byzantine sphere, and Islam in the Arab world. Each placed its unique stamp upon the classical tradition to which all three fell heir. The articles in this unit concentrate on the Byzantine and Muslim civilizations. The medieval culture of Europe is treated in the next unit.

Western perceptions of Islam and Arabic civilization have been clouded by ignorance and bias. To European observers during the medieval period, Islam seemed a misguided or heretical version of Christianity. In the wake of Arab conquests, Islam increasingly came to represent terror and devastation, a dangerous force loosed upon Christendom. Reacting out of fear and hostility, Christian authors were reluctant to acknowledge the learning and high culture of the Arabs.

Muslim commentators could be equally intolerant. Describing Europeans, one wrote: "They are most like beasts than like men….Their temperaments are frigid, their humors raw, their bellies gross…they lack keenness of understanding…and are overcome by ignorance and apathy."

The stereotypes formed in the early encounters between Christians and Muslims survived for generations. Centuries of hostility have tended to obscure the extent of cultural exchange between the Arab world and the West. Indeed, as historian William H. McNeil has observed, "Muslims have been written out of European history."

The lands of Islam encroached upon too many points for the two cultures to remain mutually exclusive. In Western Europe Islam swept over Spain, crossed the Pyrenees, and penetrated France; in the central Mediterranean, it leaped from Tunis to Sicily and then into Southern Italy; in Eastern Europe, Islam broke into Asia Minor, the Balkans, and the Caucasus. In its expansion, early Islam was exposed to Jewish, Christian, and classical influences. History and geography determined that there would be much cross-fertilization of Islam and the West.

Yet there is no denying the originality and brilliance of Islamic civilization. The religion of Muhammad is unquestionably one of the world's most influential faiths. "In the Beginning There Were the Holy Books" highlights essentials of that faith. Additional evidence of Arab creativity can be found in the visual arts, particularly in the design and decoration of the great mosques. The Arabs also made significant contributions in philosophy, history, geography, science and medicine.

The medieval West borrowed extensively from the Arabs. The magnificent centers of Islamic culture—Baghdad, Cairo, Cordoba, and Damascus outshone the cities of the West. Their administration of Andalusia was a model of successful governance. Islamic scholars surpassed their Christian counterparts in astronomy, mathematics, and medicine—perhaps because the Arab world was more familiar than medieval Europe with the achievements of classical Greece. European scholars eventually regained access to the Greek heritage at least partially through translations from Arabic.

As for the Byzantine Empire, it was for nearly 1,000 years, a Christian bulwark against Persians, Arabs, and Turks. Charles Freeman recounts the great contributions to the Christian faith by Constantine the Great in "The Emperor's State of Grace." It also made important cultural contributions. The beautiful mosaics and icons of Byzantine artists set the pattern for later visualizations of Christ in the West. Byzantine missionaries and statesmen spread Orthodox Christianity, with its unique tradition of Caesaro-Papism, to Russia. Byzantine scholars and lawmakers preserved much of the classical heritage. Even hostile Islam was subject to a constant flow of ideas and traditions from the Byzantines.

The Emperor's State of Grace

Charles Freeman considers whether Constantine's famous adoption of Christianity was a spiritual conversion or an act of political expediency.

THE STORY OF CONSTANTINE and Christianity is often simply told. It is AD 312. Constantine, the Augustus or senior emperor of the western Roman empire, confronts the usurper Maxentius who holds Rome and the African provinces. Alerted by a vision that the Christian God is on his side, Constantine decorates the shields of his men with a cross and goes into battle at the Milvian Bridge just north of Rome. The result is a stunning victory, all the western empire falls into Constantine's hands and a conversion of Constantine to Christianity follows. Then with the emperor of the east, Licinius, Constantine issues the Edict of Milan which declares toleration for Christianity throughout the empire and underlines this with massive commitments to the Christian communities. Within twelve years, and now sole emperor, Constantine is presiding at the first empire-wide council of bishops, which produces the earliest version of the Nicene creed and soon to be the badge of Christian orthodoxy.

Many studies of this extraordinary turnaround in Christian affairs (there had been brutal persecutions of Christians under Diocletian only a few years before) make the assumption that Constantine accepted Christianity on its own terms. However, the evidence suggests instead that Constantine treated the God of Christianity as if he were similar to the pagan gods, such as Apollo, to which he had already given allegiance. As he began to grasp the distinctive nature of Christianity, he acted to bring the Church directly under his control, giving himself special roles as a bishop outside the Church and later as 'the thirteenth apostle' in order to maintain his distance from, and dominance over, it.

An early clue to Constantine's beliefs can be found in the Edict of Toleration itself. In it Constantine and Licinius 'grant both to Christians and to all men unrestricted right to follow the form of worship each desired, to the end that whatever divinity there may be on the heavenly seat may be favourably disposed and propitious to us and all those placed under our authority'. So this was genuinely an Edict of Toleration and a true Christian brought up in the tradition that the polytheistic world was evil could hardly have supported it. One reason for such a wide-ranging decree was that Constantine had to maintain the support of Licinius but it seems clear that he had not appreciated that Christians energetically rejected all other gods.

There is another important theme here: Constantine is suggesting that by giving appropriate honour to the 'divinity on the heavenly seat', he will get that divinity's support. This need remained paramount in the years that followed. But what drew Constantine to Christianity in the first place? A simple answer would be the vision before the Milvian Bridge. Yet the accounts of this vision date from years later and are contradictory. In the earliest account (*c*.415) Lactantius, himself a convert to Christianity, reported that Constantine had had a dream the night before the battle in which he was commanded to place the 'heavenly sign of god', the Chi-Rho sign, on his soldiers' shields and he did so. Many years later Constantine told his biographer Eusebius—and under oath Eusebius tells us—a somewhat different version of the story. At some moment before the battle a cross of light appeared in the skies above the sun. It was inscribed, 'By this, conquer,' and this command was confirmed in a dream when Christ himself appeared to Constantine and asked him to inscribe a cross on his standards as a safeguard against his enemies.

Yet in Eusebius's *Life of Constantine* another story is developed and it links Constantine's adherence to Christianity directly to his father, Constantius. His father was enormously important to Constantine's legitimacy. When Constantius had been appointed Caesar or junior emperor (in the Tetrarchy set up by Diocletian, there were four emperors: two senior, known as Augusti, and two junior, known as Caesars) in the west in

293, his son Constantine, then about twenty, had remained in the east and cut his teeth on campaigns against the frontier tribes along the Danube. Constantine only rejoined his father some years later, in York where the latter was dying. On Constantius's death in 306, Constantine was immediately proclaimed Augustus in his place by his men, although this elevation was only accepted three or four years later by Galerius, Augustus in the east. Meanwhile the Tetrarchy was disintegrating and the politically astute Constantine set out to establish his legitimacy independently of it. Panegyrics to Constantine which survive from the years immediately after Constantius's death assume the latter is in heaven and Constantine, 'similar to you [Constantius] in appearance, in spirit and in the power of empire,' holds power on earth as a symbol of his father's immortality.

Constantine believed the god of the Christians was on his side, but this did not mean a rejection of other gods.

Next Constantine stretched Constantius's own legitimacy back to an early third-century emperor, Claudius Gothicus (r. AD 268–270), whose victory over the Goths at Naissus (coincidentally Constantine's birthplace, present-day Nish in Yugoslavia) in 269 blunted their strength for over a century. With a line of descent from an earlier emperor and divine support assumed through his father, Constantine now claimed to rule the western empire in his own right. Yet there is another vital ingredient. Constantine came to believe that his father was Christian. The evidence on which he based his belief, as reported by Eusebius, was circumstantial. Constantius had refrained from enforcing the edicts of persecution, he was known to talk of a single God, and his very survival (in comparison to the fates of other emperors in these troubled years) confirmed that he enjoyed his God's favour. The apparent visions before the Battle of the Milvian Bridge, followed by the great victory, were enough to confirm for Constantine that it was the God of the Christians who was on his side.

Yet for Constantine this did not mean a rejection of other gods. The triumphal arch in 315, erected by the senate of Rome in Constantine's honour three years after his 'conversion', makes the point well. The arch is traditional in form and is notable for its use of reliefs from monuments to earlier emperors, Trajan, Hadrian and Marcus Aurelius. There are reliefs of Mars, Jupiter and Hercules and Constantine's victory at the Milvian Bridge is associated with the power of the sun and the goddess Victory, but there is no hint of any Christian symbol and no mention of Christ. (Alistair Kee, in his *Constantine versus Christ*, goes so far as to argue that Christ played no part in the religion of Constantine.) An inscription on the arch credits Constantine's victory to the 'instigation of the Divinity', but the 'Divinity', like the 'Supreme Deity', is a vague term used by pagans and Christians alike. In 313 Licinius had used it in a prayer before his troops when it appears that he was referring to Jupiter. Constantine clearly had no inhibitions about using this phrase alongside traditional pagan symbols.

Whatever Constantine believed the 'Divinity' might be, he desperately needed its support and feared that any form of disunity among Christians might threaten it. Toleration was followed by the granting of special favours to the clergy, in particular exemption from the heavy burden of holding civic office, so that, in Constantine's words, the clergy 'shall not be drawn away by any deviation and sacrifice from the worship that is due to the divinity, but shall devote themselves without interference to their own law… *for it seems that, rendering the greatest possible service to the deity, they most benefit the state.*' (My italics). When, for instance the Donatist dispute broke out over whether a bishop who had surrendered the scriptures at a time of persecution was legitimate, Constantine supported those who said he was, but in a letter to an official he expressed his real concerns, particularly his fear that his own position as the ruler favoured by God would be jeopardised by internal squabbles. 'I consider it absolutely contrary to the divine law that we should overlook such quarrels and contentions,' he wrote, 'whereby the Supreme Divinity may perhaps be roused not only against the human race but also against myself, to whose care he has by his celestial will committed the government of all earthly things.'

By 324 Constantine had defeated Licinius and was sole ruler of the empire. In view of his concern that the Christian churches should be unified he must have been shocked by what he found. The Greek speaking east had always been a hotbed of lively debate, theological controversy and rivalry between the great bishoprics. Constantine's victories would have made him more convinced that the god of the Christians was on his side, yet this relationship was threatened by the endemic political and theological disunity of the east.

Almost immediately he was confronted by a major dispute between a bishop, Alexander of the important see of Alexandria, and a presbyter in the diocese, one Arius. It concerned a central problem of Christian doctrine, the relationship between God the Father, and Jesus Christ the Son. Arius claimed that Jesus, though fully divine, was a subsequent creation of God the Father and hence subordinate to him. An alternative, monotheistic, view was to suggest that Jesus had been part of the Godhead since the beginning of time. The dispute erupted when Arius, who had a well-developed sense of drama, loudly interrupted one of Alexander's sermons and Alexander, with the backing of other bishops, excommunicated him. Constantine was irritated by the dispute and wrote to Alexander and Arius urging them to stop their idle and trivial speculations. By this time, however, the controversy had spread as other bishops had associated themselves with one side or the other and Constantine realised that only by summoning a council of bishops could he hope to enforce a solution. The bishops were to assemble at Nicaea in Asia Minor, where there was an imperial palace with an audience hall. Constantine would pay their travel expenses and preside himself.

By now the Emperor's aura and reputation were overwhelming. When he arrived at the Council he was described by Eusebius as 'like some heavenly messenger of God, clothed in a shining raiment, which flashed as if with glittering rays of light… and adorned with the lustrous brilliance of gold and precious stones'. Those who beheld him were 'stunned and amazed at the sight—like children who have seen a frightening apparition'. Later Byzantine mosaics and frescos (as in the refectory of the Great Lavra on Mount Athos) show Constantine as the central figure of the council, larger than the bishops assembled around him.

It is impossible to know what went on at Nicaea because the accounts are so fragmentary. The assumption has to be that the determination of Constantine to resolve the issue, his dominating presence, and the growing dependency of the Church on him for patronage combined to give him an overwhelming position. Eusebius describes him working assiduously to get an agreement. The Creed which emerged declared that Christ 'is of the substance *[ousia]* of the Father,… true God of true God,… consubstantial *[homoousios]* with the Father…'. Then, at the end, it contained a number of anathemas condemning specific Arian beliefs, notably that there was a time that Jesus had never existed or that Jesus was of a different substance from the Father. What had happened in effect was that Christ had been brought into the Godhead, and was no longer subordinate to it as in previous Church tradition. It was, as Hanson in his *The Search for the Origins of Christian Doctrine* puts it; 'a startling innovation' but a united Godhead, of one substance, provided a more effective theological backing for an autocratic political order than one whose powers were divided between God and Jesus as a lesser divine figure.

Constantine enforced the creed by excommunicating those attending the Council who refused to sign it. 'Thus,' wrote Eusebius, 'the Faith prevailed in a unanimous form…' and he concludes '…When these things were finished, the Emperor said that this was the second victory he had won over the enemy of the Church, and held a victory-feast to God.' Constantine later came to realise that he had created a false unity, and he accepted Arius back into the Church, and received his own baptism at the hands of an Arian bishop, before his death.

Constantine's allegiance to his God was backed by massive patronage. Emperors had always honoured their favoured gods with benefactions and buildings. Constantine's patronage was so lavish that he had to strip resources from temples to fund it. One of his early foundations in Rome was the church of St John Lateran, whose apse was to be coated in gold. Around 500 pounds weight of it were needed at a cost of some 36,000 *solidi*. This sum, which might be translated into approximately £60 million today, could have fed about 12,000 poor for a year (according to calculations from Dominic Janes' *God and Gold in Late Antiquity*). Another 22,200 *solidi* worth of silver (3,700 lbs was required for light fittings and another 400 pounds of gold for fifty gold vessels. The costs of lighting were to be met by estates specifically granted for the purpose which brought in 4,390 *solidi* a year. Everything in these new churches had to be of the highest quality. While early Christian decoration, in the catacombs or house churches, for instance, had been painted walls, now nothing less than mosaic was appropriate. In order to make the effect more brilliant the mosaics were made of gold, silver or precious stones set within glass. It was an enormously

delicate and costly business. Studies of the original floor mosaics at the Church of the Nativity in Bethlehem, one of Constantine's foundations in the Holy Land, reveal the care and cost lavished on decoration. While the normal pattern of high-quality mosaics in Palestine is 150 tesserae per 10cm square, the ratio in the nave is 200 and in the Octagon at the end of the nave, some 400. In their size and opulent decoration, the basilicas echoed the great audience halls of the emperors. The transformation in a religion whose founder had been so committed to the poor was shocking to many. 'Parchments are dyed purple, gold is melted into lettering, manuscripts are dressed up in jewels, while Christ lies at the door naked and dying,' wrote the horrified Jerome. But by the end of the century the Church had accepted its buildings and the scriptures had been reinterpreted to justify the fortunes spent on them.

There were, of course, tensions with the pagan senatorial aristocracy over these transformations, particularly in Rome (where Constantine's two major churches, St John Lateran and St Peter's on the Vatican Hill, were build outside the city centre). There was also deep shock in the city over the mysterious execution of Constantine's son Crispus and Crispus's stepmother, Constantine's second wife Fausta, in 326, on suspicion of treason. The pagan writer Zosimus even suggested that the pilgrimage of the Emperor's mother Helena to the Holy Land had been ordered as a Christian penance for her part in allegedly drowning Fausta in a bath.

Such opprobrium, and a desire to celebrate his own glory, must have been one reason why Constantine was so determined to create a city where he could be personally supreme. He chose an ancient Greek foundation, Byzantium, which occupied a stunning and well defended site overlooking the southern end of the Bosphorus and which was well placed on the main routes between east and west. As its name suggests Constantinople was Constantine's city. Eusebius, in his attempt to assert the Christian commitment of Constantine, went so far as to claim, misleadingly, that Constantinople was always a wholly Christian city without a single pagan temple. For its founder, however, this was the city of Constantine, not of Christ.

Many elements of the foundation were traditional. Constantine traced the line of the future walls of the city with a spear just as a Greek founder would have done. Statues and classical monuments were brought from all over the world to grace the public spaces. The protecting goddesses Rhea, the mother of Olympian gods, and Tyche, the personification of good fortune, were honoured with new temples. Constantine's most ambitious plans, however, were to create a central complex of forum, hippodrome and imperial palace as a setting for his own majesty. In the circular forum, on one of the highest hills of the city, Constantine erected a great porphyry column twenty-five metres high, topped with a gold statue of himself.

All this was dedicated on a great day of celebration in May 300 and it was as much a celebration of Constantine as of his city. A gold coin was struck to mark the occasion showing Constantine gazing upwards in a pose made famous by Alexander the Great, his head crowned by an opulent diadem. The ceremonies began in the presence of the Emperor with the lifting of the great gold statue onto its column. Dressed in magnificent robes and wearing a diadem encrusted with jewels (another spiritual allegiance of Constantine's, to the sun, a symbol of Apollo, first known from 310 was expressed through rays coming from the diadem). Constantine processed to the imperial box. Among the events that followed one stood out: the arrival in the hippodrome of a golden chariot carrying a gilded statue of the emperor. In his hands was a smaller statue of Tyche. For the next two hundred years the ritual drawing of the statue and chariot through the hippodrome was to be re-enacted on the anniversary of the dedication.

He built a circular mausoleum with a tomb surrounded by twelve sepulchres, symbolic burial places for the apostles.

Where did Christianity fit into all this? In the original celebrations hardly at all. Space was put aside for churches in the centre of the city but their titles, Hagia Sophia, Holy Wisdom, Hagia Eirene, Holy Peace and Hagia Dynamis, Holy Power, suggest that Constantine was still using epithets which were as comprehensible to the pagan world as to the Christian. The only saints honoured with churches were local martyrs. The pagan elements of the city were not erased until later in the century, under Theodosius I, when Rhea and Tyche were absorbed into the cult of the Virgin Mary, the new protectress of the city.

In April 337 Constantine realised he was dying. Then, and only then, did he allow himself to be baptised. In the last weeks of his life (he died on May 22nd) he discarded the imperial purple and dressed himself in the white of the newly baptised Christian. He had already built his final resting place within Constantinople and it provided a fitting testimonial to how he saw himself in relation to God and Christ. It was a circular mausoleum with a tomb left for the emperor under the central dome. Placed around the tomb were twelve sepulchres—each a symbolic burial place of one of the original apostles. Constantine was to be the thirteenth apostle. To orthodox Christians this might seem blasphemous but it made sense in terms of Constantine's own perception of himself in relation to the god who had given him such support.

After his death his sons issued a coin to commemorate their own *consecratio* (being made sacred as emperors). On one side it bore Constantine's veiled head and an inscription, 'The deified Constantine, father of the Augusti', on the other Constantine is seen ascending to heaven in a chariot with God's hand reaching out to welcome him. The evidence suggests that Constantine was using the Christian god as an adjunct to his own

power, much as earlier Roman emperors had done with their gods. Every victory was simply a confirmation that the relationship was intact and that the emperor was justified in maintaining his power and magnificence. Constantine kept himself at arm's length from the institutional structure of the Church. He once told the bishops, 'You are bishops of those within the Church, but I am perhaps a bishop appointed by God over those outside.' For Constantine his policy was justified by his continuing victories:

> While God was close at hand to make him Lord and Despot, the only Conqueror among the Emperors of all time to remain Irresistible and Unconquered, Ever-conquering and always brilliant with triumphs over enemies, so great an Emperor... so God beloved and Thrice blessed,... that with utter ease he governed more nations than those before him, and kept his dominion unimpaired to the very end.

When the papacy and the Roman Catholic Church came under sustained attack in the Reformation, the Medici Pope Leo X (r. 1513–21) ordered a great room to be built in the Vatican. Known as the *Sala di Constantino*, it had unashamedly propagandist aims. It frescoes, planned by Raphael, show the early popes, from Peter onwards, and then, in four great scenes, the achievement of Constantine. One fresco shows the vision of the Cross, another the battle of the Milvian Bridge itself. Leo associated himself with the victory. The *palle* from the Medici coat of arms are on Constantine's tent and lions, a reference to Leo's name, are also found on the tend with another on a standard. At a moment of crisis and confrontation, this was the event the pope chose to highlight. It was more than toleration that Constantine gave to Christianity, it was transformation. By tying in his victories to the support of the Christian God, and associating his allegiance with massive patronage, Constantine had shifted the nature of Christianity itself.

FOR FURTHER READING

D. Bowder, *The Age of Constantine and Julian* (London, 1978); Averil Cameron, *The Late Roman Empire* (London, 1993); G. Bowersock, and others, eds, *Late Antiquity: A Guide to the Postclassical World* (London, 1999); H. Pohlsander, *Constantine the Emperor* (London, 1997); Eusebius's *Life of Constantine*, trans. Averil Cameron and Stuart Hall (Oxford, 1999); Dominic Janes, *God and Gold in Late Antiquity* (Cambridge, 1998); R. Hanson, *The Search for the Christian Doctrine of God* (Edinburgh, 1988); Sabine MacCormack, *Art and Ceremony in Late Antiquity* (London, 1981); Alistair Kee, *Constantine versus Christ* (SCM Press, 1982).

Charles Freeman is author of *The Greek Achievement* (Penguin 1999) and is working on a study of the transition from the Greek to the Christian world.

This article first appeared in *History Today*, January 2001, pp. 9-15. © 2001 by History Today, Ltd. Reprinted by permission.

The Survival of the Eastern Roman Empire

Stephen Williams *and* **Gerard Friell** *analyse why Constantinople survived the barbarian onslaughts in the fifth century, whereas Rome fell*

THE OLD ATTITUDE still prevails in some quarters that what we know of as the Roman Empire was dismembered in the fifth century, and that what survived in the East was something different—Byzantium, Greek and Christian; fascinating, no doubt, but no longer the real Rome. This quite misleading picture is often accompanied by another: that the survival of the Eastern half in the terrible fifth century, when the West went under, was a more or less natural development—even unconsciously anticipated by Constantine's wise foundation of his new capital in the wealthier, more urbanised East.

The reality of course was very different. Despite the administrative division into East and West, which predated Constantine, the empire was everywhere seen as one and indivisible. At the beginnings of the fifth century both halves faced similar chronic problems: immature or inept emperors, rebellious armies, external barbarian invaders and the large and dangerous settlements of barbarian 'allies' within imperial territories. By difficult expedients and innovations the East was eventually able to overcome these problems, while the West was not. After several attempts, Constantinople accepted that it had not the strength to save the West, but it still treated it as a group of temporarily lost provinces to be recovered when the situation permitted—a view that the emperor Justinian in the sixth century took entirely literally.

After the disastrous defeat by the immigrant Visigoths at Adrianople (Edirne) in 378, the new Eastern emperor, Theodosius, was eventually able to fight and manoeuvre them into signing a treaty in 382, settling them in the Balkans as 'allies' (*foederati*), since they could not possibly be expelled. They were obliged to support the emperor, militarily, on request, but this was nonetheless a radically new departure in foreign policy, the result of Roman weakness. Instead of mere farmer-settlers under Roman administration, this was an entire armed Germanic nation established deep within Roman territory under its own tribal leaders. It could not help but be a precedent for other land-hungry barbarians. Theodosius, however, had no option but to hope that in time the Goths could be assimilated as others had been.

After Theodosius's death in 395, his two young sons, Arcadius (377–408) and Honorius (384–423), inherited the thrones of East and West respectively. Both boy-emperors were immature and incapable (Honorius was practically retarded), and although strong loyalty to the dynasty kept them on their thrones, they were entirely managed by individuals or factions within the two courts. Instead of the cooperation that was badly needed, the two governments of East and West intrigued and manoeuvred against each other like hostile states for over ten years, with damaging consequences.

On Theodosius's death the Visigoths immediately broke out of their assigned territories and ravaged the Eastern provinces, under their leader Alaric, who now declared himself king. Temporarily without their main army, the Eastern government, dominated by the eunuch chamberlain Eutropius, was able to deflect Alaric westwards by granting him a top military command in Illyricum (Yugoslavia). The combined status of Roman general and tribal warlord created yet another dangerous precedent. Alaric was able to exploit the deep hostility between the two governments, becoming a destabilising force over the next fifteen years.

In the West, real power was legitimately in the hands of the commander-in-chief Stilicho, of Vandal origin, who had been appointed guardian of the boy-emperor Honorius. He was resented and feared by the ruling circles at Constantinople, who had him declared a public enemy. Stilicho, hoping in vain to force Alaric back into his former alliance, was able to defeat him several times but not destroy him. He had to crush a revolt in Africa (encouraged by Constantinople) and then defeat an Ostrogothic invasion of Italy itself. He was by now forced to buy barbarian fighting men from any source and on any terms, often with personal promises, and even grants of land.

To defend Italy, Stilicho had to strip Britain and the Rhine frontier of troops, and at New Year 407 multiple barbarian invaders crossed the frozen Rhine into Gaul virtually unopposed, never to be expelled again. For this, Stilicho's political enemies in the Senate contrived to have him condemned and executed on the weak emperor's orders, whereupon thousands of his loyal barbarian troops, fearing for themselves and their families, fled over to join Alaric. With Stilicho removed, nothing could prevent Alaric from besieging and finally sacking Rome in 410.

The East had rid itself of the menace of Alaric by propelling him westwards, but this did not free it from other barbarian dangers. What Alaric's Visigoths could do, others could imitate. A new revolt broke out in 399 among the recently-settled Ostrogothic federates. Gainas, the general sent to suppress it, mistrusted the government and was himself of Gothic origin and the commander of other Gothic federate troops. The two Gothic groups joined forces, marched on Constantinople and occupied it, with Gainas dictating his terms to the emperor. However, he was met by a violent anti-Gothic, popular backlash and total hostility from the civil government. Having achieved nothing, he attempted a clumsy withdrawal from the capital in which many Goths and their families were massacred by the mob. Those that escaped were later defeated by loyal units (also commanded by a Goth).

These events had a profound effect on the civilian ruling circles in Constantinople. Henceforth they were determined to keep a firm grip on imperial power and curb ambitious generals, especially those of Gothic origin, even though many were entirely loyal. For several years Goths were excluded from top commands, armies were thinned in numbers, and care was taken to avoid any new settlements of barbarian federates. The Praetorian Prefect, Anthemius, the acknowledged leader of the state, invested instead in strengthening the defences on the Danube frontier, building a new and massive belt of land walls to protect Constantinople, its emperor and government, from both barbarian invasions and its own potentially dangerous armies.

The exclusion of Gothic generals did not last long. With the federate crises past, and a growing external threat from the Huns, able professional commanders such as Plinta, Aspar and Areobindus once again rose to the top *Magister* posts. The fact that they were divorced from any federate or tribal power base (unlike Alaric and Gainas) made them acceptable. They remained what they had been in the previous century—loyal members of the Roman ruling class.

The really farsighted achievement of the Eastern empire during this period was not so much the weakening of the power of the army, as the institutionalising of it within a central ruling establishment at Constantinople, which included the palace and civil bureaucracy. The Eastern field army, about 100,000 strong, was already divided into five regional mobile groups, and the commands carefully balanced between men of Gothic and Roman origin. Two of these groups—the Praesental armies—were stationed in the vicinity of Constantinople and their commanders, of whatever background, were senior members of the senate and members of the emperor's inner council of state, the Consistory.

Any successful, ambitious general was faced with a choice and a temptation. He could use external military violence to try to dominate the emperor at Constantinople, perhaps even making himself emperor, or at least military dictator. Or he could use the army's indispensability and natural leverage within the legitimate, established power structure where there was a place for him at the top table.

Gainas had attempted the first option and had been ruined. Other military leaders overwhelmingly chose the second. Though politically powerful, the army was only one of several competing, but also interlocking, forces around the throne. To break out of this careful web of power risked losing everything. Certainly, there were bitter conflicts within the Constantinople establishment. For many years the deficiencies of the pious and bookish emperor Theodosius II (408–450) were heavily compensated by his dominating sister Pulcheria, who did everything possible to keep power within the palace and the imperial family rather than the civil ministers and generals. But even she had to negotiate with these other power centres.

The solidarity of the inner establishment was strikingly demonstrated when confronted by the end of an imperial dynasty, when all the old threats of factional coup, military violence and even civil war reared their heads in the struggle to place a new emperor on the throne. Aware of what each stood to lose, palace, bureaucracy, army and, later, church found ways to fight their conflicts behind closed doors and then present an agreed imperial choice to be acclaimed by the senate, the troops, the people and the wider world.

This orderly transmission of imperial power was achieved in the elevation of Marcian in 450, Leo in 457 and Anastasius in 491, all of them dynastic breaks. Through these precedents, buttressed by an increasingly elaborate ceremony of emperor-making, violent coups and civil wars became the exception. Even if a declared rebel succeeded in gaining wide support outside, he still had to cash in his imperial claims in the capital itself, in the face of the central establishment and the city's virtually impregnable defences: if he did not already enjoy powerful allies within the city this was a daunting task.

Thus, an important factor in the durability of the establishment was simply the acknowledged geographical concentration of power and authority in a single capital, Constantinople, which was in every sense what Rome had once been. The emergence of a viable, rival power base was made very difficult, and this, as much as the city's strategic position and fortifications, contributed heavily to the stability and survival of the Eastern state.

Of all the elements in the establishment, stability was most steadfastly provided by the civil bureaucracy, which provided experience, statecraft and continuity. They kept the impersonal, administrative machine functioning even during violent conflicts within the palace, or purges of this or that faction. These senatorial mandarins, in fact, represented a new service aristocracy created by Constantine. Frequently of modest origins, they owed their power and status not to birth or landed wealth, but entirely to government service. Consequently, regardless of

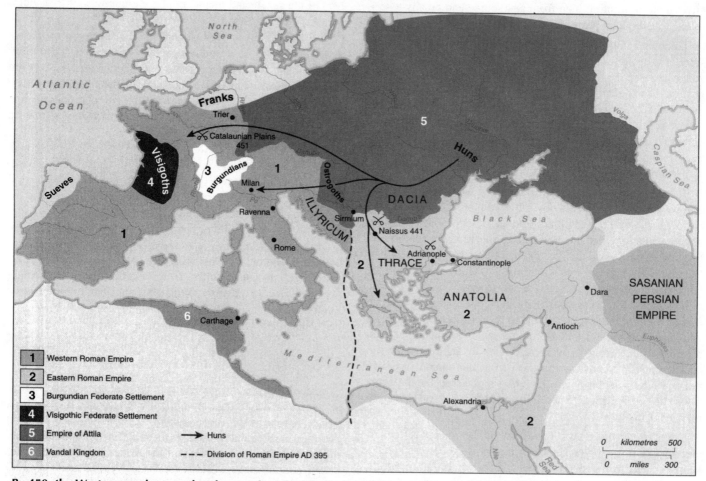

By 450, the Western empire was already a patchwork of barbarian settlements whereas the East retained its integrity.

whether a particular emperor was strong or weak, they took great care to uphold and strengthen the imperial authority itself, since their careers, and hence their prosperity, completely depended on it.

In contrast, the great Western senatorial clans such as the Anicii and Scipiones were only concerned to husband their already huge accumulated family wealth, and treated high state positions as no more than honorific perquisites. Part of the East's undoubtedly greater financial muscle, therefore, was due not just to its inherently greater wealth but also to these mandarins' more honest management of the tax machine, even when it bore on their own aspiring social order.

In the West, the response to the problem of a weak unmilitary emperor was quite different. Real power was concentrated in a military strongman such as Stilicho who ruled on his behalf and enjoyed extraordinary authority, making appointments and issuing laws in the emperor's name. The long reign of the feeble Honorius, the multiple military emergencies and the need to raise and move armies rapidly made this new ruling figure indispensable. After a few years of turmoil the general Constantius stepped into this new position, now vaguely designated 'Patrician' and perhaps better described as military dictator or *generalissimo*. After him came Aetius. Both were patriotic and energetic rulers but had no legally acknowledged position beyond their monopoly of military force, and no regular way of

transferring their power to a successor. Each had to intrigue or fight his way to dominant power, which was destructive and destabilising.

Inevitably they came to depend more on their personal popularity and prestige among the troops, whom they recruited and paid. A gulf steadily grew up between the real power of the warlord with his army, and the symbolic, legal authority with the emperor in his palace. During the invasion of Italy, Stilicho had persuaded Honorius to shift the imperial capital from Milan to the safe refuge of Ravenna, creating a geographical split in addition to the political one.

Constantius achieved a degree of stability in the West, but at enormous cost. Visigoths, Burgundians, Franks, Suevi and Vandals were all settled as federates on large tracts of Gaul and Spain, and were evolving into Germanic kingdoms under only the most nominal Roman overlordship. Constantius and Aetius skillfully exploited their rivalries to maintain some ascendancy. But having relinquished control of so much taxable land and its populations, the regular Roman armies were only one force among many, and no responsible leader could do more than hold the balance, and avoid risking this force if possible.

The Hun menace took on an entirely new dimension with Attila, who had unified them under a single king and subjected all the remaining tribes to Hun rule. His object was not land to settle, but plunder, tribute and glory, and once again the blow fell initially on the East. His hordes ravaged the Balkans three times in the 440s, sacking and ruining many major cities and enslaving their populations. The Roman armies that met him in the field were repeatedly beaten by his cavalry, but he was always deterred by Constantinople whose defences he could not storm. After each invasion he had to be bought off by an increasingly ignominious 'treaty' and larger annual payments, involving heavier taxation of the senatorial classes. In all, the East paid him about nine tons of gold, until the new emperor Marcian finally tore up the treaties and defied him.

Yet here, the two great resources of the East came to the rescue: the impassable fortifications of Constantinople and the enormous taxable wealth of the Asiatic provinces—Anatolia, Syria, Palestine, Egypt. So long as this great land gate was kept shut and so long as these provinces remained secure—meaning peaceful relations with Persia—Attila could always be bought off and much of the Balkan territories temporarily lost without mortal damage to the empire.

Relations with Persia were always a crucial consideration if the empire was to avoid the perils of fighting on two frontiers simultaneously. Unlike other potential enemies, Persia was a centralised, sophisticated state, and both empires were continually involved in a chess game of military and diplomatic manoeuvres which at intervals broke down into open war. In set battle the Romans could usually win, but at quite huge logistical costs. The 1,400-mile frontier zone along the Euphrates was already the most expensive in terms of providing troops and resources. The danger was not so much that Persia would conquer the Roman provinces, as that they would disrupt the whole delicate defensive system of Arab alliances and force the empire to a great commitment of forces, imperilling other frontiers.

But, although Persia tried to take advantage of the empire's difficulties elsewhere, its war aims were limited and it was usually amenable to negotiation. After nearly twenty years of peace, a brief Persian attack in 441 was halted and led to a new treaty involving Roman payments. At the same time, Persia's ambitions were severely checked by pressure from their own northern enemies, the Ephthalite horse peoples, akin to the Huns, who were tacitly encouraged by Constantinople. Whatever martial propaganda they still broadcast to their peoples, the two empires gradually came to accept the advantages of avoiding costly and unrewarding wars, and sought if possible to resolve conflicts by other means. As a result, a mature and structured diplomacy became as important as the military strategy.

Finally, after suffering heavier casualties in battle for diminishing returns of plunder, Attila decided to cut his losses and invade westward. Here Aetius, with all his carefully cultivated barbarian friendships, performed a diplomatic miracle in uniting and commanding the mutually hostile Germanic kingdoms in a great coalition to stop Attila in 451. After a huge and bloody battle on the Catalaunian plains of northern Gaul, Attila was forced for the first time to retreat. The next year he mounted an abortive invasion of Italy. Soon afterwards, he died suddenly in a drunken stupor. Within a short time his always personal and charismatic 'empire' collapsed.

In the West, Aetius was immediately concerned to disperse the more numerous and powerful Germanic armies as quickly as possible. But now that the main barbarian threat seemed removed, he was treacherously murdered by the emperor Valentinian III (425–455) who had long hated him. In revenge, Aetius's partisans assassinated Valentinian shortly afterwards, ending the Theodosian dynasty.

The next *generalissimo* figure, Ricimer, was himself a barbarian and naturally well-qualified to deal with the overwhelmingly barbarian army and allies. He was related both to the Visigoth and Sueve royal houses, and very willing to allow more federate settlements. Ricimer was a leader spanning two worlds. He saw the Roman empire more as a prestigious, unifying symbol than a political reality, and he set up and deposed puppet emperors at will. In the end it was only logical that a barbarian king should step into the ruling role of patrician and *generalissimo*. When that happened there was no need to retain even a figurehead emperor in the West. In 476 the barbarian king Odovacer forced the emperor Romulus Augustulus to abdicate, and sent an embassy to Constantinople declaring that he would henceforth rule as the viceroy of the Eastern emperor. The fiction of a single united Roman empire was still retained.

The East had tried, and partially succeeded, in arranging the fragments of Attila's old empire to its advantage, but it had been forced to accept two large blocs of Ostrogoths, formerly subjects of Attila, as federates in Illyricum (Yugoslavia) and Thrace (Bulgaria-Romania). These were a destabilising element, each too strong to be defeated by a single Roman field army. In the confused reign of Zeno (474–491) all the dangerous elements erupted again: open conflict in the imperial family, civil wars for the throne, rebellion by the Gothic federates. At one point there was fighting within the capital itself. There seemed a real danger that the Ostrogoths would carve out permanent kingdoms for themselves in the way this had happened in the West.

For a time, the central establishment lost control, but they had several strong advantages. There was always a strong core of regular Roman troops to balance the federates, and they continued to be steadily recruited. All the soldiers, Roman or federate, could only be paid from the central treasuries, which were a potent lever in negotiations, as were timely bribes of gold. The Goths also suffered periodic food shortages which the imperial government, with its network of cities and supply depots, naturally exploited. The two Gothic blocs were often in competition and could easily be played off against each other. Their aims were opportunistic and their long-term goals uncertain. One king, Theoderic (471–526), wanted larger, more secure territories for his people, while the other, Strabo, aimed at a top Roman command and a seat at the centre of government.

By the time Zeno had managed to crush or conciliate his other domestic enemies, by adroit and unscrupulous manoeuvring, Strabo was dead and all the Goths followed Theoderic. In 488, with only one king to deal with, Zeno played the masterstroke. Instead of poor and precarious lands in the Balkans, he invited Theoderic to take Italy from Odovacer. Theoderic did so, finally freeing the East of the federate problem.

It was left to the next emperor Anastasius (491–518) to consolidate these gains. Himself a civil bureaucrat who knew the government machinery intimately, he overhauled and improved the entire fiscal system to produce considerably greater sums for the treasury without injuring the mass of taxpayers. With these funds he expanded the armies by raising pay, built new defences, revived and repopulated much of the Balkans, and fought a successful war against Persia, still leaving a healthy surplus. It was with these great resources that Justinian was soon to embark on his ambitious schemes of reconquest.

The East had certain long-term advantages: a strategically placed capital, shorter vulnerable frontiers, a wealthier agricultural base. But it demanded a high order of statecraft to overcome all the external and internal threats of the fifth century. Individually, its leaders were no more skilful than their Western counterparts, but they managed to evolve institutions and practices which applied these skills and perpetuated them. The Constantinople establishment; the constitutional rituals of imperial succession; the integration of the top army commands; the op-position to federate settlements; the centralised pool of administrative, fiscal and diplomatic experience—all these enabled the East to avoid the unravelling process of diminishing control which occurred in the West.

FOR FURTHER READING

A.H.M. Jones, *The Later Roman Empire* (2 vols, Oxford University Press, 1990); J.B. Bury, *History of The Later Roman Empire*, (Dover paperbacks, 1958); R.C. Blockley, *East Roman Foreign Policy* (ARCA, 1992); J.H.W.G. Liebeschuetz, *From Diocletian to the Arab Conquest*, (Oxford University Press, 1990); J.H. W.G. Liebeschuetz, *Barbarians and Bishops: Army, Church and State in the Age of Arcadius and Chrysostom* (Oxford University Press, 1991); C. Mango, *Byzantium. The Empire of New Rome* (London, 1980).

Stephen Williams and Gerard Friell are also the authors of Theodosius: the Empire at Bay *(Batsford, 1994).*

This article first appeared in *History Today*, November 1998, pp. 40-46. © 1998 by History Today, Ltd. Reprinted by permission.

In the Beginning, There Were the HOLY BOOKS

The Bible and the Qur'an both reveal the word of God.
Both speak of prophets, redemption, heaven and hell.
So why the violence? Searching the sacred texts for answers.

By Kenneth L. Woodward

He was a pious family man, a trader from Mecca who regularly retreated into the hills above the city to fast and pray. In his 40th year, while he was praying in a cave on Mount Hira, the angel Gabriel spoke to him, saying, "Muhammad, you are the Messenger of God," and commanded him to "Recite!" Muhammad protested that he could not—after all, he was not gifted like the traditional tribal bards of Arabia. Then, according to this tradition, the angel squeezed him so violently that Muhammad thought he'd die. Again Gabriel ordered him to recite, and from his lips came the first verses of what eventually became the Qur'an, regarded as the eternal words of God himself by some 1.3 billion Muslims around the world.

Until that moment, 13 centuries ago, the Arabs were mostly polytheists, worshiping tribal deities. They had no sacred history linking them to one universal god, like other Middle Eastern peoples. They had no sacred text to live by, like the Bible; no sacred language, as Hebrew is to Jews and Sanskrit is to Hindus. Above all, they had no prophet sent to them by God, as Jews and Christians could boast.

Muhammad and the words that he recited until his death in 632 provided all this and more. Like the Bible, the Qur'an is a book of divine revelation. Between them, these two books define the will of God for more than half the world's population. Over centuries, the Bible fashioned the Hebrew tribes into a nation: Israel. But in just a hundred years, the Qur'an created an entire civilization that at its height stretched from northern Africa and southern Europe in the West to the borders of modern India and China in the East. Even today, in streets as distant from each other as those of Tashkent, Khartoum, Qom and Kuala Lumpur, one can hear from dawn to dusk the constant murmur and chant of the Qur'an in melodious Arabic. Indeed, if there were a gospel according to Muhammad, it would begin with these words: in the beginning was the Book.

But since the events of September 11, the Qur'an and the religion it inspired have been on trial. Is Islam an inherently intolerant faith? Does the Qur'an oblige Muslims to wage jihad—holy war—on those who do not share their beliefs? And who are these "infidels" that the Muslim Scriptures find so odious? After all, Jews and Christians are monotheists, too, and most of their own prophets—Abraham, Moses and Jesus especially—are revered by Muslims through their holy book. Listening to the rants of Osama bin Laden and other radical Islamists, Jews and Christians wonder who really speaks for Islam in these perilous times. What common ground—if any—joins these three "Peoples of the Book," as Muslims call their fellow monotheists? What seeds of reconciliation lie within the Qur'an and the Bible and the traditions that they represent? Does the battle of the books, which has endured for centuries between Muslims and believers in the West, ensure a perpetual clash of civilizations?

The Qur'an does contain sporadic calls to violence, sprinkled throughout the text. Islam implies "peace," as Muslims repeatedly insist. Yet the peace promised by Allah to individuals and societies is possible only to those who follow the "straight path" as outlined in the Qur'an. When Muslims run into opposition, especially of the armed variety, the Qur'an counsels bellicose response. "Fight them [nonbelievers] so that Allah may punish them at your hands, and put them to shame," one Qur'anic verse admonishes. Though few in number, these aggressive verses have fired Muslim zealots in every age.

To read the Qur'an is like entering a stream. At any point one may come upon a command of God, a burst of prayer, a theological pronouncement or a description of the final judgment.

The Bible, too, has its stories of violence in the name of the Lord. The God of the early Biblical books is fierce indeed in his support of the Israelite warriors, drowning enemies in the sea. But these stories do not have the force of divine commands. Nor are they considered God's own eternal words, as Muslims believe Qur'anic verses to be. Moreover, Israeli commandos do not cite the Hebrew prophet Joshua as they go into battle, but Muslim insurgents can readily invoke the example of their Prophet, Muhammad, who was a military commander himself. And while the Crusaders may have fought with the cross on their shields, they did not—could not—cite words from Jesus to justify their slaughters. Even so, compared with the few and much quoted verses that call for jihad against the infidels, the Qur'an places far more emphasis on acts of justice, mercy and compassion.

Indeed, the Qur'an is better appreciated as comprehensive guide for those who would know and do the will of God. Like the Bible, the Qur'an defines rules for prayer and religious rituals. It establishes norms governing marriage and divorce, relations between men and women and the way to raise righteous children. More important, both books trace a common lineage back to Abraham, who was neither Jew nor Christian, and beyond that to Adam himself. Theologically, both books profess faith in a single God (Allah means "The God") who creates and sustains the world. Both call humankind to repentance, obedience and purity of life. Both warn of God's punishment and final judgment of the world. Both imagine a hell and a paradise in the hereafter.

DIVINE AUTHORITY

AS SACRED TEXTS, however, the Bible and the Qur'an could not be more different. To read the Qur'an is like entering a stream. At almost any point one may come upon a command of God, a burst of prayer, a theological pronouncement, the story of an earlier prophet or a description of the final judgment. Because Muhammad's revelations were heard, recited and memorized by his converts, the Qur'an is full of repetitions. None of its 114 suras, or chapters, focuses on a single theme. Each sura takes its title from a single word—The Cow, for example, names the

THE ANNUNCIATION

In the Qur'an and the Bible the angel Gabriel is God's announcer. Through Gabriel, Muhammad hears the revelations that, for Muslims, is the Word of God made book. In the Bible, Gabriel tells the Virgin Mary she will give birth to Jesus who, for Christians, is the Word of God made flesh.

CREATION

Both the Qur'an and the Bible tell the story of Adam and Eve in the Garden of Eden. But for Muslims, as for Jews, their 'original sin' of disobedience is not passed on to humankind, so they don't require salvation through the sacrifice of Jesus on the cross—a central doctrine of Christianity.

THE ASCENSION

In one story extrapolated from a verse in the Qur'an, the Prophet Muhammad ascends to the throne of God, the model for the Sufis' flight of the soul to God. In the Bible, Jesus ascends to the Father after he is resurrected from the dead. For Muhammad, it was inconceivable that Allah would allow one of his prophets to be executed as a criminal.

HOLY PLACES

The Temple Mount is the holiest shrine for Jews. At first Muhammad directed his followers also to face Jerusalem when they prayed. But after the Jews of Medina refused him as their prophet, he directed Muslims to bow in the direction of the Kaaba [Ka´aba] in Mecca, now the holiest shrine in Islam.

PEACE AND WAR

Muhammad was not only a prophet but a military commander who led Muslim armies into battle. Jesus, on the other hand, refused even to defend himself against the Roman soldiers who arrested him in the Garden of Gethsemane after he was betrayed with a kiss by Judas, one of his own disciples. The difference helps explain the contrasting attitudes toward war and violence in the Qur'an and the New Testament.

longest—which appears only in that chapter. When Muhammad's recitations were finally written down (on palm leaves, shoulders of animals, shards of anything that would substitute for paper) and collected after his death, they were organized roughly from the longest to the shortest. Thus there is no chronological organization—this is God speaking, after all, and his words are timeless.

Nonetheless, scholars recognize that the shortest suras were received first, in Muhammad's Meccan period, and the longest in Medina, where he later became a political and military leader of the emerging community of Muslims. As a result, the longer texts take up matters of behavior and organization which are absent in the shorter, more "prophetic" suras that announce the need to submit. ("Muslim" means "submission" to God.) The Qur'an's fluid structure can be confusing, even to Muslims. "That's why one finds in Muslim bookstores such books as 'What the Qur'an says about women' or 'What the Qur'an says about a just society'," observes Jane McAuliffe of Georgetown University, editor of the new Encyclopaedia of the Qur'an.

Like the Bible, the Qur'an asserts its own divine authority. But whereas Jews and Christians regard the Biblical text as the words of divinely inspired human authors, Muslims regard the Qur'an, which means "The Recitation," as the eternal words of Allah himself. Thus, Muhammad is the conduit for God's words, not their composer. Moreover, since Muhammad heard God in Arabic, translations of the Qur'an are considered mere "interpretations" of the language of God's original revelation. "In this very important sense," says Roy Mottahedeh, professor of Middle Eastern history at Harvard, "the Qur'an is *not* the Bible of the Muslims." Rather, he says, it is like the oral Torah first revealed to Moses that was later written down. In gospel terminology, the Qur'an corresponds to Christ himself, as the *logos*, or eternal word of the Father. In short, if Christ is the word made flesh, the Qur'an is the word made book.

Compared with the few and much quoted verses that call for jihad against the 'infidels,' the Qur'an places far more emphasis on acts of justice, mercy and compassion.

The implications of this doctrine are vast—and help to explain the deepest divisions between Muslims and other monotheisms. For Muslims, God is one, indivisible and absolutely transcendent. Because of this, no edition of the Qur'an carries illustrations—even of the Prophet—lest they encourage idolatry *(shirk)*, the worst sin a Muslim can commit. Muslims in the former Persian Empire, however, developed a rich tradition of extra-Qur'anic art depicting episodes in the life of Muhammad, from which the illustrations for this story are taken. But for every Muslim, the presence of Allah can be experienced here and now through the very sounds and syllables of the Arabic Qur'an. Thus, only the original Arabic is used in prayer—even though the vast majority of Muslims do not understand the language. It doesn't matter: the Qur'an was revealed through the Prophet's ears, not his eyes. To hear those same words recited, to take them into yourself through prayer, says Father Patrick Gaffney, an anthropologist specializing in Islam at the University of Notre Dame, "is to experience the presence of God with the same kind of intimacy as Catholics feel when they receive Christ as consecrated bread and wine at mass."

'PEOPLE OF THE BOOK'

WHY THEN, DOES THE Qur'an acknowledge Jews and Christians as fellow "People of the Book," and as such, distinguish them from nonbelievers? Contrary to popular belief, "the Book" in question is not the Bible; it refers to a heavenly text, written by God, of which the Qur'an is the only perfect copy. According to the Qur'an, God mercifully revealed the contents of that book from time to time through the words of previous Biblical prophets and messengers—and also to other obscure figures not mentioned in the Bible. But in every case those who received his revelations—particularly the Jews and Christians—either consciously or inadvertently corrupted the original text, or seriously misinterpreted it. On this view, the Qur'an is not a new version of what is contained in the Bible, but what Jane McAuliffe calls a "rerevelation" that corrects the errors of the Hebrew and Christian Scriptures. Readers of the Bible will find in the Qur'an familiar figures such as Abraham, Moses, David, John the Baptist, Jesus and even the Virgin Mary, who appears much more often than she does in the New Testament, and is the only woman mentioned in the Qur'an by name. But their stories differ radically from those found in the Bible. In the Qur'an all the previous prophets are Muslims.

Abraham (Ibrahim), for example, is recognized as the first Muslim because he chose to surrender to Allah rather than accept the religion of his father, who is not mentioned in the Bible. Neither is the Qur'anic story of how Abraham built the Kaaba [Ka´aba] in Mecca, Islam's holiest shrine. Abraham's importance in the Qur'an is central: just as the Hebrews trace their lineage to Abraham through Isaac, his son by Sarah, the Qur'an traces Arab genealogy—and Muhammad's prophethood—back through Ishmael, a son Abraham had by Hagar.

The Qur'anic Moses (Musa) looks much like his Biblical counterpart. He confronts the pharaoh, works miracles and in the desert ascends the mountain to receive God's commandments. But in the Qur'an there is no mention of the Passover rituals, and among the commandments one of the most important for Jews—keeping the Sabbath—is absent. Obedience to parents is stressed repeatedly, but as in the Qur'anic story of Abraham, disobedience is required when parents are polytheists.

As a prophet rejected by his own people, the Qur'anic Jesus (Isa) looks a lot like Muhammad, who was at first rejected by the people of Mecca. He preaches the word of God, works miracles, is persecuted and—what is new, foretells his successor: Muhammad. But the Qur'an rejects the Christian claim that he is the son of God as blasphemous and dismisses the doctrine of the Trinity as polytheistic. The Crucifixion is mentioned in passing, but according to the Qur'an Jesus mysteriously does not die. Instead, Allah rescues him to heaven from where he will descend in the last days and, like other prophets, be a witness for his community of believers at the Final Judgment.

What Muhammad may have known about the Bible and its prophets and where he got his information is a purely scholarly debate. The Qur'an itself says that Muhammad met a Jewish clan in Medina. He even had his followers bow to Jerusalem when praying until the Jews rejected him as prophet. Some scholars claim that Muhammad had in-laws who were Christian, and they believe he learned his fasting and other ascetic practices from observing desert monks. But Muslims reject any scholarly efforts to link the contents of the Qur'an to the Prophet's human interactions. They cherish the tradition that Muhammad could not read or write as proof that the Qur'an is pure revelation. It is enough for them that Islam is the perfect religion and the Qur'an the perfect text.

That belief has not prevented Muslim tradition from transforming the Qur'an's many obscure passages into powerful myths. By far the most significant is the story developed from one short verse: "Glory be to Him who carried His servant at night from the Holy Mosque to the Further Mosque, the precincts of which we have blessed, that we might show him some of our signs" (sura 17:1). From this Muslims have elaborated the story of Muhammad's mystical nighttime journey from Mecca to Jerusalem, where he addresses an assembly of all previous prophets from Adam to Jesus. Yet another version of this story tells of his subsequent Ascension *(mi'raj)* from Jerusalem

to the throne of Allah, receiving honors along the way from the prophets whom he has superseded. For Sufi mystics, Muhammad's ascension is the paradigmatic story of the soul's flight to God. For many Muslim traditionalists, however, the journey was a physical one. Either way, its geopolitical significance cannot be ignored because the spot where the ascension began is Islam's third holiest shrine: the Dome of the Rock on Jerusalem's Temple Mount.

In Islam's current political conflicts with the West, the major problem is not the Muslims' sacred book but how it is interpreted. Muslims everywhere are plagued by a crippling crisis of authority. The Qur'an envisioned a single Muslim community (the *umma*), but as subsequent history shows, Muslims have never resolved the tension between religious authority and Islamic governments. When Islam was a great medieval civilization, jurists learned in the Qur'an decided how to apply God's words to changed historical circumstances. Their *fatwas* (opinions) settled disputes. But in today's Islamic states, authoritative religious voices do not command widespread respect. Like freewheeling fundamentalists of every religious stripe, any Muslim with an agenda now feels free to cite the Qur'an in his support. Osama bin Laden is only the most dangerous and obvious example.

Bin Laden's Twisted Mission

A bloody misinterpretation of the Qur'an's call to arms

BY CHRISTOPHER DICKEY

WHEN OSAMA BIN Laden proclaimed his "jihad against Crusaders and Jews" in 1998, he knew he was on shaky religious ground. This was his declaration of "holy war" to justify bombing U.S. embassies in Africa a few months later and, eventually, the attacks of September 11. It was his theological license "to kill the Americans and plunder their money wherever and whenever they are found." And it was based on a lie: that Islam itself was under attack by the United States, that "crimes and sins committed by the Americans are a clear declaration of war on God, his messenger and Muslims." The fact that Americans defended Muslims against the likes of Saddam Hussein and Slobodan Milosevic was ignored because, for bin Laden's bloody-minded purposes, it had to be.

Without that lie about American aggression, none of the many verses of the Qur'an that bin Laden cites would justify violence, much less the unholy slaughter of civilians. There are many interpretations of jihad—which means, literally, "effort." Often it describes the personal struggle merely to be a better, more pious Muslim. The empire builders of Islam waged military offensives in the name of jihad as late as the 17th century, and not a few turned their righteous doctrines on each other. But according to Gilles Kepel, author of the forthcoming book "Jihad: The Trail of Political Islam," the defensive holy war that bin Laden claims to fight is the most potent and most dangerous form of all. It is seen by many Muslims, if it is justified, as a personal obligation that supersedes all others, and may ultimately challenge all authority. "It's a two-edged sword,"

says Kepel. "Once you open the gate of defensive jihad, it's very difficult to close it again."

"To those against whom war is made, permission is given to fight," says the 22d chapter of the Qur'an—especially "those who have been expelled from their homes... for no cause except that they say, 'Our Lord is Allah'." Thus in Muslim theology defensive holy war was justified against European Crusaders and conquerors who attacked Muslims in the name of Christ and imposed the Inquisition, with all its horrors. Thus, in more recent times, Afghans could wage their war against the atheistic Soviets with plenty of religious backing. Few if any Muslim scholars will speak out against jihad by Palestinians fighting Israeli occupying troops. But bin Laden, a Saudi, was never persecuted for his faith. The goals he fought for initially were political and personal: to overthrow the Muslim rulers of his own country. And the jihad he declared against the United States, in the eyes of most religious scholars, was never a holy war, it was a blatant fraud.

DECIPHERING MEANINGS

BUT THE QUR'AN HAS ITS moderate interpreters as well. Since September 11, brave voices scattered across the Middle East have condemned the terrorist acts of killing civilians and judged suicide bombing contrary to the teaching of the Qur'an. Returning to the text itself, other scholars have found verses showing that Allah created diverse peoples and cultures for a purpose and therefore intended that the world remain pluralistic in religion as well. "The Qur'an," argues Muslim philosopher Jawat Said of the Al-Azhar Institute in Cairo, "gives support and encouragement to sustain the messengers of reform who face difficult obstacles."

America, too, has a core of immigrant and second-generation Muslim scholars who have experienced firsthand the benefits of democracy, free speech and the Bill of Rights. They think the Qur'an is open to interpretations that can embrace these ideals for Islamic states as well. Islam even has feminists like Azizah Y. al-Hibri of the University of Richmond Law School, who are laying the legal groundwork for women's rights through a careful reconsideration of the Qur'an and its classic commentators.

It is precisely here that the Bible and the Qur'an find their real kinship. As divine revelation, each book says much more than what a literal reading can possibly capture. To say that God is one, as both the Qur'an and the Bible insist, is also to say that God's wisdom is unfathomable. As the Prophet himself insisted, God reveals himself through signs whose meanings need to be deciphered. Here, it would seem, lie the promising seeds of religious reconciliation. Humility, not bravado, is the universal posture of anyone who dares to plumb the mind of God and seek to do his will.

UNIT 5
The Medieval Period

Unit Selections

Key Points to Consider

- Why were the gifts sent to Charlemagne thought to be important in the scheme of international trade?

- Why is King Alfred regarded so highly in English history?

- How is our view of the Vikings changing according to recent investigations?

- Why was Spain to be thought of so highly in the tenth century?

- Who undertook the First Crusade and what did it accomplish?

- Why did the myths about witches arise?

- What do you learn about women in the Middle Ages?

- What was life like for people in England during the fourteenth century?

- Why was the introduction of the Trebuchet important in medieval warfare?

- Why did the Italian governments introduce intramural games?

- What were the effects on medieval civilization as a result of the "Black Death"?

- Where the Knights Templar seen as either "saints or sinners" in medieval Europe?

 **Links: www.dushkin.com/online/**
These sites are annotated in the World Wide Web pages.

EuroDocs: Primary Historical Documents From Western Europe
http://www.lib.byu.edu/~rdh/eurodocs/

Feudalism
http://www.fidnet.com/~weid/feudalism.htm

The Labyrinth: Resources for Medieval Studies
http://www.georgetown.edu/labyrinth/

The World of the Vikings
http://www.worldofthevikings.com

In the aftermath of barbarian invasions, Western civilization faced several important challenges: to assimilate Roman and Germanic people and cultures, to reconcile Christian and pagan views, and to create a new social, political, and economic institution to fill the vacuum left by the fall of the Roman order-in sum, to shape a new unity out of the chaos and diversity of the post-Roman world. The next millennium (550-1500) saw the rise and demise of a distinctive phase of Western experience—medieval civilization.

Medieval culture expressed a uniquely coherent view of life and the world. In theory, medieval society provided a well-ordered and satisfying life. The Church looked after people's souls, the nobility maintained civil order, and a devoted peasantry performed the work of the world. Ideally, as historian Crane Brinton explains, "a beautifully ordered nexus of rights and duties bound each man to each, from the swineherd to emperor and pope."

Of course, medieval society, like our own, fell short of its ideal. Feudal barons warred among themselves. Often the clergy was ignorant and corrupt. Peasants were not always content and passive. And medieval civilization had other shortcomings. During much of the Middle Ages there was little interest in nature and how it worked. While experimentation and observation were not unknown, science (or "natural philosophy") was subordinate to theology, which generally attracted the best minds of the day. An economy based on agriculture and a society based on inherited status had little use for innovation. Aspects of Medieval society are treated in the articles "The Ideal of Unity" and "The Most Perfect Man in History?" The articles "Hero of the Neva and Lake Peipus," and "Saints or Sinners? The Knights Templar in Medieval Europe" explore facets of medieval warfare.

All this is not to suggest that the medieval period was static and sterile. Crusaders, pilgrims, and merchants enlarged Europe's view of the world. And there were noteworthy mechanical innovations: the horse collar, which enabled beasts of burden to pull heavier loads; the stirrup, which altered mounted combat; mechanical clocks, which made possible more exact measurement of time; the compass, which brought the age of exploration closer; and the papermaking process, which made feasible the print revolution, which in turn played key roles in the Reformation and the scientific revolution. The articles "An Iberian Chemistry," and "Doctor, Philosopher, Renaissance Man" discuss the accomplishments made possible by Muslim rule in Spain, while John France's article, "The Capture of Jerusalem" shows how the Crusades began hostilities between the Muslims and Christians. Yet, the military encounter between the two faiths produced cross-cultural influences that contributed to fundamental economic, military, and political changes in the West.

The medieval order broke down in the fourteenth and fifteenth centuries. Plague, wars, and famines produced a demographic catastrophe that severely strained the economic and political systems. Charles Mee's article, "How a Mysterious Disease Laid Low Europe's Masses," explains how the Black Death affected many aspects of medieval life. During this period social discontent took the form of peasant uprisings and urban revolts. Dynastic and fiscal problems destabilized England and France. The Great Schism and the new heresies divided the Church. Emerging capitalism gradually undermined an economy based on land. Yet these crises generated the creative forces that would give birth to the Renaissance and the modern era. The nation-state, the urban way of life, the class structure, and other aspects of modern life existed in embryonic forms in the Middle Ages. It was in medieval Europe that the West prepared itself for its modern role as "chief disturber and principal upsetter of other people's way."

The Ideal of Unity

Russell Chamberlin examines the origins and development of Europe's persistent vision of unity from the birth of the Holy Roman Empire to its fall.

by Russell Chamberlin

'NEITHER HOLY, NOR ROMAN, nor an empire'. Voltaire's gibe about the Holy Roman Empire was literally true but, like all such glib gibes missed the essential point. For a thousand years people believed it existed or thought it ought to exist. For a thousand years, as they tore at each other in fratricidal wars, Europeans nevertheless nursed the idea of a unity that would bind, not destroy, their racial identities. The Treaty of Rome of 1957, which established the European Economic Community, might lack the drama of the events of Christmas Day, 800, but it shared the same dynamic, and the Treaty may yet prove more durable than the crown.

On that day, Karl der Grosse, King of the Franks, King of the Lombards, Patrician of Rome, better known to English and French posterity as Charlemagne, had bent in prayer in the basilica of St Peter's in Rome. He was startled (some said later) when, without warning, Pope Leo III advanced and placed a circlet of gold on his head. The congregation, in a well-rehearsed chorus, acclaimed him as Roman law prescribed, 'To Carolus Augustus, crowned by God, mighty and pacific emperor, be life and victory'.

The giant silver-haired Frank rose to his feet, towering above the slighter-built Latins and, according to his biographer, Einhard, protested—just a little too much, in the view of posterity. His counsellor, the Englishman Alcuin, who had wide contacts in Rome, must have been well aware of the tide moving in Rome and had surely informed his master of the plans to revive the Roman empire with him at its head. Indeed, after the acclamation the rituals of coronation went smoothly, suggesting that all had been prepared long beforehand. And whatever his private thoughts, the new Emperor voluntarily took part in the ceremonies that followed.

Whoever stage-managed the event in St Peter's had done his work well by arranging that 'acclamation' by the Roman people and clergy. Even in the most dictatorial and tyrannical days of the classical empire the emperor was in theory chosen—acclaimed—by the army and the people, and the idea that the Roman empire was a *res publica* had never been abandoned, even when it had become a formality.

Charlemagne's protests were diplomatic and political: he was objecting to the time and manner of Leo's act and its heavy symbolism. Moreover, he realised that the man who bestowed a crown could take it back. Charlemagne was having none of that. When, eleven years later, he made his last surviving son Louis co-emperor it was he who, personally, placed the crown on the young man's head. Centuries later, Napoleon took the hint and, in making himself 'emperor' of the French, took care to crown himself.

There was another reason for Charlemagne to protest: Leo's action was illegal. There could be only one *imperator* on earth and he (or, to be exact, she, Irene) was already reigning in Constantinople. Strictly speaking, the Roman Empire—the empire of Augustus, Nero, Virgil and Tacitus—endured until 1453 when the last true Roman emperor fell beneath Turkish swords. Leo's act began the long degradation of the once awesome title, so that, in due course, there would emerge an 'emperor' of Austria, an 'emperor' of Mexico, of Haiti, and, ultimate absurdity, the British style, 'king-emperor', adopted after the acquisition of the Indian Empire even as, ironically, the mighty empire itself would dwindle down to a 'loose federation of German princes under the presidency of the House of Habsburg'.

The Byzantines derided the coronation of Charlemagne. To them he was simply another barbarian general with ideas above his station. Indeed, he took care never to style himself *Imperator Romanorum*. His jurists, dredging through the detritus of empire, came up with a title which met with his approval: *Romanum gubernas imperium* 'Governing the Roman Empire'. The resounding title of this first of the post-classical Western Emperors was 'Charles, Most Serene Augustus, crowned by God, great and merciful Emperor, governing the Roman empire and by the mercy of God, King of the Lombards and the Franks'.

Although illegal, the coronation and acclamation were perhaps inevitable. In the Western world, the rule of law had broken down. Alcuin, a stickler for law and conventions, gave his opinion:

Upon you alone reposes the whole salvation of the Churches of Christ. You are the avenger of crime, the guide of the wanderers, the comforter of the mourners, the exaltation of the righteous.

A thousand years later, James Bryce, the great historian of the Holy Roman Empire, agreed that a vacuum had been created in Europe by the rise of Byzantium. The coronation of Charlemagne 'was the revolt of the ancient Western capital against a daughter who had become a mistress, an exercise of the sacred right of insurrection justified by the weakness and wickedness of the Byzantine'. That wickedness had plumbed new depths a few years earlier when the reigning emperor Constantine had been blinded and, deposed by his mother who claimed to reign as 'emperor': to Western apologists, the Byzantine throne was vacant and the Frankish monarch was merely taking up the sceptre laid down by the Latin Caesars. One of the great myths of history is the portrayal of the 'Fall of the Roman Empire' as a Hollywood-type scenario in which shaggy, skin-clad Germanic 'barbarians' hurl themselves upon elegant, toga-clad 'Romans', raping, murdering, destroying what they could not eat, wear or carry off. In reality the 'barbarians' were inferior only in culture, not intelligence. They could, and did, respond to the majesty of the Empire. For a people without written records, that Empire must have seemed, quite literally, eternal: an almost supernatural structure around which the world always had and always would revolve. But they realised that behind this outward show was a hugely complex human system that had brought stability out of chaos. In the early 5th century, the Visigothic chieftain, Arhalhauf, spoke for most of his fellow barbarians:

It was at first my wish to destroy the Roman name and erect in its place a Gothic empire. But when experience taught me that the untameable barbarism of the Goths would not suffer them to live under the sway of law I chose the glory of renewing and maintaining by Gothic strength the fame of Rome.

The Franks themselves had entered history fighting alongside the Roman army at one of its last great battles, that of Chalons in 451 AD when it turned back the invasion of Attila the Hun. The captain of the Frankish host was Merovech,

who founded the first Frankish dynasty, the Merovings, but they were gradually shouldered aside by their own Mayors of the Palace. The dynasty ended bloodlessly in 751, when Charlemagne's father Pippin appealed to Rome, asking, in effect, who should wear the crown: he who was the puppet or he who truly ruled? Pope Zarachias came down in Pippin's favour. He thus began that link between pope and Germanic king that was to dominate the notion of the Western Christian empire for centuries.

Meanwhile, a debt had been contracted and four years later the papacy sent Pippin the bill. In January 754 Pope Stephen and a small entourage braved the Alps in mid-winter to throw himself at the feet of Pippin and plead for help against Aistulf, King of the Lombards, who had dared to seize the property of the Church. Pippin avoided the tricky business of precedence between pope and monarch by sending his fourteen-year-old son to escort Stephen to the palace, thus providing posterity with its first glimpse of the future Charlemagne.

The historiography of Charlemagne is tantalising. Later, he had his own biographer, in his devoted secretary and architect Einhard. But though Einhard declared he would record nothing through hearsay, he also glossed over facts unfavourable to his hero. The surviving evidence of the development of the relationship between the papal and Frankish courts is one-sided, for while all the popes' letters survived in the Frankish archives, the letters from Pippin and his sons have disappeared from the Vatican, probably looted on the orders of Napoleon.

After Charlemagne's debut, little is heard of him directly until the death of his father in 768. He emerged on the European stage with his capture of the Lombard capital of Pavia in 774, thereby acquiring the Iron Crown of the Lombards and establishing the Frankish control beyond the Alps. The young king began to lay the foundations of what was to become an imperial regime and which, eventually, would provide a blueprint for Europe for centuries.

Distance and communication were the greatest problems he faced, as for all medieval monarchs. He tackled these by establishing *missi domini*, trusted counsellors with delegated powers who penetrated every part of his enormous realm, which ran from the Elbe to the Tiber, conveying his will in documents known as 'capitularies'. These provide a means for

historians to follow the thought processes by which he governed his expanding realm. Named after the articles or capitula into which they were divided, each was nominally concerned with a specific subject but tended to be wide-ranging, as though the King were saying, 'Oh, yes that reminds me ...'. Nothing was too small: the provision of a dowry for a young girl; the number and type of tools to be kept in a manor. Nothing was too large: the composition of the Host in the mass; the conduct of priests.

The deeply religious Charlemagne, through his relationship with a succession of six popes, strove to advance the ideal of a theocratic state governed by a priest and a king in harmony. But there was no doubt as to which he considered the dominant partner. When Pope Leo III announced that a vial of the Precious Blood had been found in Mantua the sceptical King ordered an enquiry. Nothing more was heard of the miraculous substance. His restless, questing, creative mind stimulated the so-called Carolingian renaissance, that sudden flowering of learning which was doomed to disappear after his death. But it left its permanent mark, in the form of the Carolingian miniscule script, which replaced the ugly, spiky Merovingian script, and was adopted by the humanist Poggio Bracciolini in the fifteenth century and through him became the model for all fonts of print.

The King's transmutation into Emperor made little personal difference to him. He did not fall into the trap of trying to pass himself off as a Roman and in so doing losing contact with his roots. Only twice did he wear the robes of the Patrician, both times by direct request of the pope. He dressed and acted in a manner indistinguishable from his subjects. He took literally the precept 'where the emperor is, there is Rome' and his beloved city of Aachen became the Rome of the North.

Charlemagne's imprint on Aachen remains evident over a thousand years later. The city's *rathaus* is built on the foundations of his palace, making it the world's longest occupied seat of administration. Even more astonishing is his chapel, designed by Einhard on the basis of the mystic octagon. Nothing has changed in its interior. The Emperor Frederick Barbarossa (r.1152-90) provided an immense candelabra to celebrate Charlemagne's canonisation in 1165: the Emperor Henry II (r. 1002-24) provided the golden front of the altar, but nothing else has been added. The mezzanine gallery, on which the throne is placed, is approached by a flight of stairs which could be in a modest town church. The throne itself, composed of plain slabs of stone, is unchanged; Thirty emperors have been crowned in it: each resisted the temptation to add his symbols to its simple expression of majesty.

With the death of Charlemagne in 814, cracks in the state opened up in the Empire, as warlords struggled for dominance. Yet the memory continued of that compact made on Christmas Day 800, and those boasting Carolingian blood, no matter how remote or illegitimate, advanced their claims over the rest. But without effect. It seemed that the Empire was at an end before it had started.

It was revived only by bizarre events in Rome in the mid-tenth century. By this time, Rome was on the edge of collapse. The aqueducts had long since failed, forcing the population, now shrunk to less than 20,000, to huddle in the unhealthy lower areas. Bandit families holed up in the once-great buildings, fighting each other and preying on the populace. The Donation of Constantine, an eighth-century forgery according to which the first Christian Emperor had supposedly granted the Church vast territories in central Italy, had turned the papacy into a territorial monarchy, to be fought for as any other secular prize. The papacy itself was in a state of grotesque degradation, with popes murdering or being murdered, placed on the throne by their paramours, hurled off it by their rivals. Two extraordinary women ruled both the city and the papacy, Theodora and her daughter Marozia, the probable model for the later legend of Pope Joan. The sober papal historian, Cardinal Baronius, writing in the sixteenth century, labelled this period the 'Pornocracy'. In 961 the Apostolic throne was occupied by Marozia's grandson, a dissolute twenty-year-old called John XII. Threatened by a Lombard warlord, Berengar, he summoned a Germanic monarch, the Saxon Otto I, to his aid, promising that crown of empire which—it was now believed—only a pope could bestow.

Like Charlemagne before his own imperial coronation, Otto was already a figure of European stature. At Lechfeld (955) near Augsburg, his army had destroyed an immense army of Magyars, true barbarians as murderous as the Huns. It was claimed that his warriors hailed him as *imperator* after the battle: inherently unlikely but testament to how he was seen.

Otto came at John's summons but he had no illusions about the fickle, violent Romans. He instructed his sword-bearer, Ansfried:

> When I kneel today at the grave of the Apostle, stand behind me with the sword. I know only too well what my ancestors have experienced from these faithless Romans.

But all passed smoothly. John listened contritely to the lecture on morals by the pious Saxon, and made specious promises. Yet the moment Otto withdrew from Rome to commence the campaign against Berengar, John offered the crown of empire—to Berengar. That failing, he peddled it round, with no takers. It is difficult to interpret John's lunatic actions. It is possible that he wanted to show that he could make and unmake an emperor at will. It is possible that he was mentally unbalanced. Even his *curia* revolted. Otto convened a synod to which the pope was summoned to account for himself. John dashed off a contemptuous response ignoring the emperor: 'To all the bishops. We hear that you wish to make another pope. If you do, I excommunicate you by almighty God and you have no power to ordain no one or celebrate mass. Ponderously humorous, Otto urged him to improve his morals and his grammar: 'We thought that two negatives made a positive' but followed this with a threat: unless the pope presented himself, he would be deposed. This too was ignored. At the synod a catalogue of John's crimes was presented, ranging from rape to sacrilege.

On December 1st, Pope John XII was formally deposed and a nominee of Otto's took his place. John ignored this too. In Otto's absence he returned to Rome and took bloody revenge on those who had testified against him and who had remained in the city. How the matter might have ended, with a Roman-born pope calling on the support of a Roman mob, is difficult to speculate—but a cuckold caught the Holy Father *in flagrante* and, enraged, cudgelled him to death.

The blows of the cudgel might have ended the theological debate but it did nothing to resolve the secular one. The Romans had seen their bishop, their prince, deposed by a German; and they rose in revolt. The papal crown was the symbol of Roman sovereignty and, to gain control of that symbol, emperor and city were now prepared to destroy each other and themselves. Otto subjected

Rome to a terrible vengeance; but it rose again. Again he smashed it down. Again it rose. And again. The Emperor died and his son Otto II continued to pour out German blood and wealth seeking the double goal of a purified papacy and a Roman crown.

With the approach of the millennium, there was a pause in the cycle of violence. The pope was the pious and learned Sylvester, reputed to be a magician, so versed was he in the sciences. The emperor was his pupil, the youthful Otto III (r. 983-1002) who, with his pope, swore to restore the splendours of the Roman empire infused with Christian belief. He built himself a palace on the Aventine, dressed in the toga, cast a medal with the legend 'Otto Imperator Augustus' and on the reverse the proud claim *Renovatio Imperii Romanorum*. But the Romans rose against him, drove him and his pope out of the city, and reverted to murderous anarchy. He died outside the city in January 1002, not quite twenty-two years of age. Sylvester survived his brilliant but erratic protégé by barely sixteen months. His epitaph summed up the sorrow that afflicted all thoughtful men at the ending of a splendid vision:

> The world, on the brink of triumph, its peace now departed, grew contorted in grief and the reeling Church forgot her rest.

The failure of Otto III and Sylvester marked the effective end of the medieval dream of a single state in which an emperor ruled over the bodies of all Christian men, and a pope over their souls. At Canossa in 1077 Pope Gregory VII avenged the deposition of John XII when the Emperor Henry IV was forced to beg for forgiveness in the snow. In 1300 Pope Boniface VIII displayed himself to pilgrims robed in imperial trappings, calling out 'I, I am the emperor'. But he, too, was eventually destroyed.

Looking down through the long perspective of the Holy Roman Empire is a melancholy experience of watching the dream fall apart. The Italians fought endless civic wars under the banner of Guelph or Ghibelline, Pope or Empire, but they were little more than pretexts for strife. Yet as the actual power of the emperor waned, the ideal of the universal monarch increased so that the imperial nadir coincided with its most able apologia, Dante's *De Monarchia*. Henry VII (r. 1312-13) came in 1310 in answer to

Dante's summons to resolve the conflict, but became trapped in the complexities of Italian politics and died shamefully.

Dante's call for the risen majesty of empire became its requiem. Nevertheless, in 1354 a Germanic emperor was again summoned to Italy to take the crown and bring peace to a tortured land—but where Henry had come in majesty, the progress of his son Charles IV 'was more as a merchant going to Mass than an emperor going to his throne', as the Florentine merchant Villani observed sardonically. Petrarch, who had implored him to come, joined Villani in condemning him. 'Emperor of the Romans but in name, thou art in truth no more than the king of Bohemia'. But Petrarch was looking back to a mythical Golden Age, while Charles accepted he was living in an Age of Iron.

Shrugging off the criticism he returned home and promulgated his Golden Bull, which effectively turned the crown of empire into a German crown.

The last word is perhaps best left to the sardonic Edward Gibbon:

> It is the duty of a patriot to prefer and promote the exclusive interest and glory of his native country; but a philosopher may be permitted to enlarge his views and to consider Europe as one great Republic.

FOR FURTHER READING

In 1965, Aachen put on an exhibition, embodied in four volumes edited by Wolfgang Braunfells, *Karl der Grosse: Lebenswerk und Nachleben*, D.A. Bullough, *Age of Charlemagne* (1965); James Bryce, *The Holy Roman Empire*. (8th ed. 1887); Russell Chamberlin, *Charlemagne, Emperor of the Western World*. (2nd ed. 2003); F.L. Ganshof, *Frankish Insitutions under Charlemagne*: trans S. Bruce and Mary Lyon. (1968); Gregorovius, Ferdinand *History of the City of Rome in the Middle Ages*, trans. Annie Hamilton. (1912); Thomas Hodgkin, *Italy and her Invaders* (1899); Friedrich Heer, *The Holy Roman Empire* (Phoenix, 2003); Horace K. Mann, *The Lives of the Popes in the Early Middle Ages* (1902-32); W Ullman, *Medieval Papalism* (1949).

RUSSELL CHAMBERLIN is the author of some thirty books on European travel and history. He has been awarded an honorary degree by the University of Surrey.

The Most Perfect Man in History?

Barbara Yorke considers the reputation of King Alfred the Great—and the enduring cult around his life and legend.

King Alfred of Wessex (r.871–99) is probably the best known of all Anglo-Saxon rulers, even if the first thing to come into many people's minds in connection with him is something to do with burnt confectionery. This year sees the 1100th anniversary of his death on October 26th, 899, at the age of about fifty. The occasion is being marked with conferences and exhibitions in Winchester, Southampton and London, but the scale of celebrations will be modest compared with those which commemorated his millenary, and culminated in the unveiling by Lord Rosebery of his statue in Winchester.

Alfred's reputation still stands high with historians, though few would now want to follow Edward Freeman in claiming him as 'the most perfect character in history' (*The History of the Nor-*

man Conquest of England, 5 volumes, 1867–79). Alfred is someone who has had greatness thrust upon him. How and why did he acquire his glowing reputation, and how does it stand up today?

There can be no doubt that Alfred's reign was significant, both for the direction of the country's development and for the fortunes of his descendants. After the kingdoms of Northumbria, East Anglia and Mercia had fallen to the Vikings, Wessex under Alfred was the only surviving Anglo-Saxon province. Alfred nearly succumbed to the Vikings as well, but kept his nerve and won a decisive victory at the battle of Edington in 879. Further Viking threats were kept at bay by a reorganisation of military service and particularly through the ringing of Wessex by a regular system of garrisoned fortresses. At the same time Alfred

promoted himself as the defender of all Christian Anglo-Saxons against the pagan Viking threat and began the liberation of neighbouring areas from Viking control. He thus paved the way for the future unity of England, which was brought to fruition under his son and grandsons, who conquered the remaining areas held by the Vikings in the east and north, so that by the mid-tenth century the England we are familiar with was ruled as one country for the first time.

His preservation from the Vikings and unexpected succession as king after the death of four older brothers, seem to have given Alfred a sense that he had been specially destined for high office. With the help of advisers from other areas of England, Wales and Francia, Alfred studied, and even translated from

Latin into Old English, certain works that were regarded at the time as providing models of ideal Christian kingship and 'most necessary for all men to know'.

Alfred tried to put these principles into practice, for instance, in the production of his law-code. He became convinced that those in authority in church or state could not act justly or effectively without the 'wisdom' acquired through study, and set up schools to ensure that future generations of priests and secular administrators would be better trained, as well as encouraging the nobles at his court to emulate his own example in reading and study. Alfred also had the foresight to commission his biography from Bishop Asser of Wales. Asser presented Alfred as the embodiment of the ideal, but practical, Christian ruler. Alfred was the 'truthteller', a brave, resourceful, pious man, who was generous to the church and anxious to rule his people justly. One could say that Asser accentuated the positive, and ignored those elements of ruthless, dictatorial behaviour which any king needed to survive in ninth-century *realpolitik*. Alfred and Asser did such a good job that when later generations looked back at his reign through their works they saw only a ruler apparently more perfect than any before or after. Alfred is often thought to have provided his own epitaph in this passage from his translation of the *Consolation of Philosophy* by Boethius:

I desired to live worthily as long as
I lived, and to leave after my life,
to the men who should come after
me, the memory of me in good
works.

Alfred, particularly as presented by Asser, may have had something of a saint in him, but he was never canonised and this put him at something of a disadvantage in the later medieval world. The Normans and their successors were certainly interested in presenting themselves as the legitimate heirs of their Anglo-Saxon predecessors, but favoured the recognised royal saints, especially Edmund of the East Angles, killed by the Danish army which Alfred defeated, and Edward the Confessor, the last ruler of

the old West Saxon dynasty. St Edmund and St Edward can be seen supporting Richard II on the Wilton diptych, and members of the later medieval royal houses were named after them. Nor were Alfred's heroic defeats of the pagan Vikings enough to make him the favoured military hero of the post-Conquest period. None of the Anglo-Saxon rulers qualified for this role. After Geoffrey of Monmouth's successful promotion, the British Arthur was preferred—a man whose reputation was not constrained by inconvenient facts, and who proved extremely adaptable to changing literary conventions. However, Alfred was lauded by Anglo-Norman historians, like William of Malmesbury, Gaimar and Matthew Paris, and their presentations, and occasional embellishments, of his achievements would be picked up by later writers. Alfred's well-attested interest in learning made him the obvious choice to be retrospectively chosen as the founder of Oxford University when that institution felt the need to establish its historical credentials in the fourteenth century.

Alfred's lack of a saintly epithet, a disadvantage in the high Middle Ages, was the salvation of his reputation in a post-Reformation world. As a pious king with an interest in promoting the use of English, Alfred was an ideal figurehead for the emerging English Protestant church. The works he had commissioned or translated were interpreted as evidence for the pure Anglo-Saxon church, before it had become tainted by the false Romanism introduced by the Normans. With a bit of selective editing, Anglo-Saxon ecclesiastical provision came to bear an uncanny resemblance to Elizabethan Anglicanism. Archbishop Matthew Parker did an important service to Alfred's reputation by publishing an edition of Asser's *Life of Alfred* in 1574, even if he could not resist adding the story of the burnt cakes which came from a separate, later, Anglo-Saxon source. Perhaps even more significant for getting Alfred's reputation widely known was the enthusiastic notice of him in John Foxe's *Book of Martyrs* (1570 edition), where material derived from sources of Alfred's own time was mixed with stories with a later currency, such as

his visit to the Danish camp as a minstrel which was first recorded in a post-Conquest account. It was also writers of the sixteenth century who promoted the designation of Alfred as 'the Great', an epithet that had never been applied to him in the Anglo-Saxon period.

Comparable claims of the contribution of the Anglo-Saxons to English life were used to support radical political change in the seventeenth century, when it was argued, for instance, that the right of all freemen to vote for representatives in Parliament was a lost Anglo-Saxon liberty. The relative abundance of sources from Alfred's reign, including his surviving law-code and Asser's description of his interest in law and administration, naturally meant that attention was drawn to him by those searching for an ancient constitution to serve contemporary needs. Alfred himself was an unlikely champion for the more radical movements, and was more readily adopted by those who wanted to show Stuart, and eventually Hanoverian, rulers, how they could become successful constitutional monarchs by emulating their most famous Anglo-Saxon ancestor. Robert Powell, in his *Life of Alfred*, published in 1634, attempted to draw parallels between the reigns of Alfred and Charles I, something which often called for considerable ingenuity, and his hope that Charles would share the same respect for English law as that apparently shown by Alfred proved misplaced. Rather more impressive as a work of scholarship was Sir John Spelman's *Life of King Alfred*, which drew upon an extensive range of primary material and itself became a source for later biographers. The work was dedicated to the future Charles II when Prince of Wales, and was completed during the Civil War in 1642, in the royalist camp at Oxford. Spelman was to die the following year of camp fever, and publication of the biography was delayed until more propitious times. In fact, any attempts to interest Stuart monarchs in their Saxon forebears had only a limited success. The Stuarts' preferred cultural reference points were from the classical world rather than the history of their own islands.

The common Saxon heritage of the Hanoverians and the Anglo-Saxons provided more fertile ground for the promotion of a cult of King Alfred. His first aristocratic and royal backers came from the circle which gathered around Frederick, Prince of Wales (1707–51), the eldest son of George II, and was united by the opposition of its members to the prime minister Robert Walpole. Walpole's opponents called themselves 'the Patriots', and Alfred was the first 'Patriot King', who had saved his country from tyranny, as it was devoutly hoped Frederick himself would do when he succeeded his father. A number of literary works centred upon Alfred were dedicated to the prince. Sir Richard Blackmore's *Alfred: an Epick Poem in Twelve Books* (1723) enlivened the conventional accounts of Alfred's reign with an extensive description of his imaginary travels in Europe and Africa, in which were concealed many heavy-handed compliments to Prince Frederick. Of much more lasting worth was Thomas Arne's masque *Alfred*, which was first performed in 1740 at the prince's country seat of Cliveden. The main text was provided by two authors already active in Frederick's cause, James Thomson and David Mallett, but included an ode by Viscount Bolingbroke, one of the leaders of the opposition to Walpole who had defined their political philosophy in his essay 'The Idea of a Patriot King' (1738). A visual representation of this political manifesto was provided in Lord Cobham's pleasure grounds at Stowe. Alfred's bust was included alongside those of other Whig heroes in 'The Temple of British Worthies' completed in 1734–35 by William Kent. Alfred is described as 'the mildest, justest, most beneficent of kings' who 'crush'd corruption, guarded liberty, and was the founder of the English constitution', in pointed reference to qualities which George II was felt to lack. Alfred's bust was placed next to that of the Black Prince, a Prince of Wales whose noble qualities were perceived as having been inherited by Frederick, particularly if he followed the example of King Alfred rather than that of his father.

The Stowe landscape gardens also contain a Gothic Temple, in which 'Gothic' should be understood as ancient Germanic. The building was dedicated 'to the Liberty of our Ancestors', and was surrounded by statues of Germanic deities (albeit in Classical pose), while the ceiling of the dome was decorated with the arms of the earls of Mercia from whom Lord Cobham claimed descent. This new interest in the Germanic past began to trickle down to other sectors of society. Those who could not afford to erect their own monuments to Alfred's greatness might nevertheless find remembrances of him in the Wessex landscape. In 1738, the antiquarian Francis Wise, hoping to improve his promotion prospects at the University of Oxford, produced a pamphlet 'concerning some antiquities in Berkshire' in which he argued that the White Horse of Uffington had been cut to commemorate Alfred's victory over the Vikings at the battle of Ashdown, and that all other visible antiquities nearby had some connection with the campaign. His claims were entirely spurious, but helped to publicise the idea that Alfred's influence permeated the very fabric of the country. Those who could not have a Saxon memorial in their grounds or in the nearby countryside could at least own a print of the new genre of History painting. Alfredian topics, especially 'Alfred in the neatherd's cottage' (the cake-burning episode), were among those frequently reproduced.

Alfred at Stowe was also remembered as one 'who drove out the Danes, secur'd the seas', and his role as defender of the country and supposed founder of the British navy ensured him increasing fame as the country found itself embroiled in frequent foreign wars as the reign of Frederick's son, George III, progressed. A series of patriotic Alfred plays, opera and ballets were performed, particularly during the French Wars (1793–1815). More often than not they ended with the rousing anthem which had closed Arne's *Alfred*, 'Rule Britannia', which became increasingly popular as an expression of loyalty to the crown under the threat of foreign attack. It was from this period that 'Alfred' became favoured as a Christian name at all levels of society.

As in other European countries, a new national pride in nineteenth-century England had an important historical dimension, and an accompanying cult of the heroes who had made later success possible. The English, it was believed, could trace language and constitutional continuity back to the fifth century when they had defeated the effete Romans, and it became increasingly felt that other, positive, facets of 'the national character' could be traced back this far as well. These characteristics were felt to have made those of Anglo-Saxon descent uniquely programmed for success, and to rule other less fortunately endowed peoples, and the best of them were represented by King Alfred himself. Alfred was fast being rediscovered as 'the most perfect character in history', and alongside his defence of constitutional liberties, his country and true religion, was added renewed admiration for his Christian morality and sense of duty.

Anglo-Saxonism, and the accompanying Alfredism, could be found on both sides of the Atlantic. Thomas Jefferson had ingeniously argued that, as the Anglo-Saxons who had settled in Britain had ruled themselves independently from their Continental homelands, so the English settlers of America should also be allowed their independence. He believed both countries shared an Anglo-Saxon heritage, and proposed a local government for Virginia based on a division into hundreds, an Anglo-Saxon institution widely believed then to have been instituted by Alfred. A less attractive side of this fascination with Anglo-Saxon roots was that it helped foster a belief in racial superiority, as celebrated in a shortlived periodical called *The Anglo-Saxon* (1849–50), which aimed to demonstrate how 'the whole earth may be called the Fatherland of the Anglo-Saxon. He is a native of every clime—a messenger of heaven to every corner of this Planet.'

One of the chief supporters of *The Anglo-Saxon*, who wrote large segments of it if no other copy was available, was Martin Tupper, the author of several volumes of popular, highly sentimental and moralistic verses. Alfred was one of Tupper's particular heroes, largely because he felt many of the King's writings anticipated his own, and it was through his impetus that the millenary of Alfred's birth at Wantage was celebrated in 1849, one of the earliest of all such jubilees.

The event was not the success for which Tupper had hoped, largely because he left arrangements rather late in the day and had no influential backers. Many of the details were still not fixed on the eve of the event to the indignation of the few local gentry inveigled into attending, but the event still managed to attract crowds estimated at 8,000–10,000 who enjoyed traditional games and an oxroast, as well as Tupper's specially composed Jubilee song:

Anglo-Saxons!—in love are we met To honour a name we can never forget! Father, and Founder, and King of a race That reigns and rejoices in every place, Root of a tree that o'ershadows the earth First of a Family blest from his birth Blest in this stem of their strength and their state Alfred the Wise, and the Good, and the Great!

During the reign of Victoria, who gave birth to the first Prince Alfred since the Anglo-Saxon period (b.1844), King Alfred was accepted as founder of the nation and its essential institutions to such an extent that one commentator was moved to complain 'it is surely a mistake to make Alfred, as some folks seem to do, into a kind of ninth-century incarnation of a combined School Board and County Council'. Alfred was no longer a mirror for princes, but an exemplar for people at all levels of society and, above all, for children. Charles Dickens's *A Child's History of England* (1851–53) can stand for many such works where Alfred was used to demonstrate the best of the English character:

The noble king... in his single person, possessed all the Saxon virtues. Whom misfortune could not subdue, whom prosperity could not spoil, whose perseverance, nothing could shake. Who was hopeful in defeat, and generous in success. Who loved justice, freedom, truth and knowledge.

So much had Alfred become the epitome of the ideal Victorian that Walter Besant, in a lecture on Alfred in 1897, thought it entirely appropriate to apply to him verse that Alfred, Lord Tennyson had written to commemorate Prince Albert.

Alfred was no longer the totem of one political party. In 1877 Robert Loyd-Lindsay, Conservative MP for Berkshire and a perfect exemplar of the paternal landlord of Disraeli's 'Young England' movement, provided Wantage with the statue that Tupper had hoped to raise in 1849, but for which he had failed to get funds. Wantage also got the grand occasion it had missed then as Edward, Prince of Wales, to whom Lindsay had once been an equerry, unveiled the statue carved by Count Gleichen, one of the Prince's German cousins. In 1901, the year of Queen Victoria's death, there were even greater celebrations to commemorate the millenary of that of Alfred. Problems with the calculation of Anglo-Saxon dates meant it was widely believed then that Alfred had died in 901, rather than 899, which is now recognised as the true date of his death, but at the time it seemed particularly apposite to many that the great Queen and her illustrious forebear had died a thousand years apart. On the surface the Alfred millenary appeared to fulfil its aim, as advertised in the National Committee's prospectus, of being 'a National Commemoration of the king to whom this Empire owes so much'. The procession through the heart of Winchester to the site of Hamo Thornycroft's giant statue of the King, included representatives of Learned Societies and Universities 'from all lands where the English speaking-race predominate' (needless to say, they were all white males) and members of the different armed forces. Alfred was further commemorated in the same year by the launching of a new Dreadnought, the HMS *King Alfred*.

But in 1901 Britain was embroiled in the Boer War, and the priority was the reality of the present rather than an imagined past. The National Committee did not raise nearly as much money as it had expected and had to abandon many of its ambitious plans, including one for a Museum of Early English History. Many were worried at the direction Britain's imperial policy was taking. Charles Stubbs, Dean of Ely, took advantage of the millenary year to suggest that Alfred's standards were not only in advance of his own age, but in advance of those of many statesman of the present day, especially in their conduct of the Boer War, which had been prompted by 'insolence of pride ... by passion of vengeance... by lust of gold'. But there was also a more positive side to the celebrations when Alfred was used, as he had been in the past, as a cloak for the introduction of change in society. It was not by chance that the statue was unveiled by the Liberal leader Lord Rosebery, for the former Whig support for British Worthies had never completely died away, and Liberals were prominent in the many commemorations of the latter part of the nineteenth century. It was a row over the statue of Oliver Cromwell, commissioned in 1895 by Rosebery from Thornycroft for the House of Commons, that precipitated the former's resignation as Prime Minister. The most active members of the National Committee were leading Liberals and others, like the positivist Frederic Harrison and litterateur Walter Besant, who were associated with them in the promotion of Working Mens' Colleges or the London County Council, formed in 1888 with Lord Rosebery as its first Chairman. Most active of all in the promotion of Alfred was the secretary of the National Committee and mayor of Winchester, Alfred Bowker, who used the millenary as an opportunity to develop the profile and scope of the Corporation of Winchester by, for instance, purchasing the site of Alfred's final resting-place at Hyde Abbey with adjoining land that could be used for public recreation (as it still is today).

Lord Rosebery commented that the statue he was to unveil in Winchester

can only be an effigy of the imagination, and so the Alfred we reverence may well be an idealised figure.... we have draped round his form... all the highest attributes of manhood and kingship.

Alfred, though no doubt gratified by his posthumous fame, would have trouble recognising himself in some of his later manifestations, and would find it difficult to comprehend, let alone approve, some of the constitutional developments he was supposed to have championed. One hopes that it will not be possible for such a wide divorce between an idealised Alfred and the reality of Anglo-Saxon rule to occur again, but it is possible that Alfred's symbolic career is not over. Now that Britain is relapsing into its regional components, who better than Alfred, the champion of the English language and Anglo-Saxon hegemony, to be a figurehead of the new England?

FOR FURTHER READING:

R. Abels, *Alfred the Great: War, Kingship and Culture in Anglo-Saxon England* (Longman, 1998); J.W. Burrow, *A Liberal Descent: Victorian Historians and the English Past* (Cambridge University Press, 1981); R. Horsman, *Race and Manifest Destiny: The Origins of American Racial Anglo-Saxonism* (Harvard University Press, 1981); S. Keynes and M. Lapidge (eds.), *Alfred the Great: Asser's Life of King Alfred and Other Contemporary Sources* (Penguin, 1983); R. Quinault, 'The Cult of the Centenary, 1789–1914', Historical Research 71 (1998), 303–23; B.A.E. Yorke, *Wessex in the Early Middle Ages* (Leicester University Press, 1995).

Barbara Yorke is Reader in History at King Alfred's College, Winchester. Her latest book is *Anglo-Saxons* (Sutton Pocket Histories, 1999).

This article first appeared in *History Today,* October 1999, pp. 8-14. © 1999 by History Today, Ltd. Reprinted by permission.

An Iberian chemistry

It was a time and place to blend Muslim and Jewish cultures

By Fouad Ajami

Long before the rise of Spain and Spanish culture, before that special run of historical events that took the Iberian Peninsula from the Catholic sovereigns Ferdinand and Isabella to the golden age of Cervantes and El Greco and Velázquez, there was another golden age in the peninsula's southern domains. In Andalusia's splendid and cultured courts and gardens, in its bustling markets, in academies of unusual secular daring, Muslims and Jews came together—if only fitfully and always under stress—to build a world of relative tolerance and enlightenment. In time, decay and political chaos would overwhelm Muslim Spain, but as the first millennium drew to a close, there had arisen in the city of Cordova a Muslim empire to rival its nemesis in the east, the imperial world around Baghdad.

We don't know with confidence the precise population of Cordova in the closing years of the 10th century. The chroniclers and travelers spoke of a large, vibrant city, which could have had a population of some 250,000 people. One 10th-century traveler wrote with awe of a city that had no equal in Syria, Egypt, or Mesopotamia for the "size of its population, its extent, the space occupied by its markets, the cleanliness of its streets, the architecture of its mosques, the number of its baths and caravansaries." Cordova had no urban rival in Western Europe at the time. Its equiva-

lents were the great imperial centers of Baghdad and Constantinople, and cities in remote worlds: Angkor in Indochina, Tchangngan in China, Tollán in Mexico.

LOUVRE, PARIS—GIRAUDON/ART RESOURCE

An age of artistic richness

City life. A Pax Islamica held sway in the Mediterranean region, and Cordova's merchants and scholars took part in the cultural and mercantile traffic of that world. In fact, the city made a bid of its own for a place in the sun in the early

years of the 10th century. One of its great rulers, Abd al-Rahman III, had taken for himself the title of caliph— or successor to the prophet Mohammed—and staked out Cordova's claim to greatness.

In the seven or eight decades that followed, the city would become a metropolis of great diversity. Blessed with a fertile countryside, the city had some 700 mosques, 3,000 public baths, illuminated streets, luxurious villas on the banks of the Guadalquivir River, and countless libraries. Legend has it that the caliph's library stocked some 400,000 volumes.

Andalusia was a polyglot world, inhabited by Arabs, Jews, Berbers from North Africa, blacks, native Christians, and Arabized Christians called Mozarabs, as well as soldiers of fortune drawn from the Christian states of Europe. The Jews did particularly well in this urban world of commerce, philosophy, and secularism. The Jewish documents of that age depict a truly cosmopolitan world in which Jewish merchants traveled between Spain and Sicily, to Aden and the Indian Ocean, from Seville to Alexandria. Jewish academies were launched in Cordova, Granada, Toledo, and Barcelona. By the end of the 10th century, Iberian Jews had declared their independence from the Talmudists of the Babylonian academies in Baghdad. A rich body of Judeo-Arabic literature became the distinctive gift of this age.

VILLAS & MOSQUES

Constructing Andalusia

Andalusia's architects thrived on Cordova's cultural stew, and their work fused myriad regional and cultural styles. The city's villas, built around patios and lined by terraces, are imitated to this day. The Jewish quarter was home to synagogues inspired by the sun-baked edifices of North Africa. But the most spectacular triumphs were the mosques, and chief among them was La Mezquita, or Great Mosque, a 6-acre giant built to hold 35,000.

When the Moors arrived in 711, the existing temples were plain affairs. The newcomers remade mosque interiors with marble columns taken from Roman and Visigothic ruins, creating dense thickets of pillars to support wooden roofs; it is said that one caliph asked his architects to simulate palm tree groves, as a reminder of his native Syria. A vital innovation, adapted from the Visigoths, was the horseshoe arch, a semicircular support that became the Moorish trademark. In the Great Mosque, these arches were made from alternating bands of red brick and white stone, a pattern that tricks the eye into perceiving the interior as limitless in size.

Brendan I. Koerner

A mingling of cultures in Andalusia's golden age

GRANGER COLLECTION

JEWS AND MUSLIMS, though always wary of one another, built a unique world of relative tolerance and enlightenment.

Terror and plunder. Even given these great cultural accomplishments, the success—and the hazards—of the Andalusian world are best seen through the deeds and valor of the Muslim soldier and strongman of Cordova, Almanzor. Cordova's de facto ruler, the first minister of the court in the final years of the 10th century, Almanzor was an able and ambitious ruler descended from the early Arab conquerors of Spain. He had risen to power in 976 and made the caliphate an instrument of his own ambi-

tions. By some estimates, Almanzor led more than 50 expeditions against neighboring Christian states. In 997 he undertook his most daring symbolic campaign, sacking Santiago de Compostela, the Christian shrine and pilgrimage center in Galicia. He laid waste to the church and took the church bells for the Great Mosque of Cordova. Three years later, in the year 1000, he cut a swath of terror through much of Castile and plundered Burgos. He died on horseback in 1002, on his way back to Cor-

dova from a military campaign in La Rioja.

Almanzor had given Cordova's political center a military vocation but undone its prosperity at the same time. He had brought into this Andalusian setting wholesale contingents of Berber tribesmen from North Africa, and the enmity between Berbers and Arabs would push the Cordovan world into its grave. What unity the Andalusian political structure had once possessed was irretrievably lost. The opening years of the 11th cen-

LIFE ON THE MARGIN

A Zionist in Andalusia's golden age

The Spanish rabbi-poet Judah Halevi lived in a society in which he and other Jews were socially powerless and influenced heavily by the dominant Islamic culture. Still, he used his poetry to explore both conflict and harmony among Arabs and Jews. An outgoing physician and court poet with many friends, he wrote a collection of secular poetry and a huge body of religious verses, some of which have made their way into modern Jewish prayer books. (His famed *Ode to Zion* has been read for centuries in religious services.) The poetry brought forth a deeper sense of Jewish spirituality that had been unheard of in previous generations

With Islam and Christianity locked in a battle of religious giants, the Jewish minority in medieval Spain was left with few privileges. Although some Jews felt at

GRANGER COLLECTION

Some Spanish Jews felt at home in Islamic society.

home in an Islamic society, many, like Halevi, longed for a world in which their own people could rise to the top.

In fact, the years between 900 and 1200 in Spain and North Africa are known as the Hebrew "golden age," a sort of Jewish Renaissance that arose from the fusion of the Arab and Jewish intellectual words. Jews watched their Arab counterparts closely and learned to be astronomers, philosophers, scientists, and poets.

Signs of status. But this was a time of only partial autonomy. Jews were free to live in the Islamic world as long as they paid a special tax to Muslim rulers and submitted to an order forbidding them to own Muslim slaves. Jews had their own legal system and social services, were forbidden to build new synagogues, and were supposed to wear identifying clothing.

These restrictions led to a profound sense of alienation for some Jews. It was, says Raymond Scheindlin, professor of medieval Hebrew literature at New York's Jewish Theological Seminary, a demoralizing daily reminder "that you are part of a losing team." Halevi reacted to that message. To him, life in Spain—though comfortable in between harrowing bouts of persecution—was like slavery compared with the life intended for Jews in Palestine.

Allied neither with the crescent nor the cross, Halevi instead focused on a different destiny. To him, the Jews were a calamitous and wounded people, unsure of their place in human history. He wanted Jews to believe what he was confident of: that Hebrew was superior to Arabic, Palestine to Spain, and they were the chosen people.

When he was 50, Halevi underwent an emotional upheaval and decided to devote himself to God by going on a pilgrimage to the Holy Land. Legend has it that he met his death upon finally arriving in Israel, where he was run over by an Arab horseman. With the vision of Jerusalem set before him, he recited the last verse of his *Ode to Zion*.

—Lindsay Faber

tury would be terrible years for Cordova. The city was sacked by Catalan mercenaries in 1010; the Guadalquivir overflowed its banks in the year that followed; and a terrible mass slaughter took place in 1013 when merciless Berber soldiers besieged the city, put a large number of its scholars to the sword, and torched its elegant villas. Many of the city's notables, Muslims and Jews alike, took to the road.

One of these exiles was a talented Jewish child of Cordova, one Samuel Ibn Neghrela. He was given the gift of Cordova's greatness: He was a poet, learned in Arabic and Hebrew and Latin, the Berber and Romance tongues. But he also inherited the legacy of Cordova's collapse. He fled Cordova's upheaval to the coastal city of Málaga, then made his way to the court of Granada, where he prospered as courtier and chief minister. He saw through the splendor and the hazards of that world. In a poignant poem, entitled "A Curse," he wrote of his wandering and exile: "Heart like a pennant / On a ship's mast, in a storm; / An exile is ink / In God's book. Across my soul, and every shore; / And all on whom wandering is written / Are driven like Jonah, and scavenge like Cain."

Distant memory. It twisted and turned, that world that had risen in the West. Ten years after Neghrela's death, his son and heir, Joseph, was killed by a mob in Granada, in an anti-Jewish riot in which some 1,500 Jewish families perished. By then the unity of the Andalusian world had become a distant memory. The age that followed was dubbed the *mulak al-tawa'if*, a time when warlords and pretenders carved up Muslim Spain into petty, warring turfs. No fewer than 30 ministates claimed what had once been a coherent dominion. The robust mercantile economy eroded.

Calamity soon struck this world. In 1085, Toledo, the ancient capital of the Visigothic kingdom, was conquered by Alfonso VI, King of León. For Christians this was a sign of divine favor, and the conqueror claimed no less than that. "By the hidden judgment of God," a charter of Alfonso read, "this city was for 376 years in the hands of the Moors, blasphemers of the Christian faith…. Inspired by God's grace I moved an army against this city, where my ancestors once reigned in power and wealth." Cordova itself fell in 1236. Its conqueror, Ferdinand III of Castile, claimed the Great Mosque of Cordova in a "purification" ceremony, and his bishops consecrated it for Christian worship as the Catedral de Santa María. The foundations of the Great Mosque had been laid down in the closing years of the eighth century, and successive rulers had adorned and enlarged it. It was the symbol of Andalusian authority, a sublime architectural wonder into which rulers and patrons poured their reverence and ambition, their desire for a new Muslim frontier as grand as the best Baghdad or Damascus could boast. In the peninsula, one people's golden age was always another's decline. What had once been a land of three faiths would in time be cleansed of its Muslims and Jews. A militant new doctrine—called *limpieza de sangre*, or "purity of blood"—would dispense with all that tangled past and its richness.

From *U.S. News & World Report*, August 16–23, 1999, pp. 44, 48, 50. Copyright © 1999 by Fouad Ajami. Reprinted by permission of the author.

The Capture of Jerusalem

John France recounts the against-the-odds narrative of the capture of the Holy City by the forces of the First Crusade.

On Tuesday, June 7th, 1099, the First Crusade arrived before the city of Jerusalem and began a siege which would end with its capture on Friday July 15th. It was a moment of great rejoicing in the crusader host, because Jerusalem was the Holy Place for whose liberation they had set out on the long and bitter journey some three years before.

After Pope Urban's appeal for a military expedition to the East in November 1095, Western Europe had been swept by a wave of enthusiasm which inspired about 100,000 men, women and children to leave their homes. Many turned back, others died even as they began their journey: Fulcher of Chartres saw 400 drown at Brindisi when a pilgrim ship sank. Even so the group of armies which gathered before Nicaea in June 1097 was some 60,000 strong, including roughly 6–7,000 knights. Not since Roman times had such a host gathered in Europe, though this was not a single army like that of Rome, but a collection of armed bands massively encumbered with non-combatants.

The major armies were commanded by the great princes— Raymond of Toulouse, Godfrey of Bouillon, Robert Duke of Normandy, Robert Count of Flanders, Stephen of Blois, Hugh of Vermandois and Bohemond, son of Robert Guiscard. But there were many others with their own warbands who owed little loyalty to such men, and new leaders emerged during the journey. Bohemond's nephew Tancred enjoyed an independent command at Jerusalem, while Godfrey's younger brother Baldwin seized the principality of Edessa in March 1098.

There were people of so many nationalities on the crusade that they found it difficult to understand one another, and since there was no overall commander the crusade was run by a committee of its most important members, presided over by the papal legate Adhémar of Le Puy who died, however, on August 1st, 1098. The result was a host of quarrelling nationalities presided over by bickering lords: the only unity came from the sense of a common mission reinforced by the dire peril to which they were exposed in the hostile Middle East. But even this mission was a cause of strife. Urban II had wanted his great expedition to aid the Byzantine emperor Alexius Comnenus in his struggle with the Turks who had seized Asia Minor, to rescue

the Christians of the East from their captivity under Islam and to liberate Jerusalem. But many of the crusaders came to regard Alexius as little more than a traitor who had failed to live up to his promises of help: the Count of Toulouse, commander of the biggest army, disagreed and was permanently at odds with his fellows. Few of the crusaders had a high opinion of the native Christians. As a result Jerusalem became the sole focus of their endeavours because it was the one objective on which they could all agree.

Jerusalem had a special place in the religion and culture of medieval Europe for it was the place where Christ had died and his empty tomb in the Church of the Holy Sepulchre was the very symbol of Christian belief. The people of the eleventh century were burdened by a profound sense of their own sinfulness, a perception increased by the confused state of theological ideas about penance. Heaven was a place for which 'Many are called but few are chosen' and the common fate of mankind must have seemed to be eternal punishment. Fear of hell has never prevented men from sinning, but at moments of crisis or illness eternal torment loomed large. In the late eleventh century the church preached peace to an upper class whose *métier* and delight was war—the signs are that the tension engendered by this contradiction was unbearable. Pilgrimage was one deeply satisfying ritual of escape.

Travel in the Middle Ages was hazardous and in such a context to undertake an ordeal voluntarily was admired as a commitment to Christ. The pilgrim took a public vow to complete his journey and assumed a special dress and badges. He left behind his loved ones, submitted to a self-denying discipline and went to a place where heaven and earth met—the shrine of a holy saint—to atone for his sins. Of all pilgrimages the most distant, difficult and therefore respected, was that to the holiest of all places, Jerusalem, which was regarded as wiping a man's slate clean of sin. When Urban launched his crusade he offered to all who participated this special 'remission of sins'. He offered a vision of Jerusalem suffering under the tyranny of Islam and demanded that the military aristocracy avenge Christ for this suffering and recapture His most holy place. This was an

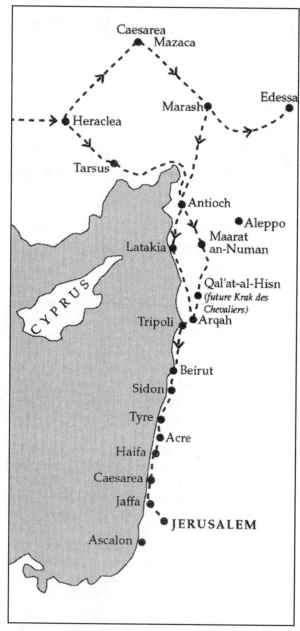

HT MAP BY COLIN BARKER

Road to salvation: map showing the final phase of the First Crusade.

even these could have argued that righteous war meant rightful plunder. The army which rejoiced as it reached the gates of Jerusalem on that June day was driven by a heady cocktail of greed and devotion.

In their self-righteousness the crusaders gave little thought to the fact that this same Jerusalem was sacrosanct to Jew and Muslim also. The leaders were not totally ignorant of Islam. The Emperor Alexius had advised them to ally with the Fatimids of Egypt against the Seljuk Turks who dominated Syria and ruled Jerusalem. That alliance served them well, for when they broke it in May 1099 and entered the Fatimid lands of Palestine, the Egyptians were so surprised that they could offer no resistance to their march and even demolished the fortifications of Jaffa, the port of Jerusalem because they could not defend it.

The Fatimids had profited from the Seljuk conflict with the crusaders to seize Jerusalem in August 1098 and now they were faced with defending it against their former allies. For Jerusalem is sacred to Islam: its name al-Kuds, 'the city of the sanctuary', refers to the important shrine we now call the Dome of the Rock, built in 691, whence the angel Gabriel took Mohammed through the heavens. Its great golden dome and the magnificent al-Aksa mosque built nearby in 780 dominate the enormous structure of the Temple Mount which towers over Jerusalem: its western wall is the famous 'Wailing Wall' sacred to Judaism.

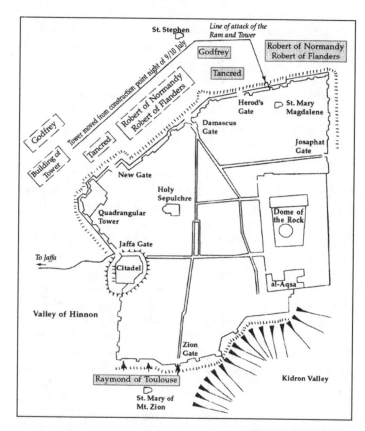

HT MAP BY COLIN BARKER

Plan of Jerusalem, showing the final attack of July 13th–15th, 1099.

opportunity for a warlike class to expunge their sins by a single convulsive act of violence.

In this 'new religion' the business of fighting and killing was meritorious, equal to the traditional 'good works', prayer, fasting and charity to the poor. Those who went on this fighting pilgrimage regarded their sufferings as part of a ritual which freed individuals from sin and purified the army as a whole to be the 'chosen of the Lord'—and their ultimate trial was Jerusalem. Of course there were other motives. One eye-witness noted that as they approached the Holy City only 'a few who held God's command dear marched along barefooted, sending up deep sighs to God', while many others indulged in 'a mad scramble caused by our greed to seize castles and villas', but

The Jews had their own quarter in the north-east of the city and they were probably aware that Christian fanatics had mas-

'The chosen of the Lord': Christians and Muslims in mortal combat (from the 14th-century *Romans de Godefroy de Bouillon*); the latter attempting to defend Jerusalem from the warrior pilgrims' bloody sanctioned quest to 'avenge Christ'.

sacred the Jews of the Rhineland cities even before setting out on the crusade, because Jews manned the walls in their own quarter and perished in the great massacre which followed the crusader capture. But the crusaders were not interested in the claims of other religions. Most of those from northern Europe would have known nothing of Islam before their journey to the East and the circumstances of that journey would not have encouraged curiosity. The defenders of the city stood in the way of their path to salvation, loot and land. In later years when they ruled Jerusalem the Dome of the Rock became the Temple of the Lord and the al-Aksa, the Palace of Solomon. History was rewritten to obliterate the memory of Islam, and the despised Jews were excluded from the city.

In attacking Jerusalem the crusaders faced a formidable task. The city is set upon a steep spur dividing the Kidron valley, which falls away southwards towards the Dead Sea. To the east the Valley of Josaphat cuts an enormous gash between the city and the Mount of Olives, while to the west the Valley of Hinnon provides a similar if less dramatic protection. Apart from a level stretch of some 250–300 metres around the Zion Gate, the land before the southern wall falls sharply to the Kidron valley: it was here that the Count of Toulouse chose to mount his attack, but he faced a deep ditch between the wall and his camp. The most vulnerable aspect of the city is the northern wall, about a kilometre long, which is built well below the brow of the hill; here the rest of the army gathered. The whole city was surrounded by a wall, three stories high studded with projecting towers; the relative vulnerability of the northern wall was protected by an outer wall and beyond it a ditch extending from the citadel, called the 'Tower of David' by Jaffa Gate on the west side, to the platform over the Valley of Josaphat at the northeast corner.

War, disease and desertion had reduced the once enormous crusader host to about 1,200 knights and 12,000 on foot.

Through circumstance they had become efficient and seasoned soldiers, but there were not enough of them to surround the city. They were bitterly divided between the Provençals and the rest; only on the eve of the final assault were Raymond of Toulouse and Tancred publicly reconciled. The nearest Christian outpost was 500 kilometres away. The garrison had scorched the land about the city and blocked wells forcing the attackers to bring water from afar; according to Albert of Aachen some of this had leeches in it and when crusaders 'swallowed down the slippery water-worms they were killed by a swollen throat or stomach'. Worst of all the garrison had destroyed or hidden every piece of wood, which was essential for the building of siege machinery. And the whole enterprise was a desperate race against time, for the Egyptians were known to be raising a relief army, a fact which encouraged the garrison recently reinforced by 400 cavalry. They were strong enough to defend the city, but not strong enough to mount sorties against the crusaders, and seem to have relied on forces already at Ascalon to harass the besiegers.

When Tancred, struck by dysentery, sought privacy in a cave and discovered enough wood to build one ladder, the leaders were so anxious about the Egyptian threat that they mounted an attack on the northern wall on June 13th. It failed and Reybold of Chartres, the first on the ladder, had his hand cut off. This forced the crusaders to prepare a more deliberate assault, made possible by the arrival of a Genoese fleet at Jaffa on June 17th, bringing food, timber and above all, skilled labour. The Ascalon garrison attacked the crusader convoy going to Jaffa, but their defeat, near Ramla, ended the harassment of the crusaders. Throughout the crusade sea-power had been a vital factor and never more so than now as siege machinery could be built.

The Count of Toulouse employed the Genoese engineer William Ricau to construct a siege-tower by Zion Gate. At the north-west corner of Jerusalem, Godfrey and the northern French built another, together with a ram to breach the outer wall. These great wooden towers were about four storeys high mounted on wheels or rollers. Brought close to the wall they could clear off the defenders by missiles, enabling others to attack by ladders and mining the walls, though they did not have drawbridges to mount an assault themselves. The defenders on the north wall did not sit idly by. They raised a wooden tower at the anticipated point of attack and brought up beams and padding to protect their defenders. Nine catapults, high-trajectory weapons which hurled stones in a great arc, were deployed against the Provençals, and five against the northern French along with a number of *balistae*, (giant crossbows). The crusaders also built a few catapults and *balistae*, and sent out every man, woman and child to bring light timber for the construction of ladders and mantelets, large shields to cover the attackers' advance to the wall.

In the fever of preparations visions were seen, including one of the dead legate, Adhémar, who commanded that before the assault a solemn procession should be made around the city in the manner of Joshua before Jericho; this duly took place on July 8th, raising morale. But the decisive event in the siege occurred on the night of July 9th–10th, when Godfrey's tower was dismantled and rebuilt at a weak spot on the northeastern corner of the city, almost a kilometre away from where it had been built. The defenders hastened to relocate their forces but they had little time to elaborate their defences before, on Wednesday July 13th, the grand assault began.

By modern standards the whole business must have been painfully slow. The clumsy machines had been assembled as close as possible to the wall, towards which gangs of men pushed and dragged them on wheels or rollers. Before they could be brought into action the northern French had to flatten the ground along the line of attack, while the Provençals faced a large ditch which took three days to fill, with the labourers paid a penny for every three stones moved. Here on Mount Zion there was little room for manoeuvre, for the Provençal camp and the city wall were no more than fifty metres apart. Raymond's mobile tower was severely battered by the nine machines deployed against it, one of which threw blazing balls of pitch and straw not merely at the tower but also into the camp and ultimately set the tower alight: this fire-thrower was dragged off its mounting on the wall when the Provencals improvised a hook mounted on a beam with a chain to drag it. By Friday July 15th, this southern attack was stalled, but it had diverted forces from the north. At the north-east corner of the city the ram lumbered up to the outer wall, its crew supported by bowmen and groups with scaling ladders. Godfrey used a crossbow to set fire to the protective padding hung down the wall front. The Egyptians replied with streams of arrows from the wall-head and stones fired from catapults inside the city, and tried to set fire to the ram while the crusaders organised relays of waterbearers.

The fighting at the fore-wall lasted all of Wednesday and into Thursday when the wall was penetrated—and then ensued a pantomime. The tower, slowly dragged up behind, now found its route to the main wall blocked by the ram which could not be cast aside because the outer wall was probably no more than 10 metres from the powerfully defended main curtain. The crusaders set fire to the ram, and now it was the turn of the garrison to throw water from the main wall, but in the end it was burned. Only on Friday, July 15th, did the tower approach the main wall. Wet hides hanging around it defeated enemy fire attack while its osier covering cushioned somewhat the rain of stones. Even so it was badly damaged and the crusaders decided to push the tower right up against the wall. As a counter-measure the defenders hung a great tree blazing with naphtha, pitch and sulphur, on chains down the front of the wall but the crusaders managed to grapple this down and to manoeuvre the tower against the wall.

Now the defects of the improvised defences were felt. Because of the sudden change in the crusader point of attack, the Egyptians had not had time to build platforms on the wall on which to mount their catapults: they were simply stationed in the streets of the city. These machines had thrown their missiles over the wall, but when the wooden tower moved up to it, their stones, moving slowly at the peak of their arc, merely bounded off onto their own men on, and behind, the wall: lack of time had not permitted demolition of houses to enable them to adjust their range. The crusaders in the siege tower, led by Godfrey with his crossbow, now engaged in a fire-fight with a nearby

Greed and devotion: the pillage and plunder of Jerusalem, depicted in this 14th-century illustration, did not appear to disturb the consciences of those triumphant at freeing the Holy City from the Infidel.

tower, supported by three catapults and numerous archers and ladder teams, while others tried to mine the wall. Then two Flemish brothers, Ludolf and Engelbert of Tournai, climbed out from the top storey of the siegetower, improvising a bridge by cutting down logs used to reinforce its front, and established a bridgehead on the wall which rapidly expanded.

As news of this breakthrough spread, resistance to the Provençals melted away and the garrison of the Tower of David surrendered in return for their lives. In the north there was a massacre as the crusaders poured through the Jewish quarter where the main synagogue was burned over the heads of those who took refuge there. Muslims fled to the Temple Mount where so many were killed that crusaders 'rode in blood to the knees and bridles of their horses'. Tancred offered quarter to those who took refuge on the al-Aksa roof, doubtless hoping to ransom them, but in the morning, and much to his anger, they too were massacred. After a week in which they cleared the corpses from Jerusalem, the bickering crusader leaders elected Godfrey de Bouillon on July 22nd, as Advocate of the Holy Sepulchre 'so that he might fight against the pagans and protect the Christians'. The conquest, however, remained provisional until, on August 12th, the crusader army surprised the relief

force led by the Vizier of Egypt, al-Afdal, at Ascalon and destroyed it. Afterwards, the greater part of the host returned to the West.

In terms of eleventh-century behaviour in war, the massacre at Jerusalem was not unusual. Later in the twelfth century Muslim writers spoke of 70,000 being killed at the al-Aksa alone, but this was propaganda for the holy war, *Jihad*, against the Franks. Not all the Muslims of Jerusalem were killed: many fled to form a suburb of Damascus taking with them the famous Koran of Uthman. Letters from the Cairo synagogue bear witness to the ransoming of Jerusalem Jews in the wake of the fall of the city. Most native Christians had been expelled before the siege, but those left behind welcomed the crusaders into the city.

However horrible it may seem, what happened in Jerusalem was not then exceptional. The city had a strong garrison which could hope for relief—until the last minute they were receiving messages of support from Ascalon. Possibly they had heard exaggerated stories of crusaders' cannibalism at Ma'arrat an Nu'man in Syria, a wholly exceptional event, which may well have stiffened their resistance. The truth was that in the Middle Ages any garrison which held out to the bitter end was liable to bring down massacre on its stronghold. This could hardly be prevented, for armies were poorly disciplined and, in the heat of a breakthrough, impossible to control. In 1057 the Turks massacred or enslaved the whole population of Christian Melitene. William the Conqueror harried the north of England so savagely that a contemporary thought 100,000 had perished, and so ruthlessly did he destroy Mantes in 1087 that many believed his death there was the vengeance of God.

It is not simply the fact of the massacre and its scale which is shocking, but the fact that the crusaders rejoiced in it, as Raymond of Aguilers, who was present at the fall of Jerusalem, describes:

> How they rejoiced and exulted and sang a new song to the Lord! For their hearts offered prayers of praise to God, victorious and triumphant, which cannot be told in words. A new day, new joy, new and perpetual gladness, the consummation of our labour and devotion, drew forth from all new words and new songs. This day, I say, marks the justification of all Christianity, the humiliation of paganism, and the renewal of our faith. 'This is the day which the Lord hath made, let us rejoice and be glad in it', for on this day the Lord revealed Himself to His people and blessed them.

This passage may shock, but it should not surprise us. Each crusader was convinced that every Muslim he cut down represented a step nearer to paradise, for the essence of Urban's message, which was the driving force of the whole expedition, was that killing Muslims was meritorious. To hack down a child, as many must have done in Jerusalem, was an act whose merit was equal to that of the Good Samaritan. These were rational people performing what they believed to be the will of God and certain that it would contribute to their own salvation. Such absolute self-righteousness cloaked much self-interest. Tancred seized Bethlehem as a prize of war as the army neared Jerusalem, and during the sack he plundered the treasures of the Dome of the Rock.

But the real horror of the sack of Jerusalem is its legacy to us all. In the short-run the Christian crusade revived in ever fiercer form the Muslim *jihad*, which soon had plenty of massacres to its credit. Before the crusade most Western Christians had only a vague knowledge of Islam, which was not really relevant to their daily lives. Centuries of crusade propaganda changed that to a latent hatred. Islam and Christianity were in contact in Spain before the crusade, and relations between the two had never been simply characterised by conflict. On July 10th, 1099, as the crusaders prepared to attack Jerusalem, *El Cid*, Rodrigo Diaz de Vivar, died. He was well-versed in Islamic law and culture and had carved out a great career for himself in the service of Muslim and Christian alike. In the twelfth century his life had to be rewritten to make him a champion of Christendom and a worthy hero of the Spanish *Reconquista* in the new age. For the spirit of crusade, symbolised by the fall of Jerusalem, insisted on an absolute hatred of Islam.

The inheritance of the crusades in the West is one of deep suspicion, very evident in our media's portrayal of 'Islamic Fundamentalism'. The inheritance of the capture of Jerusalem in the East is that it is fatally easy for those who would defend Islamic culture to be fearful of the West and to see in any intrusion evidence of a new crusade, and to react in the same way as they did to the old.

FOR FURTHER READING:

J.A. Brundage, *The Crusades, a documentary survey* (Milwaukee, 1962); S.B. Edgington, *The First Crusade*, Historical Association 'New Appreciations in History' No. 37 (London, 1996); J. France, *Victory in the East: a Military History of the First Crusade* (Cambridge, 1994), A. Maalouf, *The Crusades through Arab eyes* (London, 1984); J. Riley-Smith, *The Crusades: a short history* (London, 1987).

John France *is Senior Lecturer in Medieval History at the University of Wales and author of* Victory in the East: a Military History of the First Crusade *listed above.*

Doctor, Philosopher, Renaissance Man

Written by Caroline Stone

A man can be adopted by a civilization other than his own and can there become a symbol of something very different from that which he signifies to his own civilization. This was the case with Abu 'I-Walid Muhammad ibn Rushd, who came to be known to the west as Averroës. And just as the medieval Arab world and the medieval European world knew him by two names, so did they value two different aspects of his schlorships: In the Arab world, he is remembered primarily as a medical pioneer, while the West esteemed his philosophy.

Ibn Rushd was born in Córdoba, in southern Spain, in 1126. His family was one of those dynasties with a multi-generational tradition of learning and service to the state that were so much a part of the Arabic-speaking world. The Crusades had begun, and when Ibn Rushd was young, Jerusalem was a Crusader state.

Al-Andalus—as Muslim Spain was called—was splintered into numerous petty principalities and local kingdoms, independent but vulnerable, known as the "*taifa* kingdoms" (from the Arabic *ta'ifah*, meaning "party" or "faction"). Weak as they were, many of them were nonetheless admirable cradles of learning and the arts, as each ruler tried to outdo the others in the magnificence and prestige of his court and the caliber of the scholars he could attract to it. From the north, however, the newly unified Christians had embarked on the reconquest of Spain from the Muslims that would finally conclude in 1492. The *taifa* kings urged two successive North African dynasties to support the Muslims of Spain against the resurgent Christians. The resulting northward influx of people and puritanical ideas—secular learning, science and music were increasingly viewed with suspicion—along with the consequent social upheavals and greatly increased contacts with Morocco would all be of consequence to Ibn Rushd.

The Christian-Muslim rivalry also took peaceful forms, symbolized by the impressive construction activity of this time. The great Cathedral of Santiago de Compostela in northwest Spain, the third most important pilgrimage site in the Christian world, was completed in the year that Ibn Rushd was born. During his middle years, working in Marrakech, he must have watched the construction of that city's most famous mosque, the Kutubiyyah, or Booksellers', Mosque. As an old man in Seville, he would have witnessed, rising from its foundations, the Giralda, still the symbol of the city to this day. During his lifetime, two of the three cities he loved best, and to which he was most closely linked, were building their greatest monuments.

Although these buildings physically proclaimed the differences between the faiths, the intellectual activities of these years often took a far less competitive direction. This was a time when thoughtful men were searching for areas of common ground where they might escape destructive fanaticism from either side. Hence the many translations that each culture made of the other's works, and the rising awareness that sciences, such as mathematics, medicine or astronomy, could be a terrain where exciting and productive work could be done and differences of faith at least briefly forgotten. This attitude was very different from the confident intellectual curiosity of ninth-century Baghdad that had triggered the first wave of translations from the classics into Arabic, preserving many of them in the only form we have today. Those efforts established the roots, while the works of al-Andalus were fundamentally new creations, new intellectual ventures. They were the shoots, and their ultimate blossoming would be the time we call the Renaissance.

The political disturbances of Ibn Rushd's years would also lead to the dispersal across Europe of learned men from southern Spain who, as they moved, scattered new ideas, new techniques and new books like seeds. These would be nurtured especially in the new, relatively secular institutions of learning called "universities" that had been founded at Bologna, Oxford and Salerno. There students were taught the works of the great scholars—many of them Muslims—together with the Greek learning at their roots. Among those scholars, Ibn Rushd was one of the most admired, perceived by the West as a bridge between two faiths and between past and present. The ultimate fruitfulness of the many individual hardships that must have informed this intellectual diaspora can perhaps be compared to the extraordinary flourishing of American science in the wake of the disruptions of World War II. Certainly this period of dissemination and cultural cross-fertilization definitively shifted the balance of intellectual initiative from south to north.

A good deal is known of Ibn Rushd's family background, but very little about his own life or upbringing. His grandfather was a well-known jurist of the Maliki school of Islamic law. One of the most prestigious of the positions he held was that of *qadi*, or chief justice, of Córdoba. Ibn Rushd was appointed to the same position in 1180 and earlier served as *qadi* of Seville in 1169. These were appointments of great importance, for the *qadi* held a three-fold responsibility: he was the religious authority, the representative of the ruler and the upholder of civic order. That Ibn Rushd held the position in not one but two cities indicates the respect in which he was held and testifies to the soundness of his legal training. But he moved on: In addition to his service in law, Ibn Rushd studied medicine, and it is for this aspect of his learning and writing that he was most esteemed in the Islamic world.

In 1148, the North African Almohad dynasty began its—initially welcomed—takeover of al-Andalus. The Almohad capital was at Marrakech, in today's Morocco, a city founded only some 80 years earlier and which the Almohad ruler was anxious to make a center of the arts and scholarship. To this end, he encouraged education, and Marrakech, like Córdoba, was already famous for its bookshops and libraries when Ibn Rushd traveled therein 1153. He received his first official appointment as inspector of schools there.

Ibn Rushd was to produce more than 100 books and treatises in his lifetime, and it was in Marrakech that he began his first philosophical work, sometime before 1159. This was quickly followed by his substantial *Compendium of Philosophy (Kitab al-Jawami' al-Sighar fil-Falsafa)* with its sections on physics, heaven and earth, generation and corruption, meteorology and metaphysics—some of the main interests that would occupy him the rest of his life. It has been suggested among scholars that Ibn Rushd's work may have been inspired by the desire to prove that man is rational and can learn, that nature is intelligible and its interpretation a legitimate task of man, and that ultimately science and divine revelation need not be at odds. Part of this philosophy is derived from the Greeks, especially from Plato and Aristotle, whom Ibn Rushd admired and on whose works he wrote numerous commentaries and paraphrases—books that to a large extent won him the respect he enjoyed in the West, where the struggle to reconcile science and faith still goes on.

The other major work which he produced during these years at Marrakech was the first draft of his *Compendium of Medical Knowledge (Kitab al-Kulliyat fil-Tibb)*. Written at the request of the sultan, it is divided into seven books:

anatomy, health, disease, symptoms, food and medicines, preservation of health and treatment of illness. Excellently arranged, though not on the whole the fruit of original research, this compilation brought together the work of the best physicians from both the classical Greek and the Islamic traditions, and became a standard text for generations of physicians in both East and West. As Averroes, Ibn Rushd appears, along with many of his main sources, in the list of authorities used by Chaucer's doctor in the General Prologue to the *Canterbury Tales*—a measure of the extent to which he had become a household word in England 200 years later:

> Well knew he the old Esculapius
> And Dioscorides and also Rusus,
> Old Hippocras, Hali and Galen
> Serapion, Rasis and Avicen,
> **Averrois**, Damascene and Constantine,
> Bernard and Gatesden and Gilbertine.

It is to the *Kulliyat* and other medical works that Ibn Rushd owes his fame in the East today, where he is remembered as a great doctor. His philosophical works, which fascinated and influenced the West, were of relatively little interest to the Muslim world outside Al-Andalus. In a way this is surprising, for Islam too has been concerned since its beginning with the vision of a perfect society, albeit one based on the *shar'iah*, or holy law, as revealed in the Qur'an. The Islamic rejection of Ibn Rushd as a philosopher is no doubt partly because of the criticism that he subordinated religion to philosophy, suggesting that scientific research could teach people more than the revelations of faith—a criticism also leveled at him by the Catholic church in the West.

The *Kulliyat*, however, was a great success for Ibn Rushd. (Indeed, versions of it were still appearing on medical school reading lists around Europe as recently as 100 years ago.) In 1168, his teacher Ibn Tufayl, a scholar of Aristotle and follower of Ibn Sina (known in the West as Avicenna), introduced Ibn Rushd to the new Almohad ruler, Abu Ya'qub Yusuf. The following year, Yusuf appointed Ibn Rushd *qadi* of Seville, and Ibn Rushd returned to al-Andalus.

His years in Seville were apparently happy and productive. He wrote numerous works on natural science and philosophy there, many of which—though they are paraphrases or commentaries on classical texts—need to be understood not as derivative but as truly original works. They were perceptive "updates" of some of the greatest thinkers of the classical world, men who provide models for how we think about things and study them even today. It is fascinating to compare Ibn Rushd's versions with the originals.

Ibn Rushd's great importance to western thought lies in his making available many of the philosophical works of ancient Greece, particularly those of Plato and Aristotle, but his most notable work is his commentary on Plato's *Republic*. It was this book, with its idea that society is perfectible and its discussion of how society can and should be changed, that worried some secular rulers no less than the Muslim 'ulama and the Catholic theologians, all of whom were inclined to see the order of the world as preordained and immutable. The Almohad rulers of al-Andalus, however, were more relaxed than the earlier Almoravid dynasty, and they allowed discussion of these questions—up to the limit of challenging their authority. It was thus largely Ibn Rushd's texts that inspired the thinkers of the Renaissance, such as Tomaso Campanella and Sir Thomas More, to produce their theories of Utopia, or the ideal state. The notion that this ideal is something definable, and that it can be attained through human endeavor and wise leadership—rather than only as a matter of God's grace or mere good luck—has inspired reformers and socially conscious governments to the present day. Though his name—once a household word—is barely known in the West today, and though his works are now largely unread, the impact of this man's thought remains immeasurable.

In 1171, at age 45, Ibn Rushd returned to Córdoba. There, for the rest of his life, he maintained his main residence and his library. His visits to Seville were frequent and long, and perhaps he was present when, five years later, the Great Mosque, designed to rival that of Córdoba in size and splendor, was inaugurated. He would have enjoyed its nearby Patio of the Oranges, where he would have meditated and debated with his friends.

Those were productive years for him. The ongoing political tensions caused by the Almohad conquest of Al-Andalus and the struggles with the Christians to the north seem not to have much affected the relative peace and prosperity of Seville and Córdoba, and Ibn Rushd produced a stream of works on a wide range of subjects, from his paraphrase of the *Nicomachaean Ethics (Kitab al-Akhlaq)*, which has not survived intact, to his discussion of Aristotle's *Poetics* (from the *Talkhis Kitab al-Shi'r*), as well as his *Supplement to Questions on Ancient Science (Damima li-Mas'alat al-Ilm al-Qadim)* and further medical treatises. His work on Ptolemy's *Almagest* may also belong to this period.

After another visit to Marrakech, Ibn Rushd was appointed *qadi* of Córdoba in 1180 and personal physician to Sultan Abu Ya'qub Yusuf at the Almohad's new capital in Seville. Between the demands of these two appointments, he found time to write one of his most famous works, his parry of al-Ghazali's *Incoherence of the Philosophers*, titled *Incoherence of the Incoherent Philosophy of al-Ghazali (Tahafut al-Tahafut al-Falasifa lil-Ghazali)*.

It was a time of expansion and optimism in the Muslim world. Saladin retook Jerusalem from the Crusaders in 1187; in Spain, a Christian coalition was routed at Alarcos eight years later. Ibn Rushd's fame was spreading into the eastern Islamic world, and by 1190 his books were available and under discussion in Cairo.

Four years later, he wrote one of his most controversial works, the paraphrase of Plato's *Republic*. While the original implies criticism of the existing social order and studies ways to perfect it, Ibn Rushd's version courageously applied Plato's theories to Ibn Rushd's own times, citing chapter and verse of where the political system had failed. He pointed out, for example, that, strictly speaking, the government of Córdoba should have been considered a tyranny from 1145 onward—that is, since the end of Almoravid rule and the accession of the current Almohad dynasty, whose head was his patron. The following year, complaints were made against Ibn Rushd on various counts. He was briefly exiled, and the authorities burned his books. They forbade him to write on philosophy, politics or religion. It is probably fair to assume that the main reasons for his falling into disfavor were his defense of rationalism and the outspokenness of his social criticism. Perhaps too many people agreed with him.

This period of disfavor, however, did not last long. The ban against him was repealed, but as far as is known, he wrote no more, though his son began to publish about this time. The questions of how he was inspired to begin his life's work and where he found his texts, as well as many of the most basic details of his personal world, remain largely unknown.

Ibn Rushd died at Marrakech on December 11, 1198. Three months later his body was returned, as he had wished, to rest in his beloved Córdoba. His rival, the mystic Ibn al-Arabi, describes the funeral: "When the coffin with his body was laid upon the bier, they put his works on the opposite side to serve as a counterweight. I was standing there…and I said to myself, 'On one side the master and on the other his works. But, tell me, were his desires at last fulfilled?'"

CAROLINE STONE divides her time between Cambridge and Seville. She is working on a Gulf-based project to map pre-modern cultural contacts and build a website to teach world history. She has recently returned from Uzbekistan and is also working with Paul Lunde on translations of the Arab sources about the Vikings and peoples of the North and of 'Abd al-Latif al-Baghdadi's description of Egypt

The Emergence of the Christian Witch

P.G. Maxwell-Stuart examines the impact of early Christianity on notions of magic and definitions of witchcraft.

As CHRISTIANITY BEGAN to make an impact on the Roman world, the new religion faced two major struggles. On the one hand, it faced a series of deviations from orthodox theology, in the form of heresies principally concerned with the exact nature of Jesus and his relation to God the Father. Second came the challenge of magic. Magical practitioners were ubiquitous in the pagan world, and their stock in trade consisted of claims to exercise powers beyond the merely natural or human.

Prospective converts looked to Christian priests and monks to work magic more effectively than their pagan equivalents, and this remained a requirement as long as there were sizeable areas of Europe to be converted, that is, until at least the twelfth century. Saints played a major role in this preternatural activity. They worked wonders, cured the sick, expelled evil spirits and, when death took them, their relics continued the good work. Hence, amulets of all kinds, re-cast in Christian guise, pursued the miraculous or magical ends once sought purely by pagan magic.

Yet when non-Christians realised that Jesus himself was credited with miraculous cures and exorcisms, and that the new Church was offering rituals, such as baptism and the Eucharist, which purported to protect its converts by driving away evil spirits, and to change bread and wine into the body and blood of the new god, they maintained that Jesus himself had been a magician, a wonder-worker of a familiar type, and that what his Church called 'sacraments' were no different from rites of magic.

This posed a problem for the Church. Christian missionaries could draw on pagan willingness to accept the possibility of the miraculous more or less without reservation, and hence belief in Christ's resurrection and the efficacy of the sacraments; but they also had to explain why the miracles of Christ himself, or those of the Apostles or later saints were genuine, whereas those of pagan magicians such as the first-century AD Simon Magus or his contemporary, Apollonius of Tyre, were fraudulent.

As well as being accommodated by the Christians, magic was also reinterpreted in the light of the new religion's developing theology. Crucial to this re-interpretation were the figures of Satan and the *daimones*, spirits, conceived as intermediaries between the spiritual and material worlds of paganism. Dai-

mones became evil spirits and in that guise were associated with every branch of magic because of the supposed pact between them and human beings. The Christian perception of creation itself underwent a change as everything took on a Manichaean aspect: God was mirrored by Satan, (even though Satan was always acknowledged, at least in theory, to be weaker and not divine); creation became a battle-ground between good and evil, with humans allowed, by free will, to choose which side they would fight upon; and angels were divided into ranks and had their counterparts in Hell.

Sources of malicious preternatural power, such as the evil eye, continued to exercise potent sway over people's belief and imagination, although now they could be countered by rites and symbols made Christian, while those who inflicted the effects of the evil eye and malicious magical intention upon their neighbours were likely to be seen as adherents of Satan, and therefore idolaters and apostates from the Christian faith.

As a result, the early Christian state came to treat magicians of any kind and their clients as potential trouble-makers or even enemies. The collection of edicts known as the Theodosian Code (AD 428), which contained legal *pronunciamenti* from more or less the whole of the fourth century, forbade consultation of magicians or diviners, regarded necromancy as highly dangerous, since it sought to foretell the future by raising and communicating with the dead, and imposed the death penalty on practitioners of magic. Those who confessed to working harmful or poisonous magic (*maleficium* and *veneficium*), or had been found guilty thereof by due process of law, were not allowed to appeal against their sentences and their families were liable to lose any possible inheritance; nor were convicted defendants able to benefit from any Imperial pardons issued in honour of Easter or to celebrate a birth in the Imperial family. Indeed, being a worker of harmful magic was considered sufficient cause for a woman to sue her husband for divorce, as though he were a murderer or a violator of graves, and some of the edicts went as far as to describe magic in medical terms, as a pollution which contaminates those who come into contact with it.

The state, being the state, consistently attached the death penalty to such practices as these. The Church, however, did not. Its condemnations were just as consistent and just as vehement, but it felt unable, whatever the provocation, to inflict the ultimate penalty. Eager to cure rather than punish what was perceived as spiritual illness, the Church tended to administer, in a spirit of stern rebuke tempered by maternal concern, spiritual remedies in the form of prescribed fasting and prayer. From a plethora of church councils between the fourth and eighth centuries, we can derive a picture of the range of magical activities [that] attracted the wrath of the Christian Church. Women were forbidden to keep watch in cemeteries, presumably for fear that they might rifle the graves or invoke the ghosts of the dead; people were not to call angels by names not to be found in Scripture, a prohibition clearly aimed at the long-standing habit of including Hebrew and Egyptian names in magical invocations; while excessive devotion to certain legitimate angels, such as Michael, was also forbidden, presumably on the grounds that this might be mistaken for something akin to pagan worship.

In late antiquity, anyone,
cleric or layman, might practise
magic in some form and at some time.

'Witches', magicians, diviners and the other practitioners of the occult sciences did not exist on the margins of society in late antiquity; nor were they confined to a particular group by virtue of their age, sex, or education. Anyone at all, cleric or layman, might practise magic in some form at one time or another. We should also avoid drawing strict boundaries between magic, religion and the natural sciences. Parents with a sick child, for example, might offer prayers for its recovery, turning to the priest for exorcism if the illness were of a kind which warranted that assistance, and seeking the help of an apothecary or amateur herbalist for infusions or poultices whose ingredients might or might not be gathered in accordance with astrological calculations, and put together and administered to the accompaniment of prayers or magical formulae or both. Magic was not an exotic recourse to which people turned when religion or 'science' in the form of medicine had failed or seemed to fail them. It was a valid alternative way of seeking to exercise power, or tap into the hidden forces of creation, for personal benefit, even if the official line of both church and state declared that magic was a dubious activity best left alone. In practice, even those very officials might ignore their own prohibitions and behave as everyone else. No one questioned the possible reality of at least some of the effects of magic. Yet it was the danger to the soul and body inherent in that reality that caused the church and state to fear the effects of magic; hence their condemnations, decrees and punishments against it.

In the world of late antiquity or the early Middle Ages, it is impossible to define someone as a witch (as opposed, for example, to an amateur herbalist, a heretic or a scold), and none of the legislation of the time attempted to do so. Offenders were designated offenders by virtue of their performing various actions or wearing certain objects declared by the legislation to be condemned or forbidden. For all practical purposes, the 'witch' had not yet been invented. There were only practitioners of various kinds of magic, both male and female, who might belong to any rank of ecclesiastical or lay society, and whose actions might, or might not, bring them within the compass of canon or secular law, depending on external factors which were usually local but could, from time to time, be more general.

Perhaps the most important factor to influence ecclesiastical and state authority in relation to magic was the ever-present problem of heresy. Deviation from doctrinal orthodoxy had been fought by the Church ever since the earliest years of its establishment, and it was therefore inevitable that it would take a dim view of any manifestations of magic which it did not itself approve or control. Thus, for example, Christian prayers offered with a view to affecting the weather were approved; pagan prayers and rituals offered to achieve the same were not. As a result magic and heresy were almost bound to be perceived as two sides of the same coin.

The consequences of this were significant. The more closely the two were associated, the more likely it was that official perceptions of magic would resemble official perceptions of heresy. Paganism and magic would come to be seen, not as hitherto a loose diversity of questionable activities which depraved or foolish individuals persisted in doing for their own selfish ends, but more an organised movement with its own quasi-theology and liturgy, a distorted mirror of the true faith and the true Church, one with its own god, its own angels, its own 'miracles', and its own worshippers. Once perceived in this way, the impulse to uproot heresy, as it was later to come to be uprooted with the help of the secular authorities doing their pious duty, became potentially very strong. Thus, in 1437, Pope Eugenius IV issued a bull addressed to all inquisitors, deploring the fact that so many people were practising various forms of magic, worshipping evil spirits, and making pacts with them. In consequence of this, he said, these people were to be arrested, brought before inquisitorial tribunals and, with the assistance of the local bishops, tried in accordance with canon law, after which they were to be punished. If necessary, the Pope added, the secular authorities should be called on to render their assistance.

By the later Middle Ages Christian teaching on *daimones* had become a key element in explaining how witches were able to operate and why God allowed them to do so. Alfonso de Spina (died 1469), writing in Latin but recording some Spanish terms for spirits and witches, noted some of their names and types.

> Just as good angels and blessed souls are divided into nine ranks, so evil spirits fell from these nine into another nine categories, and damned souls along with them. Those evil spirits who belonged to the higher grades of the [heavenly] hierarchy became correspondingly worse and more inferior in that part of the meridian whose ruler the Psalmist has called 'the destruction that wastes at noonday'. But there are popular names for many of these spirits and their various grades. Some are called fates, others (in Spanish)

The first known depiction of a witch flying on a broomstick is from Martin le Franc's *Champion des Dames*, 1440. In the manuscript she is described as a *Vaudoise* (Waldensian heretic).

duende, others *incubi* and *succubi*. Some of them cause wars; others eat and drink with human beings and appear in their dreams. Some are said to be generated from the smell given off by a man and a woman during sexual intercourse, or from planetary rays. Some are hermaphrodites; some are clean and others filthy. Some deceive men and women who are called *jorguinas* or *brujas* in Spanish. Many people claim to have seen spirits of this type and stick to the truth of their assertion.

The significance of this for witches is plain. The daimones, in pre-Christian times neutral or even benign figures, had gradually been re-interpreted as evil spirits who mirrored in their organisation and graded powers the angelic hierarchy. By their fall from Heaven through the increasingly inferior stages into which the material world was divided, they arrived in the sublunary, elemental region, where they degenerated and suffered the same imperfections as humankind, though to a lesser degree and without the same limitations. They became associated with the practice of magic in any form, and the conception of magic was so tainted by this association that it became virtually impossible for Christian theologians to dissociate the practice of magic from traffic with evil spirits; when de Spina discussed *jorguinas* and *brujas* (different words for 'witch'), he used a verb *illudere* capable of more than one meaning. The spirits, he said, 'deceive' them in the sense of 'playing with' them or 'making fools of' them, as well as 'using them for sexual pleasure'. His is thus a complex description of a sinister relationship.

The notion of a pact between human beings and daimones became deep-seated, and in consequence any act of magic was liable to be interpreted as the effect of a diabolical alliance between an evil spirit and the human operator. Moreover, as the Middle Ages proceeded, the habit of blaming evil spirits for any kind of misfortune grew. God might be all-powerful and all-merciful, but he was prepared to permit Satan and his evil spirits

to punish people's sins or to test their faith, as the biblical case of Job demonstrated. The serried ranks of angels and evil spirits became opposing armies in a continual war between good and evil; it could therefore be argued that any human being who practised magic was liable to be doing so with the help of Satan and thus to be an enemy of God.

The situation was summed up by the fifteenth-century theologian, Pedro Ciruelo:

> Anyone who maintains a pact or treaty of friendship with the Devil commits a very grave sin because he is breaking the first commandment and is sinning against God, committing the crime of treason or *lèse majesté*. His action is also contrary to the religious vow he made when he was baptised. He becomes an apostate from Christ, and an idolater who renders service to the enemy of God, the Devil.

Matters had now begun to reach the stage where the image of what is now seen as the typical early modern witch of the Sabbat could begin to emerge, although the grounds for the details of her behaviour had been laid a long time before the fifteenth century. In *c*.1115, for example, Guibert de Nogent recorded in his autobiography *Monodiae* (Solitary Songs) details of the behaviour of certain heretics from Soissons. They would meet, he said, in underground chambers where they would light candles and then, coming up behind a woman who was lying on her stomach with her naked buttocks on view for everyone to see, they would 'present the candles to her' (by which Guibert probably meant they inserted them briefly into her anus). After these ritual acts, the candles were extinguished, everyone shouted 'Chaos!' and indiscriminate sexual intercourse took place. Any baby which might result from this copulation was then brought to another meeting and thrown from one person to another through the flames of a large fire until the child was dead, after which its body was reduced to ashes, made into bread, and eaten as a kind of blasphemous sacrament.

These details were by no means unique, and similar tales had long been told of all kinds of heretics and, in the early days, of Christians themselves. Yet they were adapted with only certain changes to give the picture of witches' Sabbats, which rapidly became the norm. By the beginning of the fifteenth century, for example, the heretical sect known as 'Waldensians' or 'Vaudois' had become identified with sorcerers and witches, and Vauderie and Vaudoiserie were used as synonyms of 'sorcery' or 'witchcraft'; the amalgamation of the notion of heresy with the notion of magic was now complete and with magic, it seems, as a whole, although the emphasis did tend to be upon its maleficent operations.

But if the Sabbat itself could be related to anti-heretic propaganda, the witches' flight thither had other, folkloric roots. A description of something similar is to be found in the *Canon Episcopi*, a piece of canon law dating from *c*.906.

> Certain wicked women turn themselves round to face the other way behind Satan and, led astray by hallucinations and figments of their imaginations created by

Serried ranks of angels surround the celestial spheres in this pre-Copernican cosmology.

evil spirits, believe and maintain that during the hours of night they ride upon certain beasts along with Diana (a goddess of the pagans), or with Herodias and an innumerable host of women, traversing many areas of the earth in the silent dead of night; that they obey her commands as though she were their mistress, and that on specific nights they are called to her service.

Perhaps the most notable aspect of records concerning the flight is the degree of scepticism which attended them. The *Canon Episcopi* itself calls such stories hallucinations and figments of the imagination. Burchard of Worms, in the early eleventh century, condemned these and other claims to magical ability, and prescribed a penance of forty days on bread and water for seven consecutive years for anyone admitting to believe in them; while in the twelfth century John of Salisbury, in a passage devoted to dreams and visions, declared that there were some people, driven by their sins and the free rein they gave to their wickedness, who were allowed by God to come to such a pitch of madness that they believed (in the most wretched and lying manner) that something they were experiencing in spirit was actually happening to them bodily. He gives as an ex-

ample attendance at a Sabbat in the train of the pagan goddess Herodias. The Dominican Jordanes of Bergamo introduced medical explanations into the discussion and in *c.*1460 gave it as his opinion that evil spirits worked upon the witch's humours, stirring them up so that they ascended to the brain and there created all kinds of imaginings, which caused the witch to believe that he or she had the power to work magic, be transported from place to place, and attend the Sabbat to worship the Devil.

Despite these doubts, however, the story of witches' flights had a certain allure. Thus in the mid-thirteenth century Thomas of Cantimpré recounted the anecdote of a nobly-born girl who, at the same hour each night, was carried away bodily by evil spirits, and although her brother, a monk, did his best to prevent this from happening by grasping her firmly in his arms, as soon as the hour arrived she disappeared. In the early fifteenth century, Johannes Nider, whose *Formicarius* is an important repository of key ideas in the development of the theory of witches' behaviour, was told about the experience of a fellow-Dominican who arrived at a village to be confronted by a woman who claimed that at night she flew with Diana; and although neither Nider nor his informant believed her story, the fact of its being pletely at variance with earlier conceptions and models of the magical operator, but which tended to concentrate on certain newly developed 'theatrical' (as opposed to everyday magical) aspects of her behaviour. In much of the literature which was beginning to specialise in these aspects, the witch now seems to have been visualised more or less as distinctively female. What is more, her activities were described as those of a person who was less a depraved individual and more a willing member or adherent of an organised anti-Christian sect of Devil-worshippers whose aim was to help Satan corrupt the society of the faithful and thereby swell the ranks of the damned in Hell.

Courtesy of the author

A witch is carried off by the devil on horseback in this 16th-century woodcut.

told is enough to indicate that belief in such flight was common. Then in *c*.1440 Martin le Franc, secretary to the anti-Pope Felix V, wrote a long poem, *Champion des Dames*, in which two speakers exchanged views on witches and their wicked practices. One of them described women going to the Sabbat on foot or on sticks, 'flying through the air like birds', and the manuscript illustrated the point with two marginal miniatures showing one woman astride a besom and the other riding a long, stout staff. Significantly, they flew under the heading 'Vaudoises'.

By the second half of the fifteenth century, then, there had come into existence a notion of the witch which was not com-

FOR FURTHER READING

B. Ankarloo & S. Clark (eds.), *The Athlone History of Witchcraft and Magic in Europe, Vol. 2* (Athlone Press, 1999); V. Flint, *The Rise of Magic in Early Mediaeval Europe* (Clarendon 1991); S. Houdard, *Les sciences du diable: quatre discours sur la sorcellerie* (Cerf, Paris 1992); N. Jacques-Chaquin & M. Préaud (eds.), *Le sabbat des sorciers en Europe, xve-xviiie siècles* (Grenoble, 1993); H. Maguire (ed.), *Byzantine Magic* (Dumbarton Oaks, 1995); P.G. Maxwell-Stuart, *Witchcraft in Western Europe and the New World, 1400–1800*, (Macmillan, 2000) and *Witchcraft: A History* (Tempus, 2000).

P.G. Maxwell-Stuart is honorary lecturer at St Andrews University. His new book *Witchcraft: A History* is published by Tempus in November 2000 at £19.99/$32.50. Call 01453-883300 (UK) or 1-888-313-2665 (USA).

Lackland

The loss of Normandy in 1204

Nick Barratt argues that Normandy's loss in the reign of
King John has had a far-reaching impact on Britain.

by Nick Barratt

BRITONS ARE DRAWN TO events when their independence and freedom have been under threat, yet overwhelming odds have been defied. The Second World War brought the evacuation of the Dunkirk beaches, the Battle of Britain and D-Day. Victories at Trafalgar and Waterloo safeguarded Britain from Napoleon. The defeat of the Spanish Armada cemented the reputation of Queen Elizabeth. The dates we remember most are usually linked with triumph, or at least the aversion of disaster. In contrast one of the most important dates in English history—one which represents one of the greatest catastrophes ever to befall an English monarch—has been airbrushed from national consciousness.

Eight hundred years ago, in 1204, the political map of Western Europe was redrawn in the space of a few months when John, king of England and ruler of territories covering roughly two-thirds of modern France, was expelled from most of these continental lands by the French king, Philip Augustus. The consequences of this humiliating defeat still reverberate, particularly in relations between the English and their neighbours in the British Isles, attitudes to continental Europe, lingering concepts of British imperialism, and the significance of Magna

Carta as a symbol of human rights. I believe this humbling defeat should be seen as a key turning point.

The kings of England from 1066 considered themselves first and foremost as landowners in Normandy and nominal subjects of the King of France but who, as a result of William the Conqueror's invasion, had also acquired a royal title and access to England's riches. The relative unimportance of England to them is illustrated by William's division of his lands before his death in 1087; his eldest son Robert received the Duchy of Normandy, while his second son William Rufus took the secondary prize, becoming William II of England. Nevertheless, the fledgling Anglo-Norman realm was re-united under one ruler, when the Conqueror's third son Henry I inherited England after Rufus's death in 1100 and then defeated and imprisoned his brother Robert at the battle of Tinchebrai in 1106. A cross-Channel aristocracy developed, holding lands in both territories and having a vested interest in keeping them united in one ruler. The wars of Stephen's reign (1135-54) emphasised this; he failed to win over the Norman aristocracy and thereby made the task of hanging on to England much harder. Unification was achieved under Henry II (r.1154-89), but now the Anglo-Norman

realm became part of an even larger accumulation of titles.

Henry II, son of the Empress Matilda and Geoffrey of Anjou, was the nominal ruler of lands stretching from the borders of Scotland to the Pyrenees. He inherited England partly through conquest, partly through his mother's birthright as daughter of Henry I; Normandy had been conquered by his father and Henry was invested as duke of Normandy some time between November 1149 and March 1150; Anjou also passed to him on Count Geoffrey's death in 1151. Perhaps the most audacious acquisition was the strategically important duchy of Aquitaine when Henry married its heiress Eleanor in 1152. This was a gamble; not only was Eleanor eleven years older than the nineteen-year-old Henry, but also she was the repudiated wife of Louis VII, king of France. One of the grounds for the annulment was that she had failed to produce a male heir, a serious issue when dynastic continuity depended on a brood of healthy sons.

Thus, through dynastic accident and shrewd marriage, within five years Henry had gained control of unprecedented resources, often referred to as the Angevin Empire. In 1158 he added lordship of Brittany, and claimed lordship of Ireland following an invasion in 1171 and subsequent settlement by English adventurers. To secure the borders of these lands, Henry forged a complicated network of alliances, paid for by a steady flow of money from England's treasury. Indeed a cynic might argue that money from England's cash-rich economy was more important to Henry than the prestige that its royal title brought.

Thus Henry was an international figure with multiple calls on his time; England was only a constituent part of this territorial jigsaw and it is not surprising that he spent most of his reign abroad. He was a French lord several times over; his place of birth was Le Mans in the province of Maine; his education was as a French nobleman, his first language was French and his leading advisers and courtiers were all French. He was naturally more concerned with affairs on the continent, and spent most of his life defending his acquisitions against external foes such as the King of France, and ambitious sons.

Henry had no intention of keeping the lands together, yet his policy of partially handing the governance of key territories to each of his sons without fully releasing control, led to bitter resentment and open warfare amongst his offspring. On Henry's death in 1189 the vast conglomeration passed virtually in tact to his son Richard, but this was down to the untimely deaths of Richard's brothers Henry and Geoffrey. Only one brother remained—Henry's youngest son John, unkindly described by historians as the runt of the Angevin litter, whom Henry had only entrusted with the lordship of Ireland, still a frontier land in the Angevin territories. Henry's last few years had been spent in open warfare with Richard, who was never a favourite of his father; it was the news that John had joined Richard's revolt in 1189 that broke the old king's heart. Wearied by old age and treachery, Henry was forced to acknowledge Richard as his heir. His last words to his estranged son had a prophetic ring: 'May the Lord spare me until I have taken vengeance upon you.' Henry's time had run out—he died a few days later on July 6th, 1189, but Richard had inherited a poisoned chalice.

Arguably, Richard I was an even more famous figure than his father, win-ning renown and the nickname 'Lionheart' as a Crusader in the Middle East and locking horns with Saladin. Whilst Richard's fame as a warrior and general has endured, his reputation as a competent ruler has come under scrutiny, particularly in the context of the loss of Normandy, the traditional heartland of the Anglo-Norman realm. The Duchy was fundamentally destabilised during Richard's reign on a number of levels—financial, political and structural—through the excessive militarisation of Normandy's frontiers. Furthermore the French king Philip Augustus, 1179-1223, one of Western Europe's most astute and opportunist monarchs, had constantly sought to exploit his position as Henry and Richard's feudal overlord to undermine their position as Duke of Normandy. He had often acted as catalyst in the arguments between father and son. Despite little material success in the ensuing conflicts, the effects on the duchy of Philip's constant military, political and diplomatic barrage was further to destabilise relations between the leading barons and their Angevin princes. The ambivalence of the Norman barons can be traced back to Geoffrey of Anjou's conquest of Normandy, which had forcibly ended many years of open enmity between the two territories. For as long as Henry II and Richard remained successful, the Norman aristocracy proved loyal, albeit grudgingly. However, during Richard's captivity on his way back from Crusade (1193-94), Philip forged an alliance with Prince John, who handed over key castles such as Evreux to the French king, allowing Philip to seize large sections of the French-Norman frontier. Richard spent the rest of his life trying to win them back, whilst the Norman aristocracy never forgot John's treachery.

In the face of Philip's aggression, Richard embarked on a massive programme of fortification along a disputed section of the Norman border called the Vexin. Castle after castle was constructed to provide a strategic network, at the heart of which was Château Gaillard—literally the 'saucy castle'. Built on Les Andelys, an island in the Seine, Château Gaillard was personally designed by Richard, who boasted that its defences were so well conceived that he could defend the castle even if its walls were made of butter. It protected strategic routes to the ducal capital of Rouen: whilst Château Gaillard stood intact, Normandy was safe.

Richard's castle-building programme came at an enormous cost. The duchy's finances were pushed to breaking point, and large drafts of cash from England were required to complete the construction. Norman ducal revenues were insufficient to meet even the cost of garrisoning its defences and so, to fund Richard's seemingly never-ending wars against Philip, England was subjected to unprecedented levels of financial exaction. Worst of all, Richard fatally undermined England's fiscal base, namely revenue from royal demesne lands, at a time when Philip Augustus was vastly expanding the French royal demesne.

On Richard's death in 1199, the new king John faced an unenviable position—committed to unsustainable levels of expenditure in Normandy that could only be funded by huge cash injections from England, drawn largely from politically sensitive sources. Contemporary chroniclers reveal a hitherto unrecognised level of resentment directed against Richard, and in contrast, the first years of John's reign saw praise heaped on the new king as the bringer of peace to a people wearied from heavy taxation and constant warfare. Yet within a few years, John's reputation was in tatters.

Amongst English monarchs, perhaps only Richard III can claim to have been vilified at a level similar to John. There are so many low points of John's reign it is difficult to know where to begin. Here was a man who was alleged to have murdered his nephew with his own bare hands; who lusted after and married a thirteen-year-old heiress, much to the disgust of her fiance, a key ally; who lost territories that had been in his family's possession for centuries; whose actions in England brought the wrath of the Pope onto his God-fearing subjects during the great Interdict of 1208-14, when all church doors were locked; who managed to alienate so many leading English subjects that they declared war on him, having first attempted to tie him to written guidelines for good-government; and who was so disliked that a foreign prince—Louis, son of Philip Augustus—with no legitimate claim to the throne was preferred as a potential monarch by the rebels, who offered him the throne. Even taking into account the difficult political and financial situation bequeathed to him, John was indisputably the architect of his own misfortune.

A chain of events was set in motion by John's marriage in 1200 to Isabella d'Angoulême, betrothed at the time to one of his leading vassals in Aquitaine, Hugh le Brun, Lord of Lusignan. The ensuing squabble quickly turned to full-scale revolt, and as supreme overlord of both John and Hugh, Philip Augustus was provided with an easy opportunity to intervene directly in Angevin affairs. His demands for John to grant justice to Hugh were ignored; and thus, as a disobedient vassal, in 1202 John was formally stripped of all lands held of Philip except Normandy. Philip handed them to Arthur, John's nephew, and promptly embarked on raids against Normandy's borders. In an astonishingly decisive response, John won a victory more stunning than any achieved by his father or brother, and at the castle of Mirabeau captured Arthur along with all the leading Lusignan rebels. All were imprisoned, Arthur at Falaise; but in the words of the Margam chronicler, 'after King John had captured Arthur and kept him alive in prison for some time, at length, in the castle of Rouen, after dinner on the Thursday before Easter [April 3rd, 1203], when he was drunk and possessed by the devil, he slew him with his own hand, and tying a heavy stone to the body cast it into the Seine.' Rumours of this barbaric act, and the treatment of other noble prisoners, sealed John's fate.

The erosion of Norman confidence in their duke had been growing during Richard's last years, but under John, loyalty sank to a new low. Sensing this, Philip continued his assault on John's lands throughout 1203, and quickly seized control of Anjou, Maine and large sections of Aquitaine. More significantly, he made heavy inroads into the Norman defences, seizing castle after castle. John acted like a rabbit caught in headlights and, (correctly) fearing treachery from the Norman nobles, fled

the duchy on December 5th, 1203. Philip had already begun his assault on Chateau Gaillard in August. In one sense Richard's boasts about the defensive capability of Château Gaillard were proved accurate; while opposition to Philip had melted away like butter, the walls of this key defence held out until March 1204. For as long as Château Gaillard held there was hope, as control of Normandy depended on its possession. However, John continued to cower in England, and by the time he had begun to make preparations for a return, it was too late. After a lengthy siege during which local residents were condemned to a horrific existence of depravation and starvation, trapped between the castle walls and the besieging army, Philip Augustus stormed the fortress on March 6th, 1204. He then mopped up resistance in the south and west of the duchy, taking the symbolically important towns of Falaise and Caen, before heading east. He reached Rouen, the ducal capital, in May; with the rest of Normandy in French hands and with no realistic hope of relief from John, resistance seemed futile and the city surrendered on June 24th, 1204. The heart had been ripped out of the Angevin Empire.

John devoted the remainder of his reign to the recovery of his lands. The next ten years were spent frantically gathering resources to mount a campaign of reconquest. Trapped in England, he traversed his kingdom selling royal justice, privilege and office, raising heavy taxes and imposing massive financial penalties on leading magnates to secure the King's 'goodwill'. This was particularly odious given the arbitrary nature of the exactions; and John's treatment of William de Braiose, who was hounded out of his lands and his wife and children starved to death in the dungeons of Windsor Castle on John's orders, left few in doubt of the need for compliance. By 1214 John's arbitrary exactions had secured an enormous war chest. He was risking everything on a military gamble to recover his lost lands. Succeed, and the means would justify the ends; fail, and the consequences were unthinkable.

The funds bought an impressive array of allies, including John's nephew and Holy Roman Emperor, Otto of Brunswick.

John had planned a two-pronged assault, and led the southern attack himself. Predictably, he made little headway and, deserted bv his Poitevin vassals, he was forced to withdraw. Nevertheless, a momentous encounter took place on July 27th, 1214, at Bouvines in Flanders, where Philip squared up to Otto and John's northern allies. In a pitched battle fought on a hot summer's day, Philip's victory was crushingly decisive; God had delivered his verdict on the battlefield, and John slunk back to England to face the consequences.

The date of the battle of Bouvines deserves to be as famous as Hastings, mainly because it decided the direction of England's future development as a nation. First and foremost, the floodgates of political protest in England were opened, leading directly to the creation of Magna Carta in 1215. Although large sections of the document simply attempted to limit the financial exactions of the Crown, several key clauses still have significance as defining civil liberty: 'No freeman shall be arrested or imprisoned or 1 disseised or outlawed or exiled or in any way destroyed, neither will we set forth against him or send against him, except by the lawful judgement of his peers and by the law of the land'; and 'To no one will we sell, to no one will we refuse or delay right or justice.' These statements of justice and the rule of law are enshrined in constitutions around the world, and have been used as rallying cries against oppression. Without John's actions after the loss of Normandy, it is entirely possible that Magna Carta would never have materialised.

Secondly, Bouvines confirmed the end of the Anglo-Norman realm. The cross-Channel aristocracy were forced to choose on which side of the fence they belonged. Thus for the first time the English nobility focused solely on the acquisition and consolidation of possessions within England. Their attention to their English estates led to greater political and social integration, as well as the development of a sense of Englishness that hitherto had been largely absent. Within forty years, John's son Henry III found himself facing a political crisis of his own because he had surrounded himself with non-English courtiers. Although the kings of England retained some continental lands, most importantly Gascony, they were now for the first time resident rulers, with a greater role to play in England's development.

More ominously, the severance of the Anglo-Norman reign had left John free to turn his attention to Wales and Ireland. After successful campaigns, one chronicler remarked that 'Ireland, Scotland and wales all bowed to his nod—a situation which, as is well known, none of his predecessors had achieved—and he would have thought himself as happy and successful as he could have wished, had he not been despoiled of his continental possessions and suffered the Church's curse.' Although the Angevin monarchs no longer had most of their Angevin lands, their grand dynastic visions had not diminished. John's grandson Edward I undertook the conquest of Wales (complete with a castle-building programme of which Richard I would have been proud), and an abortive attempt to estab-

lish sovereignty over Scotland. Similarly, the gradual extension of English rule in Ireland continued. Thus the tone for English imperialism within the British Isles was set in the early years of the thirteenth century.

Finally, the events of 1204 and the battle of Bouvines had created an enmity between the kings of England and France that remained until the nineteenth century. Although Henry III recognised the loss of Normandy, Anjou and Aquitaine under the terms of the Treaty of Paris in 1259, the terms by which he was permitted to hold on to Gascony stored up problems for future generations. The impractical nature of one sovereign having to perform homage as a vassal to another, with ties of fealty that theoretically prevented an independent foreign policy, were unworkable and was a major cause of the Hundred Years War. It was only in 1801 that the British monarchy formally relinquished its claim to the French throne.

Thus without the ineptitude of King John, no modern debate that takes in British devolution, British sovereignty and role within Europe, trial by jury, civil liberty, or even sporting rivalry with the French would be possible. We owe much to the humiliating events of 1203-4, and should celebrate this, one of the least glorious chapters in our history.

FOR FURTHER READING

J. Gillingham *The Angevin Empire* 2nd edition, (Arnold, 2001); S.D. Church, ed., King John: *New Interpretations* (Boydell, 2003); J. Holt, *The Northerners* (Oxford UP, 1961); D. Bates and A Curry, eds., *England and Normandy in the Middle Ages* (Woodbridge, 1994)

NICK BARRATT has written numerous articles about the reigns of Richard I, John, Henry III and Edward I. He currently works as a historical consultant and researcher to the media.

This article first appeared in *History Today*, March 2004, pp. 32–37. Copyright © 2004 by History Today, Ltd. Reprinted by permission.

Hero of the Neva and Lake Peipus

Aleksandr Nevsky defended Russia against enemies from the east and the west—by knowing when to fight and when not to.

By Donald O'Reilly

But for Aleksandr Nevsky, there might not be a Russia today. His story remains a significant part of Russia's ambivalence toward the west since the 13th century, when Russians were simultaneously menaced by Mongol invaders from the east, Swedes from the north and Germans from the west.

Aleksandr was born on May 30, 1219 at Peryaslavl, a fief of his father, Prince Yaroslav II of the house of the Grand Prince of Suzdal. As were all Russian princes at that time, Aleksandr Yaroslavich was a descendant of the family of Ryurik, an eastern Scandinavian Viking who had settled on Russian soil to rule the city of Novgorod in 860. In the 13th century, however, Russia was not a nation, but a people descended from Vikings and Slavs, scattered over a region the size of western Europe. From the grasslands of Ukraine to the deep taiga oak, fir and birch forests of their heartland to the north, the Rus held a common bond only in their Slavic language and the Orthodox Christian faith. Towns were the center of political power, each ruled by a prince, or *kniaz*, with a hired bodyguard of Rus, Germans, Turks, Bulgars, Poles and other professional warriors called the *druzhina* ("companions"). The most powerful prince ruled from the city of Vladimir. Aleksandr's father, and later his brother, would hold that title.

Novgorod ("new city"), the key link in Russia's trade with Europe, was part of Yaroslav's domain. Its council of guildmasters, local landlords and churchmen, called the *veche*, represented a civil middle class that was unique in Russia at that time. Equally unique was the council's right to choose or depose their city's prince. In 1222, Yaroslav was elected prince of Novgorod and moved to take up residence there. The veche met three times a week in the church of St. Sophia, and there young Aleksandr learned about politics by observing the stormy disputes between its members. On four occasions, he saw his father sent packing to Peryeslavl, only to be recalled by the *veche*. He

developed a distaste for dissent and an acute consciousness of the danger that constant discord posed to his homeland. He also developed a profound spiritual life, spending hours reading the Old and New Testaments.

Disgusted with the incessant quarreling in St. Sophia, Yaroslav left Novgorod in 1228 and only returned for short visits, leaving 9-year-old Aleksandr and his elder brother Fyodor under the guardianship of certain Novgorod nobles, with a tutor to handle their education. Fyodor later died prematurely on the eve of his wedding in 1228. When Yaroslav became Grand Prince of Kiev by right of succession in 1236, Aleksandr inherited the fief of Novgorod—with all its attendant headaches. In the following year, however, the northern Rus faced the gravest threat to their existence since they had settled in the region. The Mongol invasion began in earnest, and it would only be the harbinger of other horrors to follow.

Contact with the rising empire of Genghis Khan had first occurred in 1225, when Russians and Cuman Turkish tribesmen defeated a Mongol raiding party at the River Khalka. That encounter should have served as a warning for the people of the region to unite against future incursions. Instead, during the next 12 years the princes and boyars remained preoccupied with feuds, intrigue and civil war, during which they also forfeited their tenuous alliance with the Cumans.

What the Rus were apparently unaware of was that at that same time, the Mongols had been concentrating their growing power toward the conquest of China and the consolidation of an empire encompassing the largest land area in human history. In 1237, they were ready to move west. Legend has it that Genghis Khan gave his sons flags signifying by color the regions they were to rule. In 1243, for example, Batu was given a golden banner before being dispatched to Russia. The Golden Horde was born.

Nomadic horsemen of Turkish languages had long clashed with Slavic farmers over control of the steppe grasslands. Batu, with only 4,000 warriors at his command, succeeded in uniting those wandering bands under his banner. Most of the Golden Horde was, in fact, comprised of Turkic peoples, rather than pureblooded Mongols.

The Mongol *ordu*, or horde, was organized in units of 10 fighting men, each choosing its leader. If one man fled in combat, all 10 would be executed. Mongols avoided the use of lance and sword, preferring to use a double curved composite bow, made of laminated wood, bone and leather, as their primary weapon. Each warrior traveled with a string of horses, alternating between them on the move, so that no one of them would be burdened with a rider for too long. This allowed the Mongols to travel over great distances and gave the horde the appearance of many times the number of men that it actually had. Terror was a key Mongol tactic. Genghiz Khan adopted a policy of sparing cities or kingdoms that submitted to his rule without a fight. The penalty for resistance, however, was for entire populations to be systematically tortured and killed. Slaves were acquired as tribute, for the Mongols did not customarily take prisoners in battle.

Tatar, derived from a Chinese term meaning, literally, "fight-fight," became a common term throughout central Asia and Europe for the Mongols and all the nomadic horsemen who joined them east of the Great Wall of China. Their towns were mobile camps of tents and wagons. The Golden Horde lacked the numbers to settle the regions that it overran. Instead, Batu ruled through the local Slavic leaders who yielded to him. Sarai, built where the Volga and Don rivers came closest to one another—not far from present-day Volgograd—became the Golden Horde's capital, a repository for taxes and slaves from the subject territories all around it.

Ryazan, the first Russian town to face the Mongols in 1237, asked other towns for help. None came and Ryazan was reduced to a smoldering graveyard. Some cities fought one another even as the Golden Horde advanced on them, putting one after another to the torch. The only city they spared was Novgorod. In March 1238, following a winter distinguished by heavy rains, the Mongols approached within 50 miles of the city before the sight of their horses sinking in the marshes surrounding it compelled them to retreat—for the time being.

Aleksandr spent the next year trying to combat the separatist tendencies within the *veche*. In an attempt to undermine the boyars' economic power, he intervened in their system of administering justice by seizing the right to levy a tribute on furs over a vast region to the north of the city. While engaged in centralizing his power, Aleksandr found the time to marry the daughter of the prince of Polotsk in 1239. He also reputedly hunted bears, armed with only a sling, for recreation.

During the summer of 1240, while the Mongols laid plans to attack Kiev, 21-year-old Aleksandr found himself facing another threat. Pope Gregory IX had offered to aid the Rus against the Mongols if they accepted the authority of the Catholic Church in Rome.

When no response was forthcoming, the pope accused Novgorod of interfering with Christian efforts to convert the pagan peoples of adjacent Finland, and on December 14, 1237, he issued a papal bull to the bishop of Upsala, Sweden, calling for a crusade against the Rus. In response to that edict, King Erik Eriksson spent the next two and half years assembling an army of knights, professional soldiers, churchmen and common thieves, which, under the command of his son-in-law, Birger, landed at Abo (now Turku in Finland). After adding local adventurers to his ranks, Birger led the Swedish fleet up the River Neva and landed north of Novgorod. Unctuous self-justifications were clearly not Birger's style, as he sent Alexandr a message that was blunt and to the point: "If you have courage, come here to fight me. Behold, I have taken your land and intend to keep it."

Postponing his original plan to aid Kiev in its hour of dire need, Aleksandr mobilized fighting men from the towns and provinces around Novgorod and Lake Ladoga, and from Karelian and Ingrian vassals. Even with its ranks swelled by Finns who had fled the Swedish invasion, the army he managed to assemble was outnumbered, but Aleksandr judged it vital to attack before the Swedes could establish a fortified bridgehead on the Neva. Reviewing his troops before the march, Aleksandr inspired them with an allusion to the Psalms: "God is not on the side of force, but of the just cause, the truth."

As he force-marched his army to meet the enemy, Aleksandr was aided by intelligence from Pelguse, an Ingrian chieftain who had been baptized into the Orthodox Christian faith. The final approach to the Swedish camp was a difficult trek over marshy ground, but the Novgorodians reached it before dawn on July 15, 1240. There, along the mist-shrouded banks of the Neva, Pelguse claimed to have seen a boat coming slowly toward the shore, bearing the martyred princes Boris and Gleb, propelled by heavenly oarsmen to help their "brother Alexandr."

Of more tangible help to Aleksandr was Swedish overconfidence. Convinced that Novgorod, with the Suzdal army busily engaged with the Mongols, would be too weak to challenge him, Birger and his knights were resting comfortably in a gold-embroidered tent, with the main body of his force still on the other side of the Neva. Consequently, when Aleksandr led a lightning charge into the Swedish camp at sunrise, the result was more of a massacre than a battle. While most of Aleksandr's warriors wrought havoc among the panicking Swedes, other cut the gangways joining their boats to the river bank. Russian accounts claim that Aleksandr, riding at the head of his men, directly challenged Birger to single combat and "impressed his seal upon the face" of his opponent with his lance. Thrown from the saddle, the wounded Swedish commander was rescued by some of his men and carried to safety on the other side of the Neva. After another fight—between themselves over who was to blame for the debacle—the Swedes fled for home that night. In spite of his ignominious defeat, Birger later managed to attain an earldom and founded the city of Stockholm in 1253.

For his victory at the Neva, Aleksandr Yaroslavsky was dubbed Nevsky thereafter. Nevertheless, the Novgorodians soon fell out with him, resentful of his princely ways and of his diplomatic appeasement of the Tatars, who while he was off battling the Swedes had sacked and destroyed Kiev. Aleksandr had adopted his appeasement policy after taking the measure of his foes and making the hard but necessary choice of who to fight and who to buy off. Merciless though they were to any who resisted them, the seemingly invincible Mongols could be dealt with through tokens of submission and payments of tribute. The European crusaders, justifying their rapaciousness with religious zeal, were not open to negotiation. Interpreting Aleksandr's decision as weakness and betrayal, the *veche's* town meetings became unruly and often dominated by the mob. Unwilling to use his household guard to enforce his authority, the chagrined prince returned to his ancestral home of Suzdal.

Late in 1241, however, Aleksandr's choice was vindicated when a greater threat to Novgorod arose. German knights of the Teutonic order, including the Livonian Knights and the Brotherhood of the Sword, seized Izborsk, then marched on Pskov, a town on the southern shore of Lake Peipus locally referred to as "Novgorod's younger brother." After the Germans burned the outskirts of the city, Pskov's boyars opened its gates to them. Once again, the burghers of Novgorod pleaded for Aleksandr to come to their aid.

Like other military-religious orders of that time, the Teutonic Knights had emerged during the crusades to the Holy Land. Unlike the other, more international orders, such as the Templars and Hospitalers, the Teutonic Knights were almost exclusively German. In the Holy Land, they jealously rivaled the other military-religious orders to the point of armed conflict. By the 13th century, the Teutonic Knights had lost most of their holdings there, but had shifted their focus to the conquest and evangelization of the pagan regions of the eastern Baltic. The order soon ruled eastern Germany after exterminating the Prussian tribes who had originally lived there, and became a law unto itself, defying any other authority, religious and secular.

Raising an army in Suzdal and bolstering it with levies from Novgorod and the surrounding countryside, Aleksandr set off for the western frontier. The Teutonic Knights were fighting elsewhere when he arrived at Pskov, which he liberated and punished those of its populace who had collaborated with the invaders. Then, rather than allow the townspeople to endure another siege, Aleksandr went over to the offensive, invading Livonia and, in the absence of any enemy army to stop him, dispersing his forces to lay waste the countryside. That proved to be a mistake, however, for amid those activities his Novgorod militia, under Domash

Tverdislavich, was ambushed and routed by a German force led by Bishop Hermann of Dorpat at Mooste Bridge. That setback compelled Alekandr to withdraw back to Russia, but soon he had an aroused and reunited force of Teutonic Knights and Danes, as well as Bishop Hermann's forces, in hot pursuit. Skirting the southern shore of Lake Peipus in present-day Estonia, Aleksandr took up a position on the eastern shore to make a stand.

Although it was inflated to epic proportions in later centuries, the forces engaged at the lake were dwarfed in comparison to those involved in a typical Mongol battle. At that time, the entire Livonian branch of the Teutonic Order numbered about 131 knights, mostly of the Sword Brethren, a separate order that was absorbed by the Teutonic Order following a disastrous engagement at Saule in 1236, in which it lost 49 of its 120 brother knights at the hands of the Samogitians. To that was added a reinforcement of 60 knights from the Teutonic Order under Hermann Balke, who had become the Livonians' *Landmeister* in 1237. Of those, many would have been distributed among the various garrisons throughout the province. A modern estimate of the Teutonic Order's forces at the battle would be about 100 brother knights and sergeants, to which would be added many times that number in attendant men-at-arms.

It was April 5, 1242 when the battle began, but Lake Peipus was still frozen solid. Open fields were scarce in the region, so the Teutonic Knights saw an advantage in advancing on horseback over the lake itself. They were astonished to discover an unimpressive rabble of ragged armed peasants, bolstered by a cadre of professional Rus warriors, waiting to meet them in a narrow channel at the edge of the lake. If the ice held up to their weight, the situation favored the armored knights, who would be able to mount a devastating shock cavalry charge.

The Teutonic Knights attacked in a wedged-shaped formation described as a "pig's snout." Five armored lancers rode in the front rank, seven in the second, nine in the third and so on, in widening ranks. Behind them, infantry and a rabble of lightly armed teenage skirmishers and scavengers ran to follow through the breach that the knights would punch through the enemy line.

Aleksandr had placed his archers in the center of his line, along with his militiamen. In spite of their appearance, many of them had served in the Neva campaign and had great confidence in their leader. Aleksandr had stationed his personal infantry units and militia from Novgorod at the flanks of his line, but his ace in the hole, his *druzhina* cavalry, waited in the wings, hidden in the lakeside forest.

Crashing into the Russian center, the Germans were elated to see its ranks split wide before their lances, only to realize too late that that had all been part of Aleksandr's plan. Suddenly, the knights found themselves assailed from both sides by a barrage of arrows, javelins and throwing axes. The Germans pressed on, facing Russian horsemen who fought Mongol style, tempting the knights to charge and then veering off to avoid them. Some, armed with hooked spears, pulled Teutonic riders from their mounts. Still the knights advanced, until Aleksandr judged the time ripe to spring the trap and signaled his *druzhina* to fall upon the German rearguard.

Caught in flank from two directions, the Teutonic Knights broke—and according to legend, so did the ice, at least in some places, resulting in numerous heavily armored Germans plunging to their death in the freezing waters below. It should be noted, however, that neither of the most contemporary sources, the *Livonian Rhymed Chronicle* and the *Novgorod Chronicle*, mention knights crashing through the ice, suggesting that the frozen climax, immortalized in Sergei Eisenstein's film, is an apocryphal touch added in later years.

As for casualties, the *Novgorod Chronicle* stated that "countless Chuds fell, and four hundred *Nemtsy*." The term Chuds referred to the Estonian levies that accompanied the forces of the Danish crown and the Bishop of Dorpat. *Nemtsy* was a collective term used to include all the Germans and Danes as well as the Teutonic Knights, suggesting that the battle cost the Crusaders 400 casualties in total. The *Livonian Rhymed Chronicle* gives the Teutonic Order's losses as 20 brother knights killed and six captured. The remainder of their losses would have been Danish knights and vassals of the Teutonic Order or the Bishop of Dorpat, along with their sergeants, both mounted and on foot.

However exaggerated its size may have been, Aleksandr had won a convincing victory over the most feared warriors in central Europe, with his lighter cavalry pursuing the fleeing survivors. He returned to Novgorod in triumph, with numerous German and Danish nobles ignobly tied and tossed across horses' backs like sacks of grain. In contrast to the Teutonic Knights' policy of killing or enslaving the peoples they vanquished, Aleksandr treated his prisoners humanely, ransoming the knights and freeing the men-at-arms.

The Battle of Lake Peipus marked the zenith of Aleksandr Nevsky's military career, but it was by no means the end of it. The Livonian Knights, who had established themselves in Lithuania, made seven incursions across the Novgorodian frontier between 1242 and 1245. Again, Aleksandr showed his belief that the best defense was a good offense by thwarting each invasion in turn with a lightning counterattack, until a final, decisive rout at the hands of his *druzhina* and militia neutralized the Livonian threat.

At that point, however, Aleksandr's attention was necessarily drawn to the east, because his victories had caught the notice of Batu Khan. The leader of the Golden Horde was troubled by the subsequent Russian boast, "Who can stand against God and great Novogorod?" He decided it time to summon the Prince of Novgorod to Sarai for a reckoning.

The Mongol khans made it a standard policy to compel the rulers within their empire to journey to their courts from time to time to "beat earth with their foreheads" in fealty. None of Russia's contentious princes were allowed to war against one another without a Mongol nod. Subjects appointed as tax collectors were given profitable commissions. The Mongols purchased goods and became virtually the only source of money in the local economies. Nevertheless, they ruled as if playing a chess game, carefully calculating their moves, based on their appraisal of each vassal. Batu Khan had an additional reason to reassess Aleksandr's measure, however—in 1246 his father, Grand Prince Yaroslav, died while on his way back from the Mongol capital of Karakorum after answering a summons from the Great Khan, Guyuk. Russian chroniclers assert that he had been poisoned by his hosts. Whenever there was an issue of succession, the Mongols wanted to know all about the new ruler with whom they would have to deal. Aleksandr's surviving eldest brother, Andrei, seemed to be the logical choice to inherit his father's title, but at that point, Batu Khan wanted to see both brothers.

Again faced with the dilemma of whether to fight or submit, Aleksandr turned to the higher clergy for counsel. The Metropolitan Cyril gave his approval for Aleksandr to do whatever it took to appease the Mongols, short of denying his Christian faith and worshipping their animist gods. Aleksandr was in no position to dictate terms, however. Friar Giovanni di Plano Carpini, a Franciscan papal envoy to Karakorum, wrote of one audience at Sarai in 1246, in which Mikhail Vyevolodovich, Prince of Kiev, was ordered to worship the Mongol gods of fire. When he refused, Batu Khan had him wrapped in blankets and trampled to death by horsemen, since the Mongols regarded it as sacrilege to spill the blood of royalty.

Sacrificing his pride for the survival of Novgorod and its people, Aleksandr joined Andrei for the journey to Sarai. There, he found that his reputation had preceded him and the Mongols, impressed by his past exploits, afforded him the honors due his rank. Nevertheless, Batu Khan did not mince words after Aleksandr had settled down in his quarters. "Prince of Novgorod," he said, "do you not know that God has submitted a great number of people to us? Will you alone remain free and independent? If you wish to reign peacefully come at once to my golden tent to acknowledge the glory and greatness of the Tatars." Aleksandr did so, and to his relief his host did not demand that he worship the Mongol deities, declaring the Russian's deep faith in his own God was proof of the integrity of his promises. Batu did press him further, however, by demanding that he and Andrei follow their father's footsteps to Karakorum, a round trip that would take them more than two years. After receiving the brothers at his capital in 1247, Guyuk Khan, suspicious of Batu's preference for Aleksandr, appointed Andrei as Lord of Vladimir and Prince of Suzdal, while Aleksandr was made prince of Kiev. The latter was a dubious honor—during his travels to and from Karakorum, Carpini passed by Kiev years after its fall and remarked that for miles around there were more unburied skeletons than living people.

Ultimately, however, Aleksandr's diplomatic mission was a success. The Mongols had occupied the Ukrainian steppes, but avoided the Russian forests where their horsemen might be at a disadvantage. Their seeming invincibility lay largely in knowing their limitations. Aleksandr was equally shrewd. Both he and his Mongol overlords came to a mutual agreement that each was better bought than fought.

Guyuk died in 1248 and after the Mongols elected Möngke as the new Great Khan, he summoned the Yareslavich brothers to Karakorum. Aleksandr went, but Andrei refused. In 1252, the Mongols sent tax collectors, under armed guard, to visit every Russian province to take a census of the human and farm population. From that, they levied a 10 percent tribute of grain, with no flexibility for subsequent years that might see poor crops. The Novgorodian freemen rejected the census and the tithe. Mongols who entered the city gates were mobbed. When he learned of the incident, Batu Khan was livid with rage and threatened terrible reprisals.

Aleksandr appeared before the *veche* amid an uproar of protest. One of his own sons declared him a traitor. With characteristic calm, however, he persuaded the people that the Tatars must be obeyed, lest Novgorod be reduced to ruins as Ryazan, Vladimir, Kiev and other towns had already been. Grudgingly, his subjects yielded in respect to him, if not his argument. He personally accompanied the Mongol envoys through Novgorod's streets to protect them from the mob. The census was taken and the tribute paid. Aleksandr also appointed his son Vasily prince of Novgorod. Later, when Vasily was ousted by *veche* members who still opposed acquiescence to the Mongols, Aleksandr sent an army to reinstall him in power.

Even while the census proceeded in Novgorod, Andrei was defying the Mongols. Sartak, son of the aging Batu, sent troops to crush the futile revolt and took dreadful vengeance on the people of Suzdal. Aleksandr journeyed to Sarai and pleaded for Sartak to forgive his foolish, headstrong brother. Sartak spared Andrei's life, but sent him fleeing into exile in Sweden and appointed Aleksandr prince of Vladimir. Theoretically, at that point Aleksandr ruled all of Russia—albeit under Mongol suzerainty, a bitter honor under the circumstances.

Batu Khan died in 1255 and in 1258, the Mongols took a new census of Novgorod. Then, in 1262, they unwisely raised the tribute. Again, Suzdal rebelled and killed the Mongol tax collectors. As the spreading revolt reached a kindling point, Aleksandr traveled to Sarai once more, this time convincing the Mongols to reduce the taxes and cease conscripting Russians into the Golden Horde. While returning from Sarai in 1263, he was visiting the Volga domain of his younger brother, Yaroslav III of Tver, when he died, his health evidently worn down from the constant stresses of war and peace, at age 43. Aleksandr's youngest son, age 2, was given the backwoods settlement of Moscow as his meager share of his inheritance.

After Aleksandr Nevsky's demise, Russia slipped ever deeper into Mongol oppression. Any householder who refused to pay his yearly tribute to the Golden Horde could have his children seized and sold into slavery. The first ruler addressed by Russians as *tsar* ("caesar") was not a Russian, but the khan at Sarai. Russian leaders were Mongol agents, obeyed not with civic pride or patriotism, but with dread and hatred.

Russians would not successfully resist the Mongols until 1380, when Dmitri Donskoy led them in battle at Kulikovo, a bloody standoff that nevertheless marked the first ebb of the Mongol tide. Poles, Galicians and Lithuanians crusaded against the Horde too late to save Russia from its ordeal. Mongol armies repeatedly assailed Europe thereafter, but their only major attack on Russia was a venture against Moscow in 1399.

Under the Mongol yoke, the Orthodox Church became the font of Russian patriotism and isolationism, deeply distrustful of western Christianity and unwilling to try evangelizing the Tatars. By the 1400s, most of the Golden Horde had become Muslim.

The lasting cultural memory of the West's stab in the back during the original Mongol invasion rankles Russians to this day. Russia emerged as the child of Europe and central Asia, denied by both.

Aleksandr Nevsky never lost a battle or campaign. Although he never fought the Mongols, he never lost a diplomatic test of will with them. He kept their hordes from invading the Russian heartland, and time and again fended off demands that could bring greater oppression. By having the courage to fight, the prudence to submit and the wisdom to recognize which situation warranted the appropriate response, he earned a place in Russian history as both an Orthodox saint and a national hero.

Donald O'Reilly has a Ph.D. in history and teaches at Rockland Community Collage, N.Y. For further reading, he suggests *History of Russia, Vol. III*, by G. Vernadsky; and *Formation of the Great Russian State*, by A.E. Presniakov.

Spreading the gospel in the Middle Ages

Bernard Hamilton unravels the complex tale of the spread of the Christian faith and its competing hierarchies.

by Bernard Hamilton

ALTHOUGH WESTERNERS did not set out to explore the world until the fifteenth century, their beliefs had long since penetrated far and wide. When Constantine the Great and his colleague Licinius had declared Christianity a lawful religion in the Roman Empire in AD 313, they ended almost three centuries of sporadic but sometimes severe persecution. There were many different Christian sects in the fourth century, but the largest and best organised called itself the Catholic (or universal) church and in 392 Theodosius I made Catholic Christianity the official religion of the Empire. The other sects had died out by c.700 and almost all the churches of the medieval world traced their descent from the Catholic church of the fourth century. They accepted the same Biblical books as canonical; their public worship centred on the eucharist, and authority in all of them was vested in bishops. Medieval Christianity in all its forms was deeply influenced by monasticism, a practice that had spread from fourth-century Egypt to all parts of the Christian world, and men and women who lived as religious solitaries were held in particularly high esteem.

The Catholic church, which worshipped in Latin and acknowledged the pope as its senior bishop, was the only institution that survived the collapse of Roman power in the western provinces during the fifth century and the formation of independent kingdoms there by Germanic settlers. By the seventh century all those rulers had been converted to Catholicism, which had also spread beyond the former imperial frontiers to the Celtic lands in Scotland and Ireland. Medieval Western Europe may have been politically fragmented but it remained united in a shared religious faith.

Catholic Europe proved resilient to attacks from new enemies in the years 800-1000—the Vikings from the north, the Magyars from the east and the Muslims of North Africa from the south. Partly as a result of intermarriage between the invaders and Western Christians, the Catholic religion spread throughout Scandinavia and also to the new lands which the Vikings had discovered and settled in the north Atlantic, notably Iceland and Greenland, where a bishopric was established in 1112. Similarly, the Magyars, together with the other peoples of central Europe, such as the Bohemians and the Poles, were converted to Catholicism by c.1000. Sicily, Iberia and the Balearic islands were recaptured from the Muslims in a series of wars supported by the Papacy, which began in the eleventh century but only ended when Granada fell to the Catholic kings of Spain in 1492. Although there were Jewish communities in some cities and groups of Muslims in some southern frontier regions, by 1050 the vast majority of the inhabitants of western Europe were members of the Catholic Church. Small dissenting movements developed during the eleventh century and a tradition of dissent lived on throughout the rest of the Middle Ages, but its impact was limited except in some areas such as thirteenth-century Languedoc and fifteenth-century Bohemia.

In the early medieval centuries the Western church had been the custodian of literacy in a barbarian world and it inevitably became involved in the work of secular government, since rulers relied on the clergy to draft laws and keep records. The Church worshipped in Latin and preserved the Classical tradition of learning in some of its monastic and cathedral schools. Western Catholic civilisation reached maturity in the twelfth and thirteenth centuries, when its growth of scholarship found institutional expression in the emergence of universities where students were trained to argue in terms of Aristotelian logic. In time this led to the reformulation of Christian doctrine by theologians such as St Thomas Aquinas, who sought to demonstrate that there was no necessary conflict between human reason and divine revelation.

The foundation of the Dominican and Franciscan Orders of friars in the thirteenth century transformed the spiritual life of the Western Church. Their members took the traditional monastic vows, but devoted their lives to pastoral work, aiming to produce a well-instructed and devout laity. They encouraged men and women to seek holiness not in the traditional way by renouncing the world, but by remaining in the world and consecrating their everyday lives to God's service.

The Church always patronised the arts. Romanesque, and later Gothic, churches were decorated with frescoes and embellished with stained glass, a distinctively Western form of religious art. Traditional plainsong accompaniment of the liturgy was augmented in the fourteenth century by polyphony. It was therefore natural that, when a revival of interest in the literature and art of classical Greece and Rome developed in fourteenth-century Italy, the Church should share this enthusiasm and by 1500 Rome had become the centre of the Renaissance as well as the religious capital of Western Europe.

The Church developed in different ways in the eastern provinces of the Roman Empire ruled from Constantinople, which Constantine the Great had made his capital in 325. This part of the Roman state, which survived until the Turkish conquest of 1453, took its name from Byzantium, the former Greek name for Constantinople. Here the emperor was regarded as the vicegerent of Christ the King in temporal affairs, while the patriarch of Constantinople was head of the church hierarchy and custodian of the Orthodox faith (as the church became known in the Middle Ages).

Constantinople was the largest city in the medieval Christian world and its cathedral, the church of the Holy Wisdom (Hagia Sophia), commissioned by Justinian I (527-65), was a masterpiece of engineering in which a huge dome was suspended above a large basilica. The interior was clad in marble and decorated with mosaics and the church could provide the most magnificent liturgy in Christendom. In the ninth century, Orthodox missions from Constantinople converted the Bulgars, Serbs and Slavs, tribes who had invaded and settled the Balkan provinces some 200 years before. In the ninth century saints Cyril and Methodius devised a written form of the Slav language and the new churches came to use translations of the Orthodox liturgy into the Old Slavonic language made by their disciples. Byzantine Orthodoxy in the Old Slavonic rite also spread to Russia after Prince Vladimir of Kiev was baptised in 988.

Monasticism occupied an important place in the Byzantine Church and when St Athanasius founded the Grand Laura on Mount Athos near Thessalonica in 963 and the monks were given control over the thirty-five mile long peninsula, this became the spiritual centre of the Orthodox world. Communities from the Balkans, the Caucasus and Russia, as well as from the Greek provinces, were soon established there.

No other civilisation has ever approached the degree of aesthetic and technical mastery which the Byzantines achieved in the production of mosaics, but that was an elite form of religious art because it was so costly. Icons, or religious paintings on wooden panels, which are focuses of devotion in Orthodox churches and homes, have occupied an important role in devotional life at all social levels since the eighth century. These have had a spiritual significance since the Second Council of Nicaea in 787 defended the use of religious representational art by arguing that Christ, through his incarnation, had made it possible for the entire material creation to be consecrated to the glory of God and to become a vehicle of grace.

Although in the early Middle Ages the Byzantine and Western churches were united in matters of faith, they later came to understand some parts of that faith (for example, the role in the universal Church of the pope as successor of St Peter) in different ways. Political tensions between the West and Byzantium culminated in the sack of Constantinople by the Fourth Crusade in 1204, and exacerbated those differences and in the thirteenth century led to a schism which has not yet been healed.

A third centre of Christianity developed in late antiquity, when Antioch in Syria, which had occupied an important place in the history of the early Church, was one of the greatest cities in the eastern Mediterranean. By the fifth century its bishop had been given the title of Patriarch and was regarded as their head by all the churches of Asia.

Monasticism flourished in fifth-century Syria and asceticism took some extreme forms. St Symeon Stylites left his monastery in 423 and spent the remainder of his life atop a series of increasingly high columns, on the last of which, 60 feet high, he remained for twenty years, absorbed in prayer, until his death in 459. Huge numbers of people visited him to seek intercession for their illnesses and afflictions and on occasion the emperor in Constantinople sent to ask his advice.

During the fifth century serious divisions arose among the Christians of the East. These grew out of disagreements between theologians, who sought to define the traditional belief that Christ was both the Son of God and the son of Mary, in Greek philosophical terminology. Some of the decisions about these disputes, were ratified by General Councils of the Church and proved acceptable in the Greek provinces, were rejected by some bishops in the eastern provinces for reasons that were often more semantic than substantive; but those dissenting bishops attracted a wide following among the non-Hellenic population which had little sympathy with the Imperial Church in Constantinople. Attempts to find a compromise broke down in the sixth century and divisions became permanent. While some people remained faithful to the Orthodox patriarchs of Antioch, who were in communion with Constantinople, large numbers seceded to form the Jacobite church, named after its first bishop, Jacob Baradeus, which had its own patriarch and worshipped in Syriac—the common speech at the time. In the seventh century matters were further complicated when the Maronites, found chiefly in Mount Lebanon, also broke away from the Orthodox church and appointed their own patriarch.

The bishop of Jerusalem, who had been given the title of patriarch in 451 by the Council of Chalcedon, had jurisdiction over Palestine. That province remained largely Orthodox. Jerusalem, the mother-church of Christendom, was a spiritual focus for the whole Christian world. In 325 Constantine the Great ordered a church to be built on what were traditionally believed to be the sites of Calvary and of Christ's tomb in Jerusalem. This great shrine, known to the Byzantines as the Anastasis or church of the Resurrection, and to Western Christians as the church of the Holy Sepulchre, immediately became a focus of pilgrimage and remained so throughout the Middle Ages despite frequent changes of secular ruler. Adherents of churches throughout the world met and worshipped at the shrine of their founder.

When in c.640 the Arab followers of the Prophet Muhammad conquered Syria and Palestine, they tolerated all forms of Christianity equally, but forbade Christians to proselytise Muslims on pain of death. Although in 800-950 there were large-scale conversions to Islam, Christians still remained a significant minority in those regions. The First Crusade (1096-99) brought much of this area under Western (Frankish) rule for some 200 years. The Franks established the Catholic Church in their kingdom, but tolerated all forms of eastern-rite Christianity. During this period the Maronite Church came into full communion with the Western Church; it preserved its own hierarchy, liturgy and canon law and its patriarch was made directly subject to the pope. That union has lasted to the present day. Although the

Franks were finally driven out of the Holy Land in 1291, a Catholic presence was restored there in 1336 when the sultan of Egypt allowed the Franciscans to establish the Custodia Terrae Sanctae to minister to Western pilgrims visiting the Holy Places.

Moving further east, Christianity had reached the Caucasus in the fourth century. Armenia, where King Tiridates III was converted by St Gregory the Illuminator in *c*.314, justly claims to be the first Christian state, since in the Roman Empire at that time Christianity, though tolerated, was not the established religion. In the neighbouring kingdom of Iberia (Georgia), the introduction of Christianity in the fourth century was traditionally ascribed to St Nino, the only woman who has ever been given the honorary title of Apostle. Both Caucasian churches came to adopt a vernacular liturgy, but whereas the Georgian church remained in communion with the Orthodox church of Byzantium, the Armenian church refused to recognise the General Council of Chalcedon of 451 at which it had not been represented, and became independent under its own Catholicus in the early seventh century. The Armenians, despite being widely dispersed throughout the Levant and the Near East during the Middle Ages, preserved their religious identity and their church developed distinctive forms of liturgy, chant and canon law.

Christians were always in a minority in the Persian Empire, where Zoroastrianism was the established religion, and Christians there were initially subject to the patriarchs of Antioch; but they became involved in the Christological disputes of the fifth century and in the 480s most of them seceded to form an independent church with its own patriarch. They are often, but wrongly, called Nestorians. They called themselves the Church of the East, and are also known as Chaldean Christians.

The Arab conquest of the seventh century, which led to the establishment of Islam, made little difference to their status. Many Persian Christians became Muslims in the ninth and tenth centuries, but these losses were offset by the missionary activity of the church of the East outside the Arab Empire. A stele at Xian in China records the arrival in 635 of a Christian mission from Persia and relates how the Emperor Taizong had the Christian scriptures translated and, finding the new faith 'mysterious, wonderful and calm', gave permission for a monastery to be founded in his capital. The Church of the East flourished in China until 845 when it was proscribed by the Emperor Wuzong, a devout Daoist. Meanwhile churches had been founded along the trade routes linking Persia and China and in 795 the patriarch Timothy I had consecrated a bishop for Tibet. In *c*.1000 the ruler of the Keraits, a Mongol-Turkic people, became a Christian, and that religion then spread not only among his own tribe, but also among the neighbouring peoples of central Asia, the Naimans and the Merkits.

Thus when Genghis Khan became ruler of the Mongol confederacy in 1206, he numbered Christian princes among his vassals. His successors, while not themselves becoming Christians, favoured the Church of the East. When they conquered China they allowed Christian clergy to operate there, and when they sacked Baghdad in 1258 the entire population was put to the sword—except for the patriarch of the East and his flock. The Mongols appointed Christians to positions of authority in the Muslim lands which they conquered because they trusted them and under Mongol rule the Church of the East reached the pinnacle of its power.

This Christian ascendancy was deeply resented by the non-Christian subjects of the Mongols. After the Mongol Ilkhan of Persia was converted to Islam in 1295 the church of the East was severely persecuted by the Muslim majority there, and similarly, when the native Ming dynasty overthrew Mongol rule in China in 1368, Christians lost favour and were driven underground. Thereafter the once great church of the East fell into decline, and by 1500 had relatively few adherents.

The one part of the Arab Empire in which Christians were not tolerated was Arabia. In late antiquity there had been numerous churches in many of the coastal provinces of the peninsula, as well as along the borders with Syria and Mesopotamia, but it was later claimed that Muhammad, when dying, had expressed a wish that all Arabs (and therefore by implication the whole of Arabia) should be of one faith. That policy was only slowly implemented, but by AD 1000 no traces of organised Christianity were to be found on the Arabian mainland, although the island of Socotra, between Arabia and Horn of Africa, was still inhabited by Chaldean Christians when the Portuguese annexed it in 1507.

From at least the fourth century there were Christian churches on the Malabar coast of South India which claimed to have been founded by the Apostle Thomas. Although that claim is not impossible, it rests on tradition alone. Very little evidence has survived about the history of these South In-

dian Christians during the Middle Ages, but when the Portuguese reached India in the early sixteenth century they found that the St Thomas's Christians worshipped in Syriac and were ruled by Persian bishops appointed by the patriarch of the church of the East in Baghdad. The lower clergy were South Indians and their church had accepted the caste system of the dominant Hindu culture in which they lived. Thus, although untouchables were baptised by them, they were not allowed to worship with the rest of the community. This practice was challenged by the Western Catholic clergy who ministered to the Portuguese.

In late antiquity Christianity had also been strongly rooted in north Africa, which had produced such notable theologians as St Cyprian and St Augustine. All the provinces to the west of Cyrene (in modern Libya) formed part of the Western church and worshipped in Latin. In the sixth century successful missions were conducted among the nomads of the Sahara, and some of the Garamantes became Latin Christians. Yet after the Arab conquest the North African churches began to decline. This was a slow process, and popes continued to appoint bishops to sees like Carthage and Tripoli until the middle of the twelfth century, but traces of organised, indigenous Christian communities become rare after that time.

Cyrene and Egypt formed part of the Hellenistic world. Christians there worshipped in Greek and were subject to the patriarch of Alexandria. In the fourth century Egypt was gripped by monastic fervour. The land of the pharaohs was transformed; the festival hall of Thutmosis III in the temple of Karnak was turned into a church, while Christian anchorites (hermits) lived in some of the royal tombs in the Valley of the Kings.

The Christological controversies of the fifth century proved as divisive in Egypt as in Syria and from the 530s a schism developed between the Hellenised population living in some of the cities of the Nile delta, who remained in communion with the Orthodox patriarchs of Alexandria, and the rest of the population, who formed the Coptic church of Egypt with its own patriarch. Coptic, a late form of ancient Egyptian language, was the common speech of Egypt and was used by the Coptic church in its liturgy. The Coptic church was a sister-church of the Jacobite church of Syria.

The Arabs who conquered Egypt in the 640s recognised both churches. Islam later made many converts, and by the tenth century, Egyptian Christians had become a minority, albeit a substantial one, but the Coptic patriarchs continued to be treated with respect by the Muslim rulers because they were the acknowledged heads of the churches in the kingdoms of Nubia, to the south of Egypt along the Nile. Early Arab attempts to annex Nubia failed and after 650 the Egyptian frontier was fixed at Philae. To the south were two independent kingdoms: Makuria, which extended from Philae to the sixth cataract of the Nile, and Alwa, whose capital was at Soba on the Blue Nile, near modern Khartoum. Both kingdoms had become Christian in the sixth century, and throughout Nubia the Nile was lined with churches and monasteries, decorated with vivid and distinctive frescoes, in which the liturgy of Alexandria was sung in Greek. The churches in both kingdoms acknowledged the Coptic patriarch as their head and he consecrated their metropolitan bishops. These vigorous Christian cultures only collapsed towards the end of the Middle Ages when royal power grew weak in both kingdoms and church organisation broke down.

The kingdom of Axum, from which the medieval kingdom of Ethiopia evolved, became Christian during the reign of King Ezana (r. 325-52). In the Middle Ages the Abuna, or head of the Ethiopian church, was always an Egyptian monk appointed by the Coptic patriarch, but apart from this link Ethiopian Christianity developed largely in isolation and in a distinctive way. In the seventh century the church abandoned Greek and adopted the vernacular language Geeze in its liturgy. In accordance with a vision of the worship of Paradise granted to St Yared, sistrums or sacred rattles were shaken and drums beaten to accompany the chant in ecclesiastical processions, while colourful liturgical umbrellas were held over the clergy to protect them from the sun.

The ascetic tradition of early Egyptian monasticism was preserved in Ethiopia. Many monasteries were built on the tops of sheer-sided rock formations, or on narrow ledges high on the sides of mountains, and were approachable only by climbing up ropes lowered by the brethren. Although such locations were chosen partly for reasons of security, the monks also wished to live in places which were as remote as possible from the world.

The Egyptians thought of Ethiopia as a distant and exotic land from which embassies sometimes came to Cairo bringing unusual gifts, such as that sent in 1209 by King Lalibela with an elephant, a giraffe, a hyena and a zebra for the sultan and a crown of pure gold for the Coptic Patriarch. Like most medieval Christians, Lalibela believed the church was the new Israel. At his capital, Roha (now called Lalibela), he commissioned the construction of a large number of shrine churches hewn from the living rock. This was to be a centre of pilgrimage and a symbol to his people of Holy Zion, for many of the churches were named after the chief shrines of Jerusalem. The earliest written evidence for the Ethiopian epic, the *Kebra Nagast* (*The Glory of the Kings*), dates from his reign, and relates how the kings of Ethiopia are descended from Menelik, son of Solomon and the Queen of Sheba, who is said to have brought the Ark of the Covenant from Jerusalem to Ethiopia.

In the later Middle Ages every church in Ethiopia had a *tabot*, a portable altar-slab symbolising the Ark of the Covenant, and when a tabot was carried in procession outside a church the clergy danced before it as King David had once danced before the Ark, but the true Ark was believed to rest in the cathedral at Axum. Alone among the churches of Africa, that of Ethiopia increased in size and power during the Middle Ages by evangelising the huge areas conquered by the crown in the province of Shoa to the south and around Lake Tana to the west.

FOR FURTHER READING

P. Brown, *The Rise of Western Christendom, Triumph and Diversity 200-1000* (Blackwells, 1996); J.M. Hussey, *The Orthodox Church in the Byzantine Empire* (Oxford UP, 1986); I. Gillman, and H-J Klimkeit, *Christians in Asia before 1500* (Curzon Press, 1999); G. Gerster, *Churches in Rock: Early Christian Art in Ethiopia* (Phaidon 1970); J. Farnell, *A History of the Russian Church to 1448* (Longman, 1995).

Bernard Hamilton is Emeritus Professor of Crusading History at the University of Nottingham.

Saints Or Sinners? The Knights Templar in Medieval Europe

During the trials that destroyed one of 14th-century Europe's most celebrated crusading military orders, witnesses claimed all manner of abuses had been going on for years. But how true were these claims? And what did contemporaries think about them and the other military orders—such as the Knights Hospitaller and Teutonic Knights? Helen Nicholson investigates.

In October 1307, by order of Philip IV of France, all the Knights Templar within the French domains were arrested. In November, Pope Clement V sent out orders for the arrest of the Templars throughout Europe. The brothers were accused of a variety of crimes, which were said to be long-established in the order. There were, it was claimed, serious abuses in the admission ceremony, where the brothers denied their faith in Christ. The order encouraged homosexual activity between brothers. The brothers worshipped idols. Chapter meetings were held in secret. The brothers did not believe in the mass or other sacraments of the church and did not carry these out properly, defrauding patrons of the order who had given money for masses to be said for their families' souls.

What was more, it was alleged that the Templars did not make charitable gifts or give hospitality as a religious order should. The order encouraged brothers to acquire property fraudulently, and to win profit for the order by any means possible.

During the trial of the Templars witnesses claimed that the order's abuses had been notorious for many years and under interrogation, including torture, many brothers confessed to at least some of these crimes. In March 1312, Pope Clement dissolved the Order of the Temple, giving its property to the Order of the Hospital, and assigning the surviving brothers to other religious orders. Despite this, the question of the order's guilt has never been settled. Just what were the accusations made against the Templars before 1300, and were these related to the trial? What did contemporaries think about the other military orders, such as the Knights Hospitaller and the Teutonic Knights?

The Order of the Temple was a military order, a type of religious order. It had been founded in the early twelfth century, in the wake of the Catholic conquest of the Holy Land, to protect pilgrims travelling to the holy places against bandits. This role soon grew to protecting Christian territory in Spain as well as the Holy Land. The order gained its name because the King of Jerusalem had given the brothers his palace in the al-Aqsa mosque, which the Christians called 'the Temple of Solomon', to be their headquarters. In Europe the members' lifestyle was much like that of ordi-

nary monks. The order's rule laid down a strict regime on clothing, diet, charitable giving and other living arrangements. In theory only men could join the order, but in practice some women were also admitted.

The Order of the Temple was the first military order, but others soon followed. The Order of the Hospital of St John of Jerusalem had been founded as a hospice for pilgrims in the eleventh century, but by the 1130s the Hospital was employing mercenaries to protect pilgrims from bandits, and was soon involved in the defence of the frontiers of the Kingdom of Jerusalem alongside the Order of the Temple. These brothers became known as the Hospitallers.

The Hospital of St Mary of the Teutons was set up at the siege of Acre during the Third Crusade (1189–92) to care for German pilgrims and was then relaunched in 1198 as a military order. The brothers were known as the Teutonic Knights. These were the most famous of the international military orders, but the concept was so popular that others were founded wherever Christians confronted non-Christians: in Spain, where the Muslim frontier was slowly retreating, and in the Baltic and Prussia where pagan tribes threatened Christian settlements and converts. From the 1230s onwards the Teutonic order became prominent in the Baltic area.

The concept of the military order was a natural development from the concept of the crusade. Rather than taking up weapons for a short period to defend Christ's people, the members of a military order did so for life. In return, they expected to receive pardon for their sins and immediate entry into heaven if they died in action against the enemies of their faith.

In western Europe, far from the battlefield, some of the clergy were doubtful whether a military order could be a valid religious order. Around 1150, the Abbot of Cluny wrote to Pope Eugenius III that he and many of his monks regarded the brothers of the Temple as only knights, not monks, and believed that fighting the Muslims overseas was less important than suppressing bandits at home. Letters written to encourage the early Templars also hint at this sort of opposition. But the bulk of the surviving evidence is warmly in praise of the Templars, and clergy and knightly classes alike welcomed the new order with generous donations. In fact the Hospital of St John seems to have attracted more donations as it became more of a military order. By 1200 the military orders had become part of the religious establishment and criticism of the concept ceased.

However, other criticism arose which tended to fluctuate with events. During a crusade, while crusaders wrote home with accounts of the military orders' courage and self-sacrifice, criticism was overlooked. Between crusades, as Europeans received news of territorial losses to the Muslims, they forgot the military orders' heroism and concluded that these defeats were God's punishment for sin. For surely God would not allow godly men to suffer such setbacks.

Political views also shaped criticism, especially during the period 1229–50, while pope and emperor were at loggerheads. The Temple, and to a lesser degree the Hospital, supported the pope, while the Teutonic order supported the emperor. So observers sympathetic to the emperor's policies in the Holy Land,

such as Matthew Paris, chronicler of St Albans abbey, criticised the Templars and Hospitallers. Yet there was praise from those who opposed the emperor in the Holy Land, such as Philip of Novara and the Powerful Ibelin family of Cyprus who were Philip's lords.

Chroniclers tended to be critical, for they wished to draw a moral from contemporary events for the edification of future generations. In other forms of literature, romance, epic or farce, the Templars, Hospitallers and Teutonic Knights appeared as brave knights of Christ combating the Muslim menace, or as helpers of lovers, or as good monks. It is interesting that although monks and parish priests came under heavy criticism for their immorality in the 'fables' or farces, the military orders were not criticised. Obviously they were not regarded as womanisers.

Between the Second and Third Crusades of 1148–49 and 1189, the generous donations of money and privileges to the Templars and Hospitallers became a major cause of resentment. This was hardly surprising. All religious orders aroused complaints about their privileges, and the Templars and Hospitallers never attracted such severe criticism as the Cistercians and friars.

But the Templars and the Hospitallers caused particular annoyance because their houses were so widely scattered. Their legal privileges were especially resented. In 1236 Pope Gregory IX wrote to the Templars and hospitallers in western France ordering them not to abuse the privileges granted to them by the papal see. The brothers had been summoning their legal opponents to courts in far-off places which they had no hope of reaching by the specified day, so that they were then fined for failing to appear. The brothers had also been taking annual payments for clergy and laity in return for allowing them to share their legal privileges.

Forty years later, when Edward I's commissioners were conducting the Hundred Roll inquiries to establish where royal rights had been usurped in each locality, there were similar protests. Some people who had no proper connection with the Templars and Hospitallers were claiming their privileges, in Warwick-

shire and Derbyshire there were complaints that the orders' privileges 'impede and subvert all common justice and excessively oppress the people', while the burghers of Totnes and Grimsby had been summoned to courts in the four corners of England by the Hospitallers and Templars respectively.

Despite their extensive possessions, the Templars and Hospitallers were always claiming to be poverty-stricken. They sent out alms-collectors on a regular basis, to collect money from lay-people and clergy for their work in the Holy Land. Matthew Paris was probably expressing a widely-felt discontent when he wrote around 1245:

> The Templars and Hospitallers… receive so much income from the whole of Christendom, and, only for defending the Holy Land, swallow down such great revenues as if they sink them into the gulf of the abyss…

Whatever did they do with all their wealth? Some Europeans concluded that they must be using their resources very inefficiently.

The orders were not only wealthy and privileged, they were proud and treacherous. Pride, the first of the seven deadly sins, was already the military orders' most infamous vice by the 1160s. As the years passed it became a stock complaint against the Templars and Hospitallers, as if it was 'their' sin. Pride made the orders jealous of each other and of other Christians, so that they fought each other instead of fighting the Saracens. The Templars and Hospitallers' quarrels became notorious, although in fact the orders went to great lengths to ensure peaceful relations. The troubadour, Daspol, writing in around 1270, neatly summed up the problem: because the Templars and Hospitallers had become proud and greedy and did evil instead of good, they were unable or unwilling to defend the Holy Land against the Saracens.

In 1289 a Flemish satirist, Jacquemart Giélée, depicted the Templars' and Hospitallers' bitter quarrels in his satire, *Renart le Nouvel*, the new Renart, based on the old theme of the unscrupulous fox. A

Hospitaller is shown denigrating the Templars in order to win Renart for his order. After the final loss of Acre in 1291, Pope Nicholas IV suggested that the military order's quarrels had been a contributory factor in the defeat, and many chroniclers and churchmen agreed.

The charge that the Order of the Temple encouraged the brothers to acquire property fraudulently and to win profit by all possible means clearly reflects these complaints against the Templars and Hospitallers. For at least 150 years contemporaries had accused the military orders of lying and cheating because of their greed for wealth. In 1312 the same old criticisms against the Hospitallers arose again at the Council of Vienne, as the pope planned to bestow on them the former property of the Templars.

Interestingly, no critic before 1300 accused the Templars of immorality. In the mid-thirteenth century an English poet, writing in Anglo-Norman French, surveyed the whole of society and accused most of the clergy of womanising, even dropping hints about the Hospitallers. But he exempted the Templars, who were too busy making money to have time for sex:

The Templars are most doughty men and they certainly know how to look after themselves, but they love pennies too much; when prices are high they sell their wheat instead of giving it to their dependants. Nor do the lords of the Hospital, have any desire for buying women's services, if they have their palfreys and horses, I don't say it for any evil…

A more explicit charge of immorality against the Hospitallers appeared in March 1238, when a French crusade was preparing to depart for the Holy Land. Pope Gregory IX wrote a letter of rebuke to the Hospitallers in Acre. He had heard that the brothers kept harlots in their villages, had been cheating the dying into bequeathing their property to them and (among other crimes) that several of the brothers were guilty of heresy. As for the Templars, he only complained that they

were not keeping the roads safe for pilgrims!

Although the Templars were not accused of immorality, they were linked with traditional romantic love. A late thirteenth-century French verse romance, *Sone de Nausay*, depicts the Master of the Temple in Ireland as the go-between in a love affair, while a French Arthurian romance of the same period, *Claris et Laris*, depicts the Templars as friends to lovers. But this was a wholly sympathetic view, and saw the Templars as servants of lovers rather than as lovers themselves. None of the military orders were accused of sodomy, although such accusations were occasionally made against ordinary monks.

There were many other complaints against the military orders before 1300. Perhaps the most significant were the divided opinions over their record of fighting the Muslims (and other non-Christians). Many complained that they were not sufficiently enthusiastic about defending Christendom and winning back lost territory, while others complained that they were too eager to fight those who could be won to Christ by peaceful means.

Some contemporaries alleged that the military orders were unwilling to fight the Muslims because they were secretly in alliance with them. The military orders certainly did make alliances with Muslim rulers on various occasions, but these alliances were intended to promote the Christian cause, not to hinder it.

The chroniclers also alleged that the Muslims exploited the brothers' greed. There was a legend in circulation which recounted how the Christians had failed to capture a Muslim fortress because some of the Christian leaders had been bribed by Muslim gold to raise the siege. This gold subsequently turned out to be copper. This story appeared in various forms and with various parties in the role of dupe from the mid-twelfth century onwards. By the early thirteenth century the Templars had become the dupes, and by the mid-thirteenth century the Hospitallers had joined them. The fortress also changed identity several times! In fact this is a very old story, and versions of it appear in Gregory of Tours' *History of the Franks*, written in the sixth century,

and in the collection of ancient Welsh legends known as the *Mabinogion*.

Many accusations that the military orders were unwilling to attack the Muslims arose from a misunderstanding of the true situation in the Holy Land. The Templars were criticised for refusing to help the Third Crusade besiege Jerusalem in 1191–92, but the brothers believed that the city could not be held after the crusaders had returned home, and that the security of the holy places were better served by attacking Egypt. In 1250, during the crusade of Louis IX of France, Count Robert of Artois decided to lead the vanguard of the crusading army to attack the Muslims in Mansourah. The Templars and Hospitallers advised against this, whereupon the count accused them of laziness and trying to impede the Christian cause and advanced. Anxious not to be accused of cowardice, the military orders accompanied him and, as they had predicted, the Christian army was cut to pieces. This was a terrible defeat, but something of a propaganda coup for the military orders, who had fearlessly died for Christ against hopeless odds.

Other critics felt that the military orders were *too* eager to fight. Thirteenth-century literature depicted the ideal knight as one who only fought when necessary. The military orders' self-sacrifice for Christ seemed rash and irrational. Some of the clergy believed that the orders' love of violence and domination impeded or prevented conversions. This accusation was made against the Templars in the 1180s by Walter Map, Archdeacon of Oxford, and against the Teutonic order by some unknown critics and around 1266–68 by Roger Bacon, an English Franciscan friar imprisoned in Paris for his unorthodox views.

The unknown critics may have been the Polish princes who opposed the expansion of the Teutonic order's power in Prussia. In 1258, letters were sent to Pope Alexander IV from the order's friends in Poland and Prussia, defending them against various accusations. Apparently the brothers had been accused of forbidding the preaching of Christianity to the pagan Prussians, preventing the establishment of churches, destroying old churches, impeding the sacraments and enslaving new converts. Roger Bacon's criticisms echoed these: the Teutonic order wanted to subjugate the Prussians and reduce them to slavery, and refused to stop attacking them in order to allow peaceful preaching. He added that the order had deceived the Roman Church for many years as to its true motives in Prussia.

The peak of criticism of the military orders came around 1250. After this they faded from the chronicles and critical writings. Many critics of the church omitted them. Others showed little actual knowledge of them. Although there was a vast number of newsletters coming from the Holy Land, so the chroniclers could hardly have been short of information on events, they seem to have chosen to ignore this. News was almost invariably bad, and chroniclers probably believed that the loss of the Holy Land was only a matter of time. There were many crises closer to home to occupy their pens.

As a result, after 1250, the image of the military orders expressed in the chronicles and other writing shows a relative improvement. Day-to-day relations between the military orders and their neighbours and the authorities were usually peaceful. Bishops' registers, royal administrative records and the records of the nobility where these survive, show that although there were disputes generally the military orders were obedient subjects and reliable servants. As Walter Map had remarked, whatever the Templars did in the Holy Land, in England they lived peacefully enough.

Despite the sorry state of the Latin Christian settlement in the Holy Land, after 1250 the military orders were still well regarded in Europe. Donations to the orders had fallen in most areas, but all religious orders were suffering in this respect. Some commentators, while agreeing that even the Templars had declined in spirituality along with all other religious orders, depicted them as having previously been among the most spiritual of the religious orders. This was a far cry from their original foundation, when some had doubted that the order could have a spiritual dimension at all!

So, how far were the Templars' accusers of 1307 justified in their case against the order? Contemporaries would certainly have agreed with the charge that they lied and cheated in order to satisfy their greed. Yet there is no hint before 1300 that the Templars did not carry out the sacraments; although the Teutonic order were accused of impeding the sacraments in Prussia. It was true that the proceedings of the order's chapter meetings were kept secret, but this was the custom among military orders.

The accusation that the order did not practice charity and hospitality may have sprung from the rivalry between the Temple and the Hospital. The Hospitallers were always at pains to emphasise their dual hospitable-military role, in contrast to the solely military role of the Templars. A few contemporaries were struck by the difference: a German pilgrim, John of Würzburg, remarked dismissively in around 1170 that the Temple's charitable giving was not a tenth of the Hospital's. Of course, the Order of the Temple did practise charity, as it was obliged to do under its religious rule, but most contemporaries seemed to have regarded the defence of pilgrims as charity in itself.

There is no indication before 1300 of public scandal over the order abusing admission procedures, or of heresy, idolatry or homosexuality within the order. Only the Hospital was accused of heresy. Interestingly, the Teutonic Knights' rivals in Livonia were accusing them of pagan practices and witchcraft by 1306. This suggests that such charges were politically motivated, rather than based on fact.

The accusations of denial of Christ, sodomy and idolatry had been standard accusations against heretics for centuries, most recently against the Waldensians and the Cathars. Therefore, to accuse a rival of such crimes was to accuse them of heresy. Orthodox Christian belief was believed to be essential for the health of society and to ensure God's favour. Heresy was seen as a disease which must be eradicated before it overcame the whole Christian body. Powerful political rivals could use the charge of heresy with devastating effect against their opponents: it had been deployed by Pope Innocent IV against the emperor Frederick II during the 1240s, and from 1303 by Philip IV's government against Pope Boniface VIII, who had infuriated Philip by asserting the supremacy of the church over secular rulers. Boniface was accused of heresy, sodomy, witchcraft and magic. Later Guichard, Bishop of Troyes, and Louis of Nevers, son of the Count of Flanders, were accused of similar crimes after incurring Philip's enmity.

Certainly any wealthy, privileged religious order with close ties to the papacy, such as the Cistercians, Friars, Hospitallers or Templars, was likely to incur a monarch's enmity. Yet the Templars were no more disliked than other military orders, and less criticised than some other religious orders. They had a long history of faithful service to the French crown. So why were they singled out for attack?

The Templars had a special position in the defence of the Holy Land. According to Jacquemart Giélée, the brothers claimed to be sole 'Defenders of the Holy Church'. They were depicted as principal defenders of the Holy Land by the Parisian poet Rutebeuf in 1277. Templars were mentioned in chronicles and literature in general more than other military orders. They were invariably listed first whenever anyone thought about military orders. They had been the first military order, and were one of the richest and most far-flung. Yet this particular prominence also left them particularly vulnerable when they failed in their duty.

When the city of Acre finally fell to the Muslims in May 1291, several reports of the disaster depicted the Templars as chiefly responsible for the defence of the city. The chronicler of Erfut, writing in the summer of 1291, depicted the Templars dying like true knights of Christ, fighting to the last. Thaddeo of Naples, a priest, praised the courage of the brothers of the military orders who died, and portrayed the death of the master of the Temple, William of Beaujeu, as the decisive blow which led to the loss of the Holy Land. For after Acre fell, the remaining Latin Christian possessions in the East surrendered to the Muslims.

ANNUAL EDITIONS

But the order's prominence could also be its undoing. The most popular account of the defeat, which was reproduced in many chronicles, dismissed the Templars as totally ineffective and only concerned to save their treasure. The true hero of the tragedy was now Brother Matthew of Claremont, marshal of the Hospital, who was 'a faithful warrior, knight of Christ', and died a martyr's death. Ricoldo of Monte Cruce, a Dominican Friar who was on a preaching mission in the Middle East when he heard of the disaster, compared William of Beaujeu to the notorious King Ahab, husband of Queen Jezebel and the worst king of Israel in the Old Testament. Certainly he was an excellent soldier, but God rejected him because of his sins.

The loss of Acre was not mentioned among the charges brought against the Templars in 1307, but it was understood that the brothers' alleged abuses were responsible for the disaster.

From the evidence, the famous, shocking charges brought against the Templars in 1307 were unknown before 1300. The order was certainly guilty of fraud and unscrupulous greed, but so too were other religious orders. The brothers' real crime was their failure to protect the Holy Land after claiming to be solely responsible for its defence.

FOR FURTHER READING:

M. Barber, 'Propaganda in the Middle Ages: the charges against the Templars', *Nottingham Medieval Studies*, 17 (1973); M. Barber,

The Trial of the Templars (Cambridge University Press, 1978); M. Barber, *The New Knighthood: a History of the Order of the Temple* (Cambridge University Press, 1993); H. Nicholson, *Templars, Hospitallers and Teutonic Knights: Images of the military orders, 1128–1291* (Leicester University Press, 1993); J. Upton-Ward, (trans.) *The Rule of the Templars: the French text of the Rule of the Order of Knights Templar* (Boydell Press, 1992).

Helen Nicholson lectures in history at the University of Wales College of Cardiff. She is currently working on a translation of the Itinerarium Peregrinorum et Gesta Regis Ricardi, *a chronicle of the Third Crusade.*

This article first appeared in *History Today*, December 1994, pp. 30–36. © 1994 by History Today, Ltd. Reprinted by permission.

How a Mysterious Disease Laid Low Europe's Masses

In the 1300s, a third of the population died of plague brought by fleas, shocking the medieval world to its foundations.

Charles L. Mee Jr.

In all likelihood, a flea riding on the hide of a black rat entered the Italian port of Messina in 1347, perhaps down a hawser tying a ship up at the dock. The flea had a gut full of the bacillus *Yersinia pestis*. The flea itself was hardly bigger than the letter "o" on this page, but it could carry several hundred thousand bacilli in its intestine.

Scholars today cannot identify with certainty which species of flea (or rat) carried the plague. One candidate among the fleas is *Xenopsylla cheopis*, which looks like a deeply bent, bearded old man with six legs. It is slender and bristly, with almost no neck and no waist, so that it can slip easily through the forest of hair in which it lives. It is outfitted with a daggerlike proboscis for piercing the skin and sucking the blood of its host. And it is cunningly equipped to secrete a substance that prevents coagulation of the host's blood. Although *X. cheopis* can go for weeks without feeding, it will eat every day if it can, taking its blood warm.

One rat on which fleas feed, the black rat *(Rattus rattus)*, also known as the house rat, roof rat or ship rat, is active mainly at night. A rat can fall 50 feet and land on its feet with no injury. It can scale a brick wall or climb up the inside of a pipe only an inch and a half in diameter. It can jump a distance of two feet straight up and four horizontally, and squeeze through a hole the size of a quarter. Black rats have been found still swimming days after their ship has sunk at sea.

A rat can gnaw its way through almost anything—paper, wood, bone, mortar, half-inch sheet metal. It gnaws constantly. Indeed, it *must* gnaw constantly. Its incisors grow four to five inches a year: if it were to stop gnawing, its lower incisors would eventually grow—as sometimes happens when a rat loses an opposing tooth—until the incisors push up into the rat's brain, killing it. It prefers grain, if possible, but also eats fish, eggs, fowl and meat—lambs, piglets and the flesh of helpless infants or adults. If nothing else is available, a rat will eat manure and drink urine.

Rats prefer to move no more than a hundred feet from their nests. But in severe drought or famine, rats can begin to move en masse for great distances, bringing with them any infections they happen to have picked up, infections that may be killing them but not killing them more rapidly than they breed.

Rats and mice harbor a number of infections that may cause diseases in human beings. A black rat can even tolerate a moderate amount of the ferocious *Yersinia pestis* bacillus in its system without noticeable ill effects. But bacilli breed even more extravagantly than fleas or rats, often in the millions. When a bacillus finally invades the rat's pulmonary or nervous system, it causes a horrible, often convulsive, death, passing on a lethal dose to the bloodsucking fleas that ride on the rat's hide.

THE ULTIMATE BACILLUS BREEDER

When an afflicted rat dies, its body cools, so that the flea, highly sensitive to changes in temperature, will find another host. The flea can, if need be, survive for weeks at a time without a rat host. It can take refuge anywhere, even in an abandoned rat's nest or a bale of cloth. A dying rat may liberate scores of rat fleas. More than that, a flea's intestine happens to provide ideal breeding conditions for the bacillus, which will eventually multiply so prodigiously as finally to block the gut of the flea entirely. Unable to feed or digest blood, the flea desperately seeks another host. But now, as it sucks blood, it spits some out at the same time. Each time the flea stops sucking for a moment, it is capable of pumping thousands of virulent bacilli back into its host. Thus bacilli are passed from rat to flea to rat, contained, ordinarily, within a closed community.

For millions of years, there has been a reservoir of *Yersinia pestis* living as a permanently settled parasite—passed back and forth among fleas and rodents in warm, moist nests—in the wild rodent colonies of China, India, the southern part of the Soviet Union and the western United States. Probably there will always be such reservoirs—ready to be stirred up by sudden climatic change or ecological disaster. Even last year, four authentic cases of bubonic plague were confirmed in New Mexico and Arizona. Limited outbreaks and some fatalities have occurred in the United States for years, in fact, but the disease doesn't spread, partly for reasons we don't understand, partly because patients can now be treated with antibiotics.

And at least from biblical times on, there have been sporadic allusions to plagues, as well as carefully recorded outbreaks. The emperor Justinian's Constantinople, for instance, capital of the Roman empire in the East, was ravaged by plague in 541 and 542, felling perhaps 40 percent of the city's population. But none of the biblical or Roman plagues seemed so emblematic of horror and devastation as the Black Death that struck Europe in 1347. Rumors of fearful pestilence in China and throughout the East had reached Europe by 1346. "India was depopulated," reported one chronicler, "Tartary, Mesopotamia, Syria, Armenia, were covered with dead bodies; the Kurds fled in vain to the mountains. In Caramania and Caesarea none were left alive."

Untold millions would die in China and the rest of the East before the plague subsided again. By September of 1345, the *Yersinia pestis* bacillus, probably carried by rats, reached the Crimea, on the northern coast of the Black Sea, where Italian merchants had a good number of trading colonies.

From the shores of the Black Sea, the bacillus seems to have entered a number of Italian ports. The most famous account has to do with a ship that docked in the Sicilian port of Messina in 1347. According to an Italian chronicler named Gabriele de Mussis, Christian merchants from Genoa and local Muslim residents in the town of Caffa on the Black Sea got into an argument; a serious fight ensued between the merchants and a local army led by a Tartar lord. In the course of an attack on the Christians, the Tartars were stricken by plague. From sheer spitefulness, their leader loaded his catapults with dead bodies and hurled them at the Christian enemy, in hopes of spreading disease among them. Infected with the plague, the Genoese sailed back to Italy, docking first at Messina.

Although de Mussis, who never traveled to the Crimea, may be a less-than-reliable source, his underlying assumption seems sound. The plague did spread along established trade routes. (Most likely, though, the pestilence in Caffa resulted from an infected population of local rats, not from the corpses lobbed over the besieged city's walls.)

In any case, given enough dying rats and enough engorged and frantic fleas, it will not be long before the fleas, in their search for new hosts, leap to a human being. When a rat flea senses the presence of an alternate host, it can jump very quickly and as much as 150 times its length. The average for such jumps is about six inches horizontally and four inches straight up in the air. Once on human skin, the flea will not travel far before it begins to feed.

The first symptoms of bubonic plague often appear within several days: headache and a general feeling of weakness, followed by aches and chills in the upper leg and groin, a white coating on the tongue, rapid pulse, slurred speech, confusion, fatigue, apathy and a staggering gait. A blackish pustule usually will form at the point of the fleabite. By the third day, the lymph nodes begin to swell. Because the bite is commonly in the leg, it is the lymph nodes of the groin that swell, which is how the disease got its name. The Greek word for "groin" is *boubon*—thus, bubonic plague. The swelling will be tender, perhaps as large as an egg. The heart begins to flutter rapidly as it tries to pump blood through swollen, suffocating tissues. Subcutaneous hemorrhaging occurs, causing purplish blotches on the skin. The victim's nervous system begins to collapse, causing dreadful pain and bizarre neurological disorders, from which the "Dance of Death" rituals that accompanied the plague may have taken their inspiration. By the fourth or fifth day, wild anxiety and terror overtake the sufferer—and then a sense of resignation, as the skin blackens and the rictus of death settles on the body.

In 1347, when the plague struck in Messina, townspeople realized that it must have come from the sick and dying crews of the ships at their dock. They turned on the sailors and drove them back out to sea—eventually to spread the plague in other ports. Messina panicked. People ran out into the fields and vineyards and neighboring villages, taking the rat fleas with them.

When the citizens of Messina, already ill or just becoming ill, reached the city of Catania, 55 miles to the south, they were at first taken in and given beds in the hospital. But as the plague began to infect Catania, the townspeople there cordoned off their town and refused—too late—to admit any outsiders. The sick, turning black, stumbling and delirious, were objects more of disgust than pity; everything about them gave off a terrible stench, it was said, their "sweat, excrement, spittle, breath, so foetid as to be overpowering; urine turbid, thick, black or red...."

Wherever the plague appeared, the suddenness of death was terrifying. Today, even with hand-me-down memories of the great influenza epidemic of 1918 (SMITHSONIAN, January 1989) and the advent of AIDS, it is hard to grasp the strain that the plague put on the physical and spiritual fabric of society. People went to bed perfectly healthy and were found dead in the morning. Priests and doctors who came to minister to the sick, so the wild stories ran, would contract the plague with a single touch and die sooner than the person they had come to help. In his preface to *The Decameron*, a collection of stories told while the plague was raging, Boccaccio reports that he saw two pigs rooting around in the clothes of a man who had just died, and after a few minutes of snuffling, the pigs began to run wildly around and around, then fell dead.

"Tedious were it to recount," Boccaccio thereafter laments, "brother was forsaken by brother, nephew by uncle, brother by sister and, oftentimes, husband by wife; nay what is more and scarcely to be believed, fathers and mothers were found to abandon their own children, untended, unvisited, to their fate, as if they had been strangers...."

In Florence, everyone grew so frightened of the bodies stacked up in the streets that some men, called *becchini*, put themselves out for hire to fetch and carry the dead to mass graves. Having in this way stepped over the boundary into the land of the dead, and no doubt feeling doomed themselves, the *becchini* became an abandoned, brutal lot. Many roamed the streets, forcing their way into private homes and threatening to carry people away if they were not paid off in money or sexual favors.

VISITING MEN WITH PESTILENCE

Some people, shut up in their houses with the doors barred, would scratch a sign of the cross on the front door, sometimes with the inscription "Lord have mercy on us." In one place, two lovers were supposed to have bathed in urine every morning for protection. People hovered over latrines, breathing in the stench. Others swallowed pus from the boils of plague victims. In Avignon, Pope Clement was said to have sat for weeks between two roaring fires.

The plague spread from Sicily all up and down the Atlantic coast, and from the port cities of Venice, Genoa and Pisa as well as Marseilles, London and Bristol. A multitude of men and women, as Boccaccio writes, "negligent of all but themselves... migrated to the country, as if God, in visiting men with this pestilence in requital of their iniquities, would not pursue them with His wrath wherever they might be...."

Some who were not yet ill but felt doomed indulged in debauchery. Others, seeking protection in lives of moderation, banded together in communities to live a separate and secluded life, walking abroad with flowers to their noses "to ward off the stench and, perhaps, the evil airs that afflicted them."

It was from a time of plague, some scholars speculate, that the nursery rhyme "Ring Around the Rosy" derives: the rose-colored "ring" being an early sign that a blotch was about to appear on the skin; "a pocket full of posies" being a device to ward off stench and (it was hoped) the attendant infection; "ashes, ashes" being a reference to "ashes to ashes, dust to dust" or perhaps to the sneezing "a-choo, a-choo" that afflicted those in whom the infection had invaded the lungs—ending, inevitably, in "all fall down."

In Pistoia, the city council enacted nine pages of regulations to keep the plague out—no Pistoian was allowed to leave town to visit any place where the plague was raging; if a citizen did visit a plague-infested area he was not allowed back in the city; no linen or woolen goods were allowed to be imported; no corpses could be brought home from outside the city; attendance at funerals was strictly limited to immediate family. None of these regulations helped.

In Siena, dogs dragged bodies from the shallow graves and left them half-devoured in the streets. Merchants closed their shops. The wool industry was shut down. Clergymen ceased administering last rites. On June 2, 1348, all the civil courts were recessed by the city council. Because so many of the laborers had died, construction of the nave for a great cathedral came to a halt. Work was never resumed: only the smaller cathedral we know today was completed.

In Venice, it was said that 600 were dying every day. In Florence, perhaps half the population died. By the time the plague swept through, as much as one-third of Italy's population had succumbed.

In Milan, when the plague struck, all the occupants of any victim's house, whether sick or well, were walled up inside together and left to die. Such draconian measures seemed to have been partially successful—mortality rates were lower in Milan than in other cities.

Medieval medicine was at a loss to explain all this, or to do anything about it. Although clinical observation did play some role in medical education, an extensive reliance on ancient and inadequate texts prevailed. Surgeons usually had a good deal of clinical experience but were considered mainly to be skilled craftsmen, not men of real learning, and their experience was not much incorporated into the body of medical knowledge. In 1300, Pope Boniface VIII had published a bull specifically inveighing against the mutilation of corpses. It was designed to cut down on the sale of miscellaneous bones as holy relics, but one of the effects was to discourage dissection.

Physicians, priests and others had theories about the cause of the plague. Earthquakes that released poisonous fumes, for instance. Severe changes in the Earth's temperature creating southerly winds that brought the plague. The notion that the plague was somehow the result of a corruption of the air was widely believed. It was this idea that led people to avoid foul odors by holding flowers to their noses or to try to drive out the infectious foul odors by inhaling the alternate foul odors of a latrine. Some thought that the plague came from the raining down of frogs, toads and reptiles. Some physicians believed one could catch the plague from "lust with old women."

Most Christians believed the cause of the plague was God's wrath at sinful Man.

Both the pope and the king of France sent urgent requests for help to the medical faculty at the University of Paris, then one of the most distinguished medical groups in the Western world. The faculty responded that the plague was the result of a conjunction of the planets Saturn, Mars and Jupiter at 1 P.M. on March 20, 1345, an event that caused the corruption of the surrounding atmosphere.

Ultimately, of course, most Christians believed the cause of the plague was God's wrath at sinful Man. And in those terms, to be sure, the best preventives were prayer, the wearing of crosses and participation in other religious activities. In Orvieto, the town fathers added 50 new religious observances to the municipal calendar. Even so, within five months of the appearance of the plague, Orvieto lost every second person in the town.

There was also some agreement about preventive measures one might take to avoid the wrath of God. Flight was best: away from lowlands, marshy areas, stagnant waters, southern exposures and coastal areas, toward high, dry, cool, mountainous places. It was thought wise to stay indoors all day, to stay cool and to cover any windows that admitted bright sunlight. In addition to keeping flowers nearby, one might burn such aromatic woods as juniper and ash.

The retreat to the mountains, where the density of the rat population was not as great as in urban areas, and where the weather was inimical to rats and fleas, was probably a good idea—as well as perhaps proof, of a kind, of the value of empirical observation. But any useful notion was always mixed in with such wild ideas that it got lost in a flurry of desperate (and often contrary) stratagems. One should avoid bathing because that opened the pores to attack from the corrupt atmosphere, but one should wash face and feet, and sprinkle them with rose water and vinegar. In the morning, one might eat a couple of figs with rue and filberts. One expert advised eating ten-year-old treacle mixed with several dozen items, including chopped-up snake. Rhubarb was recommended, too, along with onions, leeks and garlic. The best spices were myrrh, saffron and pepper, to be taken late in the day. Meat should be roasted, not boiled. Eggs should not be eaten hard-boiled. A certain Gentile di Foligno commended lettuce; the faculty of medicine at the University of Paris advised against it. Desserts were forbidden. One should not sleep during the day. One should sleep first on the right side, then on the left. Exercise was to be avoided because it introduced more air into the body; if one needed to move, one ought to move slowly.

By the fall of 1348, the plague began to abate. But then, just as hopes were rising that it had passed, the plague broke out again in the spring and summer of 1349 in different parts of Europe. This recurrence seemed to prove that the warm weather, and people bathing in warm weather, caused the pores of the skin to open and admit the corrupted air. In other respects, however, the plague remained inexplicable. Why did some people get it and recover, while other seemed not to have got it at all—or at least showed none of its symptoms—yet died suddenly anyway? Some people died in four or five days, others died at once. Some seemed to have contracted the plague from a friend or relative who had it, others had never been near a sick person. The sheer unpredictability of it was terrifying.

In fact, though no one would know for several centuries, there were three different forms of the plague, which ran three different courses. The first was simple bubonic plague, transmitted from rat to person by the bite of the rat flea. The second and likely most common form was pneumonic, which occurred when the bacillus invaded the lungs. After a two- or three-day incubation period, anyone with pneumonic plague would have a severe, bloody cough; the sputum cast into the air would contain *Yersinia pestis*. Transmitted through the air from person to person, pneumonic plague was fatal in 95 to 100 percent of all cases.

The third form of the plague was septocemic, and its precise etiology is not entirely understood even yet. In essence, however, it appears that in cases of septocemic plague the bacillus entered the bloodstream, perhaps at the moment of the fleabite. A rash formed and death occurred within a day, or even within hours, before any swellings appeared. Septocemic plague always turned out to be fatal.

Some people did imagine that the disease might be coming from some animal, and they killed dogs and cats—though never rats. But fleas were so much a part of everyday life that no one seems to have given them a second thought. Upright citizens also killed gravediggers, strangers from other countries, gypsies, drunks, beggars, cripples, lepers and Jews. The first persecution of the Jews seems to have taken place in the South of France in the spring of 1348. That September, at Chillon on Lake Geneva, a group of Jews were accused of poisoning the wells. They were tortured and they confessed, and their confessions were sent to neighboring towns. In Basel all the Jews were locked inside wooden buildings and burned alive. In November, Jews were burned in Solothurn, Zofingen and Stuttgart. Through the winter and into early spring they were burned in Landsberg, Burren, Memmingen, Lindau, Freiburg, Ulm, Speyer, Gotha, Eisenach, Dresden, Worms, Baden and Erfurt. Sixteen thousand were murdered in Strasbourg. In other cities Jews were walled up inside their houses to starve to death. That the Jews were also dying of the plague was not taken as proof that they were not causing it.

Very rarely does a single event change history itself. Yet an event of the magnitude of the Black Death could not fail to have an enormous impact.

On the highways and byways, meanwhile, congregations of flagellants wandered about, whipping themselves twice a day and once during the night for weeks at a time. As they went on their way they attracted hordes of followers and helped spread the plague even farther abroad.

The recurrence of the plague after people thought the worst was over may have been the most devastating development of all. In short, Europe was swept not only by a bacillus but also by a widespread psychic breakdown—by abject terror, panic, rage, vengefulness, cringing remorse, selfishness, hysteria, and above all, by an overwhelming sense of utter powerlessness in the face of an inescapable horror.

After a decade's respite, just as Europeans began to recover their feeling of well-being, the plague struck again in 1361, and again in 1369, and at least once in each decade down to the end of the century. Why the plague faded away is still a mystery that, in the short run, apparently had little to do with improvements in medicine or cleanliness and more to do with some adjustment of equilibrium among the population of rats and fleas. In any case, as agents for Pope Clement estimated in 1351, perhaps 24 million people had died in the first onslaught of the plague; perhaps as many as another 20 million died by the end of the century—in all, it is estimated, one-third of the total population of Europe.

Very rarely does a single event change history by itself. Yet an event of the magnitude of the Black Death could not fail to have had an enormous impact. Ironically, some of the changes brought by the plague were for the good. Not surprisingly, medicine changed—since medicine had so signally failed to be of any help in the hour of greatest need for it. First of all, a great many doctors died—and some simply ran away. "It has pleased God," wrote one Venetian-born physician, "by this terrible mortality to leave our native place so destitute of upright and capable doctors that it may be said not one has been left." By 1349, at the University of Padua there were vacancies in every single chair of medicine and surgery. All this, of course, created room for new people with new ideas. Ordinary people began wanting to get their hands on medical guides and to take command of their own health. And gradually more medical texts began to appear in the vernacular instead of in Latin.

AN OLD ORDER WAS BESIEGED

Because of the death of so many people, the relationship between agricultural supply and demand changed radically, too. Agricultural prices dropped precipitously, endangering the fortunes and power of the aristocracy, whose wealth and dominance were based on land. At the same time, because of the deaths of so many people, wages rose dramatically, giving laborers some chance of improving their own conditions of employment. Increasing numbers of people had more money to buy what could be called luxury goods, which affected the nature of business and trade, and even of private well-being. As old relationships, usages and laws broke down, expanding secular concerns and intensifying the struggle between faith and reason, there was a rise in religious, social and political unrest. Religious reformer John Wycliffe, in England, and John Huss, in Bohemia, were among many leaders of sects that challenged church behavior and church doctrine all over Europe. Such complaints eventually led to the Protestant Reformation, and the assertion that Man stood in direct relation to God, without need to benefit from intercession by layers of clergy.

Indeed, the entire structure of feudal society, which had been under stress for many years, was undermined by the plague. The three orders of feudalism—clergy, nobility and peasantry—had been challenged for more than a century by the rise of the urban bourgeoisie, and by the enormous, slow changes in productivity and in the cultivation of arable land. But the plague, ravaging the weakened feudal system from so many diverse and unpredictable quarters, tore it apart.

By far the greatest change in Western civilization that the plague helped hasten was a change of mind. Once the immediate traumas of death, terror and flight had passed through a stricken town, the common lingering emotion was that of fear of God. The subsequent surge of religious fervor in art was in many ways nightmarish. Though medieval religion had dealt with death and dying, and naturally with sin and retribution, it was only after the Black Death that painters so wholeheartedly gave themselves over to pictures brimming with rotting corpses, corpses being consumed by snakes and toads, swooping birds of prey appearing with terrible suddenness, cripples gazing on the figure of death with longing for deliverance, open graves filled with blackened, worm-eaten bodies, devils slashing the faces and bodies of the damned.

Well before the plague struck Europe, the role of the Catholic Church in Western Europe had been changing. The Papacy had grown more secular in its concerns, vying with princes for wealth and power even while attempts at reform were increasing. "God gave us the Papacy," Pope Leo X declared. "Let us enjoy it." The church had suffered a series of damaging losses in the late 1200s—culminating in 1309 when the Papacy moved from Rome to Avignon. But then, the Black Death dealt the church a further blow, for along with renewed fear and the need for new religious zeal came the opposite feeling, that the church itself had failed. Historical changes rarely occur suddenly. The first indications of change from a powerful catalyst usually seem to be mere curiosities, exceptions or aberrations from the prevailing worldview. Only after a time, after the exceptions have accumulated and seem to cohere, do they take on the nature of a historical movement. And only when the exceptions have come to dominate, do they begin to seem typical of the civilization as a whole (and the vestiges of the old civilization to seem like curiosities). This, in any case, is how the great change of mind occurred that defines the modern Western world. While the Black Death alone did not cause these changes, the upheaval it brought about did help set the stage for the new world of Renaissance Europe and the Reformation.

As the Black Death waned in Europe, the power of religion waned with it, leaving behind a population that was gradually but certainly turning its attention to the physical realm in which it lived, to materialism and worldliness, to the terrible power of the world itself, and to the wonder of how it works.

From *Smithsonian* magazine, February 1990, pp. 67–74, 76, 78. © 1990 by Charles L. Mee, Jr. Reprinted by permission of the author.

UNIT 6
Renaissance and Reformation

Unit Selections

Key Points to Consider

- What does the career of Jacques Coeur tell us about the basic elements of early capitalism?

- Why was the career of Masilio Ficino important in the Renaissance era?

- How did politics change at the beginning of the modern era?

- Did Renaissance humanism influence the place of women in European life? Explain.

- How is Martin Luther viewed?

 **Links: www.dushkin.com/online/**
These sites are annotated in the World Wide Web pages.

Burckhardt: Civilization of the Renaissance in Italy
   http://www.idbsu.edu/courses/hy309/docs/burckhardt/burckhardt.html
Elizabethan England
   http://www.springfield.k12.il.us/schools/springfield/eliz/ elizabethanengland.html
1492: An Ongoing Voyage/Library of Congress
   http://lcweb.loc.gov/exhibits/1492/
History Net
   http://www.thehistorynet.com/THNarchives/AmericanHistory/
The Mayflower Web Pages
   http://www.mayflowerhistory.com/
Reformation Guide
   http://www.educ.msu.edu/homepages/laurence/reformation/index.htm
Sir Francis Drake
   http://www.mcn.org/2/oseeler/drake.htm
Society for Economic Anthropology Homepage
   http://nautarch.tamu.edu/anth/sea/

The departure from medieval patterns of life was first evident in Renaissance Italy. There, the growth of capital and the development of distinctly urban economic and social organizations promoted a new culture. This culture, which spread to other parts of Europe, was dominated by townsmen whose tastes, abilities, and interests differed from those of medieval clergy and feudal nobility.

The emerging culture was limited to a minority—generally those who were wealthy. But even in an increasingly materialistic culture it was not enough just to be wealthy. It was necessary to patronize the arts, literature, and learning, and to demonstrate skill in some profession. The ideal Renaissance man, as Robert Lopez observes in (*The Three Ages of the Italian Renaissance*, University of Virginia Press, 1970) "came from a good old family, improved upon his status through his own efforts, and justified his status by his own intellectual accomplishments."

The new ideal owed much to the classical tradition. Renaissance man, wising to break out of the otherworldly spirituality of the Middle Ages, turned back to the secular naturalism of the ancient world. Indeed, the Renaissance was, among other things, a heroic age of scholarship that restored classical learning to a place of honor. It was classical humanism in particular that became the vogue. And in the new spirit of individualism, however, humanism was transformed. None better illustrate these traits better than the articles, "Machiavelli," and on Leonardo in "Virtue and Beauty The Renaissance Image of the Ideal Woman."

Civic humanism was another Renaissance modification of the classical heritage. It involved a new philosophy of political engagement, a reinterpretation of political history from the vantage point of contemporary politics, and the recognition that men would not simply imitate the ancients but would rival them.

Renaissance art and architecture reflected the new society and its attitudes. Successful businessmen were as likely as saints to be subjects of portraits. Equestrian's statues of warriors and statesmen glorified current heroes while evoking memories of ancient Rome. Renaissance painters rediscovered nature, which generally had been ignored by medieval artists, often depicting it as an earthly paradise—the appropriate setting for humanity in its new image. And in contrast to the great medieval cathedrals, which glorified God, Renaissance structure focused on humanity.

Some of these developments in art and architecture indicate the changes in the role of Christianity and the influence of the Church, which no longer determined the goals of Western civilization as they had during the medieval period. Increasingly, civil authorities and their symbols competed with churchmen and their icons, while Machiavelli and other writers provided a secular rationale for a new political order. Nonetheless, most Europeans, including many humanists retained a deep and abiding religious faith.

The Reformation, with its theological disputes and wars, is a powerful reminder that secular concerns had not entirely re-

LUTHER SCHLÄGT DIE 90 SÄTZE AN.

placed religious ones, especially in northern Europe. The great issues that divided Protestants and Catholics—the balance between individual piety and the Church's authority, the true means of salvation—were essentially medieval in character. Indeed, in their perceptions of humanity, their preoccupation with salvation and damnation, and their attacks upon the Church's conduct of its affairs, Martin Luther, John Calvin, Ulrich Zwingli, and other Protestant leaders echoed the views of medieval reformers. These Protestant reforms are treated in the articles, "Martin Luther's Ninety-Five Theses," "Explaining John Calvin," and "The Development of Protestantism in 16th Century France."

Taken together, then, the Renaissance and Reformation constituted a new compound of traditional elements—classical and medieval, secular and religious—along with elements of modernity. The era was a time of transition, or as Lynn D. White describes it, "This was a time of torrential flux, or fearful doubt, making the transition from the relative certainties of the Middle Ages to the new certainties of the eighteenth and nineteenth centuries."

THE FALL OF CONSTANTINOPLE

Judith Herrin tells the dramatic story of the final moments of Byzantine control of the imperial capital.

by Judith Herrin

"At this moment of confusion, which happened at sunrise, our omnipotent God came to His most bitter decision and decided to fulfil all the prophecies, as I have said, and at sunrise the Turks entered the city near San Romano, where the walls had been razed to the ground by their cannon ... anyone they found was put to the scimitar, women and men, old and young, of any conditions. This butchery lasted from sunrise, when the Turks entered the city, until midday ... The Turks made eagerly for the piazza five miles from the point where they made their entrance at San Romano, and when they reached it at once some of them climbed up a tower where the flags of Saint Mark and the Most Serene Emperor were flying, and they cut down the flag of Saint Mark and took away the flag of the Most Serene Emperor and then on the same tower they raised the flag of the Sultan ... When their flag was raised and ours cut down, we saw that the whole city was taken, and that there was no further hope of recovering from this."

With these words, and much longer descriptions of the slaughter that followed, the Venetian Nicolo Barbaro recorded the fall of Constantinople to the Ottoman Turks. His eyewitness account describes the progressive stranglehold devised by the Turks and the sense of fatalism that developed within the city. As the major trading partner of the empire, Venice had strong links with Constantinople and its citizens fought bravely in its defence. Barbaro's account of their loyalty is impressive. Although he is less favourably inclined to the Genoese, who also played a leading role in the defence of the city,

his account has the immediacy of one who lived through the siege.

There is no shortage of records of the fall, although some were concocted long after the event and claim a presence that turns out to be quite inauthentic. Greeks, Italians, Slavs, Turks and Russians all composed their own versions; they cannot possibly be reconciled. But those written closer to the date, May 29th, 1453, and by people involved in some capacity all share a sense of the disaster they documented. Taking account of many of their variations and contradictions, they permit a basic outline of events to be constructed.

The leaders of what became such a mythic battle were both younger sons who had never expected to become rulers. The Ottoman sultan Mehmet II, born in 1432, was made sole heir at the age of eleven by the death of his two elder brothers; Constantine XI, born in 1404, was the fourth of six sons of Manuel II, whose imperial authority was inherited by the eldest John VIII. When John died in 1448, the Empress-Mother Helena insisted that Constantine should be crowned in a disputed succession. His two younger brothers, Demetrios and Thomas, were appointed Despots in the Morea (southern Greece), and took no interest in the fate of Constantinople. In 1453 the Sultan was twenty-one years old, the Emperor forty-nine, and the Ottomans far out-numbered the Christian forces who undertook the defence of the city.

The imperial capital dedicated by Constantine I in AD 330 had resisted siege on numerous occasions. The triple line of fortifications constructed on the land side in the fifth century had held off attacks by Goths, Persians, Avars, Bulgars, Russians, and especially Arabs. Even today they make an impressive sight. Over the centuries new aqueducts and cisterns were built to ensure an ample water supply, and the imperial granaries stored plentiful amounts of grain.

From the first attempt by the Arabs to capture the city in 674-78, Muslim forces aimed to make Constantinople their own capital. Using this ancient foundation as their base, they hoped to extend their power across Thrace and the Balkans into Europe, in the same irresistible way that they advanced across North Africa into Spain. Frustrated in these efforts, the centre of their operations was moved to Baghdad, and they occupied the Fertile Crescent and vast areas further east. In the eleventh century these same ambitions were taken up by Turkish tribes from central Asia, who constantly harried the empire. First Seljuks and later Ottomans maintained pressure on Constantinople, hoping to take a symbol of unconquered strength and great strategic importance.

Their aim was not merely political and military. For centuries Constantinople was the largest metropolis in the known world, the impregnable core of a great empire, served by a deep-water port that gave access to the sea. Known as New Rome and the Queen City, it had been built to impress, its magnificent public monuments, decorated with statuary set in an elegant classical urban landscape. Its apparent invincibility and famous reputation made it a great prize. The city was also reputed to be hugely wealthy. While the Turks had no interest in its famous collection of Christian relics, the fact that many were made of solid gold and silver, decorated with huge gems and ancient cameos, was of importance. Their existence added weight to the rumour that Constantinople contained vast stores of gold, a claim which cannot have been true by 1453. By the early fifteenth century the city had lost all its provinces to Turkish occupation and was totally isolated. The surviving Greek territories of Trebizond and the Morea were similarly surrounded and made no effort to assist the ancient capital.

It is notoriously difficult to reconstruct the early history of the Ottoman Turks from the sparse sources that survive. They seem to have been a tribe of *ghazi* warriors (men devoted to holy war) who gradually adopted a more organised monarchy. Their leader Osman (1288-1326) gave his name to the group, which is now associated with one of the most successful empires of all time. During the fourteenth century these Ottoman Turks took full advantage of the civil war in Byzantium. From his capital at Nikomedia Sultan Orhan offered assistance to John VI, claimant to the throne, and married his daughter Theodora, thus setting up an excellent excuse for invading the empire.

At the same time, he was able to exploit unexpected developments at Gallipoli when an earthquake shook the castle fortifications so violently that they collapsed in 1354. Orhan ferried an entire army across the Dardanelles and opened a bridgehead on the European shore. The conquest of Thrace, the last province loyal to the empire, and the capture of Adrianople, which became the Ottoman capital as Edirne, meant that the Turks were now in a position to threaten the capital from the west. Once they

could mount an attack by land as well as by sea, Constantinople was totally surrounded. This stranglehold on the empire was symbolised by the treaty of 1373, which reduced the emperor to the status of a Turkish vassal. John V agreed to pay Sultan Murad an annual tribute, to provide military aid whenever it was required, and to allow his son Manuel to accompany the Turks back to their court as a hostage.

Despite a surprising defeat by the Mongols in 1402, Ottoman attempts to capture Constantinople continued. In preparation for the campaign of 1452-53, Sultan Mehmet II ordered the blockade of the city. Since the southern entrance to the Bosphorus from the Aegean at the Dardanelles was already in Ottoman hands, he concentrated on the northern entrance from the Black Sea. Two castles were constructed close to the mouth of the Bosphorus on the Asian and European shores, to prevent any aid arriving from the Black Sea. Barbaro gives a vivid description of how the garrison at Rumeli Hisar on the European shore tried to control shipping by firing on any galleys entering the Bosphorus until they lowered their sails:

> From the walls of the castle, the Turks began to shout 'Lower your sails, Captain' ... and when they saw that he was unwilling to lower them, they began to fire their cannon and many guns and a great number of arrows, so that they killed many men ... After he had lowered his sails, the Turks stopped firing, and then the current carried the galleys towards Constantinople. And when they had passed the castle and the Turks could not reach them any longer with their cannon, the captain quickly raised his sails and got through safely.

Ships also carried oars so that sailors could row with the current in order to avoid the blockade.

Byzantine rulers had made too many appeals to Western powers to come to the aid of their Christian city. The crusading movement had been exhausted by numerous military disasters. After the failure of the crusade of 1396 at Nicopolis on the Danube, the young emperor Manuel II made a long tour of western capital cities between 1399 and 1403 in the hope of gaining financial and above all military support for the defence of the city. In Paris he noticed a fine tapestry hanging in the palace of the Louvre and wrote a letter to his old tutor describing its beauty. In London he was invited to the Christmas dinner hosted by Henry IV at the palace of Eltham. Manuel's attempts to obtain aid were enhanced, as so many times before, by a promise to unite the Latin and Greek churches.

In this respect Manuel and his son John VIII proved that they could achieve the desired ecclesiastical union. At the Council of Ferrara-Florence in 1438-39 the union of the churches was finally realised. But even after this major compromise, help from the papacy, the Italian city republics and the monarchs who had received Manuel during his trip was slow to materialise. In the autumn of 1452, the

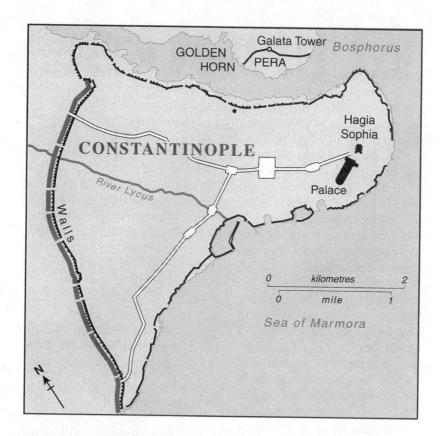

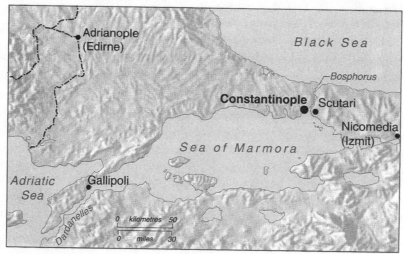

papal legate Cardinal Isidore and Bishop Leonard of Chios arrived in the city with a body of archers recruited and paid for by the papacy. The Cardinal then celebrated the official union of the Latin and Greek churches in the cathedral of Hagia Sophia on December 12th.

As Bishop Leonard of Chios reports the event:

> Through the diligence and honesty of the said Cardinal, Isidore of Kiev, and with the assent (if it was not insincere) of the emperor and the senate, the holy union was sanctioned and solemnly celebrated on December 12th, the feast of Saint Spiridon, the bishop.

But even with the union in place, Western promises to assist the last great Christian centre in the East Mediterranean proved empty, while a large portion of the Greek population of Constantinople remained obstinately opposed to it.

Among those who joined the Greek inhabitants in the city to defend it against the expected siege, were numerous representatives of the Italian republics of Venice and Genoa. Both enjoyed commercial privileges from trading in Constantinople but were staunch rivals. Some of those who fought had been residents for many years, had adopted Byzantine citizenship and married Greek wives. A significant number of Armenians were present and the resident Catalan traders took part under their consul. Prince Orhan, pretender to the Ottoman throne, who had lived for years as a guest of the Byzantine court, offered his services with his Turkish companions. Ships from Ancona, Provence and Castile added to the naval forces, and a group of Greeks from Crete elected to remain in the city. When they saw what would happen, though, on February 26th, 1453, six of their ships slipped away with one Venetian.

The inhabitants were greatly cheered by the arrival in January 1453 of the Genoese *condottieri*, who braved the Turkish blockade and got through with his two ships and about 700 men. This was Giovanni Giustiniani Longo, identified in many sources as Justinian, a friend of the emperor, whose determination to assist the city was greatly appreciated. Constantine XI put him in charge of the weakest part of the land walls, the section by the Gate of Romanos, and, as Nestor-Iskander says:

> ... he invigorated and even instructed the people so that they would not lose hope and maintain unswerving trust in God ... All people admired and obeyed him in all things.

After masterminding the defence Justinian was hit on the chest during the last days of the assault. The Genoese managed to get him out of the city on one of the first ships to leave after the capture but he died at Chios. His disappearance lowered the spirits of the Christian forces.

Also among the defenders was a young man called Nestor, who had been taken captive by a Turkish regiment in Moldavia, southern Russia, forcibly converted to Islam and enrolled in the unit. Since he had some education, Nestor, renamed Iskander, was employed in military administration and learned about Turkish artillery practices. He accompanied the unit on its march to Constantinople and then ran away, 'that I might not die in this wretched faith'. His account of the siege may have been written many years later when he was a monk in a Greek monastery, but it has the quality of a lived experience, a first-hand account of what he witnessed as a noncombatant. It has been suggested that he was attached to Giustiniani's forces at the Romanos Gate and helped them to identify the Ottoman commanders and their weaponry.

Siege warfare was revolutionised in the fifteenth century by the invention of cannon. In the 1420s when the Byzantines had their first experience of bombardment by cannon, they reduced the effectiveness of the new weapon by suspending bales of material, wood and anything that might absorb and diffuse its impact. But the fifth-century fortifications of Constantinople presented an easy target. Now Byzantium needed new technology as well as new warriors to match the enemy. Appreciating this vital combination, in 1451 Constantine XI employed a Christian engineer, a Hungarian named Urban, to assist with the first, while he sent numerous appeals to the West for extra soldiers. But when he failed to pay Urban adequately, the cannon expert offered his skills to the Turkish side. The former allies of the Empire, meanwhile, sent little or no assistance.

It was undoubtedly Byzantine inability to invest in this technology of warfare that sealed the fate of the city. Once Urban was in the employ of the Sultan, who was happy to pay what he asked, the Hungarian cast the largest cannon ever produced, a 29 foot-long bore which fired enormous stones variously identified as weighing 1,200-1,300 lbs. This was called Imperial (*Basilica*) and was so heavy that a team of sixty oxen had to haul it from Edirne. It could only be fired seven times a day because it overheated so greatly. But once correctly positioned opposite the Gate of Romanos and fired, it brought down the ancient walls and created the historic breach through which the Ottoman forces entered the city on the morning of May 29th.

Against this monster weapon, the defenders set up their own much smaller cannon. But when fired they caused more damage to the ancient structures of the city than to the enemy. All the regular techniques of siege warfare were employed: the attackers dug tunnels under the walls, and built tall siege towers which they rolled up to the walls, in order to fix their scaling ladders. The defenders dug counter tunnels and threw burning material into those of the invaders; they poured hot pitch from the walls and set fire to anything wooden set against them. The smoke of fires, as well as cannon, meant that the combatants fought without seeing clearly what was around them.

In 1453 Easter was celebrated on Sunday April 1st, and the next day the Emperor ordered the boom which protected the city's harbour on the Golden Horn to be set in place. Once it was stretched between Constantinople and the Genoese colony of Pera it prevented ships from entering the harbour. As they watched the Turks bringing up their forces, the inhabitants must have realised that battle was about to commence. From April 11th, the cannon bombardment began and the following day the full Turkish fleet of 145 ships anchored two miles off from Constantinople. Fighting occurred on land and sea, with a major onslaught on the walls on April 18th, and a notable naval engagement on April 20th. After the land battle Constantine XI ordered the clergy and monks to gather up the dead and bury them: a total of 1,740 Greeks and 700 Franks (i.e. Westerners) and Armenians, against 18,000 Turks. This duty was repeated on April 25th, when 5,700 defenders were slain, and 35,000 enemy. While the figures (which vary from source to source) are not reliable, the sense of loss and disaster permeates all accounts. Constantinople had been under siege in effect for many years. In 1453 the actual conquest took forty-six days.

Towards the middle of May after stalwart resistance, the Sultan sent an envoy into the city to discuss a possible solution. Mehmet still wished to take the city, but he announced that he would lift the siege if the Emperor paid an annual tribute of 100,000 gold bezants. Alternatively, all the citizens could leave with their possessions and no one would be harmed. The Emperor summoned his council to discuss the proposal. No one seriously believed that such a huge sum could be raised as tribute, nor were they prepared to abandon the city. As in many earlier meetings he had with Cardinal Isidore and the clergy of Hagia Sophia, the Emperor refused to consider flight. Further discussion on the issue was useless. He had embraced his heroic role.

One aspect of the siege emphasised by many authors is the immense din of battle. The Turks made their dawn prayers and then advanced with castanets, tambourines, cymbals and terrifying war cries. Fifes, trumpets, pipes and lutes also accompanied the troops. Three centuries later this manifestation of Turkish military music inspired Mozart to some of his most exciting compositions. In response to the Turks' percussive noise, the Emperor ordered the bells of the city to be rung, and from the numerous churches the tolling of bells inspired the Christians to greater zeal. Trumpets blared at the arrival of troops in support of the city. Nestor-Iskander records how the sound of church bells summoned the non-combatants, priests, monks, women and children to collect the crosses and holy icons and bring them out to bless the city. He also says that women fought among the men and even children threw bricks and paving stones at the Turks once they were inside the city. His account reminds us of the long clash of Muslim and Christian forces which can still be heard today.

George Sprantzes, Constantine XI's loyal secretary, recorded the outcome of the final battle and the way the last emperor of Byzantium conducted himself:

> On Tuesday May 29th, early in the day, the sultan took possession of our City; in this time of capture my late master and emperor, Lord Constantine, was killed. I was not at his side at that hour but had been inspecting another part of the City according to his orders … What did my late lord the emperor not do publicly and privately in his efforts to gain some aid for his house, for the Christians and for his own life? Did he ever think that it was possible and easy for him to abandon the City, if something happened? … Who knew of our emperor's fastings and prayers, both his own and those of priests whom he paid to do so; of his services to the poor and of his increased pledges to God, in the hope of saving his subjects from the Turkish yoke? Nevertheless, God ignored his offerings, I know not why or for what sins, and men disregarded his efforts, as each individual spoke against him as he pleased.

In many respects the city of Constantinople which had for so long eluded the Arabs and Turks was no longer the great Queen of Cities it had once been. That city had already been destroyed in 1204 by Western forces of the Fourth Crusade who had plundered its wealth and then occupied it for fifty-seven years. When the Byzantines reconquered their capital in 1261, they attempted to restore its past glory but could never recreate its former strength. As the Ottomans closed in on their prize, Constantinople became the last outpost of Christian faith in the Middle East, and its inhabitants had to face their historic destiny. The battle between Christianity and Islam was joined around the city.

Constantine XI was the first to realise this and his disappearance during the last day of fighting heightened the myth of 1453. Although a head was solemnly presented to Sultan Mehmet and a corpse given to the Greeks for formal burial, Constantine's body was never found. As a result many stories of his escape and survival circulated. The idea that he had found shelter within the walls of the city and would emerge to triumph over the Muslims is typical. The prolonged resistance and bravery of the defenders made heroes of them all. And within a few years, to have been present in the city on May 29th, 1453, became a badge of honour, claimed by many who had been elsewhere. By the same token Sultan Mehmet would have delighted in the nickname which recognised his role in the fall: from the late fifteenth century onwards, and even today, 550 years later, he is still known as Mehmet the Conqueror.

FOR FURTHER READING

J. R. Melville Jones, *The Fall of Constantinople 1453: Seven Contemporary Accounts* (Amsterdam 1972); J. R. Jones, *Nicolo Barbaro: A Diary of the Siege of Constantinople 1453* (New York 1969); Nestor-Iskander, *The Tale of Constantinople (of Its Origin and Capture by the Turks in the Year 1453)*, translated and annotated by Walter K. Hanak and Marios Philippides (New Rochelle NY and Athens 1998); M. Philippides, *The Fall of the Byzantine Empire: A Chronicle by George Sphrantzes 1401-1477* (Amherst, 1980); Steven Runciman, *The Fall of Constantinople 1453* (Cambridge 1965); Mark Bartusis, *The Late Byzantine Army: Arms and Society, 1204-1453* (Philadelphia, 1992)

Judith Herrin is Professor of Late Antique and Byzantine Studies at King's College London. Her most recent book is *Women in Purple. Rulers of Medieval Byzantium* (Weidenfeld and Nicolson, 2002).

This article first appeared in *History Today*, June 2003, pp. 12–17. Copyright © 2003 by History Today, Ltd. Reprinted by permission.

Machiavelli

Would you buy a used car from this man?

Vincent Cronin

Machiavelli—the most hated man who ever lived: charged, down the centuries, with being the sole poisonous source of political monkey business, of the mocking manipulation of men, of malfeasance, misanthropy, mendacity, murder, and massacre; the evil genius of tyrants and dictators, worse than Judas, for no salvation resulted from *his* betrayal; guilty of the sin against the Holy Ghost, knowing Christianity to be true, but resisting the truth; not a man at all, but Antichrist in apish flesh, the Devil incarnate, Old Nick, with the whiff of sulphur on his breath and a tail hidden under his scarlet Florentine gown.

Machiavelli is the one Italian of the Renaissance we all think we know, partly because his name has passed into our language as a synonym for unscrupulous schemer. But Niccolò Machiavelli of Florence was a more complex and fascinating figure than his namesake of the English dictionary, and unless we ourselves wish to earn the epithet Machiavellian, it is only fair to look at the historical Machiavelli in the context of his age.

He was born in 1469 of an impoverished noble family whose coat of arms featured four keys. Niccolò's father was a retired lawyer who owned two small farms and an inn, his mother a churchgoer who wrote hymns to the Blessed Virgin. Niccolò was one of four children; the younger son, Totto, became a priest, and the idea of a confessional occupied by a Father Machiavelli is one that has caused Niccolò's enemies some wry laughter.

Niccolò attended the Studio, Florence's university, where he studied the prestigious newly-discovered authors of Greece and Rome. Like all his generation, he idolized the Athenians and the Romans of the Republic, and was to make them his models in life. This was one important influence. The other was the fact that Florence was then enjoying, under the Medici, a period of peace. For centuries the city had been torn by war and faction; but now all was serene, and the Florentines were producing their greatest achievements in philosophy, poetry, history, and the fine arts.

This point is important, for too often we imagine the Italian Renaissance as a period of thug-like *condottieri* and cruel despots forever locked in war. We must not be deceived by the artists. Uccello and Michelangelo painted bloody battles, but they were battles that had taken place many years before. If we are to understand Machiavelli, we must picture his youth as a happy period of civilization and peace: for the first time in centuries swords rusted, muscles grew flabby, fortress walls became overgrown with ivy.

In 1494, when Machiavelli was twenty-five, this happiness was shattered. King Charles VIII of France invaded Italy to seize the kingdom of Naples; Florence lay on his route. In the Middle Ages the Florentines had fought bravely against aggressors, but now, grown slack and effete, they were afraid of Charles's veterans and his forty cannon. Instead of manning their walls, they and their leading citizen, Pietro de' Medici, meekly allowed the French king to march in; they even paid him gold not to harm their country.

This debacle led to internal wars, to economic decline, in which Niccolò's father went bankrupt, to much heart-searching, and to a puritanical revolution. Savonarola the Dominican came to rule from the pulpit. Thundering that the French invasion was punishment for a pagan way of life, he burned classical books and nude pictures and urged a regeneration of Florence through fasting and prayer. The French just laughed at Savonarola; he lost the confidence of his fellow citizens and was burned at the stake in 1498.

In that same year, Machiavelli became an employee of the Florentine Republic, which he was to serve ably as diplomat and administrator. Machiavelli scorned Savonarola's idea of political regeneration through Christianity; instead, he persuaded the Florentines to form a citizen militia, as was done in Republican Rome. In 1512 Florence's big test came. Spain had succeeded France as Italy's oppressor, and now, at the instigation of the Medici, who had been exiled from Florence in 1494 and wished to return, a Spanish army of five thousand marched against Tuscany. Four thousand of Machiavelli's militia were defending the strong Florentine town of Prato. The Spaniards, ill-fed and unpaid, launched a halfhearted attack. The Florentines, instead of resisting, took to their heels. Prato was sacked, and a few days later Florence surrendered without a fight. The Medici returned, the Republic came to an end, Machiavelli lost his job and was tortured and exiled to his farm. For the second time in eighteen years he had witnessed a defeat that was both traumatic and humiliating.

In the following year an out-of-work Machiavelli began to write his great book *The Prince*. It is an attempt to answer the question implicit in Florence's two terrible defeats: what had gone wrong? Machiavelli's answer is this: for all their classical buildings and pictures, for all the Ciceronian Latin and readings from Plato, the Florentines had never really revived the essence of classical life—that military vigor and patriotism unto death that distinguished the Greeks and Romans. What then is the remedy? Italy must be regenerated—not by Savonarola's brand of puritanism, but by a soldier-prince. This prince must subordinate every aim to military efficiency. He must personally command a citizen army and keep it disciplined by a reputation for cruelty.

But even this, Machiavelli fears, will not be enough to keep at bay the strong new nation-states, France and Spain. So, in a crescendo of patriotism, Machiavelli urges his prince to disregard the accepted rules of politics, to hit below the belt. Let him lie, if need be, let him violate treaties: "Men must be either pampered or crushed, because they can get revenge for small injuries but not for fatal ones"; "A prudent ruler cannot, and should not, honor his word when it places him at a disadvantage and when the reasons for which he made his promise no longer exist"; "If a prince wants to maintain his rule he must learn how not to be virtuous."

Machiavelli develops his concept of a soldier-prince with a couple of portraits. The first, that of the emperor Alexander

Severus, is an example of how a prince should not behave. Alexander Severus, who reigned in the third century, was a man of such goodness it is said that during his fourteen years of power he never put anyone to death without a trial. Nevertheless, as he was thought effeminate, and a man who let himself be ruled by his mother, he came to be scorned, and the army conspired against him and killed him. Machiavelli scorns him also: "Whenever that class of men on which you believe your continued rule depends is corrupt, whether it be the populace, or soldiers, or nobles, you have to satisfy it by adopting the same disposition; and then *good deeds are your enemies.*"

Machiavelli's second portrait is of Cesare Borgia, son of Pope Alexander VI, who carved out a dukedom for himself and then brought it to heel by appointing a tough governor, Ramiro. Later, says Machiavelli, Cesare discovered that "the recent harshness had aroused some hatred against him, and wishing to purge the minds of the people and win them over... he had this official (Ramiro) cut in two pieces one morning and exposed on the public square... This ferocious spectacle left the people at once *content and horrified.*"

The words I have italicized show Machiavelli's peculiar cast of mind. He grows excited when goodness comes to a sticky end and when a dastardly deed is perpetrated under a cloak of justice. He seems to enjoy shocking traditional morality, and there can be little doubt that he is subconsciously revenging himself on the Establishment responsible for those two profound military defeats.

Machiavelli wrote *The Prince* for Giuliano de' Medici. He hoped that by applying the lessons in his book, Giuliano would become tough enough to unite Italy and drive out the foreigner. But Giuliano, the youngest son of Lorenzo the Magnificent, was a tubercular young man with gentle blue eyes and long sensitive fingers, the friend of poets and himself a sonneteer. He was so soft that his brother Pope Leo had to relieve him of his post as ruler of Florence after less than a year. Preparations for war against France taxed his feeble constitu-

tion; at the age of thirty-seven he fell ill and died. Machiavelli's notion of turning Giuliano into a second Cesare Borgia was about as fantastic as trying to turn John Keats into a James Bond.

This fantastic element has been overlooked in most accounts of Machiavelli, but it seems to me important. Consider the *Life of Castruccio Castracani*, which Machiavelli wrote seven years after *The Prince*. It purports to be a straight biography of a famous fourteenth-century ruler of Lucca, but in fact only the outline of the book is historically true. Finding the real Castruccio insufficiently tough to embody his ideals, Machiavelli introduces wholly fictitious episodes borrowed from Diodorus Siculus's life of a tyrant who really was unscrupulous: Agathocles. As captain of the Syracusans, Agathocles had collected a great army, then summoned the heads of the Council of Six Hundred under the pretext of asking their advice, and put them all to death.

Machiavelli in his book has Castruccio perform a similar stratagem. Just as in *The Prince* the second-rate Cesare Borgia passes through the crucible of Machiavelli's imagination to emerge as a modern Julius Caesar, so here a mildly villainous lord is dressed up as the perfect amoral autocrat. In both books Machiavelli is so concerned to preach his doctrine of salvation through a strong soldier-prince that he leaves Italy as it really was for a world of fantasy.

Machiavelli had a second purpose in dedicating *The Prince* to Giuliano de' Medici (and when Giuliano died, to his almost equally effete nephew Lorenzo). He wished to regain favor with the Medici, notably with Pope Leo. This also was a fantastic plan. Machiavelli had plotted hand over fist against the Medici for no less that fourteen years and was known to be a staunch republican, opposed to one-family rule in Florence. Pope Leo, moreover, was a gentle man who loved Raphael's smooth paintings and singing to the lute; he would not be interested in a book counseling cruelty and terror.

How could a man like Machiavelli, who spent his early life in the down-to-earth world of Italian politics, have yielded to such unrealistic, such fantastic hopes? The answer, I think, lies in the fact that he was also an imaginative artist—a playwright obsessed with extreme dramatic situations. Indeed, Machiavelli was best known in Florence as the author of *Mandragola*. In that brilliant comedy, a bold and tricky adventurer, aided by the profligacy of a parasite, and the avarice of a friar, achieves the triumph of making a gulled husband bring his own unwitting but too yielding wife to shame. It is an error to regard Machiavelli as primarily a political theorist, taking a cool look at facts. *The Prince* is, in one sense, the plot of a fantastic play for turning the tables on the French and Spaniards.

What, too, of Machiavelli's doctrine that it is sometimes wise for a prince to break his word and to violate treaties? It is usually said that this teaching originated with Machiavelli. If so, it would be very surprising, for the vast majority of so-called original inventions during the Italian Renaissance are now known to have been borrowed from classical texts. The Florentines valued wisdom as Edwardian English gentlemen valued port—the older the better.

In 1504 Machiavelli wrote a play, which has been lost, called *Masks*. It was in imitation of Aristophanes' [The] *Clouds*, the subject of which is the Sophists, those men who claimed to teach "virtue" in a special sense, namely, efficiency in the conduct of life. The Sophists emphasized material success and the ability to argue from any point of view, irrespective of its truth. At worst, they encouraged a cynical disbelief in all moral restraints on the pursuit of selfish, personal ambition. Florentines during their golden age had paid little attention to the Sophists, preferring Plato, who accorded so well with Christianity and an aesthetic approach to life; but after the collapse in 1494 it would have been natural for a man like Machiavelli to dig out other, harder-headed philosophers.

The source for his doctrine of political unscrupulousness may well have been the Sophists as presented in Aristophanes' play. The following sentence from one of Machiavelli's letters in 1521 is close to many lines in *The Clouds:* "For that small matter of lies," writes Machiavelli, "I am a doctor and hold my degrees. Life has taught me to confound false and true, till no man knows either."

In *The Prince* this personal confession becomes a general rule: "One must know how to color one's actions and to be a great liar and deceiver."

How was it that an undisputably civilized man like Machiavelli could advise a ruler to be cruel and deceitful and to strike terror? The answer lies in the last chapter of *The Prince*, entitled "Exhortation to liberate Italy from the barbarians." Often neglected, it is, in fact, the most deeply felt chapter of all and gives meaning to the rest. "See how Italy," Machiavelli writes, "beseeches God to send someone to save her from those barbarous cruelties and outrages"—he means the outrages perpetrated by foreign troops in Italy, a land, he goes on, that is "leaderless, lawless, crushed, despoiled, torn, overrun; she has had to endure every kind of desolation."

Machiavelli is a patriot writing in mental torment. He seldom mentions the deity, but in this chapter the name God occurs six times on one page, as an endorsement for this new kind of ruler. Machiavelli really believes that his deceitful prince will be as much an instrument of God as Moses was, and this for two reasons. First, Italy is an occupied country, and her survival is at stake; and just as moral theologians argued that theft becomes legitimate when committed by a starving man, so Machiavelli implies that deceit, cruelty, and so on become legitimate when they are the only means to national survival.

Secondly, Machiavelli had seen honest means tried and fail. Savonarola had hoped to silence cannon by singing hymns; Machiavelli himself had sent conscripts against the Spaniards. But the Italians had been then—and still were—bantams pitted against heavyweights. They could not win according to the rules, only with kidney punches. And since they had to win or cease to be themselves—that is, a civilized people as compared with foreign "barbarians"—Machiavelli argues that it is not only right but the will of God that they should use immoral means.

We must remember that *The Prince* is an extreme book that grew out of an extreme situation and that its maxims must

be seen against the charred, smoking ruins of devastated Italy. The nearest modern parallel is occupied France. In the early 1940's cultivated men like Camus joined the Resistance, committing themselves to blowing up German posts by night and to other sinister techniques of *maquis* warfare. Like Machiavelli, they saw these as the only way to free their beloved country.

But the most original and neglected aspect of Machiavelli is his method. Before Machiavelli's time, historians had been the slaves of chronology. They started with the Creation, or the founding of their city, and worked forward, year by year, decade by decade, chronicling plague, war, and civil strife. Sometimes they detected a pattern, but even when they succeeded in doing so, the pattern was *sui generis*, not applicable elsewhere. Machiavelli was the first modern historian to pool historical facts from a variety of authors, not necessarily of the same period, and to use these facts to draw general conclusions or to answer pertinent questions.

He applies this method notably in his *Discourses on Livy*, and among the questions he answers are these: "What causes commonly give rise to wars between different powers?" "What kind of reputation or gossip or opinion causes the populace to begin to favor a particular citizen?" "Whether the safeguarding of liberty can be more safely entrusted to the populace or to the upper class; and which has the stronger reason for creating disturbances, the 'have-nots' or the 'haves'?"

Machiavelli does not wholly break free from a cyclical reading of history—the term Renaissance is itself a statement of the conviction that the golden age of Greece and Rome had returned. Nor did he break free from a belief in Fortune—what we would now call force of circumstance—and he calculated that men were at the mercy of Fortune five times out of ten. Nevertheless, he does mark an enormous advance over previous historical thinkers, since he discovered the method whereby man can learn from his past.

Having invented this method, Machiavelli proceeded to apply it imperfectly.

He virtually ignored the Middle Ages, probably because medieval chronicles were deficient in those dramatic human twists, reversals, and paradoxes that were what really interested him. This neglect of the Middle Ages marred his study of how to deal with foreign invaders. Over a period of a thousand years Italy had constantly suffered invasion from the north; the lessons implicit in these instances would have helped Machiavelli to resolve his main problem much better than the more remote happenings he chose to draw from Livy. For example, at the Battle of Legnano, near Milan, in 1176, a league of north Italian cities won a crushing victory over Frederick Barbarossa's crack German knights. The Italians didn't employ duplicity or dramatic acts of terrorism, just courage and a united command.

So much for Machiavelli's teaching and discoveries. It remains to consider his influence. In his own lifetime he was considered a failure. Certainly, no soldier-prince arose to liberate Italy. After his death, however, it was otherwise. In 1552 the Vatican placed Machiavelli's works on the Index of Prohibited Books, because they teach men "to appear good for their own advantage in this world—a doctrine worse than heresy." Despite this ban, Machiavelli's books were widely read and his political teaching became influential. It would probably have confirmed him in his pessimistic view of human nature had he known that most statesmen and thinkers would seize on the elements of repression and guile in his teachings to the exclusion of the civic sense and patriotism he equally taught.

In France several kings studied Machiavelli as a means of increasing their absolutism, though it cannot be said that he did them much good. Henry III and Henry IV were murdered, and in each case on their blood-soaked person was found a well-thumbed copy of *The Prince*. Louis XIII was following Machiavelli when he caused his most powerful subject, the Italian-born adventurer Concini, to be treacherously killed. Richelieu affirmed that France could not be governed without the right of arbitrary arrest and exile, and that in case of danger to the state it may be well that a hundred innocent men should perish. This was *raison d'état*, an exaggerated version of certain elements in *The Prince*, to which Machiavelli might well not have subscribed.

In England Machiavelli had little direct influence. England had never been defeated as Florence had been, and Englishmen could not understand the kind of desperate situation that demanded unscrupulous political methods. The political diseases Machiavelli had first studied scientifically were in England called after his name, rather as a physical disease—say Parkinson's—is called not after the man who is suffering from it but after the doctor who discovers it. Machiavelli thus became saddled with a lot of things he had never advocated, including atheism and any treacherous way of killing, generally by poison. Hence Flamineo in Webster's *White Devil*:

> O the rare trickes of a Machivillian!
> Hee doth not come like a grosse plodding slave
> And buffet you to death: no, my quaint knave—
> Hee tickles you to death; makes you die laughing,
> As if you had swallow'd a pound of saffron.

The eighteenth century, with its strong belief in man's good nature and reason, tended to scoff at Machiavelli. Hume wrote: "There is scarcely any maxim in *The Prince* which subsequent experience has not entirely refuted. The errors of this politician proceed, in a great measure, from his having lived in too early an age of the world to be a good judge of political truth." With Hume's judgment Frederick the Great of Prussia would, in early life, have agreed. As a young man Frederick wrote an *Anti-Machiavel*, in which he stated that a ruler is the first servant of his people. He rejected the idea of breaking treaties, "for one has only to make one deception of this kind, and one loses the confidence of every ruler." But Frederick did follow Machiavelli's advice to rule personally, to act as his own commander in the field, and to despise flatterers.

Later, Frederick began to wonder whether honesty really was the best policy. "One sees oneself continually in danger of being betrayed by one's allies, forsaken by one's friends, brought low by envy and jealousy; and ultimately one finds oneself obliged to choose between the terrible alternative of sacrificing one's people or one's word of honor." In old age, Frederick became a confirmed Machiavellian, writing in 1775: "Rulers must always be guided by the interests of the state. They are slaves of their resources, the interest of the state is their law, and this law may not be infringed."

During the nineteenth century Germany and Italy both sought to achieve national unity, with the result that writers now began to play up Machiavelli's other side, his call for regeneration. Young Hegel hails the author of *The Prince* for having "grasped with a cool circumspection the necessary idea that Italy should be saved by being combined into one state." He and Fichte go a stage further than Machiavelli: they assert that the conflict between the individual and the state no longer exists, since they consider liberty and law identical. The necessity of evil in political action becomes a superior ethics that has no connection with the morals of an individual. The state swallows up evil.

In Italy Machiavelli's ideal of a regenerated national state was not perverted in this way and proved an important influence on the *risorgimento*. In 1859 the provisional government of Tuscany, on the eve of national independence, published a decree stating that a complete edition of Machiavelli's works would be printed at government expense. It had taken more than three hundred years for "a man to arise to redeem Italy," and in the event the man turned out to be two men, Cavour and Garibaldi. Both, incidentally, were quite unlike the Prince: Cavour, peering through steel-rimmed spectacles, was a moderate statesman of the center, and Garibaldi a blunt, humane, rather quixotic soldier.

Bismarck was a close student of Machiavelli, but Marx and Engels did not pay much attention to him, and the Florentine's books have never exerted great influence in Russia. In contemporary history Machiavelli's main impact has been on Benito Mussolini. In 1924 Mussolini wrote a thesis on *The Prince*, which he described as the statesman's essential vade mecum. The Fascist leader deliberately set himself to implement Petrarch's call quoted on the last page of *The Prince*:

> Che l'antico valore
> Nell' italici cor non è ancor morto.
> Let Italians, as they did of old,
> Prove that their courage has not
>   grown cold.

After a course of muscle building, Mussolini sent the Italian army into Ethiopia to found a new Roman Empire. He joined Hitler's war in 1940, only to find that he had failed to impart to modern Italians the martial qualities of Caesar's legions. The final irony occurred in 1944, when the Nazis were obliged to occupy northern Italy as the only means of stopping an Allied walkover, and Italy again experienced the trauma of 1494 and 1512. Mussolini's failures discredit, at least for our generation, Machiavelli's theory that it is possible for one man to effect a heart transplant on a whole people.

What is Machiavelli's significance today? His policy of political duplicity has been found wanting in the past and is probably no longer practicable in an age of democracy and television. His policy of nationalism is also beginning to date as we move into an era of ideological blocs. His insistence on the need for military preparedness has proved of more durable value and is likely to remain one of the West's key beliefs. His technique for solving political problems through a study of the past is practiced to some extent by every self-respecting foreign minister of our time.

Was Machiavelli, finally, an evil man? He made an ethic of patriotism. In normal times that is a poisonous equation, but defensible, I believe, in the context of sixteenth-century Italy. Machiavelli wrote on the edge of an abyss: he could hear the thud of enemy boots, had seen pillage, profanation, and rape by foreign troops. Imaginative as he was, he could sense horrors ahead: the ending of political liberty and of freedom of the press, which put the lights out in Italy for 250 years. He taught that it is civilized man's first duty to save civilization—at all costs. Doubtless he was mistaken. But it is not, I think, the mistake of an evil man.

From *Horizon*, Autumn 1972. Reprinted by permission of American Heritage, Inc., 1972.

Virtue & Beauty

The Renaissance Image of the Ideal Woman

by Mary O'Neill

When the beguiling, young Ginevra de' Benci appeared before him in all her aristocratic finery in her family's Florentine palazzo circa 1475, Bernardo Bembo, the Venetian ambassador to Florence, was instantly smitten. Though Ginevra was recently wed, and Bembo more than twice her age and also married, he launched a determined campaign to win her affection. He evidently succeeded, since Ginevra's "crimson lips," "snow-white brow" and, above all, her chastity were celebrated in nearly a dozen poems addressed to Bembo and Ginevra by writers in the Medici circle. One gentlemanly poet, Cristoforo Landino, wrote of them:

> He saw her, and the flame burst into the heart within him, and a dreadful trembling passed through his bones. For her face resembled what we often see when white lilies are mixed with red roses.... If you look at Ginevra's neck, you will rightly be able to scorn white snow.

From Bembo himself, one line of lyric testimony endures. In his likely commission for the painting for the reverse of Ginevra's portrait, the inscription trumpets: "Beauty Adorns Virtue." Bembo perhaps never suspected that the painting would outshine his love. Nor could he have forecast that the artist, a neophyte named Leonardo da Vinci, would use this portrait of Ginevra de' Benci as a springboard to some of the greatest achievements in the history of art.

One of the crown jewels of the permanent collection at the National Gallery of Art in Washington, D.C. and the only painting by Leonardo in the Western hemisphere, Ginevra's portrait is the centerpiece of a new exhibition at the gallery. "Virtue and Beauty: Leonardo's Ginevra de' Benci and Renaissance Portraits of Women" focuses on the phenomenal development of female portraiture in Florence from 1440 to 1540. A cross between the real and the ideal, these works are visual representations of long-established notions of feminine beauty, propagated in the literature of the time. The exhibition includes paintings, sculpture, medals and drawings by Florentine artists, as well as influential parallel works from Northern Europe that demonstrate important developments in technique and composition. The show, which is sponsored by Airbus, opens on September 30 and runs until January 6, 2002. The National Gallery is its only venue.

Leonardo apparently complied with Bembo's conception for the back panel of his portrait of Ginevra de' Benci. The artist had used juniper—*ginepro* in Italian—on the front panel as a pun on Genevra's name. Bembo, it seems, wanted to continue that play on the reverse by having a juniper sprig entwined with a wreath of laurel and palm, his own personal emblem. The word for "beauty" is artfully wrapped around the juniper, and an infrared examination has revealed another motto, *Virtus et Honor*—Bembo's own—underneath the present one. He thus succeeded in symbolically linking himself to his love for all eternity.

In fact, Bembo and Ginevra's love affair probably existed only on a symbolic level. Under the influence of the Medici dynasty, presided over by Cosimo and later by his grandson

Lorenzo the Magnificent, upper-class Florentines practiced an intricate and chaste courtship ritual with women of high rank. Though patrician men married—and kept mistresses—they reserved the art of the romantic pursuit for unattainable women, typically the wives of other gentlemen. He might have claimed to be love struck, but it is likely that Bembo dispassionately selected Ginevra as his *innamorata* to fulfill this convention. His attention was probably the bright spot in her existence. Her marriage to Luigi Niccolini, whose fortunes soon waned, produced no children—a discredit to Ginevra, who was in fragile health for much of her long life.

None of the participants expected these affairs to be consummated; indeed, the woman's incorruptible purity was the foundation of the gentleman's desire. The intricacies of the chase were well understood by all the parties, and its chief device was lyric poetry—particularly in the style of Petrarch. The Italian poet's obsession with his unattainable Laura served as the model for Renaissance lovers, and not just because of the popularity of his verses, which were written in the Italian vernacular. Petrarch was the champion, a century before the Medici, of a revived interest in the glory days of Greece and Rome. His advocacy of the "new learning"—an emphasis on studying the classics and adhering to ancient ideals—was eagerly adopted by the Medici, Tuscany's most powerful family. Lorenzo de' Medici surrounded himself with scholars, writers, architects, philosophers and artists who integrated these ideals into a prosperous Florentine republic.

Central to this courtly concept of idealized love was the determination by the Florentine humanist Marsilio Ficino, a writer revered and supported by the Medici, that beauty was the physical evidence of spiritual virtue. A beautiful woman would be modest, graceful, humble, obedient and pious, but she would also possess something indefinable that brought those attributes together. Agnolo

Firenzuola, another Florentine writer, would later delineate the physical characteristics that were sure signs of a virtuous character. The forehead should be twice as wide as it was high. (Women plucked their hairlines to achieve smoothness and proportion.) Arched brows, chestnut eyes, golden curls and a pointed (but not upturned) nose were necessary, and ears should be pale pink like roses, except at the edges, which should be the transparent red of a pomegranate seed. High, ivory cheeks should frame a small mouth, which might only occasionally reveal the woman's most potent feature—a smile that would transport the recipient to paradise. Not to be outdone, one poet declared his lover's smile would reveal six paradises. According to this canon of beauty, however, paradise would vanish if the lady showed more than six teeth.

The Medici circle set out to capture these qualities in an ideal woman by commemorating her in verse. As artists naturally began to translate these qualities visually, they faced a particular challenge in making women who were unattractive fit the formula for a virtuous appearance.

The homage accorded Renaissance women in poetry and art stood in stark contrast to their daily experience and position in society. Respectable women left their homes only to attend mass or family events. Conversing with men was considered immodest, and one writer cautioned young women against falling in love with the men they would marry. According to Ficino, "Women should be used like chamber pots: hidden away once a man has pissed in them." While Italian men were free to cultivate intellectual and cultural perfection, the peak experience for a woman was a strategic marriage to a man selected by her father or brothers. Under the dowry system, the family protected a young lady's chastity at all costs, since an advantageous marriage contract hinged on her purity. Once the men brokered that deal, the lady was expected to fulfill her true destiny: bearing as many

children (especially sons) as possible to sustain the lineage. Of particular importance in the face of the still-lingering plague, this assignment was fraught with danger, as many young women died in childbirth. The best that could be said about a woman during the Renaissance was not that she had a striking personality or possessed extraordinary qualities but that she conformed to the prescribed model of gentility and thus reflected well on her family. Even Lorenzo de' Medici's own sister, Nannina, was subject to the demands of family, state, church and merchant society. "Don't be born a woman if you want your own way," she once complained.

Portraits of women flourished in Florence because of the central importance of the marriage ritual and also because the city proved to be fertile ground for creative innovation. Florentines devoted themselves to a thriving international economy and to the world of ideas. Petrarch was part of a literary triumvirate, along with Dante and Boccaccio, that set a very high standard for Florentine intellectual life. It is estimated that by the 14th century as much as one-third of the male population was literate—an extraordinary rate during that time—and citizens were expected to participate actively in civic affairs. The urban bourgeoisie not only patronized the arts but also practiced them. Lorenzo de' Medici, one of the chief connoisseurs of the arts in all of Italy, wrote lyric poetry and treatises along-side Ficino and other scholars. By the 15th century, Florence's primacy as the center of creative and intellectual activity throughout Southern Europe was well established.

On January 29, 1475, at the height of the city's golden age, a jousting tournament (*giostra*) was organized by the Medici, and won by Lorenzo's brother Giuliano, as part of the celebration of an alliance with Venice and Milan. A lavish display of Medici wealth and power, the event was dedicated to Giuliano's platonic love, Simonetta Vespucci. Simonetta is thought to be the subject of a portrait attributed to Sandro Botticelli, whose painting of Giuliano is also included in the National Gallery exhibition. The lady is arrayed as a mythological figure, and her attributes—partly braided golden hair, creamy skin and arched eyebrows—are similar to those of Petrarch's Laura. Her hair is adorned with a beautiful net of pearls, called a *vespaio*, or wasp's nest, possibly a pun on Simonetta's surname. A certain Petrarchan sonnet seems to be the lyric parallel to or possible inspiration for the painting, though it was written in the previous century:

> Breeze that surrounds those blond and curling locks, that makes them move and which is moved by them in softness, and that scatters the sweet gold, then gathers it in lovely knots recurling, you linger in the eyes whence wasps of love sting me….

Simonetta died one year after the Giostra of Giuliano, as the joust was known, at age 23. Her early death only increased the adulation of her admirers. Botticelli's idealized portrait was painted c. 1480/1485, at least four years after her death. The same posthumous idealization characterizes his portrait of Giuliano, who was murdered by political enemies of his family at Easter Sunday mass in 1478. A charismatic 25-year-old, Giuliano was mourned as a martyr across Florence. His lowered eyelids support the theory that Botticelli's painting was completed from a death mask or drawing, and the turtledove in the lower left-hand corner signifies mourning but could also indicate fidelity to a lost love, possibly Simonetta.

Simonetta's representation as a nymph or goddess indicates the artist's emphasis on a poetic ideal of beauty rather than actual appearance. Such portraits are not psychological in the modern sense of revealing personal thoughts and feelings; rather they show the sitters in their public role as upper-class women. Although their real features were depicted, the sitters were shown as their families wanted them to be seen—as emblems of honor. Nevertheless, 15th-century artists took important steps toward authentic characterization.

The first step was prompted by a tacit challenge. Florentine painters began to consider how they could depict the inner beauty expressed so effusively by the literati. A *paragone*, or rivalry, developed between writers and painters as each aimed to immortalize Florentine women. Writers and scholars in the Medici circle doubted painting's ability to depict ideal beauty. They contended that only poetry could adequately describe the capacity of a woman's smile to transform the world. This attitude was subtly reinforced in Florentine society in the second half of the 15th century. Scholars, architects and writers received civic recognition, such as tax-exempt status or other distinctions, while most artists labored without support or renown. The Medici lodged Ficino in a country house but didn't pay promised fees to Andrea del Verrocchio, a favored sculptor.

In one of the key works in the exhibition, Domenico Ghirlandaio asserts his view on the rivalry between artists and literati. The inscription that appears just behind the sitter in his portrait of Giovanna degli Albizzi Tornabuoni translates to: "Art, would that you could represent character and mind. There would be no more beautiful painting on earth." While Ghirlandaio seems to be commenting on the limits of his profession, the painting may actually betray a touch of sarcasm in the inscription. Using the restrictive profile pose, Ghirlandaio succeeds in portraying the lady's moral character. The book and beads (likely a prayer book and rosary) are indications of her piety, and the surrounding tomblike structure seems to be illuminated as much by Giovanna's inner beauty as by any outside source. Her radiance in this dark chamber is purposeful, since Ghirlandaio completed the painting shortly after Giovanna's death in childbirth at age 19. Ten years later, the painting still hung in her husband's bedroom, serving to bring his beloved back to life.

No artist was more preoccupied with expressing intangible attributes—the "motions of the mind," as he called them—than Leonardo. He wanted to capture Ginevra's beauty and virtue in paint, not words. "Certainly one of Leonardo's major goals was to raise visual art to the level of poetry," says David Alan Brown, curator of Italian Renaissance painting at the National Gallery of Art. To this end, Leonardo broke with a long tradition of profile portraiture by boldly portraying his sitter in a three-quarter view. It has been said that modern portraiture begins with the connective gaze, and Ginevra looks out at us. While the profile pose symbolized rectitude and moral strength—an unmarried woman would not look at a man directly—the three-quarter pose disclosed the sitter's face, hinting at her psyche. The sitter thus gained a vitality that is absent in the modestly averted profile. The exhibition tracks the evolution in female portraiture from the profile to the three-quarter view, from a strictly idealized to a more expressive depiction, which began with Leonardo's innovation.

Inspired, perhaps, by a bust sculpted by his teacher Verrocchio entitled *Lady with a Bunch of Flowers*, Leonardo also, it is presumed, used hands to express character in his *Ginevra de' Benci*. For the first time in 500 years, these two works, both created in Verrocchio's studio, are reunited in the National Gallery exhibition. Verrocchio's bust extends below the standard head-and-shoulders format to include delicate fingers gracefully clasping a small bouquet. Leonardo apparently reprised the device in his portrait of Ginevra, gaining expressive force through the elegance of her hands and the symbolism of the flowers. White flowers represent chastity, the single most important attribute for aristocratic ladies. Ginevra wears a covering over her shoulders, as required by law and enforced by notaries called the Officials of the Women. A woman's access to the outdoors was restricted—hence the very pale skin depicted in these portraits.

Long before the National Gallery of Art acquired the work from the royal family of Liechtenstein in 1967, Ginevra's hands had been cut from the painting. Sometime before 1780, when the recorded measurements match the current size, it is thought that nearly eight inches were cut from the bottom of the portrait and half an inch from the side, probably because of fire or water damage. The wreath on the reverse is therefore truncated and off-center, and Ginevra's torso and hands are missing.

Brown has taken great pains to reproduce the effect of the original design. The exhibition includes a Leonardo drawing, *Study of Hands*, believed to be the artist's sketch of the hands for Ginevra's portrait. This drawing was used by Brown and the National Gallery's Department of Imaging and Visual Services to suggest the missing portion of the painting in a digital reconstruction. Advances in conservation work and digital imaging provide an unprecedented insight into Leonardo's creative process. The symmetrical composition on the reverse was a logical starting point for the technicians. With the juniper twig as the central axis, the technicians were able to "restore" the missing side digitally. After scanning Leonardo's drawing, the hands and flower were superimposed on an image of Ginevra, and details were added to her costume to achieve a computer-generated approximation of the original. Brown believes Leonardo would have approved of his efforts: "For Leonardo, hands were a central means of expression. Look at *The Last Supper*, with the apostles gesturing. For him, hands were as important as the face to create expression,

and that element was missing from Ginevra. That's what we were trying to bring back to the painting."

A 1991 cleaning also revealed the delicacy of Leonardo's execution. According to David Bull, senior consultant to the National Gallery of Art and head of the conservation team in 1991, "The sky became more blue, and we were able to see greater clarity in the juniper bush, which was just a blot before. Ginevra became more pale, so that her flesh seems to glow." The cleaning also revealed Leonardo's fingerprints in the paint. By blurring the wet paint with his fingertips, he achieved a more atmospheric effect—a technique that prefigures modern art. "He softens the transition between one passage and another, and he makes the medium do something new," says Bull.

As for Ginevra herself, one line of her poetry survives: "I ask your forgiveness and I am a mountain tiger," she wrote, perhaps in a fit of pique over Bembo's departure from Florence. As for Leonardo's portrait of her, she may have been somewhat bewildered by it. Not only was she posed facing the viewer and placed in an outdoor setting, she was presented in dreary household attire. Leonardo wanted to depict Ginevra as unified with nature, so he used earth tones and just a touch of blue for her dress. Ginevra probably expected to be portrayed in the Florentine fashion of the day, as seen in portraits by Fra Filippo Lippi and Ghirlandaio. A hub of capitalism, Florence was a society that encouraged ostentation. Extravagant deep-blue and red fabrics, richly embroidered dresses, jeweled belts, fur, necklaces with pearls and gems set in gold, sleeves slashed to reveal diaphanous chemises—such opulence could only reflect well on the family of the sitter. Women carried patrician honor on their backs, particularly during their most important public presentation—their wedding.

The amount spent on a bride's apparel could constitute 40 percent of the family's wealth. Because they were used to "mark" the woman, these dresses and jewels remained the property of her husband, who might later repossess them.

The rich textures of the ladies' costumes, as well as their hair and skin, were perfect counterparts to the technical advances in art sweeping Florence. With the development of oil painting earlier in the 15th century, Florentine artists were able to create a more tactile depiction of reality. The pigment floats in glazes of oil, and light reflects from those colors to give the image a certain depth and brilliance. Leonardo was one of the first to master this technique in Florence. As with the three-quarter pose, he was inspired by examples from Northern Europe, which he would have seen in the homes of his sophisticated patrons. Members of the patrician class, including the Medici, greatly admired Flemish painters like Rogier van der Weyden and Petrus Christus. The exhibition includes works by these Northern artists, such as Van der Weyden's *Portrait of a Lady*, which subtly forecasts an emphasis on the sitter's inner life. The lady seems barely able to breathe under the tight belt. With her taut fingers, sensuous mouth and furtive glance, it appears her rigid control will not last much longer.

Leonardo succeeded in silencing those scholars and writers who doubted painting's power to express the "motions of the mind" or the grace of a woman's smile. Some 30 years after capturing Ginevra's inner beauty, he communicated the interior world of Mona Lisa with an unforgettable image. Just as Petrarch insisted, a woman's smile held the power to transform the world.

Washington-based writer Mary O'Neill is also a docent at the National Gallery of Art.

Martin Luther's ninety-five Theses

Michael Mullett defines the role of the 95 Theses in the Lutheran Reformation.

by Michael Mullett

THE MAN AND THE THESES: AN INTRODUCTION

Martin Luther (1483-1546) is rightly regarded as the founder of the six-teenth-century Protestant Reformation—the religious, political, cultural and social revolution that broke the hold of the Catholic Church over Europe. Luther was born in Eisleben in eastern Germany in 1483. Though in later accounts of himself he liked to dwell on the lowliness of his origins, in point of fact his father had made good in the mining industry, while his mother was from a professional bourgeois background.

Historians today tend to be sceptical about claims made some years ago by the psychoanalyst Erik Erikson to the effect that the young Luther was haunted by a psychological collision with his parents, especially with his formidable father, and that he later transposed that conflict on to the fear of God's judgement that was to haunt him as a monk. What is sure, though, is that the young Luther had to stand up for himself to defy his father, who wanted him to train for the legal profession, and assert his own desire to seek his everlasting salvation. In 1505, with that aim in mind, he got

his own way when he entered the monastery, in Erfurt in Saxony, of the Augustinian Eremites, a strict order noted for its academic interests and pastoral concerns.

He was ordained priest in 1507 and proceeded to take up the academic focus of his order, becoming doctor of Sacred Scripture in 1512 and, at the same time, assuming a professorship of the bible at the newly founded University of Wittenberg in the Electorate of Saxony. Meanwhile, Luther's monastic years were haunted by a dark shadow of acute anxiety as he sought, without any sense of success, to win God's favour and forgiveness for his (largely imagined) sins through many acts of self-mortification.

Yet in lectures on Scripture texts, the Psalms of the Old Testament and the Epistle of St Paul to the Romans in the New, Luther gradually found assurance that sinners won acceptance from God the Father—were 'justified'—not actively, through their good deeds, but passively and simply by faith that Christ had died on the Cross to save them. However, by his own testimony, it may have been some years, perhaps not until as late as 1519, that he actually appropriated those insights fully to his

own condition. In the midst of that process, in 1517, came the 95 Theses against Indulgences, a document showing that Luther's practical appropriation of 'justification by faith alone' was far from fully formed at that point in time and that, although Luther disparaged papal indulgences as media of final forgiveness of sins, he was still placing considerable onus on the responsibility of the individual to secure remission of sins through contrition for them.

In the years to come, the breach that the 95 Theses opened up with the papacy by challenging its claimed divinely-endowed power to pardon widened inexorably, leading to Luther's excommunication in 1520 and his outlawry as an impenitent heretic at the Diet (German parliament) in 1521. In the same year, in the most dangerous passage of his life, Luther secured protection and a safe hiding place from the ruler of Saxony, the Elector Frederick the Wise. In the years to come, following Frederick's death in 1525, Luther resettled as professor at Wittenberg (and a married family man from 1525) and became the builder of the Lutheran Protestant Reformation. Its church structures were to be incorporated in the 'Instructions for the

Visitors of Parish Pastors in Electoral Saxony' of 1528 and its doctrines were formulated in the Augsburg Confession of 1530.

Martin Luther is a figure of titanic greatness in the history of religion, a man of insurmountable courage, a writer and preacher of vast output and great depth, with the most powerful sense of the immediacy of the divine. His character was marred by intense violence of emotion and language against all who disagreed with his religious views and he manifested rising bigotry against the Jewish people; he could be opportunistic and full of duplicity in advancing his cause. For good or ill, as both destructive revolutionary and patient builder, Luther's place in the history of Europe is assured.

THE 95 THESES: ORIGINS

If anyone remembers anything about Martin Luther, it is likely to be the fact that, in protest against a papal indulgence being hawked around Germany by the salesman friar Johann Tetzel, he nailed 95 Theses to the door of a church—the Castle Church in Wittenberg, in the German principality of Saxony—and thereby precipitated the Reformation. Indeed in all biographies of him the central importance of Luther's 95 Theses (to give them their full title, the 'Disputation on the Power and Efficacy of indulgences') has been recognised from the beginning.

First in the field was Luther's leading Reformation partner and academic colleague as professor of Greek at Luther's University of Wittenberg, Philip Melanchthon. It was Melanchthon who first assembled as a literary record what we may term the drama of the Theses. Its main ingredients were: Luther the lover of truth versus Tetzel, a father of lies; the nailing of the Theses; and the role of Providence in those events. Melanchthon recorded how:

> When Luther was in [his] course
> of study, venal indulgences
> were circulated in these regions
> by Tetzel the Dominican, a most

shameless sycophant. Luther, angered by Tetzel's impious and execrable debates, and burning with the eagerness of piety, published Propositions concerning indulgences [the 95 Theses] and he publicly nailed these to the church attached to Wittenberg Castle, on the day [31 October] before the feast of All Saints, 1517.
These were the beginnings of this controversy, in which Luther, as yet suspecting or dreaming nothing about the future change of rites [religion], was certainly not completely getting rid of indulgences themselves, but only urging moderation.

In writing this, Melanchthon showed, first, how Luther was goaded by Tetzel beyond the limits of righteous exasperation, that the Theses were nailed and, most significantly, that as yet Luther hardly knew what he was doing ('as yet suspecting or dreaming nothing'). So Melanchthon was indicating that the delivery to the world of the Theses, an action whose eventual outcome was at first not envisaged by their human instrument, had to be the working of Providence, shaping God's ends through a human agent. Thus, even though Luther himself was not to know where his actions, divinely inspired without his knowing, would lead, it was entirely valid to see in that drama of a starved monk, some paper, hammer, nails and a church door, the real, if distant, origins of the Protestant Reformation. It was Melanchthon, fixing the date of Luther's protest unmistakably to 31 October, who helped make that day, in subsequently devised annual commemorative celebrations, 'Reformation day' throughout the Lutheran world; not because that was when the Reformation really began, but because that was when God initiated, through Luther, the process that would lead to the Reformation.

God's instrument, Luther, was also a brave man and Melanchthon showed that he did what he had to do

because he was pushed beyond endurance by doctrinal abuse and 'sycophancy'. He had to nail the Theses, with all the theatre of action that such moments require. We might think of Robin Hood, forced to make a stand in brave defence of an oppressed friend; or of the part-legendary Swiss national hero Wilhelm Tell, inaugurating his nation's defiance of their Austrian overlords by refusing the degradation of saluting the hat of the local representative of Austrian power. In all these cases—Robin Hood, Wilhelm Tell, Luther—mere words, unaccompanied by brave action, were not enough for true valour, and in the Melanchthon version, which passed into posterity, Luther had to have nailed the Theses.

In the accumulating tradition of Luther biography, the act of nailing in turn represented the triumph of manly action. Thus a selection of Victorian English lives of Luther, celebrating him as a hero of virile Christian courage, related how he 'went boldly [my emphasis] down to the church, and affixed to the door ninety-five Theses against the doctrine of indulgences'. The act of nailing, 'this courageous attack', was literally striking hammer blows for freedom, and it took a courage that contrasted with Erasmus's lack of that virtue, 'for the only thing which gives a man true courage to speak what he knows to be right…. is "the fear of the Lord" …'. Again, in another example of this literary type, while the learned 'timidly' drew back from confrontation with Tetzel's aggressiveness, Luther alone, though fortified by the word of God and so 'not deficient in courage', spoke out in what another biography acknowledged was his 'audacious act'. In turn, such audacious acts—as Luther's, Robin Hood's or Tell's—may immediately become public acts, exemplary in their inspiration to large numbers of people to take heart from them.

Fact and legend collude in the image of Luther's brave action, not just in composing the 95 Theses, which were so critical of the papal power of issuing those remissions of the guilt of sin known as indulgences, but in taking the bold step of making them a public manifesto. In terms of the classification as the kind of production they were, the 95 Theses may have been one, two or all three of three things.

First, they were an attachment to an advisory letter, private and confidential and dated 31 October 1517, from Luther as a professorial expert on theology to his ecclesiastical superior, Albrecht von Hohenzollern, archbishop of Mainz, warning him of the doctrinally dubious nature of indulgences in general. There would have been little of the heroic about such a procedure, even though archbishop Albrecht, on receipt of the letter enclosing the Theses, issued a kind of gagging order against the bold professor-monk of Wittenberg.

At the same time, the Theses, a handwritten schedule in Latin, must be seen as a fairly routine announcement of, and the agenda for, a forthcoming university debate amongst theologians on the legitimacy or otherwise of indulgences, a discussion to be conducted by expert theologians. The chairman, Professor Luther, was using the 'disputation' Theses to put forward his own viewpoint and inviting others to submit theirs: 'The following heads [the 95 Theses] will be the subject of a public discussion at Wittenberg, under the presidency of the reverend father, Martin Luther, Augustinian, Master of Arts and Sacred Theology, and duly appointed Lecturer on these subjects in that place'. Universities are known for their posters advertising forthcoming events, and the door of the castle church was the recognised bulletin board for Wittenberg university. Luther, in posting the Theses, 'had no intention', he claimed, 'to give [them] so much publicity. I wished only to confer on their contents with some of those who reside with us or near us'.

A learned debate amongst academic theologians from the region's universities might have had little significance as a world-shattering event.

However, the Theses next took on a third identity. From what we might call a 'whistle-blowing' letter to a superior, to topics for a seminar, they turned next into a sensational printed artefact, precipitated fully into the public domain, to be a manifesto for change and rebellion, against papal Rome in a country seething with a mixture of religious, moral, political and financial grievances against the Roman Church. As Luther reported, '… now they are printed, reprinted, and spread far and wide, beyond my expectation'.

So, it is pretty well certain that the Theses were nailed to the door, in an ordinary act of bill-posting that came to be constructed as one of history's emblematic moments. Then, before Christmas 1517, what was intended as the syllabus for a colloquium of theologians from a group of provincial universities to discuss had been transformed into a public manifesto by two simple processes. First, using a German invention of the previous century, they were printed in such centres as Magdeburg and Leipzig and, second, in December in the great south German city of Nuremberg they were translated into German. But it is at least worth speculating that this distribution of the Theses 'far and wide' was not entirely, as Luther put it, 'beyond my expectation; so much so that I repent of their production'. On 11 November he was sending copies of the Theses to friends, and from this arose the mass printing that took place in the dying weeks of that year. Evidently intended in the first instance for a debate within academia, the propositions were not theoretical, technical or 'scholastic', in the sense of the abstruse academic method in which Luther was trained. Their tone was simple, from the opening ringing declaration 'When our Lord and Master, Jesus Christ, said "Repent", he called for the entire life of believers to be one of penitence'. That announcement in turn set the keynote for the Theses as a practical, teaching document ideal for public consumption. For, as well

as a professor, Luther was a working parish priest in Wittenberg, and his immediate worry over the indulgence of 1517 was that it dangerously deluded parishioners into the mistaken belief that their sins could be forgiven by purchasing indulgences rather than by genuine heartfelt contrition for sins.

Concern with what is known as pastoral, that is practical or applied, theology suffuses the Theses, above all in the almost incantatory overtures to Theses 42-3 and 45-51: 'Christians should be taught …'. By 1515 Luther was already no stranger to the press—he had, for example, had the scripture texts for his earliest university lectures printed for his students. So, if the 95 Theses were motions for a symposium which somehow got out into the public domain, they could not have been more skillfully drawn up for the latter use.

THE 95 THESES: CONTENTS

What, then, were their major concerns? For one thing they were not centrally concerned with the financial scam surrounding the 1517 indulgence, a complex racket to raise money for Rome and allow von Hohenzollen to pay off debts he had built up to pay for papal dispensation to hold more benefices—highly lucrative ones—than the Church's own law allowed: Luther knew nothing of that then.

Instead, the 95 Theses were insistently preoccupied with the theology and practice of indulgences, those papal remissions of the guilt still attaching to sins after the sins themselves had been absolved, primarily in the Church's sacrament of Penance. If that guilt was not somehow discharged in his life, by doing good deeds of mercy and charity or by performing penances and by such pious actions as going on pilgrimages, then before admission into heaven could be considered the same guilt would have to be cleared in intense suffering by fire for whatever duration was appropriate in the state beyond death known as purgatory. Individuals could, however, acquire in advance for themselves what we might term insurance policies in the form of indulgences so as to reduce or eliminate detention in purgatory after their deaths.

The Catholic Church had come to teach that indulgences, forged out of a massive 'treasury of merit' built up by Christ and the saints and in the custody of the Church itself to draw upon and dispense, could also be applied to the credits of friends, relations and benefactors in purgatory. In these senses, the doctrine of indulgences was part of the then current widespread anxiety over the ways that men and women, as sinners, were made acceptable and forgiven in God's sight.

Luther, on the other hand, is firmly associated with an alternative route-map towards redemption, the doctrine of justification by faith alone. He was already feeling his way towards the realisation of this doctrine in the course of University exegetical lectures on the Psalms (1513-1515) and on St Paul's Epistle to the Romans (1515-1516). According to its mature formulation, sinful people were accounted acceptable and just ('justified') in God's eyes not through the worth that they actively pursued by their own efforts, but only passively, by accepting and trusting that Christ had died to atone for their sins: the 'just' were saved by their faith.

This central 'Lutheran' perception, however, is not to the fore in the 95 Theses. Indeed, in the 'Preface to the Complete Edition of Luther's Writings', 1545, he carefully chronicled the issue of the 95 Theses before he recorded his full discovery of justification by faith. In their nature, these slow and gradual intellectual and psychological processes cannot always be precisely dated, but it seems certain that his fullest insight into justification by faith and his deepest appropriation of this doctrine to his own condition cannot have come earlier than 1518. In fact, Luther recalled, that discovery synchronised with the events of 1519, which were themselves partly the

fall-out from the 95 Theses. Though he had earlier hit upon most of the ingredients of justification by faith in a mental and doctrinal way, it was in 1519, he claimed, that he took possession of the doctrine in a sudden and direct experiential manner, appropriating it to his own spiritually distressed and hyper-anxious condition. He recalled how he had for so long, as a monk, hated the scriptural term the 'righteousness' (Justitia) of a judgmental God which he was sure convicted him and damned him:

> Though I lived as a monk without reproach, I felt that I was a sinner before God with an extremely disturbed conscience ... I did not love, yes, I hated the righteous God who punishes sinners ... At last, by the mercy of God, meditating day and night I began to understand that the righteousness of God is that by which the righteous lives by a gift of God, namely by faith ... Here I felt that I was altogether born again and had entered, paradise itself through open gates.

Yet those revolutionary, Liberating realisations, the cornerstones of the Reformation, were not fully at Luther's disposal when he drew up the 95 Theses, or if they were they did not inspire his devastating critique of indulgences. In the Theses Luther did not reveal the redundant and 'delusive' nature of indulgences on the grounds that the just were saved by faith alone and therefore, being already pardoned by the Father in recognition of the Son's atoning sacrifice, did not need those 'pardons'. Instead he required sinners to win their forgiveness, not, it is true, by their good works or by any external mechanisms, but through what came from within themselves, sorrow for sins, contrition, repentance:

> Any Christian who is truly penitent, enjoys full remission from penalty and guilt, and this is given him without letters of indulgence. [Thesis 36]

> A truly contrite sinner seeks out, and loves to pay, the penalties of his sins; whereas the very multitude of indulgences dulls men's consciences. [Thesis 40]

Conclusion: Luther's Theology in 1517

When he wrote the 95 Theses, Luther was still so largely anchored in medieval understandings of how justification was achieved that he found a place for the salvationary role of 'good works' in his Theses. 'Works of mercy ... works of love' are set against mechanical, mercenary indulgences as routes to justification. However, the starkest contrast in the 95 Theses was not that between necessary good works and unnecessary indulgences but that between vain papal indulgences and indispensable penitence, that state of mind, heart and soul in which the sinner freely acknowledges what he or she is, and bewails the fact. Luther was in fact strongly influenced by medieval analyses of the sacrament of Penance conducted by commentators such as Gabriel Biel (1418-1495). According to this approach, the Almighty responded with His full forgiveness to whatever quotient of grief for sin, no matter how paltry, the penitent could summon up: quod in se est, literally 'whatever is in one'.

In October 1517 the protester against indulgences was far from being the Protestant leader of later years and the full theology of the Reformation was to emerge from, not to give rise to, the 95 Theses.

Issues to Debate

- In what ways have Luther's 95 Theses of 1517 been dramatised by contemporaries, biographers and historians?

- Which aspects of the sales of indulgences did Luther object to and why?

- Which central features of Lutheranism are not present in the Theses?

In April 1518 Luther attended the general chapter of his order of Augustinians in Heidelberg and there delivered further Theses that reveal the growing occupancy of his mind by justification through faith and the invincible importance of God's forgiving and healing initiative towards us, known as grace: 'The one who does much "work" is not the righteous one, but the one who, without "work", has much faith in Christ.' And even in those propositions that herald the fuller articulation of Reformation theology in the future, such as 'The Freedom of a Christian' of 1520, Luther was still attached to active human striving for reconciliation with the Almighty—'stirring up the eagerness to seek the grace of Christ'. The 95 Theses, then, were only the beginning of the process by which Luther the monk became Luther the reformer.

FURTHER READING

James Atkinson, *The Trial of Luther* (Batsford, 1971)

Peter Newman Brooks, Seven-Headed Luther. Essays in Commemoration of a Quincentenary 1483-1983 (Clarendon Press, 1983)

Harro Hopfl (ed), Luther and Calvin on secular Authority (CUP, 1991)

Hans-Peter Grosshans, Luther (Harper-Collins, 1997)

Heiko A. Oberman, Luther, Man between God and the Devil (Hodder, 2000)

Keith Randell, Luther and the German Reformation, 1517-55 (Hodder, 2nd edition, 2001)

Geoffrey Woodward, The Sixteenth-Century Reformation (Hodder, 2001)

MICHAEL MULLETT is Professor of Cultural and Religious History at the University of Lancaster. His study of Luther is published towards the end of 2003 in the Routledge Historical Biographies series.

Explaining John Calvin

John Calvin (1509–64) has been credited, or blamed, for much that defines the modern Western world: capitalism and the work ethic, individualism and utilitarianism, modern science, and, at least among some devout Christians, a lingering suspicion of earthly pleasures. During [a] recent American presidential campaign, the two candidates appealed to "values" that recall the teachings of the 16th-century churchman, indicating that what William Pitt once said of England—"We have a Calvinist creed"—still may hold partly true for the United States. But the legend of the joyless tyrant of Geneva obscures both the real man, a humanist as much as a religious reformer, and the subtlety of his thought. Here his biographer discusses both.

William J. Bouwsma

Our image of John Calvin is largely the creation of austere Protestant churchmen who lived during the 17th century, the century following that of the great reformer's life. The image is most accurately evoked by the huge icon of Calvin, familiar to many a tourist, that stands behind the University of Geneva. There looms Calvin, twice as large as life, stylized beyond recognition, stony, rigid, immobile, and—except for his slightly abstracted disapproval of whatever we might imagine him to be contemplating—impassive.

Happily, the historical record provides good evidence for a Calvin very different from the figure invoked by his 17th-century followers. This Calvin is very much a man of the 16th century, a time of religious strife and social upheaval. His life and work reflect the ambiguities, contradictions, and agonies of that troubled time. Sixteenth-century thinkers, especially in Northern Europe, were still grappling with the rich but incoherent legacy of the Renaissance, and their characteristic intellectual constructions were less successful in reconciling

its contradictory impulses than in balancing among them. This is why it has proved so difficult to pigeon-hole such figures as Erasmus and Machiavelli or Montaigne and Shakespeare, and why they continue to stimulate reflection. Calvin, who can be quoted on both sides of most questions, belongs in this great company.

Born in 1509 in Noyon, Calvin was brought up to be a devout French Catholic. Indeed, his father, a lay administrator in the service of the local bishop, sent him to the University of Paris in 1523 to study for the priesthood. Later he decided that young John should be a lawyer. Accordingly, from 1528 to 1533, Calvin studied law. During these years he was also exposed to the evangelical humanism of Erasmus and Jacques Lefèvre d'Étaples that nourished the radical student movement of the time. The students called for salvation by grace rather than by good works and ceremonies—a position fully compatible with Catholic orthodoxy—as the foundation for a general reform of church and society on the model of antiquity.

To accomplish this end, the radical students advocated a return to the Bible, studied in its original languages. Calvin himself studied Greek and Hebrew as well as Latin, the "three languages" of ancient Christian discourse. His growing interest in the classics led, moreover, to his first publication, a moralizing commentary on Seneca's essay on clemency.

Late in 1533, the French government of Francis I became less tolerant of the Paris student radicals, whom it saw as a threat to the peace. After helping to prepare a statement of the theological implications of the movement in a public address delivered by Nicolas Cop, rector of the University, Calvin found it prudent to leave Paris. Eventually he made his way to Basel, a Protestant town tolerant of religious variety.

Up to this point, there is little evidence of Calvin's "conversion" to Protestantism. Before Basel, of course, he had been fully aware of the challenge Martin Luther posed to the Catholic Church. The 95 Theses that the German reformer posted in Wittenberg in 1517 attacked what Luther believed were corruptions of true Christianity and, by implication, the authors of those errors, the Renaissance popes. Luther, above all, rejected the idea of salvation through indulgences or the sacrament of penance. Excommunicated by Pope Leo X, he encouraged the formation of non-Roman churches.

In Basel, Calvin found himself drawing closer to Luther. Probably in part to clarify his own beliefs, he began to write, first a preface to his cousin Pierre Olivétan's French translation of the Bible, and then what became the first edition of the *Institutes*, his masterwork, which in its successive revisions became the single most important statement of Protestant belief. Although he did not substantially change his views thereafter, he elaborated them in later editions, published in both Latin and French, in which he also replied to his critics; the final versions appeared in 1559 and 1560.

The 1536 *Institutes* had brought him some renown among Protestant leaders, among them Guillaume Farel. A French Reformer struggling to plant Protestantism in Geneva, Farel persuaded Calvin to settle there in late 1536. The Reformation was in trouble in Geneva. Indeed, the limited enthusiasm of Geneva for Protestantism—and for religious and moral reform—continued almost until Calvin's death. The resistance was all the more serious because the town council in Geneva, as in other Protestant towns in Switzerland and southern Germany, exercised ultimate control over the church and the ministers.

The main issue was the right of excommunication, which the ministers regarded as essential to their authority but which the town council refused to concede. The uncompromising attitudes of Calvin and Farel finally resulted in their expulsion from Geneva in May of 1538.

Calvin found refuge for the next three years in Protestant Strasbourg, where he was pastor of a church for French-speaking refugees. Here he married Idelette de Bure, a widow in his congregation. Theirs proved to be an extremely warm relationship, although none of their children survived infancy.

During his Strasbourg years, Calvin learned much about church administration from Martin Bucer, chief pastor there. Attending European religious conferences, he soon became a major figure in the international Protestant movement.

Meanwhile, without strong leadership, the Protestant revolution in Geneva foundered. In September of 1541, Calvin was invited back, and there he remained until his death in 1564. He was now in a stronger position. In November the town council enacted his *Ecclesiastical Ordinances*, which provided for the religious education of the townspeople, especially children, and instituted his conception of church order. It established four groups of church officers and a "consistory" of pastors and elders to bring every aspect of Genevan life under the precepts of God's law.

The activities of the consistory gave substance to the legend of Geneva as a joyless theocracy, intolerant of looseness or pleasure. Under Calvin's leadership, it undertook a range of disciplinary actions covering everything from the abolition of Catholic "superstition" to the enforcement of sexual morality, the regulation of taverns, and measures against dancing, gambling, and swearing. These "Calvinist" measures were resented by many townsfolk, as was the arrival of increasing numbers of French Protestant refugees.

The resulting tensions, as well as the persecution of Calvin's followers in France, help to explain the trial and burning of one of Calvin's leading opponents, Michael Servetus. Calvin felt the need to show that his zeal for orthodoxy was no less than that of his foes. The confrontation between Calvin and his enemies in Geneva was finally resolved in May of 1555, when Calvin's opponents overreached themselves and the tide turned in his favor. His position in Geneva was henceforth reasonably secure.

But Calvin was no less occupied. He had to watch the European scene and keep his Protestant allies united. At the same time, Calvin never stopped promoting his kind of Protestantism. He welcomed the religious refugees who poured into Geneva, especially during the 1550s, from France, but also from

England and Scotland, from Italy, Germany, and the Netherlands, and even from Eastern Europe. He trained many of them as ministers, sent them back to their homelands, and then supported them with letters of encouragement and advice. Geneva thus became the center of an international movement and a model for churches elsewhere. John Knox, the Calvinist leader of Scotland, described Geneva as "the most perfect school of Christ that ever was on the Earth since the days of the Apostles." So while Lutheranism was confined to parts of Germany and Scandinavia, Calvinism spread into Britain, the English-speaking colonies of North America, and many parts of Europe.

Academic efforts to explain the appeal of Calvinism in terms of social class have had only limited success. In France, his theology was attractive mainly to a minority among the nobility and the urban upper classes, but in Germany it found adherents among both townsmen and princes. In England and the Netherlands, it made converts in every social group. Calvinism's appeal lay in its ability to explain disorders of the age afflicting all classes and in the remedies and comfort it provided, as much by its activism as by its doctrine. Both depended on the personality, preoccupations, and talents of Calvin himself.

Unlike Martin Luther, Calvin was a reticent man. He rarely expressed himself in the first person singular. This reticence has contributed to his reputation as cold and unapproachable. Those who knew him, however, noted his talent for friendship as well as his hot temper. The intensity of his grief on the death of his wife in 1549 revealed a large capacity for feeling, as did his empathetic reading of many passages in Scripture.

In fact, the impersonality of Calvin's teachings concealed an anxiety, unusually intense even in an anxious age. He saw anxiety everywhere, in himself, in the narratives of the Bible, and in his contemporaries. This feeling found expression in two of his favorite images for spiritual discomfort: the abyss and the labyrinth. The abyss represented all the nameless terrors of disorientation and the absence of familiar boundaries. The labyrinth expressed the anxiety of entrapment: in religious terms, the inability of human beings alienated from God to escape from the imprisonment of self-concern.

One side of Calvin sought to relieve his terror of the abyss with cultural constructions and patterns of control that might help him recover his sense of direction. This side of Calvin was attracted to classical philosophy, which nevertheless conjured up for him fears of entrapment in a labyrinth. Escape from this, however, exposed him to terrible uncertainties and, once again, to the horrors of the abyss. Calvin's ideas thus tended to oscillate between those of freedom and order. His problem was to strike a balance between the two.

He did so primarily with the resources of Renaissance humanism, applying its philological approach to recover a biblical understanding of Christianity. But humanism was not only, or even fundamentally, a scholarly movement. Its scholarship was instrumental to the recovery of the communicative skills of classical rhetoric. Humanists such as Lorenzo Valla and Erasmus held that an effective rhetoric would appeal to a deeper level of the personality than would a mere rational demonstration. By moving the heart, Christian rhetoric would stimulate human beings to the active reform of both themselves and the world.

Theological system-building, Calvin believed, was futile and inappropriate. He faulted the medieval Scholastic theologians for relying more on human reason than on the Bible, which spoke uniquely to the heart. The teachings of Thomas Aquinas, and like-minded theologians, appealed only to the intellect, and so were lifeless and irrelevant to a world in desperate need.

As a humanist, Calvin was a *biblical* theologian, prepared to follow Scripture even when it surpassed the limits of human understanding. And its message, for him, could not be presented as a set of timeless abstractions; it had to be adapted to the understanding of contemporaries according to the rhetorical principle of decorum—i.e. suitability to time, place, and audience.

Calvin shared with earlier humanists an essentially biblical conception of the human personality, not as a hierarchy of faculties ruled by reason but as a mysterious unity. This concept made the feelings and will even more important aspects of the personality than the intellect, and it also gave the body new dignity.

Indeed, Calvin largely rejected the traditional belief in hierarchy as the general principle of all order. For it he substituted the practical (rather than the metaphysical) principle of *utility*. This position found expression in his preference, among the possible forms of government, for republics. It also undermined, for him, the traditional subordination of women to men. Calvin's Geneva accordingly insisted on a single standard of sexual morality—a radical departure from custom.

Calvin's utilitarianism was also reflected in deep reservations about the capacity of human beings to attain anything but practical knowledge. The notion that they can know anything absolutely, as God knows it, so to speak, seemed to him deeply presumptuous. This helps to explain his reliance on the Bible: Human beings have access to the saving truths of religion only insofar as God has revealed them in Scripture. But revealed truth, for Calvin, was not revealed to satisfy human curiosity; it too was limited to meeting the most urgent and practical needs, above all for individual salvation. This practicality also reflects a basic conviction of Renaissance thinkers: the superiority of an active life to one of contemplation. Calvin's conviction that every occupation in society is a "calling" on the part of God himself sanctified this conception.

But Calvin was not only a Renaissance humanist. The culture of 16th-century Europe was peculiarly eclectic. Like other thinkers of his time, Calvin had inherited a set of quite contrary tendencies that he uneasily combined with his humanism. Thus, even as he emphasized the heart, Calvin continued to conceive of the human personality as a hierarchy of faculties ruled by reason; from time to time he tried uneasily, with little success,

to reconcile the two conceptions. This is why he sometimes emphasized the importance of rational control over the passions—an emphasis that has been reassuring to conservatives.

Calvin's theology has often been seen as little more than a systematization of the more creative insights of Luther. He followed Luther, indeed, on many points: on original sin, on Scripture, on the absolute dependence of human beings on divine grace, and on justification by faith alone. Other differences between Calvin and Luther are largely matters of emphasis. His understanding of predestination, contrary to a general impression, was virtually identical to Luther's; it was not of central importance to his theology. He believed that it meant that the salvation of believers by a loving God was absolutely certain.

In major respects, however, Calvin departed from Luther. In some ways he was more radical, but most of his differences suggest that he was closer to Catholicism than Luther, as in his insistence on the importance of the historical church. He was also more traditional in his belief in the authority of clergy over laity, perhaps as a result of his difficulties with the Geneva town council. Even more significant, especially for Calvinism as a historical force, was Calvin's attitude toward the everyday world. Luther had regarded this world and its institutions as incorrigible, and was prepared to leave them to the devil. But for Calvin this world, created by God, still belonged to Him; it remained potentially His kingdom; and every Christian was obliged to devote his life to make it so in reality by reforming and bringing it under God's law.

Calvin's thought was less a theology to be comprehended by the mind than a set of principles for the Christian life: in short, spirituality. He was more concerned with the experience and application of Christianity than with mere reflection about it. His true successors were Calvinist pastors rather than Calvinist theologians. Significantly, in addition to devoting much of his energy to the training of other pastors, Calvin was himself a pastor. He preached regularly: some 4,000 sermons in the 13 years after his return to Geneva.

Calvin's spirituality begins with the conviction that we do not so much "know" God as "experience" him indirectly, through his mighty acts and works in the world, as we experience but can hardly be said to know thunder, one of Calvin's favorite metaphors for religious experience. Calvin also believed that human beings can understand something of what God is like in the love of a father for his children, but also—surprisingly in one often identified with patriarchy—in the love of a mother. He denounced those who represented God as dreadful; God for him is "mild, kind, gentle, and compassionate."

Nevertheless, in spite of this attention to God's love for mankind, Calvin gave particular emphasis to God's power because it was this that finally made his love effective in the work of redemption from sin. God, for Calvin, represented supremely all the ways in which human beings experience power: as energy, as warmth, as vitality, and, so, as life itself.

Sin, by contrast, is manifested precisely in the negation of every kind of power and ultimately of the life force given by God. Sin *deadens* and, above all, deadens the feelings. Saving grace, then, must be conceived as the transfusion of God's power—his warmth, passion, strength, vitality—to human beings. It was also essential to Calvin's spirituality, and a reflection of his realism, that this "transfusion" be not instantaneous but gradual.

Calvin's traditional metaphor for the good Christian life implied activity: "Our life is like a journey," he asserted, but "it is not God's will that we should march along casually as we please, but he sets the goal before us, and also directs us on the right way to it." This way is also a struggle.

Complex as his ideas were, it is easy to see how the later history of Calvinism has often been obscured by scholars' failure to distinguish among (1) Calvinism as the beliefs of Calvin himself, (2) the beliefs of his followers, who, though striving to be faithful to Calvin, modified his teachings to meet their own needs, and (3) more loosely, the beliefs of the Reformed tradition of Protestant Christianity, in which Calvinism proper was only one, albeit the most prominent, strand.

The Reformed churches in the 16th century were referred to in the plural to indicate, along with what they had in common, their individual autonomy and variety. They consisted originally of a group of non-Lutheran Protestant churches based in towns in Switzerland and southern Germany. These churches were jealous of their autonomy; and Geneva was not alone among them in having distinguished theological leadership. Ulrich Zwingli and Heinrich Bullinger in Zurich and Martin Bucer in Strasbourg also had a European influence that combined with that of Calvin, especially in England, to shape what came to be called "Calvinism."

Long after Calvin's death in 1564, the churchmen in Geneva continued to venerate him and aimed at being faithful to his teaching under his successors, first among them Theodore de Bèze. But during what can be appropriately described as a Protestant "Counter Reformation," the later Calvinism of Geneva, abandoning Calvin's more humanistic tendencies and drawing more on other, sterner aspects of his thought, was increasingly intellectualized. Indeed, it grew to resemble the medieval Scholasticism that Calvin had abhorred.

Predestination now began to assume an importance that had not been attributed to it before. Whereas Calvin had been led by personal faith to an awed belief in predestination as a benign manifestation of divine providence, predestination now became a threatening doctrine: God's decree determined in advance an individual's salvation or damnation. What good, one might wonder, were one's own best efforts if God had already ruled? In 1619 these tendencies reached a climax at the Synod of Dort in the Netherlands, which spelled out various corollaries of predestination, as Calvin had never done, and made the doctrine central to Calvinism.

Calvinist theologians, meanwhile, apparently finding Calvin's loose rhetorical style of expression unsatisfactory, began deliberately to write like Scholas-tic theologians, in Latin, and even appealed to medieval Scholastic authorities. The major Calvinist theological statement of the 17th century was the *Institutio Theologiae Elencticae* (3 vols., Geneva, 1688) of François Turretin, chief pastor of Geneva. Although the title of this work recalled Calvin's masterpiece, it was published in Latin, its dialectical structure followed the model of the great *Summas* of Thomas Aquinas, and it suggested at least as much confidence as Thomas in the value of human reason. The lasting effect of this shift is suggested by the fact that "Turretin," in Latin, was the basic theology textbook at the Princeton Seminary in New Jersey, the most distinguished intellectual center of American Calvinism until the middle of the 19th century.

Historians have continued to debate whether these developments were essentially faithful to Calvin or deviations from him. In some sense they were both. Later Calvinist theologians, as they abandoned Calvin's more humanistic tendencies and emphasized his more austere and dogmatic side, found precedents for these changes in the contrary aspects of his thought. They were untrue to Calvin, of course, in rejecting his typically Renaissance concern with balancing contrary impulses. One must remember, however, that these changes in Calvinism occurred during a period of singular disorder in Europe, caused by, among other things, a century of religious warfare. As a result, there was a widespread longing for certainty, security, and peace.

One or another aspect of Calvin's influence has persisted not only in the Reformed churches of France, Germany, Scotland, the Netherlands, and Hungary but also in the Church of England, where he was long as highly regarded as he was by Puritans who had separated from the Anglican establishment. The latter organized their own churches, Presbyterian or Congregational, and brought Calvinism to North America 300 years ago.

Even today these churches, along with the originally German Evangelical and Reformed Church, remember Calvin—that is, the strict Calvin of Geneva—as their founding father. Eventually Calvinist theology was also widely accepted by major groups of American Baptists; and even Unitarianism, which broke away from the Calvinist churches of New England during the 18th century, reflected the more rational impulses in Calvin's theology. More recently, Protestant interest in the social implications of the Gospel and Protestant Neo-Orthodoxy, as represented by Karl Barth and Reinhold Niebuhr, reflect the continuing influence of John Calvin.

Calvin's larger influence over the development of modern Western civilization has been variously assessed. The controversial "Weber thesis" attributed the rise of modern capitalism largely to habits encouraged by Puritanism, but Max Weber (1864–1920) avoided implicating Calvin himself. Much the same can be said about efforts to link Calvinism to the rise of early modern science;

Puritans were prominent in the scientific movement of 17th-century England, but Calvin himself was indifferent to the science of his own day.

A somewhat better case can be made for Calvin's influence on political theory. His own political instincts were highly conservative, and he preached the submission of private persons to all legitimate authority. But, like Italian humanists of the 15th and 16th centuries, he personally preferred a republic to a monarchy; and in confronting the problem posed by rulers who actively opposed the spread of the Gospel, he advanced a theory of resistance, kept alive by his followers, according to which lesser magistrates might legitimately rebel against kings. And, unlike most of his contemporaries, Calvin included among the proper responsibilities of states not

only the maintenance of public order but also a positive concern for the general welfare of society. Calvinism has a place, therefore, in the evolution of liberal political thought. His most durable influence, nevertheless, has been religious. From Calvin's time to the present, Calvinism has meant a peculiar seriousness about Christianity and its ethical implications.

William J. Bouwsma, 65, is Sather Professor of History at the University of California, Berkeley. Born in Ann Arbor, Michigan, he received an A.B. (1943), an M.A. (1947), and a Ph.D. (1950) from Harvard. He is the author of, among other books, Venice and the Defense of Republican Liberty *(1968) and* John Calvin: A Sixteenth-Century Portrait *(1988).*

From *The Wilson Quarterly*, New Year's 1989 edition, pp. 68–75. © 1989 by William J. Bouwsma. Reprinted by permission of the author.

The development of Protestantism in 16th century France

Graham Noble investigates the causes of the rise and fall of French Protestantism

by Graham Noble

Within 20 years of Martin Luther pinning his Ninety-Five Theses to the door of the Castle Church in Wittenberg, a Protestant Reformation had begun to take shape in northern Europe. His ideas were never to find a natural home in France, but a different form of the religion, stemming from Calvin's Geneva, won supporters and gained coherence from the middle of the century. Churches burgeoned and congregations swelled as the Calvinist movement grew in spectacular style, attracting followers from every social class. By the 1560s, perhaps 1,250 churches were serving an adult population of 2 million so-called 'Huguenots', about 10 percent of the total population of the State, including amongst them a third of the French aristocracy. Consequently, on the eve of the Wars of Religion, the triumph of French Protestantism seemed not just possible but, to many, inexorable. According to one's faith, either a divine revelation of religious truth was at hand or the punishment of God was being loosed upon a sinful world.

Yet the Protestant miracle never took place. Around 30,000 Calvinists were slaughtered in the massacres of 1572 and, as fighting fragmented and foreign powers became increasingly involved, the cause was lost to political and military necessity. The Civil Wars, which might have led to the triumph of Protestantism, ended by sanctioning it under royal licence, constricting its development and tying its future to the goodwill of Catholic Kings of France as yet unborn. So, how are we to explain the progress that French Protestantism made in this period?

Protestantism and Church Reform

Two connected, but distinct, Protestant movements were to develop in the second half of the sixteenth century: the first, popular, largely urban, sometimes seditious, and linked more or less closely with Geneva; the second, aristocratic, often committed to its Faith but also intensely independent and political in motivation. They shared, though, a common ancestry, in the Christian Humanist and later Lutheran critics of the contemporary Church, men whose precarious existence relied upon sympathetic patronage and an ambiguity in royal policy, which could be exploited to their advantage.

Though the traditional Protestant interpretation of a decadent Gallican Church mired in abuse, attracting widespread anti-clericalism from its flock, is undoubtedly a caricature, there may well have been cause for the reformers' complaints. But evidence from the beginning of the century is difficult and contradictory: reports of incompetent or acquisitive clergymen, particularly in rural areas, and of monks whose lives were anything but monkish; of internal squabbles setting back the process of reform; of exploitative manipulation of relics and indulgences must be set beside clear indications that the Church conveyed a powerful liturgical message to a large body of pious believers and was well aware of its own shortcomings.

Nevertheless, the Catholic Church manifestly failed to reform itself from within in these crucial years and was left ill-equipped to meet the challenges of radical Protestantism. Those who sought to move forward, whether working independently or as agents of the Crown, found themselves blocked, vilified and, in some cases, persecuted. 'Georges d'Amboise, Cardinal Archbishop of Rouen and chief minister of Louis XII, set out to impose a new discipline on religious houses but met opposition at every turn. The Parlement de Paris treated him with great suspicion because of his papal and royal connections and clergymen obstructed his agents and repeatedly appealed against his judgements. He was forced to back away from reform for fear of stirring up an unacceptable level of discontent within the Church.

A decade later, Bishop Guillaume Briconnet set out to reform his own diocese of Meaux and in doing so offended local Franciscan friars. His invitation in 1521 to the noted evangelical humanist, Jacques Lefevre d'Etaples, to join him in the quest, alongside a group of like-minded scholars who became known as the Cercle de Meaux, brought matters to the attention of the Sorbonne and the Parlement. Lefevre's views veered dangerously near Lutheran heresy and, in the paranoid atmosphere of the mid-1520s, were quite intolerable. Briconnet and his associates were harassed by Gallican authorities, put on trial, and forced either to recant their errors, as he did himself, or to flee into exile.

Royal Treatment of Heresy

Francis I always opposed explicit heresy. Like all sixteenth-century rulers, he regarded religious toleration as irreconcilable with the maintenance of royal authority, though he wanted to decide for himself the degree of unorthodoxy permissible. He and his family were interested in promoting the scholarly enquiry associated with humanism and welcomed academics into the royal household, but in the law courts humanism proved hard to distinguish from the crime of heresy, particularly when alleged offenders, like Lefevre, were articulate men who had no intention of condemning themselves out of their own mouths. Choosing to assert his prerogative, Francis protected Lefevre, and others, by removing their cases from the jurisdiction of sovereign courts in order to try them before the Grand Conseil, the Royal Council sitting in its judicial capacity, whose members were selected by the King himself. A generous verdict could be guaranteed.

The intensification of official persecution, between the Affair of the Placards and the death of Henry II, failed to clear up the problem. For, during this period, Protestantism not only grew rapidly in popularity but transformed itself from an essentially inward-looking intellectual movement into a radical, political force.

The Affair was significant because it enabled, not for the last time, zealous Catholic opinion in Paris to force the hand of a King of France. Frenchmen in towns across the country had been confronted, on their way to Sunday Mass

on 18th October 1534, with a series of printed notices crudely denouncing the sacrament of the Eucharist:

> I call on heaven and earth to bear witness to the truth against this pompous and proud papal Mass by which the world (unless God soon provides a remedy) is being and will be completely destroyed, and in which our Lord is so outrageously blasphemed and the people seduced and blinded.

Responsibility for the placards rested with Antoine Marcourt, a French Protestant exiled to Neuchatel, and a group of fellow conspirators, but their actions were a gift to those of a different persuasion—the Sorbonne and the Parlement de Paris. Marcourt's Zwinglian message was so brazen and offensive to Catholic believers that it forced Francis to react unequivocally and to identify himself fully with the tide of popular, anti-Protestant hysteria which swept across France in the days that followed. With royal backing, the Parlement began its own witch-hunt, arresting suspects and organising public rites of purification. By the end of November, six alleged heretics had been burned in the city.

Calvin was still optimistic enough in 1536 to dedicate the preface of his Institutes of the Christian Religion to Francis in the hope of tempering future policy but its direction had already been decided. The chosen methods of the Crown were legislation, censorship and state-sponsored violence. Oppressive decrees were issued through the willing agencies of the provincial parlements, whose deputies were themselves given jurisdiction over many such cases. The Chambre Ardente, or Burning Chamber, was created within the Parlement de Paris to cope with increased demand. Among the crimes identified in the Edict of Chateaubriant of 1551 were peddling books, writing or sending money to French exiles, delivering letters from Geneva, failing to inform on known heretics and failing to attend church regularly. All judges, all town officials and all teachers had to be able to prove their Catholicism. The book trade was controlled and an Index of prohibited texts produced. By the Edict of Compiegne, of July 1557, the death penalty was made mandatory for all convicted heretics.

Finally, in the most appalling example of planned, sectarian violence, the Crown authorised the Parlement of Aix to arrange the slaughter of between four and eight thousand Waldensians. These people, members of simple, long-standing, peasant communities from the villages of the Durance Valley in Provence, posed no discernible threat to any other group in France but their unorthodox ideas on issues like oath swearing, purgatory and the veneration of saints were seen as an intolerable departure from sixteenth-century convention.

The Failure of Persecution

So why did the combined efforts of Crown and Church fail so completely to arrest the advance of French Protestantism? Firstly, because official persecution, callous though it might have been, was hopelessly inefficient. Royal decrees proved hard to enforce and the courts often failed to secure convictions. Of the 557 accused, examined by the Chambre Ardente between 1547 and 1549, 7 percent were burned at the stake. Only rarely was evidence presented of heretics caught in the act, and so cases often depended upon the dubious testimony of apostate Huguenots. Besides, royal authority did not reach into every corner of the kingdom. Unofficial areas of immunity from the law grew up on the estates of sympathetic noblemen. Censorship of Genevan texts was found to be virtually impossible to impose, in the face of the expansion of printing and book-selling. Though the Index of Prohibited Books was lengthened in 1545 and again in 1551, at least 12 French-language works by Calvin alone, which appeared in the intervening period, had not been recognised on the 1551 list.

Official persecution simply swelled the numbers of religious dissenters, who followed the path that Calvin had taken in 1535, and fled abroad to join the refugee communities in cities like Geneva, Strasbourg and Basel. French-speaking, Geneva became a particular focus of emigration: between three and four thousand Frenchmen arrived in the decade before the outbreak of the Civil Wars. Here they lived as a community apart, studying, fostering their religious radicalism and awaiting the opportunity to return home. Their direct impact as missionary pastors on the clandestine Huguenot communities of the 1550s is hard to assess but the appetite with which they were greeted by the faithful is unmistakable and suggestive of their value.

Persecution also failed because of the resilience of Calvinism and its appeal, which cut across barriers of class and wealth. Towns became the first focus of the Reformation in France and naturally attracted the majority of Genevan missionaries. The new Faith won supporters amongst the bourgeois elites, merchants and lawyers, often people with important functions inside municipal government, and, in far greater numbers, amongst the local artisans. In Paris, dyers and combers; in Meaux, Rouen and Amiens, textile workers; in Lyon, silk-workers and printers were all disproportionately attracted to Calvinism. Literacy may have been a factor for some. And though most artisans could not read, they could gather together to be read to, and the 'cheap print' propaganda of the day conveyed a message that was clear to all. Calvinism appeared to challenge the static nature of early modern society, dominated by royal and ecclesiastical authority, and to offer the Third Estate the possibility that the existing social order could be overturned.

The urban congregations that emerged across France were volatile, and often unwilling to listen to Calvin's direct admonitions to peace, but they remained certain of their beliefs and resistant to royal persecution. The virtue of martyrdom, propagandised by writers like Jean Crespin, meant that few Calvinists at this time abandoned their Faith under pressure. After all, the doctrine of the Elect assured them of their salvation. And the churches started to organise themselves. By 1557, the first Huguenot constitution had been drawn up in Poitiers and, two years later, the first National Synod met in Paris, in flagrant defiance of the King's will, to establish a disciplinary code and Confession of Faith in 35 articles. Though this grandly named affair in fact entailed the meeting of representatives of no more than 11 separate churches, it did presage the early development of an enduring ecclesiastical structure.

But it was noble conversions from the mid-1550s that were key to the development of the French Reformation and fundamentally changed its nature. Perhaps a third of the whole French nobility ultimately became Huguenot. They politicised the movement, armed and financed it and, unwilling to take direction from Geneva, drove it towards civil war. Why, then, was this rebellious, bourgeois creed attractive to so many French aristocrats? Materialist considerations must have played a part for some: Calvinism seemed to justify the expropriation of Church property. For most though, including Admiral Gaspard de Coligny and Louis de Conde, the Faith itself appears to have answered a spiritual need.

One conversion could bring many more, for the relationship between many nobles in the sixteenth century was governed by networks of patronage and obligation. The client families, recipients of pensions, favours and jobs, pledged their service to the patron and tended to follow his lead in political and religious matters. Frequently, they became conduits of Protestantism.

Noblewomen, like Jeanne d'Albret, Queen of Navarre, and Louise de Montmorency, sister of the Constable of France, played important proselytising roles. In the case of the latter, crucially influencing her three Huguenot sons: Coligny; Francois Dandelot, colonel general of the royal infantry; and Odet de Chatillon, cardinal-archbishop of Beauvais. They were perhaps in part responding to the opportunities for education and influence offered by Calvinism but denied to most women of this era by the Old Faith.

In the countryside, peasants were less inclined to turn to Protestantism but certainly not immune to its attractions, particularly if they lived on the estates of Huguenot or tolerant nobles. Others may have been motivated by the opportunity to snub their priest or even an unreformed seigneur, or by a desire to avoid traditional Catholic tithes—though it is true that the Calvinist Church imposed its own charges. But illiteracy, in combination with a low population density, and a shortage of trained pastors able to communicate effectively with the people—not one of those emerging from Geneva was from a peasant background—imposed obstacles to its wider assimilation.

The French Wars of Religion

The sudden collapse of royal government on the death of Henry II entailed the disintegration of the system of religious persecution that he and his predecessor had put in place. It did not, however, offer Huguenots the opportunity for which they had been waiting, for, at critical moments through the Wars of Religion, sectarian and political brutality left a weakened French monarchy at the mercy of Catholic militants.

Religious violence reached new levels of intensity in the first decade of the civil wars. Iconoclasm by Huguenots, and the foul desecration of Catholic churches and shrines, was countered by savage acts of retribution. Disembowelling victims was commonplace: heresy was imagined to reside in the intestines, which would be burned in an act of supposed purification. Against such a background, Catherine de Medici's 'politique' position, a determined attempt to maintain peace and stability in France, was repeatedly undermined. Her seeming willingness to compromise at Poissy in 1561, and via the January Edict of 1562, unleashed a torrent of retributive hostility which she was in no position to control.

The notorious Saint Bartholomew's Day massacres of August 1572 were initiated by the Duke of Guise but largely carried out by mobs of uncontrollable Catholic zealots across the towns and cities of France. Charles IX and his mother were given little option but to abandon conciliation and claim to have ordered the slaughters themselves. Survivors fled but regrouped, seeking revenge and eager now to embrace the antimonarchical theories of Francois Hotman, Theodore Beza and Philippe Du Pleissis Mornay, whose Vindiciae Contra Tyrannos (1579) asserted that 'The people ... is absolved from any charge of perjury if it publicly renounces a ruler who would rule unjustly or if it attempts, by force of arms, to evict a ruler who seeks to retain possession of the kingdom in contravention of the law.'

The authority of the Monarchy was also challenged by Catholics. In 1584, Henry III was forced by the Catholic League to disown his legitimate, Huguenot heir, Henry of Bourbon and, four years later, on the 'Day of Barricades', radical Catholic Parisians forced the King to scuttle away, humiliated, from the city. After Henry's assassination in 1589, supporters of the League were still backing the illegitimate Catholic candidate, Charles de Bourbon, ahead of his nephew, and only when Philip II of Spain muddied the waters still further, after Charles's death, by forwarding the claims of his own daughter, Isabella, did Leaguers begin the negotiations with Henry IV. The price of peace was his formal conversion to the Catholic Faith in July 1593.

At every stage the Crown had been a victim of events: the fate of French Protestantism was determined by political intimidation and popular bloodshed.

The Edict of Nantes

The edict of toleration, which was agreed at the end of the wars, represented not an established acceptance of Calvinism, let alone the creation of a permanent 'state within the state', but a short-term settlement, designed as a step towards an older monarchical ideal, religious uniformity throughout the realm.

The Edict comprised 92 general articles, 56 secret articles and two brevets. These last named were royal directives, issued under the Privy Seal and not requiring authorisation by the parlements. As such, they would expire, unless renewed by the king, after eight years. The main articles confirmed Catholicism as the national religion of France, to be practised without constraint in every part of the country. Freedom of Huguenot worship was essentially restricted to the lands of Huguenot nobles which, in practice, excluded large parts of France, including the City of Paris. Political liberties were also limited: Huguenot assemblies were allowed to meet but could not discuss affairs of state, raise taxes, levy troops or build fortifications. Military protection, a lifeline to the preservation of these rights, was offered and paid for by the Crown but only enforced by royal brevet. Henry IV had no immediate intention of revoking the promises he had made to his former friends, indeed he renewed the brevets in 1606, but he

TIMELINE	
1501	Cardinal Georges d'Amboise began his reform programme
1515	Guillaume Briconnet appointed Bishop of Meaux
1534	Affair of the Placards
1536	Calvin published his Institutes of the Christian Religion
1543	first Index of Prohibited Books published
1545	Massacre of Waldensians
1547	Chambre Ardente created
1551	Edict of Chateaubriant
1557	Edict of Compiegne
1559	first National Synod of Calvinist Church
1559	death of Henry II
1561	Colloquy of Poissy
1562	Edict of St. Germain (January Edict)
	Vassy Massacre
1563	Peace and Edict of Amboise
1567	Enterprise of Meaux
1570	Edict of St. Germain
1572	St. Bartholomew's Day Massacres
1576	Edict of Beaulieu (Peace of Monsieur)
	Catholic League founded
1579	Vindiciae Contra Tyrannos published
1584	death of Alencon-Anjou left Henry of Bourbon as heir to the throne
1585	War of the Three Henries
1588	Day of Barricades
1593	conversion of Henry IV to Catholicism
1598	Edict of Nantes
1610	death of Henry IV

must have been well aware that Nantes could not provide a lasting basis for religious co-existence. Louis XIII withdrew them in 1629, and the Edict itself was revoked in 1685. Its fate had been a foregone conclusion: implied in the manner of its formulation was the destruction of the liberties which it seemed to enshrine

Conclusion

French Protestantism never regained the energy and spirit of optimism that it had possessed in 1562 but its decline owed comparatively little to the challenge of the Monarchy. This is not perhaps surprising in the years of civil war but it was equally true of the reigns of Louis XII, Francis I and Henry II, all rightly considered powerful Renaissance Kings. They failed, however, to promote reform of their own Gallican Church; failed to protect its humanist scholars or to distinguish them from Lutherans; and failed to halt a wave of sacramentarian heresy, despite constructing an elaborate state apparatus specifically for this purpose.

A dramatic reduction in royal authority during the decades of civil war harmed the Protestant cause much more than half a century of royal strength, because it laid bare the movement to the one force that could really damage it—popular religious violence. Zealots of both faiths were left to determine the course of the Reformation. The Huguenots' unique claim to righteousness, and their provocative behaviour at all levels of society, aroused a powerful Catholic fanaticism, which successive Kings, up to and including Henry IV, had no choice but to embrace.

GRAHAM NOBLE has taught Early Modern history at Bedales School for twelve years. From September 2002, he is head of department at Kent College, Canterbury.

This article first appeared in *History Today*, September 2002, pp. 30–36. Copyright © 2002 by History Today, Ltd. Reprinted by permission.

SIEGE OF THE MOLES

The high tide of Ottoman expansion to the west saw the Turks
burrowing underground in an attempt to take Vienna.

By John Godwin

THEY HAD SWEPT DOWN FROM THE steppes of Turkestan in Central Asia, calling themselves the Ottoman Turks. And during that chilly, rainy summer of 1529, they represented the gravest peril Europe had faced in a thousand years, worse even than Attila's Huns in the fifth century. Attila's hordes had been barbarian primitives—these new invaders were more advanced and sophisticated than the Western nations in many dangerous ways, particularly in the military sphere.

Named after their first sultan, Osman, the Ottoman Turks settled in what is now Anatolia, in Asia Minor. At a glance they seemed no different from other tribes of wild horsemen in that region. But the Turks possessed two outstanding attributes that made them natural conquerors: They were excellent administrators, and they were very fast learners. The first enabled them to absorb neighboring peoples. The second gave them a rapid grasp of whatever sciences into which they came in contact—engineering, architecture, medicine, astronomy and the use of gunpowder.

In the 14th century, the Turks crossed the Dardanelles Strait into Europe and proceeded to overrun the entire Balkan Peninsula. Greeks, Serbs, Bulgarians, Romanians and Albanians all came under their domination. And in the process they created what was probably the most remarkable armed force in history.

The Turks were fervent Muslims. But they allowed Christians and Jews in their realm complete freedom of worship, providing they paid a special head tax imposed on all "infidels." The bitterly poor mountain folk of the Balkans had no money for taxes, so they were charged a "blood tribute" instead. This consisted of the biggest and strongest adolescent boys from each village, who were taken to the capital to become personal slaves of the sultan. What they actually became were janissaries ("new troops").

The boys, who had grown up in miserable shacks and reared on dry bread and onions, were housed in palaces with carpeted floors and marble bathing pools, with the choicest delicacies as daily rations. Their filthy, verminous rags were exchanged for silken robes. As the Venetian traveler Marcus Stinetti wrote: "Those youths whom I chanced to address believed they had entered paradise by accepting slavery."

But there was a reverse side to all this luxury. The young men were placed under the harshest possible military discipline and put through staged exercises nearly as fierce as actual battles. Every drill left dead bodies on the parade ground; the slightest show of hesitation was savagely punished. Within months the janissary recruits were turned into robots who would march in ranks over a cliff if ordered.

Though the boys were not compelled to change their religion, they soon learned that conversion to Islam might earn them unlimited promotions—all the way up to commanding general or grand vizier (prime minister). Slavery was no obstacle. They filled most government positions and often grew into fabu-lously rich slave owners themselves. Most of them converted readily and became more fanatical Muslims than the Turks.

The janissaries were so proud of their superior rations that they used cooking utensils as badges of rank and cauldrons instead of regimental standards. They also adopted a peculiar type of martial music: rolling drums accompanied by shrill, wailing flutes. This was the origin of the fife and drum bands, which Western armies later copied. By the 15th century, those sounds evoked sheer terror, even from a long distance, because the janissaries committed unspeakable atrocities among civilian populations. They were kept away from women in peacetime and forced to live like military monks, but campaigns meant freedom to do anything, especially to unbelievers. The results were mass rapes of young girls and boys, torture, massacres and the systematic devastation of entire countrysides. The sight of the blue tunics and tall, white woolen hats of the janissaries resulted in panicked flight wherever they appeared.

With these new soldiers, Turkey possessed the only regular standing army of the period, and an elite force at that. European countries still depended on mercenaries who had to be raised for every campaign, or feudal levies that were notoriously unreliable. The janissaries were all infantry, but to support them, the Turks built up an artillery arm such as the world had never before seen.

In 1453, the Turks moved on Constantinople, capital of the Byzantine Empire and the seat of the Eastern

Orthodox Church—the "Second Rome." Its citizens fought desperately while the Turkish guns pounded their walls to rubble, sending out frantic pleas for help to all Christian nations. None came—they were too busy warring among themselves to respond. Constantinople fell, and the sultan rode his blood-spattered horse into the venerable cathedral of St. Sophia, to proclaim the city his new capital—today's Istanbul.

From then on, the Ottoman Empire spread with the speed of a forest fire. It reached from Egypt and the Sudan in the south to the Crimea and Ukraine in the north; from Syria, Mesopotamia and Palestine in the east to Bosnia in the west. Its subject peoples included Russians, Tartars, Arabs, Persians, Armenians and Jews, black Nubians and blond Dalmatians. The Turks themselves were a minority. With every new province the stream of tribute money and the number of available soldiers swelled; all were at the command of the sultan in Constantinople. The empire resembled an avalanche that grew in weight and velocity the farther it rolled.

The 10th sultan, Suleiman II, ascended to the Ottoman throne in 1520. The Turks called him "the Lawgiver," but to foreigners he was Suleiman the Magnificent. His court, the Seraglio, comprised an entire town within the capital, housing approximately 9,000 people and boasting water fountains that danced to music and ponds of goldfish with tiny jewels attached to their fins. His harem contained 300 slave concubines representing every race and nationality in his realm.

Suleiman was the son of a Tartar harem slave. He spoke eight languages fluently, wrote exquisite Persian poetry and composed lute music as a hobby—none of which prevented him from being one of the most ruthless warlords of his age. He enjoyed battle as much as philosophical debate and led his armies personally on horseback. His grand vizier was a Greek slave named Ibrahim, an accomplished violinist who went on campaign with him and, it was rumored, frequently shared his bed. Suleiman, in other words, was the classic Renaissance prince, an Orien-

tal counterpart to the Borgias in Rome, but infinitely more powerful.

The Venetian envoy Ottaviano Bon described Suleiman as "tall and thin, with a smoky complexion and an aquiline nose above drooping mustaches. His hands were finely boned but exceedingly strong, and it is said that he can pull the tautest bowstring in the army. On his head he wore a wide oval turban with an aigrette of peacock feathers, held in place by a clasp of diamonds. His voice was sweet and pleasing, though he never smiled during our discourse."

Suleiman was kept fully informed about the bitter feuds among the Western powers, several of which secretly sought his aid. He also knew that the rise of Protestantism was tearing Christianity apart. The time seemed ripe for a final westward push by the forces of Islam.

The Turkish assault troops took the important border fortress of Belgrade with almost playful ease. Then Suleiman's army, 100,000 strong, advanced into Hungary, the gateway to Central Europe. King Lajos II of Hungary was a brave, handsome and extremely stupid young man; he ordered the Turkish ambassadors hanged when they came to demand his submission. Calling for help from other Christian monarchs, Lajos scraped together some 25,000 noble knights and retainers. From his royal colleagues he received fair promises and not a single soldier. In August 1526, he met the Ottomans at Mohács and was not so much defeated as obliterated. King Lajos and 24,000 of his men were killed in the battle. Hungary became yet another Turkish province.

Suleiman appointed a Transylvanian governor named János Zápolya as puppet king of Hungary, and it says a great deal about the state of that country that Zápolya and thousands of Hungarians fought fiercely for the Turks from then on. They had been so cruelly oppressed and impoverished by their own nobles that they felt better off under the sultan.

It took the Ottomans just three years to digest Hungary. Then Suleiman began preparations for the next meal: Austria. King Ferdinand I von Hapsburg of Austria had protested against the crowning of the puppet ruler Zápolya. Suleiman sent him a

brief and ominous reply via courier: "Tell the king that I will meet him on the field at Mohács. If he is not there I will come to Vienna to fetch him."

In the spring of 1529, the bulk of the Turkish army started massing in Bulgaria. Joined by their auxiliaries, they comprised the largest armed force ever in Europe—more than 330,000 men, 500 guns and 90,000 camels. They included 20,000 of the crack janissaries and 6,000 Christian Hungarians. Suleiman led this mass, with Ibrahim acting as seraskier (field commander, as distinct from commander in chief). It was a signal honor, since grand viziers, being politicians, usually stayed home.

That spring it rained as it hadn't rained in living memory. Day after day, week after week the torrents came down, turning the countryside into one vast morass. The Balkan roads became quagmires, the rivers burst their banks and swept away what bridges existed. The camels—creatures of the dry desert—could not gain a foothold in the slippery mud, stumbled, broke their legs and lay down to die by the thousands.

There was no way Suleiman could transport his heavy artillery under these conditions. He therefore decided to leave the big pieces behind—all 200 of them—and push on with only the light field guns. Ibrahim warned him against that move and advised him to postpone the campaign until the following year. Suleiman would not hear of it. Determined to take Vienna that summer, he replied, "It is beneath my dignity to allow the weather to interfere with my plans."

The sultan banked on the thousands of highly skilled Romanian and Serbian miners in his ranks to reduce the town through mining operations. It was his first—and fatal—mistake in the war. Another soon followed. Suleiman was suffering from hubris, the delusion of invincibility that has broken so many conquerors in the past and would undo so many more in future.

When his army reached Pest, opposite Buda on the Danube, the sultan offered its small German garrison a safe retreat if the soldiers would evacuate the stronghold. The Germans accepted and marched out between two lines of jeering janissaries. But from mutual insults the two sides came to blows, then to cold steel. Within half an hour the Turks killed every man of the garrison, then turned on the town and sabered most of the inhabitants as well.

Word of the massacre spread and acted as a terrible warning for the Austrians not to trust the sultan's promises. For Suleiman the episode held a different, equally ominous warning—that he couldn't control the janissaries once they went on a rampage.

Icy fear gripped Vienna as the Turks drew closer. Ferdinand—whose actual title was archduke of Austria, king of Hungary and Bohemia—appealed to his mighty brother, Charles V, emperor of Germany and king of Spain. But Charles was engaged fighting the French in Italy and did not have the resources for a two-front war. Ferdinand, probably remembering King Lajos' fate, scuttled off to the safety of Bohemia, leaving the Viennese to fend for themselves.

Fortunately for the Austrian capital, some help did arrive. The most valuable came in the person of Nicolas *Graf* von Salm, a cool, thoroughly experienced professional soldier, 70 years old but steady as a rock. Salm was too low on the nobility scale to be given top command—that went to a Duke Frederick, who gladly let Salm do all the work involved. With him arrived about 1,000 German *Landsknechte*—formidable, well-trained mercenary pikemen—and 700 Spaniards who were armed with the newfangled wheel-lock muskets, which fired faster than the old Turkish matchlocks.

Salm took charge of a garrison of 23,000 infantry and 2,000 mounted cuirassiers, plus a total of 75 cannons—a sorry handful compared to the Ottoman host. He inspected the defenses and found them in a miserable state. Vienna was not very large, consisting only of those inner city portions that are today enclosed by the chain of boulevards called "the Ring." Near the center towered the ancient cathedral of St. Stephen's, and all around clustered a maze of narrow, crooked, foul-smelling alleys, sprinkled with innumerable taverns and a few grandiose palaces. The city walls were 300 years old and in very bad repair. They were pierced by four gates, the obvious danger points.

Salm methodically set about preparing the city for a siege. He had fireproof magazines dug, threw up earthwork bastions for the defenders to stand on and used paving stones to erect a second wall of sorts. He tore the inflammable shingles off the roofs and heavily palisaded the four gateways. Every building beyond the walls that might provide cover for the attackers was demolished. For his command post he chose the looming spire of St. Stephen's, an extremely risky location, but one that gave him the widest possible view of the battlefield.

In order to save precious food supplies, Salm ordered 4,000 women, children and old people evacuated from the city in an escorted column. That turned out to be a tragic error, for by then the Turkish advance horsemen were swarming all over lower Austria, and at the village of Traismauer they swooped down on the convoy. They spared only young women who could be raped and then carried off to be sold as slaves. All the rest, including infants, were butchered, some spitted alive on sharpened stakes. Among the worst perpetrators were Zápolya's Hungarian scouts.

From the city walls the sentries could see the smoke of burning villages all around them. The Turks were scorching everything in their path, slaughtering or carrying off an estimated half of the peasant population. But it was not until late September, two months behind schedule, that the main body of the Ottoman army reached Vienna.

Overnight the city found itself surrounded by a mass of white tents stretching as far as the eye could see, all the way to the heights of Semmering Mountain. It was an awesome sight and helped to disguise the fact that things were not well with the Turkish army. Roughly one-third of its troops were spahis, light cavalry of very limited use in siege warfare. Of the initial 90,000 pack camels, barely 20,000 remained, and those were in bad shape. The same applied to the men, who had been drenched to the skin for months and were coughing so loudly that the sound drowned out the camp preparations.

Suleiman dispatched couriers with a demand for surrender. "I expect to sup in the city on the last day of September," his message ran. "If Vienna capitulates only my dignitaries will enter and all will be spared. If you resist, the place will be razed to the ground and all therein put to the sword." Salm sent the couriers back courteously enough, but minus any reply.

At dawn the following day, 300 cannons opened up on the city, maintaining a steady fire until dusk. The Turkish gunners displayed exemplary discipline; they had managed to keep their powder reserves dry in the torrential rains, and they loaded and fired faster than any Western artillerymen. The bombardment, however, was fairly futile. The heavy pieces, left behind in Bulgaria, would have cracked the walls, but the stone projectiles of the light field guns simply splattered, though at high elevation they curved over the walls and damaged houses. Several lodged in the tower of St. Stephen's, where they can still be seen by visitors. Salm remained calmly at his post, remarking to an aide, "These pebbles are like the little pills my medico bids me swallow."

With the balls came showers of arrows fired over the walls. The crescent-shaped Tartar bows used by the Turks were vicious weapons that could propel their arrows through chain mail or iron helmets. But again, these were typical field armament—against fortifications they had only nuisance value.

The defenders' response was a sudden sally by 100 cavalry that took the Turks by surprise. The horsemen, commanded by the daredevil Eck von Reischach, rode over two gun emplacements, cut down the crews and were back behind the walls before the besiegers could block their retreat. Vienna was holding its own... for the moment at least.

The bombardment continued for days, without any sign of a massed attack. But on October 1, a Serbian engineer who claimed Christian parentage sneaked into the town and conveyed some very disturbing information. He said that the cannonade was merely a ploy to hide the real preparations that were proceeding underground. The Turks were digging mine shafts on both sides of the Carinthian Gate, intending to blow up the structure to open the way for their assault troops.

Salm knew all about mine warfare and immediately took countermeasures. He had drums scattered with dried peas and buckets of water placed in the cellars near the walls and posted sentries beside them. The moment the peas rattled or the water showed ripples, the guards sounded the alarm and squads of men began digging down. They found that the Turks were tunneling six different saps, burrowing like moles with astonishing speed.

The counterminers shoveled until they struck the tunnels. Some were deserted, with huge bags of gunpowder stacked and ready to be exploded. The raiders carried them off as booty. In other shafts the work was still going on, and they became scenes of macabre subterranean combat. Neither side dared to fire a shot and could barely see each other by the light of shaded lanterns. The half-naked men fought with picks, spades, daggers and clubs, with bare fists and occasionally their teeth. Wounded men were trampled to death. Comrades killed comrades because they couldn't distinguish friend from foe. The low, narrow shafts allowed no room to dodge, so every thrust or blow found a target. The survivors crawled back to the surface half crazed, black with earth and covered in blood, looking, as one eyewitness described, like "devils from the nether pit of hell."

The defenders disarmed most of the saps, but new ones were being dug all the time and not all were discovered. On October 5, two mines exploded with ear-shattering roars at the Salt Gate, tearing holes large enough for a company to march through. The janissaries charged before the dust had settled but ran into a bastion behind the breach. On the bastion stood the *Landsknechte* armed with 12-foot pikes and halberds. Thrusting down with their long weapons, the pikemen had a distinct advantage over the Turks, who carried only their curved, razor-sharp scimitars. The attack was repulsed with heavy losses. The moment the Turks had withdrawn, the defenders were blocking the breach with sandbags and stone-filled baskets.

That night a new type of raiding party struck the Ottoman camp. This time the raiders came on foot and in utter silence, wearing black cloaks. Each one carried two homemade bombs—earthenware containers

filled with powder and chopped lead—which they hurled into the tents. The glowing streaks of the burning fuses were the only warning the sleepers had before the grenades exploded and the lead pellets tore into them. More than 2,000 Turks died in their shredded tents.

The mining and the charges that followed went on day after day, accompanied by gunfire. A huge mine went up under the Carinthian Gate and effectively demolished the twin guard towers. Again the Turks found a bastion already erected behind it, manned by pikemen, Spanish arquebusiers with their wheel locks and Bohemians wielding two-handed swords that could slice an opponent in half. The janissaries piled in, were cut down and climbed over the heaps of dead, only to be slaughtered in turn. When the attackers finally fell back they left a mountain of 1,200 bodies.

The fighting underground took on even more gruesome forms. The counterminers now used spades with sharpened edges, both as digging tools and weapons. A blow could take a man's head off. The Turks employed short cavalry maces, designed to smash helmets and crack skulls. On one occasion a spark exploded the stored powder prematurely, blowing up friend and foe alike in one indistinguishable mass. Nobody knows just how many men died in these nightmarish clashes beneath the earth.

Watching the battle, Sultan Suleiman could see that his mining operations were too unpredictable to be effective. Most of the mines were emptied before they could be blown. Sometimes the debris fell inward, creating new obstacles instead of clearing them. And the defenders were fighting like men possessed, fully aware that they were the last barrier of Christendom preventing the Muslim tide from flooding Western Europe. They had by now mounted their own guns on reinforced rooftops. Their fire was raking the Turkish camps, ploughing into troop formations and killing scores of horses. Several of their Viennese cannons were so-called royals, which outranged any of the besiegers weapons.

On October 11, the heavens opened again and more rain poured down. Thousands more of the camels subsequently sickened and died. The

coughing in the Ottoman army swelled as the campsites became waterlogged. Entire units fell out with fever chills. To make matters worse, food supplies were running low. The Turks had so thoroughly devastated the countryside that it could no longer support hundreds of thousands of hungry men.

Suleiman held a war council in his tent and decided on one final all-out attempt to capture the city. He intended to winter there, then continue the westward march with the coming of spring, when dry roads would enable him to bring up his heavy ordnance. This time the assault formations were reversed. The *bashi-bazouks*, an inferior militia, would go in first and tire out the defenders by the sheer press of their bodies. Then the janissaries would follow to push through into the city. The attack would be thrice renewed, regardless of the losses. The sultan also decided on the unprecedented step of offering a cash bonus of 1,000 silver aspers for each janissary. This was unheard of—hitherto those elite troops had fought only for loot and for glory, confident that death in battle would gain them immediate entry into heaven.

The attack began on the morning of October 14. *Seraskier* Ibrahim himself joined the janissaries. The drive was aimed at two points: the ruined Carinthian Gate and a protruding bastion called the Berg. One of the mines failed to blow; the other went off with a thunderous roar, hurling bodies into the air. The Turks surged forward, howling like demons, only to run into more palisades and the terrible rows of long pikes. Count Salm left his lookout position and took personal command. Almost immediately he was hit in the side and leg by stone splinters and had to be carried off. The wounds eventually killed him.

The *bashi-bazouks* fell back, were whipped forward by their *onbashes* (sergeants), fell back again, and were again driven toward the menacing spears. Their dead and wounded piled up, but they made no headway. Then the janissaries took over, only to be decimated by musket fire from both flanks. The musketeers rested their weapons on forked stands, which gave them steady aim. The attackers had pistols, but couldn't use them in the wild press. Those who did mostly hit their own comrades. They charged and charged again, breaking one line of pikes only to be confronted by another. Hand bombs with hissing fuses rained down on them, exploding with terrible effect. Two small fieldpieces positioned on the Berg spewed grapeshot into the attackers. Mounds of entangled bodies hampered the men advancing from behind, who had to climb over them while musket balls inflicted more casualties.

The janissaries reeled back, though no signal for retreat had been given. Ibrahim used his horsewhip, then his saber to drive them forward, only to be ignored or cursed. For the first time in the 200 years of their existence, the janissaries refused to obey. They flooded to the rear, first in trickles, then in swarms, not stopping until they had reached their tents. Some even began to strike the tents without orders. There was no pursuit.

During that night the Turks packed up their campsites. The people in Vienna were kept awake by dreadful shrieks coming from the camps. The Ottomans were setting fire to the baggage they couldn't carry and hurling their bound prisoners into the flames. Hundreds were roasted alive, but hundreds more managed to escape in the confusion and ran toward the city walls. They were hoisted up by ropes. The Viennese refused to open any gates. They couldn't believe that the danger was over.

The following day the sea of tents around the city had nearly disappeared. Snow began to fall, far too early in the season. The weather that year, more than anything, had saved Vienna. The Turks marched off unhampered after Sultan Suleiman announced solemnly, "Allah, in His wisdom, has not yet permitted us to capture Vienna." The Ottoman losses were estimated at between 18,000

and 25,000, several times higher than those of the garrison. But civilian casualties had been ghastly—lower Austria was virtually depopulated. In some villages the invaders left pyramids of human heads in place of inhabitants. Thousands of young girls were dragged off to the slave markets and never heard from again.

In Vienna the commanders were at first unable to believe their good fortune. They thought the Ottoman retreat was a feint to put them off guard. They also believed that the Turks had smuggled in scores of spies and saboteurs among the escaped prisoners. The provost marshal, a brute named Wilhelm von Roggendorf, had all the men examined to see whether they were circumcised, to confirm that they were Muslims. Those who bore the mark were hanged immediately. Others were tortured, and while their toes were crushed and their arms torn out of the sockets, a few poor wretches "confessed" to being Turkish agents. They were drawn and quartered in public while the audience cheered.

When the Austrians cautiously entered the Turkish campsites, they found some sacks filled with glistening black beans nobody had ever seen before. A Turkish prisoner explained that this was coffee, imported from Arabia and used by the Muslims as a stimulant, since the Koran forbade them wine. The Viennese brewed the stuff but found it too bitter for their taste. It was only after someone hit on the idea of adding honey that the new drink caught on, with a vengeance. A coffee house—the first such establishment in the West—opened in Vienna the following year.

In retrospect, the defeat at Vienna signaled the beginning of the decline of the Ottoman Empire. The invincible janissaries had been forced to retreat, and their morale was impaired. The Turks learned the hard way how dangerous such elite guards can be to their own side. The

janissaries grew more and more insubordinate, threatening and occasionally murdering their monarchs. Instead of the janissaries being slaves of the sultan, the sultan frequently became their prisoner.

For Suleiman, Vienna marked another kind of decline. He remained the Magnificent, but fell under the strange domination of a harem beauty. Little is known about her, not even her real name. The courtiers called her Roxelana, meaning "the Russian," or Khurrem, the "Laughing One." Her laughter, however, concealed a poisonous intent. Whatever the reason for the power she wielded over her master, she induced Suleiman to have his devoted grand vizier Ibrahim strangled, followed by his eldest son, Mustapha, a promising young heir. Roxelana contrived instead to gain the succession for her own offspring, Selim II. He was a warped creature nicknamed "the Sot," a confirmed alcoholic despite the Islamic ban on liquor.

Selim took over after Suleiman's death in 1566, and from then on the realm went steadily downhill. The Turks never produced another capable sultan, though there were many cruel ones. Their military prowess declined decade by decade as the Western nations rapidly improved their armaments and organization. The Turks still counted as a major power; they even staged another—disastrous—siege of Vienna in 1683. But as a menace to Europe they were finished the rainy night they folded their tents and retreated into the Balkans.

Australian-born John Godwin is a former reporter for Murdoch Press, living in San Francisco, Calif., whose books include *Alcatraz, Murder USA, Unsolved* and a dozen of the Frommer Dollar-a-Day travel guides. For further reading, he recommends: *The Battles That Changed History*, by Fletcher Pratt; and *The Wanderer*, by Mika Waltari.

The Muslim expulsion from Spain

Roger Boase looks at a Spanish example of religious and ethnic cleansing.

by Roger Boase

'**E**verything declines after reaching perfection …

The tap of the white ablution fount weeps in despair, like a passionate lover weeping at the departure of the beloved.

Over dwellings emptied of Islam, vacated, whose inhabitants now live in unbelief,

Where the mosques have become churches in which only bells and crosses are found …

O who will redress the humiliation of a people who were once powerful, a people whose condition injustice and tyrants have changed?

Yesterday they were kings in their own homes, but today they are slaves in the land of the infidel!

Were you to see them bewildered, with no one to guide them, wearing the cloth of shame in its different shades,

And were you to behold their weeping when they are sold, it would strike fear into your heart, and sorrow would seize you.

Alas, many a maiden as fair as the sun when it rises, as though she were rubies and pearls,

Is led off to abomination by a barbarian against her will, while her eye is in tears and her heart is stunned.

The heart melts with sorrow at such sights, if there is any Islam or faith in that heart!'

These words were written by the poet ar-Rundi after Seville fell to Ferdinand III of Castile (1199-1252) in December 1248. By that date many other cities, including Valencia, Murcia, Jaen and Cordoba, had been captured and it seemed that the end of Muslim Spain was imminent. However, it was not until 1492 that the Moorish Kingdom of Granada surrendered to Ferdinand V and Isabella, and the final Muslim expulsion did not take place until over a century later, between 1609 and 1614. This means that there was a large Moorish population in Spain half a millennium after the high point of Andalusian culture in the eleventh century.

Ar-Rundi might well have been responding to the plight of his co-religionists after the fall of Granada or at the time of the expulsion when

many similar atrocities were committed: homes were destroyed and abandoned, mosques were converted into churches, mothers were separated from their children, people were stripped of their wealth and humiliated, armed rebels were reduced to slavery. But by the seventeenth century the Moors had become Spanish citizens; some were genuine Christian converts; indeed many, like Sancho Panza's neighbour Ricote in Cervantes' novel *Don Quixote* (1605-15), were deeply patriotic and considered themselves to be '*mas cristiano que moro*'. Yet all were the victims of a state policy, based on racist theological arguments, which had the backing of both the Royal Council and the Church, for which the expulsion of the Jews in 1492 provided an immediate legal precedent.

According to the terms of the treaty drawn up in 1492, the new subjects of the Crown were to be allowed to preserve their mosques and religious institutions, to retain the use of their language and to continue to abide by their own laws and customs. But within seven years these terms had been broken. When the moderate missionary approach of the archbishop of Granada, Hernando de Talavera (1428-1507), was replaced by the fanaticism of Cardinal Cisneros (c.1436-1518), who organised mass conversions and the burning of all religious texts in Arabic, these events resulted in the First Rebellion of the Alpujarras (1499-1500) and the assassination of one of the Cardinal's agents. This in turn gave the Catholic monarchs an excuse to revoke their promises. In 1499 the Muslim religious leaders of Granada were persuaded to hand over more than 5,000 priceless books with ornamental bindings, which were then consigned to the flames; only some books on medicine were spared. In Andalusia after 1502, and in Valencia, Catalonia and Aragon after 1526, the Moors were given a choice between baptism and exile. For the majority, baptism was the only practical option. Henceforward the Spanish Moors became theoretically New Christians and, as such, subject to the jurisdiction of the Inquisition, which had been authorised by Pope Sixtus IV in 1478.

For the most part, conversion was nominal: the Moors paid lip-service to Christianity, but continued to practise Islam in secret. For example, after a child was baptised, he might be taken home and washed with hot water to annul the sacrament of baptism. The former Muslims were able to lead a double life with a clear conscience because certain Islamic religious authorities ruled that, under duress or threat to life, Muslims might apply the principle of *taqiyyah* or precaution that made dissimulation and hypocrisy permissible. In response to a plea from the Spanish Muslims, the Grand Mufti of Oran, Ahmad ibn Abu Juma'a, issued a decree in 1504, in which he stated that Muslims may drink wine, eat pork or do any other forbidden thing if they are compelled to do so and if they do not have the intention to sin. They may even, he said, deny the Prophet Muhammad with their

tongues provided, at the same time, they love him in their hearts—though not all Muslim scholars agreed with this advice.

Thus the fall of Granada marked a new phase in Muslim-Christian relations. In medieval times the status of Muslims under Christian rule was similar to that of Christians under Muslim rule: they belonged to a protected minority which preserved its own laws and customs in return for tribute. But there was no Scriptural basis for the legal status of Jews and Muslims under Christian rule; they were subject to the whims of rulers, the prejudices of the populace and the objections of the clergy. Before the completion of the Reconquest it was in the interests of the kings of Aragon and Castile to respect such laws and contracts. Now, however, Spain not only became, at least in theory, an entirely Christian nation but purity of faith came to be identified with purity of blood so that all New Christians or *conversos*, whether of Jewish or Muslim origin, were branded as potential heretics.

As a member of a vanquished minority with an alien culture, the *moro* became a *morisco*, a 'little Moor'. Every aspect of his way of life—including his language, dress and social customs—was condemned as uncivilised and pagan. A person who refused to drink wine or eat pork might be denounced as a Muslim to the Inquisition. In the eyes of the Inquisition and popular opinion, even practices such as eating couscous, using henna, throwing sweets at a wedding and dancing to the sound of Berber music, were un-Christian activities for which a person might be obliged to do penance. Moriscos who were sincere Christians were also bound to remain second-class citizens, and might be exposed to criticism from Muslims and Christians alike. Although *morisco* is a derogatory term, historians find it a useful label for those Arabs or Moors who remained in Spain after the fall of Granada.

In 1567 Philip II renewed an edict which had never been strictly en-

forced, making the use of Arabic illegal and prohibiting Islamic religion, dress and customs. This edict resulted in the Second Rebellion of the Alpujarras (1568-70), which seemed to corroborate evidence of a secret conspiracy with the Turks. The uprising was brutally suppressed by Don John of Austria. One of his worst atrocities was to raze the town of Galera, to the east of Granada, and sprinkle it with salt, having slaughtered 2,500 people including 400 women and children. Some 80,000 Moriscos in Granada were dispersed to other parts of Spain and Old Christians from northern Spain were settled on their lands.

By 1582 expulsion was proposed by Philip II's Council of State as the only solution to the conflict between the communities, despite some concern about the harmful economic repercussions—the loss of Moorish craftsmanship and the shortage of agricultural manpower and expertise. But as there was opposition from some noblemen and the King was preoccupied by international events, no action was taken until 1609-10 when Philip III (r.1598-1621) issued edicts of expulsion.

Royal legislation concerning the Moriscos was dictated at every stage by the Church. Juan de Ribera (1542-1611), the aging Archbishop of Valencia, who had initially been a firm believer in the efficacy of missionary work, became in his declining years the chief partisan of expulsion. In a sermon preached on September 27th, 1609, he said that the land would not become fertile again until these heretics had been expelled. The Duke of Lerma (Philip III's first minister, 1598-1618) also underwent a change of heart when it was agreed that the lords of Valencia would be given the lands of the expelled Moriscos in compensation for the loss of their vassals.

The decision to proceed with the expulsion was approved unanimously by the Council of State on January 30th, 1608, although the actual decree was not signed by the King until April 4th, 1609. Galleons of the Spanish fleet were secretly prepared, and they were later joined by many foreign merchant ships, including several from England. On September 11th, the expulsion order was announced by town criers in the Kingdom of Valencia, and the first convoy departed from Denia at nightfall on October 2nd, and arrived in Oran less than three days later. The Moriscos of Aragon, Castile, Andalusia and Extremadura received expulsion orders during the course of the following year. The majority of the forced emigrants settled in the Maghrib or Barbary Coast, especially in Oran, Tunis, Tlemcen, Tetuan, Rabat and Salé. Many travelled overland to France, but after the assassination of Henry of Navarre by Ravaillac in May 1610, they were forced to emigrate to Italy, Sicily or Constantinople.

There is much disagreement about the size of the Morisco population. The French demographer Henri Lapeyre estimated from census reports and embarkation lists that approximately 275,000 Spanish Moriscos emigrated in the years 1609-14, out of a total of 300,000. This conservative estimate is not consistent with many of the contemporary accounts that give a figure of 600,000. Bearing in mind that the total population of Spain at that time was only about seven and a half million, this must have constituted a serious deficit in terms of productive manpower and tax revenue. In the Kingdom of Valencia, which lost a third of its population, nearly half the villages were deserted in 1638.

There is equal disagreement about the number of Moriscos who perished in armed rebellion or on the journey into exile. Pedro Aznar Cardona, whose treatise justifying the expulsion was published in 1612, stated that between October 1609 and July 1611 over 50,000 died resisting expulsion, while over 60,000 died during their passage abroad either by land or sea or at the hands of their co-religionists after disembarking on the North African coast. If these figures are correct, then more

than one in six of the Moorish population perished in the space of two years. Henry Charles Lea, drawing on many contemporary sources, puts the mortality figure at between two-thirds and three-quarters.

The demographic factor was one of the decisive arguments employed in favour of expulsion by Juan de Ribera in 1602. He warned Philip III that, unless he took swift action, Christian Spaniards would soon find themselves outnumbered by Muslims, as all Moriscos married and had large families, whereas a third or a quarter of all Christians remained celibate after taking holy orders or entering military service. The Moriscos, Ribera said, think only of reproducing and saving their skins, while their temperance in food and drink gives them a high life expectancy. Ribera's fears were prompted by a census of the Valencian population that he himself had supervised that same year, which revealed that the Morisco population had increased by one-third.

At a meeting of the State Council in January 1608 the Comendador de Leon attributed the decline of the Old Christian population to their reluctance to shoulder the financial burden of marriage at a time of rising costs. He warned that soon the Moriscos would be able to achieve their objective simply by means of their population growth, without either taking up arms or receiving help from abroad. With Turkey distracted by war and with Persia and North Africa weakened by plague, drought and civil war, it was an opportune moment to take firm action. The Count of Alba de Liste then said, in a further twist of the demographic argument, that if the King, in his clemency, were to send the Moriscos to North Africa, it would be a form of death sentence because, if they did not die of drought and starvation, they would become sexually impotent.

In the minds of many, the fertility of the Morisco population was associated with the myth of Islamic sensuality and licentiousness. The

failure of the Church in its missionary efforts was attributed to this alleged aspect of Islam that offered—so they said—carnal delights both here and in the hereafter. The Moriscos came to personify the sins of the flesh, later romanticised in visions of oriental harems. But they were considered equally susceptible to 'the sins of the superego', such as pride, hypocrisy, cunning, avarice and grasping ambition, all features traditionally ascribed to the Jews. Prejudiced people will not hesitate to use mutually exclusive stereotypes to justify their dislike, and this is certainly true of many Spanish writers in the seventeenth century: the Moriscos are lazy, yet industrious; abstemious, yet lascivious; miserly, yet extravagant; cowardly, yet belligerent; ignorant, yet anxious to acquire learning in order to rise above their station.

There were, as we have seen, some genuine grounds for fearing and envying the Moriscos: their numbers were increasing rapidly; some had become successful merchants and shopkeepers, despite attempts to exclude them from these occupations; they exemplified in their conduct the virtues of thrift, frugality and hard work; the majority outwardly conformed to the religious requirements imposed on them, but by subterfuge continued to celebrate their own festivals and practise the basic rituals of Islam. It was this refusal to renounce their religious and cultural identity that many Old Christians found offensive. There was no serious attempt to understand Morisco culture and religion. Any slanderous anecdote, any insulting remark, any distortion of the truth was acceptable if it served what these Christians considered to be the laudable aim of denigrating Islam. Cultural diversity was an alien concept and assimilation was equally unacceptable.

The experience of the Moriscos varied enormously from one region to another. In some parts of Spain there were exceptionally good relations between Old and New Christians. A detailed study of Villarubia in La Mancha where the Moriscos comprised 20 percent of the population, owned the best farmland and were well integrated within the community, has shown that they were protected by their Old Christian neighbours from unwelcome visits from government inspectors. Many of those expelled managed to slip back into Spain and travelled hundreds of miles to reach their homes.

The full tale of the sufferings endured by the Moriscos has never fully been told: how those who survived the journey arrived at their destination starving and destitute because the bare necessities and money that they were permitted to take with them had been extorted from them by thieves and swindlers; how those travelling overland to France were forced by farmers to pay whenever they drank from a river or sat in the shade of a tree; how thousands of those who resisted and survived ended their days as galley-slaves; how those waiting to board ship were starved so that they would agree to sell their children in exchange for bread; how it was the official policy of the Church to separate Morisco children from their parents.

It was Juan de Ribera's original intention, approved by the Council of State on September 1st, 1609, that all children aged ten or under should remain in Spain to be educated by priests or trustworthy persons whom they would serve until the age of twenty-five or thirty in return for lodging, food and clothing, and that suckling babes should be given to Old Christian wet-nurses on the same conditions. Later in the month the age limit was reduced from ten to five years or under. The policy was at least partially executed, though it proved impossible to implement in full. Among the Moriscos who embarked at Alicante in Andalusia between October 6th, and November 7th, 1609, there seem to have been nearly 14,000 children missing (conservatively assuming an average 2.5 children per family). According to a document dated April 17th, 1610,

there were 1,832 Morisco boys and girls aged seven or under in the Kingdom of Valencia, all of whom, against the wishes of their guardians, were to be sent to Castile to serve the prelates and other notables of the realm. In July 1610 the Church recommended that all Morisco children above the age of seven in the Kingdom of Valencia should be sold as perpetual slaves to Old Christians. These included the orphans of rebels, children seized by soldiers and others concealed and cared for by people who believed they were doing an act of charity. The theologians who signed this document argued that slavery was not only morally justifiable but spiritually beneficial: these children would be less likely to become apostates, since their masters would ensure that they remained Roman Catholics and, as slaves rarely married, this would be another method of ridding Spain of 'this evil race'.

What was the significance of the age limit? It was thought that above the age of six or seven a child begins to lose his innocence and becomes more difficult to indoctrinate, whereas a younger child would have no real knowledge of his origins. The policy was justified on the grounds that innocent children baptised as Christians should not be punished for the sins of their fathers, although, paradoxically, the principle of hereditary guilt was found acceptable as a justification for expelling all adults, whether or not they were practising Christians. Furthermore, it was said that to banish children with their infidel parents would be to guarantee their confirmation as Muslims and their consignment to hellfire in the hereafter. But young Morisco children should not be educated above their proper station: apart from pupils preparing for the priesthood, they were to be brought up by artisans and farm labourers, and they should certainly not be allowed to study literature. In this way it was hoped that all memories of Islam in Spain would be wiped out forever. This point was much appreciated by Philip III.

Much has been written about the exodus of the Spanish Jews in 1492 and the plight of the many Jewish conversos who suffered at the hands of the Inquisition, but the Spanish Arabs or Moors have not received the same attention. In most people's minds, the Spanish Inquisition is associated with the persecution of Jews. It is not so widely known that Muslims were terrorised by this institution and that they too were the victims of an anti-Semitic ideology. About 12,000 Moriscos were charged with apostasy by the Inquisition, 50 percent of them in the last thirty years before the expulsion.

Racial and religious intolerance is nowhere more evident than in the reports of some of the meetings of Philip III's Council of State and in works written to justify the need for a policy of expulsion. In these works, most of them by frustrated Dominican missionaries, one finds a highly unorthodox racist theology, supported by biblical precedents: there was an attempt to judaise Islam and to depict Christian Spaniards of old Christian stock as the new Chosen Race engaged in a crusade to recover their Promised Land from the Antichrist Muhammad. One author claimed that the Prophet was the offspring of an incestuous relationship between his mother and his uncle, both, he says, Jews, in fulfilment of the prophecy that the Antichrist would be born of a dishonest woman.

It is ironic that those same Old Testament passages which have been used to support the theory that Palestine is the Jewish promised land were not only cited by apologists for a policy of mass expulsion for the Moriscos but were cited by anti-Jewish theologians in advocating the need for statutes of purity of blood. These authors regarded the Spanish Old Christians as the spiritual heirs of the Children of Israel and compared Philip III with Abraham, Moses or King David. They called him a second Abraham because, they said, he was obliged to banish his illegitimate son, that is to say the Moriscos, the descendants of

Hagar, the Egyptian slave-girl. One of their favourite biblical passages was God's message delivered by Moses to the Israelites as they were about to enter the Promised Land:

> In the cities of these nations whose land the Lord your God is giving to you as a patrimony, you shall not leave any creature alive. You shall annihilate them—Hittites, Amorites, Canaanites, Perizzites, Hivites, Jebusites—as the Lord commanded you, so that they may not teach you to imitate all the abominable things that they have done for their gods and so cause you to sin against the Lord your God. (Deut. 20: 16-18)

This passage has been cited by Jews campaigning for a Greater Israel stretching from the Euphrates to the Red Sea and was used by the Puritans in North America in the seventeenth century to justify massacring the native American Indians. Following the Jewish-Morisco analogy, one contemporary poet presented the expulsion of the Moriscos as a reversal of the Hebrew Exodus: the Moriscos will depart from the holy land of Spain and will return to the infernal land of Egypt, without any parting of the waters.

The Portuguese Dominican Damián Fonseca even suggested that God expected a burnt offering from His Catholic Majesty to appease His divine wrath. The phrase he used in 1611 was *el agradable holocausto* ('the agreeable holocaust').

To these antisemites, the Jews were descended from Judas, who betrayed Christ, not Judah, son of Jacob. They would not have admitted that Jesus was a Jew sent by God to preach to the 'lost sheep of the House of Israel'. As a result of the role that God had predestined for them, the Jews ceased to be God's chosen people and inherited the sin of deicide for which they were condemned to wander the earth.

The simplest method of vilifying the last remnants of Arab Spain was to depict Islam as a form of pseudo-Jewish heresy. Jaime Bleda, the royal chaplain and chief anti-Morisco polemicist, even suggested that the Moorish invasion of Spain was a divine punishment for the pro-Semitic policies of the Visigothic King Wittiza (698-710), who had revoked the decrees of his father by liberating the Jews from slavery and restoring to them their lands and privileges. This was cited as a legal precedent applicable to the Moriscos at the Council of State held on January 30th, 1608. However, the immediate historical precedent was the expulsion of the Jews in 1492. In April 1605, Bleda urged Philip III to follow the example of his royal predecessors Ferdinand and Isabella, who had been persuaded by Fray Thomas de Torquemada to banish the Jews from their realms and would have done the same to the Moors had they refused baptism. God, he said, rewarded the Catholic monarchs for their Christian zeal by giving them the New World.

Much of the vituperation that Bleda and other polemicists levelled against the Moriscos had previously been levelled against the Jews. Of both peoples it was said that they were inherently sinful and inferior, that they were incorrigible in their obstinate infidelity, and that their heretical depravity was a contagion which would have to be removed. Philip III is even described as a Catholic Galen, charged with the task of purging the poison and corruption of heresy from the mystical body of Christian Spain.

Spain has paid a heavy price for denying so long the Jewish and Muslim components of its cultural identity, but since the death of Franco in 1975, freedom of worship has gradually been established. In today's multi-ethnic, multi-religious Europe (it includes about 30 million Muslims and 1.5 million Jews), a new version of European history needs to be written, to include an account of the achievements and tribulations of European Jews and Muslims.

The Vatican might do more to admit the atrocities done in the name of the Church. It is hard to believe that as late as 1960 it was decided that Juan de Ribera should be canonised. At least a proposal to canonise Queen Isabella was recently dropped. The real saints were those who risked their lives to protect people persecuted for their beliefs or the beliefs of their ancestors, who died because they refused to betray others to the Inquisition, who would not renounce their faith and died in armed resistance. These people were engaged in what Muslims call *jihad*, which means both the inner struggle, the duty to resist evil and strife in the mystical path, and the outward struggle, the duty of those who are oppressed, or who have been unjustly driven from their homelands because they refuse to renounce their faith, to right in self-defence and in defence of their people. For, to paraphrase the *Qur'an*, 'If people did not have this right to defend themselves, monasteries and churches and synagogues and mosques, in which God's name is much remembered, would surely have been destroyed by now'.

FOR FURTHER READING

Roger Boase 'The Morisco Expulsion and Diaspora', *Cultures in Contact in Medieval Spain* ed David Hook and Barry Taylor (London, King's College, 1990); Henry Charles Lea, *The Moriscos of Spain: Their Conversion and Expulsion* (Bernard Quaritch, 1901); Anwar G. Chejne, *Islam and the West: The Moriscos* (State University of New York Press, 1983); Louis Cardaillac, *Morisques et chrétiens: un affrontement polémique* (1492-1640) (Klincksieck, 1977); L.R Harvey 'The Political, Social and Cultural History of the Moriscos', *The Legacy of Muslim Spain* ed. Salma Khadra Jayyusi (E.J. Brill, 1992).

Roger Boase is an Honorary Research Fellow at Queen Mary College, University of London, and author of *The Origin and Meaning of Courtly Love* (Manchester UP, 1977).

Reign On!

**Four centuries after her death, Good Queen Bess still draws crowds.
A regal rash of exhibitions and books examines her life anew**

by Doug Stewart

Though more than 400 years have passed since they were painted, her portraits are as recognizable as a movie star's: the receding red hair studded with pearls, the lace ruff hugging the neck from ears to collarbone, the ghostly white face with its haughty, confident gaze. England's exalted Queen Elizabeth I insisted her face be depicted in this way, luminous and shadow-free. A former lady-in-waiting gossiped that the queen loved to be told no one could look her full in the face because her radiance rivaled the sun's.

"There was a lot of mystique around Elizabeth," says Georgianna Ziegler, head of reference at the Folger Shakespeare Library in Washington, D.C., which claims the largest collection of Elizabethan writings and artifacts outside Britain. Popular poetry of the day celebrated the queen as Diana, the chaste goddess of the moon. To her subjects, England's maiden queen seemed slightly unnatural, more divine than mortal. "She saw herself as wedded to her realm," Ziegler says. "In a sense, for almost half a century she *was* the realm." And she managed to exploit the very peculiarity of her status as an unmarried woman to help shape the most glorious era of English history.

This year marks the 400th anniversary of the Virgin Queen's death, and a string of new exhibitions has been organized to commemorate her reign. The Folger has mounted a lavish tribute, "Elizabeth I, Then and Now," which opened in March—the month she died—and runs through August 2. At London's National Maritime Museum, a major exhibition is on view through September 14, and in Chicago, "Elizabeth I: Ruler and Legend" will open at the Newberry Library on September 30.

"Elizabeth is a figure of great interest now," says Ziegler, "because she was a powerful woman who carved out her own place and made herself a queen at a time when there weren't models for doing that successfully."

In fact, Good Queen Bess is a full-fledged pop phenomenon. New romance novels and thrillers about Elizabeth or her archrival, Mary Queen of Scots, appear almost monthly. A recent book, *Oxford: Son of Queen Elizabeth I*, posits that the Earl of Oxford was not only the author of Shakespeare's plays but also Elizabeth's secret love child. Several new biographies are due out this year, and films and plays about her reign are being revived. "Her life was a classic survival story," says Sian Flynn, curator of the London exhibition. "She was nearly executed twice by her own siblings, and she succeeded as a woman in a man's world."

And what a cutthroat world it was. Elizabeth's father was King Henry VIII, rotund, red-haired and irascible. Her mother was Anne Boleyn, a coquettish young lady of the court who was pregnant with Elizabeth when Henry was still married to Catherine of Aragon. Henry, who was Roman Catholic, established the Church of England largely so he could have his marriage to Catherine annulled and marry Anne (a marriage the Catholic Church never recognized). Princess Elizabeth was born September 7, 1533. Within three years, Henry had her mother beheaded on a trumped-up charge of adultery. He married another fetching young lady of the court, Jane Seymour, 11 days later.

Small wonder that at age 6 Elizabeth was said to have the gravity of a 40-year-old. Dignified and studious, she was educated as befitted a Renaissance princess, versed in history, geography, astronomy, mathematics and music. Throughout her life, she translated Greek and Latin for recreation and, as queen, wrote poetry and composed prayers that were printed and sold for popular consumption. The Folger exhibition includes a bound edition of one of her earliest literary efforts, a long religious poem that she translated from the French. The work was a gift to her father's sixth wife, Catherine Parr, whom he married after sending wife number five, Catherine Howard, to the block for adultery. In the preface, Elizabeth explains that she worked at "joining the sentences together as well as the capacity of my simple wit and small learning could extend themselves." She was 11 at the time.

Henry died three years later in 1547, and Elizabeth's younger half brother, Jane Seymour's son, was crowned Edward VI. Elizabeth was soon in danger. Barely two months after Henry's death, the widowed Catherine unwisely married Thomas Seymour, an ambitious uncle of the boy-king. When Catherine died in childbirth a year later, Seymour schemed to marry the 15-year-old Elizabeth (who had been living in his household), gain control over Edward and seize power for himself. He was arrested and beheaded for treason in 1549. Elizabeth was suspected of being in on the plot. Seymour had enjoyed hugging the young princess and liked to turn up in her bedroom in the early morning. She was even rumored to be carrying his child. But under interrogation Elizabeth denied misbehavior of any kind. "I do see it in her face that she is guilty," the crown's investigator fumed. "She hath a very good wit, and nothing is gotten of her but by great policy."

At 20, Elizabeth found herself in even greater peril. After Edward died in 1553 at age 15, most likely of tuberculosis, Mary Tudor, Elizabeth's staunchly Catholic half sister, ruled England with her fiancé, Philip of Spain. England had been convulsed by religious violence for decades, and under "Bloody Mary," as the queen was called, hundreds of English Protestants were burned at the stake for heresy. When a plot against the throne was uncovered in 1554, Mary was convinced that the Protestant Elizabeth—now next in line to be queen—was involved. Mary had her half sister arrested and sent to the Tower of London, the customary last stop before execution. Debarking in a wintry downpour at Traitor's Gate, Elizabeth called out, "Here landeth as true a subject, being prisoner, as ever landed at these stairs." She then dropped to the rain-soaked flagstones, saying, "It is better sitting here than in a worse place." The sodden princess refused to budge until one of her manservants broke down in tears. Disgusted by his show of weakness, Elizabeth collected herself and strode into the prison. Ultimately, Mary's fear of a Protestant rebellion probably spared Elizabeth, and she was released after two months.

Four years later, in 1558, Elizabeth took to the throne with alacrity, slipping into the royal plural on learning that Mary Tudor was dead of cancer: "This is the doing of the Lord, and it is marvellous in our eyes," she declared on becoming queen, quoting Psalm 118. After Mary's unpopular reign, much of England was elated at Elizabeth's accession. She was now 25 years old, slender, with long golden-red hair and a suitably regal comportment. Accompanied by 1,000 mounted courtiers the day before her coronation, in January 1559, she rode smiling through the streets of London. She stopped the procession from time to time to accept bouquets, a purse of coins, a Bible, even a sprig of rosemary from an old woman. "I will be as good unto you as ever queen was to her people," she vowed to the delight of onlookers.

Says Clark Hulse, dean of the graduate college at the University of Illinois at Chicago and curator of the Newberry Library's exhibition, "Elizabeth's popularity had a lot to do with her manner—riding in an open carriage and all that. If her sister Mary was sober and inclined to burn people at the stake, Elizabeth projected the idea of 'Merry England.'" Many, however, were horrified at the prospect of a queen reigning without a king. In a manifesto published the previous year, "The First Blast of the Trumpet Against the Monstrous Regiment of Women," a fiery Calvinist named John Knox had pronounced female rulers "repugnant to nature," women being "weak, frail, impatient" and "inconstant."

From the start, Parliament pressured the new queen to marry, but she was defiant. "A strange thing that the foot should direct the head in so weighty a cause," she upbraided Parliament in 1566. What to the M.P.s was a matter of state—England needed a king and princes who would grow to be kings—was to Elizabeth a near-treasonous affront.

The Folger's Ziegler says that Elizabeth's marriage would surely have led to turmoil, even if Parliament and her Privy Council failed to realize it. "She was very astute politically," Ziegler explains. "If she married a Catholic or a foreigner, that would upset a lot of people. If she married an English nobleman, it would create factions among the other nobles."

Nevertheless, the royal families of Scotland, France, Spain, Sweden and the Holy Roman Empire eyed England covetously, and various male royals courted her from afar, using ambassadors as go-betweens. "Elizabeth played along with one foreign prince or another, but it was mostly a political ploy," says Ziegler. Soon after she became queen, Elizabeth kept Spain's enmity in check by letting her late sister's husband, Philip II, now king of Spain, imagine he might marry her next. Later she kept France a wary ally against Spanish hegemony by pursuing a courtship with the French king's brother, the Duke of Alençon, complete with mutual love letters. "There is no prince in the world to whom I would more willingly yield to be his," the 45-year-old queen wrote him in 1579.

That year, the 25-year-old duke had called on Elizabeth in person, the only foreign suitor to do so. (The queen never set foot outside England.) The pair played at being courtly lovers, and Elizabeth was evidently quite fond of the gallant young man, whom she affectionately called "our frog." Ultimately, says Carole Levin, a professor of history at the University of Nebraska, "I don't think she ever wanted to marry. But I think she loved courtship and flirtation. I think she *adored* it." She is vain, wrote the Spanish ambassador in 1565, "and would like all the world to be running after her." As for men at the English court, a number of them, both married and unmarried, vied for Elizabeth's attentions with flattery and gifts. It was how one did business with the queen. Thus, wrote British historian J. E. Neale in his classic 1934 biography, *Queen Elizabeth*, "The reign was turned into an idyll, a fine but artificial comedy of young men—and old men—in love."

If Elizabeth herself ever fell passionately, foolishly in love, it was with Robert Dudley, her "sweet Robin." He was handsome and headstrong, an accomplished horseman and jouster, popular with the ladies at court and unpopular with the men. He and the queen flirted openly; the gossipy Spanish ambassador reported rumors in 1559 "that her Majesty visits him in his chamber day and night." It apparently bothered neither of them that Dudley was already married. He might well have sued for divorce in hopes of marrying the queen had his wife not been found in 1560 at the bottom of a staircase, dead of a broken neck. Though her death was more likely a suicide or an accident than a homicide, the ensuing scandal doomed Dudley's chances of ever becoming king. He remained the object of Elizabeth's affection all the same. When he knelt before her to be made Earl of Leicester (pronounced "Lester") four years later, the then 31-year-old queen couldn't resist tickling his neck. "I think she had an emotional and romantic relationship with Leicester," says Carole Levin. "I think there was some intimacy, but I don't think it ever went all the way."

Quick-witted, tough-minded and imperious, Elizabeth wrote her own speeches to Parliament and was England's chief diplomat—she spoke six languages in an age when none of the ambassadors to London spoke English. She once dressed down a Polish ambassador whom she found impertinent with a long, fluent harangue—in Latin. Her godson, Sir John Harington, wrote that she "left no doubtings whose daughter she was."

Like her father, Elizabeth was vain, manipulative and a bit coarse. She spat, swore, gambled at cards and backgammon, and picked her teeth in public. She silenced those who tried her patience, even priests in mid-sermon, with oaths like "Jesus!" and "God's death!" With questionable humor, given her mother's fate, she joked just before naval hero Francis Drake was knighted that she had "a gilded sword to strike off his head." And she was a practiced liar as well as a wit. Sometimes she lied apparently for her own amusement. In 1559, with Catholic Europe outraged at her steadfast Protestantism, Elizabeth toyed with the Spanish ambassador by telling him she wanted nothing more than "to be a nun and to pass her time in a cell praying." The Spaniard was amazed by her gall, concluding, "This woman is possessed by a hundred thousand devils."

On occasion—weighing a marriage offer, say, or a traitor's sentence—Elizabeth could be maddeningly indecisive. But in large matters, notably foreign policy and religious affairs, her shrewd, deliberate style was what England needed. With rare exceptions, she refused to commit troops to Protestant insurrections on the Continent, sending the rebels modest cash payments instead. (Elizabeth was notoriously frugal in approving outlays from the royal purse.) At home, she preferred to threaten high-ranking miscreants with exposure rather than execution. Her natural caution, coupled with luck and political savvy, gave England nearly half a century of unaccustomed peace.

"Her refusal to cater to the extremes of politics or religion, at a time when civil wars were raging through the rest of Europe, was a triumph of the via media, the middle way," says the National Maritime Museum's Sian Flynn. "Somehow Elizabeth personified many things—stability and lack of extremism, for example—that are now considered to be quintessentially English."

Thanks to the relative tranquillity of English life during her reign, the arts flourished. Two treasures in the Folger's exhibition are first-edition quartos of Shakespeare's *Love's Labour's Lost* and *The Merry Wives of Windsor*. "When Shakespeare's plays were first printed during his lifetime, they appeared as these cheap little paperbacks," Ziegler says. The title page of *Love's Labour's* notes that the text is "as it was presented before her Highness this last Christmas."

At the other extreme in the Folger's collection is an enormous English-language Bible that the archbishop of Canterbury presented to Queen Elizabeth in 1568. The tome is bound in red velvet with ornate gilt clasps embossed with Tudor roses. Oddly, the text is accompanied by hand-colored woodcuts of Elizabeth's court favorites, including Leicester. Vernacular Bibles were a potent symbol of English Protestantism in Elizabeth's day—under her Catholic sister, Mary, prayers and scripture in any language but Latin were deemed a sacrilege. Playing to the crowd during her coronation parade, Elizabeth had hugged an English Bible to her chest.

To show herself to the populace beyond London, Elizabeth undertook frequent "progresses" from one estate to another. A court on the move was like an occupying army, involving as many as 400 luggage-filled carts. "There were so many people," says Ziegler, "that they couldn't stay in one place for more than a couple of weeks because the privies became a health hazard." Learning she would pass through Sandwich in 1573, the town fathers ordered that the streets be paved, that all hogs be penned and that brewers "brew good beer." At an open-air banquet the evening of her visit, the queen endeared herself to her hosts by giving her foodtasters the night off. "She was a master of publicity," says Flynn. "She courted popularity the way Princess Diana did."

On formal occasions when dignitaries gave long-winded orations praising her virtues, Elizabeth would bite her lip and shake her head with mock humility. But once, when a speaker cited her virginity, the queen called out proudly, "God's blessing of thine heart, there continue!"

She made her chastity—real or not—a political asset, a badge of independence and incorruptibility. Then too, Elizabeth may have preferred being single. In an audience with the queen in 1564, the Scottish ambassador boldly suggested as much: "Ye think that if ye were married, ye would be but queen of England, and now ye are king and queen both. Ye may not suffer a commander." By the 1570s, says Clark Hulse, "Elizabeth had made being unmarried one of her strengths. The very people who had pushed her to get married in the 1560s were now pushing her not to marry. The nation didn't want a male who even thought he could order Elizabeth around—not that anyone could have."

Elizabeth played the role of Virgin Queen with theatricality and pomp, and England was dazzled. "As she grew older and the chances of her marrying became unrealistic," says Flynn, "she turned herself into 'Gloriana,' which is the Elizabeth that most people know, with the white-powdered face. She became the personification of state." In surveyor Christopher Saxton's grand atlas of Britain, published in 1579, an engraving of Elizabeth enthroned fills the title page. Elizabeth *was* England.

As she aged, her clothing grew more elaborate, and she took to concealing her thinning hair with red wigs topped with constructions shaped like leaves, globes or pyramids. Her clothes were an exhibition of power, says Cynthia Abel, costume director of the Shakespeare Theatre in Washington, D.C. "She dressed to look strong and be impressive."

By the time she entered her 50s, her face was gaunt and pockmarked (from a near-fatal case of smallpox at age 29), her joints stiff, her teeth rotting. Coveting her throne was a younger, more hot-blooded woman: Mary Queen of Scots. A Catholic educated at the French court and a grandniece of Henry VIII, Mary Stuart was a vivacious but arrogant woman with a knack for attracting unsavory men and no knack whatsoever for governing.

"Mary is usually portrayed as sexier-looking than Elizabeth," says Ziegler. "She had quite a cult following." Her followers, however, were mostly in France. At 25, she'd been toppled from the Scottish throne by a rebellion after she married the unpopular Earl of Bothwell in 1567. The earl was widely suspected of murdering her previous husband, Lord Darnley, an ambitious schemer and drunkard whom Mary had named king of Scotland. After her ouster, she fled south to England, where Elizabeth kept her under house arrest for the next 19 years. Mary passed her time doing embroidery and sending coded messages to one plotter or another. In 1586, England's spymaster, Sir Francis Walsingham, intercepted and decoded letters smuggled out in beer kegs in which Mary discussed plans for Elizabeth's murder and Mary's own rescue by a Spanish invasion. It was one plot too many. Elizabeth dithered for a year before reluctantly approving her cousin's execution. (For more than a century, playwrights and filmmakers have staged dramatic confrontations between the two willful queens; in fact, the women never met.) After Mary was beheaded in 1587, the Continent mourned her as a martyr to her religion.

For her part, Elizabeth was threatened by a more intimate menace. Robert Devereux, the dashing and reckless Earl of Essex, moved into her good graces on the sudden death of his stepfather, the Earl of Leicester, in 1588. Essex was 33 years younger than Elizabeth and likely never aroused her ardor the way his stepfather had. He was neither adept as a military commander nor comfortable in taking orders, least of all from a woman. Openly insubordinate to the queen after bungling a military campaign in Ireland, he was banished from court in 1599. The Folger show includes a copy of a letter from him entitled, not very apologetically, "An Apologie of the Earle of Essex, against those which jealously, and malisiously tax him to be the hinderer of the peace and quiet of his country." The author signed another appeal (possibly to Elizabeth): "a hart torne in peeces with care, greife, & travaile." The Apologie didn't work, and in February 1601, Essex and a band of followers tried to stir a popular rebellion against the queen's councillors, and perhaps the queen herself. He was arrested, tried for treason and beheaded. Elizabeth's chilly postmortem: "I warned him that he should not touch my scepter."

By this time she had wielded it for 43 years. In November 1601, in her emotional "Golden Speech" to members of Parliament, the queen, now 68, reflected on her long reign. "Though you have had and may have many princes more mighty and wise sitting in this seat," she declared, "yet you never had or shall have any that will be more careful and loving." She owed her success, she said, to the loyalty and affection of the English people. "Though God hath raised me high, yet this I count the glory of my crown—that I have reigned with your loves."

Elizabeth was no doubt sincere, but she was too smart to depend for her power purely on her subjects' affection. "Machiavelli said it's better to be feared than loved," says Clark Hulse. "Elizabeth knew it was better to be both. She used force only as a last resort, but it was always on the table. Plenty of people were hanged during her reign."

The end came a little more than a year after the Golden Speech. According to one account, "her appetite to meate grew sensibly worse & worse; whereupon she became exceeding sad, & seemed to be much grieved at some thing or other." Enfeebled by rheumatism and possibly pneumonia, the queen died March 24, 1603. She was 69.

A flood of books and poems mourned her passing. A century later, the date Elizabeth first gained the throne, November 17, was still celebrated with bonfires, and children were taught verses about a queen they never knew: "Gone is Elizabeth, / whom we have lov'd so deare, / She our kind Mistris was, / full foure and forty year." In a time when most of England no longer worshiped the Virgin Mary, the Virgin Queen was a Protestant substitute they could adore instead.

Eventually, Elizabeth's own carefully tended image was supplanted by a more romantic one: that of the pining virgin fated to rule alone. Popular tales like *The History of Queen Elizabeth and Her Great Favorite, the Earl of Essex, in Two Parts—a Romance* began appearing anonymously by the late 17th century. By the 20th, the pantomimes of courtly love in which Elizabeth and her courtiers had indulged had become dramas of passion and betrayal in which Leicester, Essex and Mary Queen of Scots were stock characters. For many today, the Earl of Essex is inseparable from Hollywood's swashbuckling Errol Flynn, who brought Bette Davis to grief in the 1939 hit *The Private Lives of Elizabeth and Essex.*

In historical terms, Queen Elizabeth I was an unsurpassed model of a learned, intelligent woman. She proved that a queen could rule and rule triumphantly. Sarah Jinner, author of a 1658 "almanack," asked, "When, or what Commonwealth was ever better governed than this by the virtuous Q. Elizabeth? I fear I shall never see the like again, most of your Princes now a dayes are like Dunces in comparison of her." In a paean from the 1640s, American poet Ann Bradstreet used the memory of "That High and Mighty Princess Queen Elizabeth" to aim a zinger at 17th-century male chauvinists:

Let such as say our sex is void of reason,
Know 'tis a slander now, but once was treason.

From *Smithsonian*, June 2003, pp. 64–72. Copyright © 2003 by Doug Stewart. Reprinted with permission from the author.

Index

Index

Test Your Knowledge Form

We encourage you to photocopy and use this page as a tool to assess how the articles in *Annual Editions* expand on the information in your textbook. By reflecting on the articles you will gain enhanced text information. You can also access this useful form on a product's book support Web site at *http://www.dushkin.com/online/*.

NAME: DATE:

_____

TITLE AND NUMBER OF ARTICLE:

_____

BRIEFLY STATE THE MAIN IDEA OF THIS ARTICLE:

_____

LIST THREE IMPORTANT FACTS THAT THE AUTHOR USES TO SUPPORT THE MAIN IDEA:

_____

WHAT INFORMATION OR IDEAS DISCUSSED IN THIS ARTICLE ARE ALSO DISCUSSED IN YOUR TEXTBOOK OR OTHER READINGS THAT YOU HAVE DONE? LIST THE TEXTBOOK CHAPTERS AND PAGE NUMBERS:

_____

LIST ANY EXAMPLES OF BIAS OR FAULTY REASONING THAT YOU FOUND IN THE ARTICLE:

_____

LIST ANY NEW TERMS/CONCEPTS THAT WERE DISCUSSED IN THE ARTICLE, AND WRITE A SHORT DEFINITION:

We Want Your Advice

ANNUAL EDITIONS revisions depend on two major opinion sources: one is our Advisory Board, listed in the front of this volume, which works with us in scanning the thousands of articles published in the public press each year; the other is you—the person actually using the book. Please help us and the users of the next edition by completing the prepaid article rating form on this page and returning it to us. Thank you for your help!

ANNUAL EDITIONS: Western Civilization, Volume 1

ARTICLE RATING FORM

Here is an opportunity for you to have direct input into the next revision of this volume.
We would like you to rate each of the articles listed below, using the following scale:

1. **Excellent: should definitely be retained**
2. **Above average: should probably be retained**
3. **Below average: should probably be deleted**
4. **Poor: should definitely be deleted**

Your ratings will play a vital part in the next revision.
Please mail this prepaid form to us as soon as possible.
Thanks for your help!

RATING	ARTICLE	RATING	ARTICLE
	1. Deciphering History		35. Virtue and Beauty: The Renaissance Image of the Ideal Woman
	2. Hatshepsut: The Female Pharaoh		36. Martin Luther's Ninety-Five Theses
	3. Past, Present, Future: Perceptions of Time Through the Ages		37. Explaining John Calvin
	4. The Coming of the Sea Peoples		38. The Development of Protestantism in 16th Century France
	5. Grisly Assyrian Record of Torture and Death		39. Siege of the Moles
	6. Fact or Fiction?		40. The Muslim Expulsion from Spain
	7. Olympic Self-Sacrifice		41. Reign On!
	8. To Die For?		
	9. Love and Death in Ancient Greece		
	10. Cleopatra: What Kind of a Woman Was She, Anyway?		
	11. The Year One		
	12. Old Age in Ancient Rome		
	13. Celtic War Queen Who Challenged Rome		
	14. The Great Jewish Revolt Against Rome, 66-73 CE		
	15. The Legacy of Abraham		
	16. The Other Jesus		
	17. Mary Magdalene: Saint or Sinner		
	18. Who the Devil Is the Devil?		
	19. The Emperor's State of Grace		
	20. The Survival of the Eastern Roman Empire		
	21. In the Beginning, There Were the Holy Books		
	22. The Ideal of Unity		
	23. The Most Perfect Man in History?		
	24. An Iberian Chemistry		
	25. The Capture of Jerusalem		
	26. Doctor, Philosopher, Renaissance Man		
	27. The Emergence of the Christian Witch		
	28. Lackland: The Loss of Normandy in 1204		
	29. Hero of the Neva and Lake Peipus		
	30. Spreading the Gospel in the Middle Ages		
	31. Saints or Sinners? The Knights Templar in Medieval Europe		
	32. How a Mysterious Disease Laid Low Europe's Masses		
	33. The Fall of Constantinople		
	34. Machiavelli		

(Continued on next page)

BUSINESS REPLY MAIL
FIRST CLASS MAIL PERMIT NO. 551 DUBUQUE IA

POSTAGE WILL BE PAID BY ADDRESEE

McGraw-Hill/Dushkin
2460 KERPER BLVD
DUBUQUE, IA 52001-9902

ABOUT YOU

Name

Date

Are you a teacher? ☐ A student? ☐
Your school's name

Department

Address   City   State   Zip

School telephone #

YOUR COMMENTS ARE IMPORTANT TO US!

Please fill in the following information:
For which course did you use this book?

Did you use a text with this ANNUAL EDITION? ☐ yes ☐ no
What was the title of the text?

What are your general reactions to the *Annual Editions* concept?

Have you read any pertinent articles recently that you think should be included in the next edition? Explain.

Are there any articles that you feel should be replaced in the next edition? Why?

Are there any World Wide Web sites that you feel should be included in the next edition? Please annotate.

May we contact you for editorial input? ☐ yes ☐ no
May we quote your comments? ☐ yes ☐ no